William Leeke

The History of Lord Seaton's Regiment, (the 52nd Light Infantry)

Vol. II

William Leeke

The History of Lord Seaton's Regiment, (the 52nd Light Infantry)
Vol. II

ISBN/EAN: 9783337141882

Printed in Europe, USA, Canada, Australia, Japan

Cover: Foto ©ninafisch / pixelio.de

More available books at **www.hansebooks.com**

LORD SEATON'S REGIMENT,

(THE 52ND LIGHT INFANTRY,)

AT

THE BATTLE OF WATERLOO;

ETC., ETC.

THE HISTORY

OF

LORD SEATON'S REGIMENT,

(THE 52ND LIGHT INFANTRY,)

AT

THE BATTLE OF WATERLOO:

TOGETHER WITH VARIOUS

Incidents connected with that Regiment,

NOT ONLY AT WATERLOO, BUT ALSO AT PARIS, IN THE NORTH OF FRANCE, AND
FOR SEVERAL YEARS AFTERWARDS;

TO WHICH ARE ADDED MANY OF

THE AUTHOR'S REMINISCENCES OF HIS MILITARY AND CLERICAL CAREERS,

DURING A PERIOD OF MORE THAN FIFTY YEARS.

BY THE

REV. WILLIAM LEEKE, M.A.,

(OF QUEEN'S COLLEGE, CAMBRIDGE,) INCUMBENT OF HOLBROOKE, DERBYSHIRE, AND RURAL DEAN,
WHO CARRIED THE 52ND REGIMENTAL COLOUR AT WATERLOO.

THE AUTHOR CLAIMS FOR LORD SEATON AND THE 52ND THE HONOUR OF HAVING
DEFEATED, SINGLE-HANDED, WITHOUT THE ASSISTANCE OF THE 1ST BRITISH
GUARDS OR ANY OTHER TROOPS, THAT PORTION OF THE IMPERIAL
GUARD OF FRANCE, ABOUT 10,000 IN NUMBER, WHICH ADVANCED
TO MAKE THE LAST ATTACK ON THE BRITISH POSITION:

THE 3RD BATTALION OF THE 1ST FOOT GUARDS, BY THE DUKE OF WELLINGTON'S ORDER, DROVE
THE SKIRMISHERS OF THE IMPERIAL GUARD OFF THE BRITISH POSITION,
THE OTHER BATTALION OF GENERAL MAITLAND'S BRIGADE OF GUARDS REMAINING STATIONARY.

IN TWO VOLUMES.—VOL. II.

WITH A PORTRAIT OF FIELD-MARSHAL LORD SEATON,
AND THREE PLANS OF WATERLOO, SHEWING THE POSITIONS AND
MOVEMENTS OF THE 52ND DURING THE ACTION.

LONDON:
HATCHARD AND CO., 187, PICCADILLY.
1866.

CONTENTS OF VOL. II.

———

CHAPTER XXVI.

1824.

FROM ST. ANDREW'S TO ENGLAND.

CHAPTER XXVII.

1824.

LEAVE THE ARMY.

CHAPTER XXVIII.

1825.

CAMBRIDGE.

CHAPTER XXIX.

1826.

MALTA AND BACK.

CHAPTER XXX.

1827—1831.

CAMBRIDGE.   WESTHAM.

CHAPTER XXXI.

1831.

BRAILSFORD, DERBYSHIRE.

CHAPTER XXXII.

1832—1837.

BRAILSFORD. THE LORD'S DAY.

CHAPTER XXXIII.

1833—1849.

SIR ANDREW AGNEW.

CHAPTER XXXIV.

1838, 1839.

THE ABOLITION OF PLURALITIES.

CHAPTER XXXV.

1833, 1834.

SABBATH PROCEEDINGS IN DERBYSHIRE.

CHAPTER XXXVI.

1831—1839.

MINISTERIAL WORK AT BRAILSFORD.

CHAPTER XXXVII.

1840—1843.

HOLBROOKE.

CHAPTER XXXVIII.

1845.

ADDRESS TO RAILWAY PROPRIETORS ON THE DESECRATION OF THE LORD'S DAY.

CHAPTER XXXIX.
1845, 1846.
JOURNEY TO VEVAY AND BACK. HOLBROOKE.

CHAPTER XL.
1845. 1851.
WILLIAM SHAW AND JOSEPH STEVENS OF HOLBROOKE.

CHAPTER XLI.
1847.
SIR HENRY LEEKE'S SERVICES.

CHAPTER XLII.
1860.
LORD'S DAY CONFERENCE MEETING AT DERBY.

CHAPTER XLIII.

1850.

FROM THE APPENDIX TO THE CONFERENCE REPORT.

CHAPTER XLIV.

1863.

SUNDAY CLOSING OF PUBLIC-HOUSES.

CHAPTER XLV.

1824, &c.

CAPTAIN ATCHISON AND LIEUT. DAWSON, AND THE ROMAN CATHOLIC CEREMONIES AT MALTA.

CHAPTER XLVI.
1794—1863.
FEILD-MARSHAL LORD SEATON.

CHAPTER XLVII.
1815.
LIST OF 52ND WATERLOO OFFICERS AND THEIR SERVICES.

CHAPTER XLVIII.
1755—1808.
SOME ACCOUNT OF THE 52ND LIGHT INFANTRY FROM ITS FORMATION.

CHAPTER XLIX.
1808, 1809.
THE 52ND IN THE PENINSULA. CORUNNA.

CHAPTER L.

1809—1811.

THE 52ND IN THE PENINSULA.

CHAPTER LI.

1812.

THE 52ND AT THE SIEGE AND ASSAULT OF CIUDAD RODRIGO, AND ALSO OF BADAJOS.

CHAPTER LII.

1813, 1814.

THE 52ND AT THE CLOSE OF THE PENINSULAR WAR.

CHAPTER LIII.

1822—1857.

GENERAL ORDERS AND OTHER DOCUMENTS COMPLIMENTARY TO THE 52ND.

CHAPTER LIV.

1857.

THE 52ND IN THE INDIAN MUTINY.

CHAPTER LV.

1815.

SUNDRY MATTERS CONNECTED WITH WATERLOO, AND WITH THE 52ND AT WATERLOO.

CHAPTER LVI.

ARTICLES CHIEFLY ON MILITARY OR NAVAL SUBJECTS.

CHAPTER LVII.

MISCELLANEOUS ARTICLES NOTED DOWN FOR PUBLICATION.

CHAPTER LVIII.

THE APPENDIX.

CHAPTER XXVI.

1824.

FROM ST. ANDREW'S TO ENGLAND.

Eastport—Great enjoyment at Little River harbour—Boston—Bunker's hill—
Providence—Deranged fellow-traveller—Albany—The Hudson—West Point
—New York—Embark for England—Curious dispute with a passenger—
Danger of giving spirits to people—Read service and sermon to the pas-
sengers, &c.—Liverpool—Dublin—Bristol—Home.

My leave arrived on the morning of the 28th of April, and at
noon I started from St. Andrew's for Eastport, on my way to
England. The next morning "I left Eastport in the St. Croix
packet for Boston; we took on board some passengers at Lubeck,
and after passing West Quoddy point and lighthouse, stood
away to the southward and westward with a good wind, but with
the weather foggy and rainy. In the evening, the wind being
slack and the tide against us, we put into Little River harbour.
It is just above Little Machias, and abreast of the most southern
point of Grand Manan. In the morning we went on shore, and
I strolled about for a couple of hours." I have not noted it in a
journal which I was then keeping, but I well recollect, during
these two hours, getting up to the top of a small rock, not far
from some of the houses of this village, where I was quite retired
and in nobody's sight or hearing but God's. I had such sweet
intercourse with Him in prayer as has never been surpassed by
anything of the kind I have ever experienced since. I was alone
with the Great Lord of all, the Maker of the universe, but also
my reconciled father and friend in Christ. I never read the
passage in John i, 45—49, and especially those words in the
latter part of the 48th verse, "Before that Philip called thee,

"when thou wast under the fig-tree, I saw thee," without thinking of that spot and that sweet intercourse. See 1 John i, 3, 7.
What condescension and mercy, that we poor, sinful, helpless
creatures are invited to hold communion and intercourse with
the Most High God, for surely the passages mean nothing short
of that. But the 6th verse of this last passage shews us that
such fellowship is only enjoyed by those who are upright in
heart, and sincerely *desirous* of giving up all sin. This we may
be, though we never shall be without sin in this world : 8th verse.
We passed a Sunday on board this packet, and the captain and
two of the passengers read a book of sermons which I lent them,
and with the mate and one of the passengers I had some interesting conversation.

We made Boston Bay in a thick fog, which cleared off, as it
did at Newfoundland, on my persuading the captain to fire a
cannon which he had on board. " On the fog clearing away we
saw Boston lighthouse about nine miles ahead of us ; we had a
fine breeze as we entered the passage by the lighthouse, and we
met about sixty sail of vessels going out. The next day, from
the top of the State-house, I had a beautiful view of Boston
harbour, Charlestown, Bunker's Hill, south Boston, and the town
of Boston itself. Almost every other house in Boston has trees
either in front or rear of it : these add much to the pleasing
appearance of the place. The common, which is in front of the
State-house, is surrounded on three sides by handsome houses,
and on the other by part of Charles river, and has a very pretty
appearance.

" May 5th. Hired a horse for a dollar and a quarter, and
rode to Rixborough, Cambridge, Prospect Hill, and Charlestown.
When the British troops occupied Boston, after their victory at
Bunker's Hill, Washington had his head quarters at Cambridge,
which is about three miles from Boston, his right at Roxbury,
and his left at Prospect Hill. The fort at Bunker's Hill appears
to have been a circular fort, not more than thirty-five paces in
diameter. There is a monument there to the memory of those
who fell in the defence of the fort. At Cambridge college there
are about 200 students : I believe this college, as to professors,
its philosophical apparatus, library, &c., is the most complete

thing of the sort in the States. I have found all classes of people in this neighbourhood to be remarkably civil and obliging.

"Providence, Rhode Island. Arrived here last night from Boston. The road is tolerably good; it put me much in mind of some of the cross-country roads in England. The "stage," which consists of a vehicle drawn by four horses, and something like the old-fashioned sociables of England, contained nine of us, there being a centre seat as in the French *diligence*. One of my companions was an Andover student, and a pious man."

On entering the hotel at Providence, no one took the least notice of me. The waiters were attending upon the people dining at a large table, and it was not until I had pitched my great coat into a chair and my hat into another, and had walked to the top of the room and rung the bell, that I received any attention. I then inquired of the waiter who came to me, if I might get some dinner at the table; he told me I could, and got me a chair, and then all the people about me were civil enough, particularly one person who was near the centre of the table, who was very attentive to my wants. I found out afterwards that he was the master of the hotel, and I saw, from his portrait in another part of the house, that he had been a captain in the United States navy. The Andover student gave me a very pleasing account of religion at Providence. He considered the great proportion of the inhabitants to be God-fearing people. He mentioned a custom which prevailed there, and I suppose also in many other places, which appeared very strange at first, and that was, that although there were Christians of almost all denominations in the town, the same bell summoned the inhabitants to their respective places of worship at the same hour.

"This morning I went with Mr. Howe to visit a very nice Christian lady, who has been almost bedridden for several years. At parting she asked me to come and see her again. I told her I believed we should meet no more in this world, as I was going far away. 'What! as a missionary?' she said. 'No,' I answered, 'I am at present in a very different position, I am a soldier.' She seemed, I thought, astonished and grieved at this, and looked as if she would say, 'Can you be a soldier and at the same time 'a Christian?' We parted in silence. I have never, I think, spent a more useful half hour than that which I passed with this poor suffering, but joyful servant of Christ.

May 8th. Left Providence at four o'clock in the morning for Springfield, on the Connecticut. One of my companions in the stage nearly the whole of the way, a distance of seventy-two miles, was a poor maniac. For the first two stages he scarcely ceased to talk for one moment. I afterwards hit upon a plan which kept him pretty quiet."

At one town a lady wished to go by the stage, but hesitated on account of the maniac. On their consulting me about it, I told them I had complete control over him, and I thought there was no reason why she should not join the party. When we arrived at his destination, he resisted with all his strength the efforts which were made to take him out of the stage. As they forced him up the passage of the house at which we had arrived, his screams and shrieks were most distressing.

"The bridge over the Connecticut at Springfield, is about a quarter of a mile in length, and is twenty-five feet wide. It is of wood, but the buttresses are of brick and stone. It is covered over. 10th. Started from Springfield for Albany on the Hudson, at two o'clock in the morning. The driver and the people of the inn wished the stage to go away last night, but as it was Sunday, and I thought it was improper as there was no sufficient reason for it, I declared that I should not accompany it; it therefore waited till this morning. I had two well-informed and apparently pious young men during different parts of my journey this day. By our conversation we were enabled to direct the attention of our fellow-travellers to the religion of Christ and the Scriptures. We crossed the Hudson in a circular ferry-boat; the river is at Albany about as wide as the Thames at Westminster.

"Everything at Albany, and for the 150 miles between that and New York, shewed that there was a brisk trade going on at all the towns on the Hudson or North River. I remained a whole day at Westpoint, where the military academy is, and where poor Major André was taken and hung as a spy. "There are 230 cadets at this academy; they must be past sixteen years of age before they can be admitted. They each receive twenty-eight dollars a month as pay, out of which they pay all their expenses. I went to their drawing studies; they learn figure, landscape, and military drawing. Their plans do not appear to be quite so highly finished as most of those done by the cadets at Sandhurst, but they are very neat. I saw them both in the artillery and infantry exercise. A cadet remains there four years, and passes each year into a fresh class. I reached New York by the steam-boat on the morning of the 13th, and took up my quarters at the City Hotel, where I found Scoones and Vivian * of the 52nd, who were just returned from Washington.

"May 15th. I had made an arrangement with Scoones to accompany him in a trip to Niagara, Montreal, and Quebec, but during a solitary walk on the battery this evening, I determined to change my plan, and to proceed forthwith to England. A steam-boat burst its boiler on its approach to the city this evening. Six ladies and one gentleman were killed, and seven or eight persons wounded. The boat is a complete wreck, the centre part being blown to atoms."

I left New York for England about the middle of May. We had a very good passage till we got within about a hundred miles of Ireland, and then, owing to contrary winds, it took us a week longer to get to Liverpool. Almost all our passengers were men. One of them was a member of congress. He was very fond of England and the English, but somewhat overbearing in his conduct towards some of the passengers. He was not so, however, with me and some others. He and I got on very well together for several days, so much so that as I was going into my cabin from the dining saloon, I heard him on one occasion say to those who were sitting at the table near him, "A very intelligent "young man that."

I was very sorry that anything should occur to interrupt the good feeling which existed between us; it will be seen, however, that it could hardly have been avoided on my part. One day

* Vivian returned to the regiment in New Brunswick. Scoones had some time before purchased a company, I think unattached, and I had succeeded by purchase to his lieutenancy. He was afterwards major of the 51st. Vivian was sent to supply my place at St. Andrew's, and there, by God's blessing on his intercourse with the Gawlers and others, became a truly religious man. How wonderfully does God carry out His purposes! "How unsearchable are his "judgments, and his ways past finding out!" Romans xi, 33.

we were sitting at dinner, when something led him to speak of a circumstance which had happened on one of his former voyages to England. He said that he saw a black steward beating a white boy, and that he had knocked him down, adding, "as I "would any other black rascal whom I saw striking a white boy." His black servant was standing behind his chair, and the black steward of the ship was standing at the door of his pantry at one corner of the saloon, and I was so indignant at hearing such a speech, that I said at once, though as quietly as I possibly could, "I do not exactly see that there is any difference between a "black man's striking a white boy, and a white man's striking a "black boy." He immediately angrily replied, "No one asked "your opinion on the subject, Sir." I said no more, but in a second or two quietly got up and went into my small cabin. We did not speak to each other for more than a week, I think.

I did a very foolish thing one day when we were about half-way across the Atlantic. For some purpose two of the passengers had gone up the main rigging, and, as I had heard of the joke of tying people up in the rigging till they had "paid their footing," I said to two of the sailors, "Can't some of you men tie those "gentlemen up till they have paid their footing?" "Aye, aye, "Sir," was the reply, and up the men went in no time. But the landsmen, getting some intimation of what was intended, first of all went higher in the rigging, and then, when they were over-taken, made fight, and drew out their knives to cut the cords with which the sailors were trying to lash their legs to the rig-ging. They were not very particular as to where they struck with their knives, and I began to be seriously afraid that we should have some accident. I forget whether it was by the cap-tain, or myself, or the mate, that the sailors were called upon to desist, and come down. The captain was very quiet about it, merely agreeing with my observation, that such jokes were better avoided; but I expected to have got into a regular scrape with the two passengers. They, however, were so proud of coming off victorious, that they took no offence at what had happened.

I very inconsiderately desired the steward to give the sailors a bottle of brandy or rum from me, which was very nearly the means of bringing about a sad catastrophe, which I should have lamented all my days. In the afternoon it came on to blow hard, and it was necessary to send all hands aloft. I think that it was in reefing the fore-topsail that something went wrong at the very end of the yard, and to my horror I saw one of the men, whom I recognised as one of my friends to whom I had given the bottle of spirits, walking right along the yard, over the men's hands, without any hold, for the purpose of rectifying what had got foul. As we expected, he missed his footing, and fell right off the yard, and there appeared to be nothing which could prevent his being dashed to pieces, when, in God's mercy, he fell right across a stay running from the main-mast to the mizen-mast. He was a very active man, and before he was clear of the stay he laid hold of it, and then worked himself up into the main rigging again, being altogether unhurt.

On the Sunday before we reached Ireland I asked the captain if he had any objection to my reading the morning service, and a sermon, to any of the passengers who were disposed to attend. He readily acquiesced in the proposal, and we had a large congregation on deck. The sermon I read was one of "Burder's "Village Sermons." After all was over, the member of congress came up to me and thanked me for reading to them such a nice sermon. I was very glad that our little difference should thus end. He landed in two or three days at Cork, or some other place in the south of Ireland, thinking to reach England sooner in that way than by the ship.

I found letters at Liverpool, which made it necessary for me to go to Dublin; from thence I went by steamer to Bristol. As we passed up the Bristol Channel, a small yacht came stern on to the steamer so close that the end of her bowsprit was within eight or ten yards of us as we looked over the side of our vessel. I clearly saw my friend Diggle and his family on board; I had left them at Sandhurst a year before, just as I was starting for Bristol, on my way to America. They gave us a cheer as we passed along, and we cheered them in return, but I was not at all sure that the Diggles had recognised me till about ten years after, when, in a letter on another subject, he said, "Do you recollect "the cheer we gave you in the Bristol Channel on your return "from America?"

CHAPTER XXVII.

1824.

LEAVE THE ARMY.

Memorial to the Commander-in-Chief—Reply—Hardship—Letter from Lord
Seaton—Vexatious treatment Lord Seaton had met with in 1814—Colonel
Gawler and South Australia—Lord Seaton's high opinion of Gawler—Major
Diggle—Obtain permission to return to Sandhurst—Circumstances occur
rendering it desirable that I should leave the army—Military glory.

THE following is a copy of the memorial I sent to the Duke of
York :—

"To His Royal Highness the Commander-in-Chief.
"The Memorial of Ensign Leeke, 52nd Light Infantry.
"SIR,—I beg leave to call your Royal Highness's attention
"to a late arrangement by which Ensign R. F. Hill, an ensign of
"four years' standing, has got his lieutenancy in this regiment
"over my head, who have seen more than eight years' service in the
"52nd, without including the two years allowed by His Majesty
"for Waterloo. I trust your Royal Highness will see the hard-
"ship of the case, and that you will deem it worthy of your
"consideration. I must premise that the half-pay lieutenancy
"in the 49th, to which Mr. Hill succeeded, was offered to me
"when at Sandhurst, but, in a letter I wrote to Sir Herbert Tay-
"lor, I declined it, from a wish to remain in the 52nd ; at the
"same time I intimated that I should be glad of promotion if I
"could be restored to my old corps.
"On my declining the half-pay lieutenancy in the 49th, from
"a wish not to leave the 52nd, it was given to Mr. Hill, who

" shortly afterwards exchanged back again. This lieutenancy I
" would most gladly have accepted on the same terms.

"Knowing your Royal Highness's attention to the feelings
" and interests of every individual in the army, I have thought it
"right to state the whole case for your consideration, trusting you
"will cause such an arrangement to be made respecting it, as
"may appear to your Royal Highness to be equitable and
" correct.

"With this view I beg leave to mention to your Royal
" Highness that, as there is a supernumerary lieutenancy which
"remained vacant at the death of Major Shedden, I should feel
" much gratified if I might be allowed to succeed to it. I further
" hope I shall not be considered by your Royal Highness as re-
" questing more than the circumstances of the case authorize, if
" I beg to have my commission dated senior to Lieutenant Hill
" in the army, and also to be placed before him in the list of
" lieutenants of this regiment. This last arrangement I trust
" your Royal Highness will allow to be made in the event of my
" succeeding to a lieutenancy in a regular way, either before or
" after the arrival of this memorial in England.

"I have the honour to be,

" Your Royal Highness's most obedient, humble servant,

" WM. LEEKE, Ensign, 52nd Light Infantry.

"St. Andrew's, New Brunswick,

"[About] November 20th, 1823."

This memorial was sent from New Brunswick about three
weeks after the above date, which, by the way, is the exact date
of my commission by purchase as a lieutenant in the 52nd, after
having been eight years and a half an ensign. Bentham, who
was the next ensign to me, remained an ensign, I have understood, till he had been altogether twelve years in that rank.

The communication between England and New Brunswick
was not kept up in those days as it is now ; and it will be seen
that nearly two months elapsed between the date of Sir John
Tylden's letter accompanying my memorial, and the date of the
following reply which he received to it :—

"Horse Guards, 3rd February, 1824.

"SIR,—I have submitted to the Commander-in-Chief your "letter of the 7th of December last, with a memorial of Lieutenant "Leeke of the regiment under your command, and His Royal "Highness desires that you will communicate to that officer the "enclosed copy of his own letter of the 27th of May last, de-"clining altogether the purchase of a half-pay lieutenancy, and "stating that he would prefer remaining in the 52nd Foot till a "lieutenancy became vacant in it, to purchasing even a *full-pay* "lieutenancy in any other corps, except with the prospect of "further promotion, or an immediate restoration to his old corps. "Lieutenant Hill did purchase the half-pay lieutenancy in the "49th Regiment, and exchanged to the 52nd, and although Lieu-"tenant Leeke has since obtained promotion in his regiment, "His Royal Highness cannot admit his claim to an ante-date, or "to being placed above Lieutenant Hill in the 52nd Foot, in "consideration of his having thought fit to decline that which "was not offered to Lieutenant Hill until he had declined it.

"I have the honour to be, Sir,
"Your most obedient, humble servant,
"HT. TAYLOR.

"Brevet-Lieut.-Colonel Sir John M. Tylden,
"52nd Regiment."

I know not whether this was done inadvertently, or whether it was known from the first at the Horse Guards, that if I refused the half-pay lieutenancy, it would be given to my junior, and that he would be allowed to exchange back into the regiment before I got my lieutenancy, but such transactions must be very injurious to the service. Here was the case of a man who was allowed to be a good and intelligent officer, and always very attentive to his duty, who had taken some considerable pains to try and improve himself in various studies calculated to be useful to him in his profession, and who had seen some good service at Waterloo; against whom nothing could be alleged, except, perhaps, that he had become very serious, and there never was the least hint that that fact had anything to do with the transaction—here was the case of a man who was the senior ensign of his regiment, who, although he was for purchase, had been nearly nine years an ensign, owing to the fact that the officers above him were so attached to their regiment that they made few vacancies in those " piping times of peace ;" and, also, owing to two lieutenancies not having been filled up, that the number of lieutenants might be reduced—here was the case of a man who had an officer four years his junior promoted to a half-pay lieutenancy, and then very soon brought back over his head into the regiment.

I at first hardly knew what to do under what I considered a cruel piece of injustice inflicted on me ; I could not, with any comfort, remain in the "glorious old regiment," as some of the officers in after days have called it. Before I had received the answer to the memorial, I had written to Lord Seaton, then Sir John Colborne, telling him my feelings in the matter, and requesting his advice, and saying that, in the event of an unfavourable reply to the memorial, which I anticipated, I should proceed as soon as I could to England. There appeared at the time a state of things in Europe which might possibly lead to our being involved in war, and I mentioned my desire to be so disposed of as might give me an opportunity of seeing any active service which might be likely to turn up. This will account for a great deal which he said in the following truly kind letter which I received from him immediately on my arrival in England :—

"Guernsey, July 11th, 1824.

"MY DEAR LEEKE,

"If your late movements have been influenced by your "calculations on the probability of war being at no great distance, "your speculations, in my opinion, are erroneous. We shall be "all old men or women before we are again called into the field. "It is true that Europe appears disturbed, but as the people of "most kingdoms are looking towards constitutions, and as princes "are fully employed in putting off the evil day, and are all in "debt, the present state of things is rather favourable to the "preservation of peace than otherwise, and as far as our own "country is concerned, poverty alone will prevent our interfering "in the disputes of our neighbours. Nothing but a positive in- "sult can involve us in a war, and as it is the interest of the "leading powers of Europe to avoid one, I am persuaded we "shall have a very long peace.

"Your prospect of promotion is certainly not bright, even
"should you remain on full-pay, but I see no probability of your
"succeeding to a company, without waiting patiently in one
"regiment, and taking your chance of the vacancies time pro-
"duces.

.   .   .   .

"If you apply to return to Sandhurst, you must mention that
"you wish to be placed on half-pay, for the purpose of following
"your studies, without receiving the difference.   It is difficult to
"give any advice that can be of the least use to you ; your own
"opinion must be better than mine, for you know your own views
"and feelings, with which I cannot be acquainted, and you see
"plainly the obstacles in the way of rapid promotion.   The fact
"is, you are tired of the inactive life of a soldier in peace, and at
"this I am not astonished.   I think also that I perceive that
"some accidental occurrences, arising perhaps in part from cer-
"tain changes, have made the 52nd less agreeable than that corps
"was in former days.   Thus between a struggle to do what you
"really wish, and a little inclination to deceive yourself with the
"notion that you are contented in your present situation, or a
"dislike to sacrifice the labour or claims of ten years, you would
"gladly find yourself in a state of repose, which may afford you
"time to look about, without being obliged to decide on the
"advantages or consequences to be expected from the step you
"are about to take.   I see your embarrassment, and scarcely
"know what to recommend.   Would it not be best to apply for
"admittance to Sandhurst again ?   And when you have passed
"some time there, and have completed your course of studies, you
"will find no difficulty in returning to full-pay.

.   .   .   .

"Believe me, sincerely yours,

"J. COLBORNE."

Lord Seaton himself had not been without his grievances at
treatment which he had met with at the Horse Guards. Many
years after the above letter was written, before he was made
field-marshal, but after he had obtained his peerage for his services,
I was talking to him at a friend's house in town, when he spoke
strongly, not about the treatment I had received, but about that

which Colonel Gawler had received from the Government, when he was superseded as governor of South Australia.* I said to him, " I suppose you, Sir, have not passed through your military " career without meeting with your mortifications and trials ?" He replied, " No, indeed ! In 1814, at the close of the Peninsu- "lar war, when they made me a K. C. B., King's aide-de-camp, " and a full colonel, I was exceedingly annoyed and vexed at

* Colonel Gawler had gone out as governor to the new colony of South Australia, when it was not in very flourishing circumstances, and, in completing the establishment of that colony, had met with several difficulties. Amongst others was that which arose from the influx of several thousands of emigrants from England, for whom it was almost impossible to find employment. By employing some on the survey, by forming an efficient corps of mounted police, which was rendered necessary in consequence of depredations and murders committed by the natives, and by building a suitable Government-house, &c., he managed to prevent an immense amount of suffering amongst the emigrants, and to enable them to remain in the colony. Under these circumstances, he felt it absolutely necessary to exceed the limit of outlay permitted by his instructions to the amount of about £200,000. When this was known at the Colonial Office, and was accompanied by unfair and untrue statements respecting Colonel Gawler's proceedings, he was superseded in his government. When he afterwards remonstrated and claimed an opportunity of refuting these published untruths, and even addressed the Prime Minister and the Crown on the subject, he was put off and at last thoroughly baffled in his repeated attempts to obtain redress. The hardship was greatly increased by his having, in consequence of his salary being only £800 a year, to expend a very large proportion of his moderate private fortune in meeting the expences of his position. And, after all, the formation of the afterwards flourishing colony of South Australia was carried out at a less expense to the mother-country than has been the case with regard to the establishment of any of the other numerous colonies of Great Britain. I believe that the mortification and annoyance arising from the unjust and cruel treatment he met with, led to Colonel Gawler's determination to retire from the army by the sale of his commission ; and thus the country lost the services of one of its most talented, experienced, and accomplished military officers.

The following is an extract from a letter I received from Lord Seaton in January, 1854, not long before the commencement of the Crimean war :—" Accept " my best thanks for your letter of the 19th. I should be delighted to hear that " my old friends of the 52nd were again in the field. If their services were required, " Gawler, I am convinced, from his ability and experience, would have been one of " the most distinguished officers in our army, had he been actively employed in " any foreign command."

Major Diggle wrote to me as follows on the subject of the treatment Colonel Gawler had experienced in the year 1841, just after the above related circumstances had occurred :—" I never can suppose that our friend Gawler can have acted with " want of judgment in expenditure or management, for a more sensible, better " fellow cannot be."

"their putting two junior lieutenant-colonels over my head in
"the list of colonels.   On my remonstrating on the unfairness of
"this proceeding, they made the excuse that these men were thus
"favoured because they had brought home despatches.   If I had
"not been a poor man—if I could have afforded it, I would have
"thrown my commission in their faces.   In after years they
"offered to place me before these men, but I then refused it."

I was glad to find that Lord Seaton had been so indignant at
receiving the very same sort of treatment which I had experienced
myself.   It seemed to sanction the indignation with which I had
always, whenever I thought of it, regarded the injustice done to
me.   I trust that in these days better feelings prevail, and that
such glaring injustice as that which I complain of is not likely,
if it occur, to be so easily passed over as has been formerly the
case.   Surely every care should be taken by high military and
naval authorities not to disgust men, perhaps deserving and pro-
mising men, with that service, the management of which has been
entrusted to them.   I have expressed myself freely, and have not
withheld Lord Seaton's strong expressions of feeling which I was
inclined to do, in the hope that the subject may attract more
attention, and that thus good may be effected.

I took an early opportunity, after my arrival in England, of
going to the Horse Guards, and seeing the Commander-in-Chief's
military secretary, Sir Herbert Taylor, on the subject of my future
proceedings.   He told me he thought there would be no objection
to my returning to Sandhurst to complete my studies there, on
the part of the Commander-in-Chief, but that I had better write
to Colonel Butler, the lieutenant-governor of the military college,
to see if there was any difficulty on the part of the college authorities to my returning there without waiting for my turn till
all those who preceded me on the list of candidates had been
admitted.   I told Sir Herbert Taylor that, on going on half-pay,
I should like to be permitted to hope that my wishes with regard
to a choice of regiments, when I should return to full-pay, would
be attended to.   His reply was, "The high character you bore at
"Sandhurst, Mr. Leeke, will always insure your wishes being
"attended to."   I then said I hoped that nothing I had done, in
the matter of the half-pay lieutenancy, was considered improper

in any way. He replied that the memorial should not have been sent, as the half-pay lieutenancy had not been given to Mr. Hill until after I had refused it. I said that I should gladly have purchased it, with the understanding that I should return again to the 52nd. Sir Herbert repeated, "It was not given to "Mr. Hill until it had been offered to you;" when I answered, "No! but not with the same proviso, Sir." I then bowed, and took my leave.

On writing to Colonel Butler, I found there would be no difficulty in my returning to Sandhurst as soon as a vacancy should occur. At the termination of my six months' leave of absence, I exchanged from the 52nd to a half-pay lieutenancy in the 42nd Highlanders. It was towards the end of December that I received the following communication from Colonel Butler:—

"Royal Military College, Dec. 25th, 1824.

"Sir,—I have great pleasure in obeying the directions of the "adjutant-general to communicate to you H. R. H. the Com- "mander-in-Chief's commands that you should join the senior "department of the Royal Military College on the 1st of February "next, and I request you will acknowledge to me the receipt of "this order, and I have the honour to be, Sir,

"Your obedient servant,

"Lieut. W. Leeke,   J. BUTLER, Lieut.-Governor.
"Half-pay, 42nd Regiment."

Just at this very time, circumstances of a private and family nature, which I have no occasion further to refer to, led me to make up my mind to leave the army altogether. I immediately wrote to the Horse Guards and to Colonel Butler to mention this, and received in reply the following letter from the Horse Guards:—

"Horse Guards, 3rd Jany., 1825.

"Sir,—I have submitted to the Commander-in-Chief your "letter of the 28th ultimo, and I am directed to acquaint you "that, under the circumstances represented, the order for you to "join the senior department of the Royal Military College has "been cancelled.

"I am, Sir, your humble servant,

"HT. TAYLOR.

"Lieut. Leeke, H. P., 42nd Regiment."

Thus ended my military career; I was what was termed "most fortunate" in the commencement of that career, having obtained my commission in one of the most renowned regiments in the service, and having very shortly afterwards borne one of its colours in its crowning victory at Waterloo—in its glorious advance on, and defeat of, single-handed, the French Imperial Guard, consisting of 10,000 men—having seen them and the whole French army in confusion and flight—having also had the honour of being close in front of those gallant chiefs, Wellington, Anglesea, and Seaton, when the 52nd was by itself, far away in front of all the other British and Allied troops, at that very moment of the great battle when these noble chiefs were said to be in the nearest proximity to the great Napoleon and some of the most renowned marshals of France—having also, within two months of my entrance into the army, been present at the capitulation of Paris, and then having formed part of the small force which occupied that capital during the ensuing four months ! Surely here was glory ! But I must not forget that "all the "glory of man is as the flower of the grass :" 1 Peter i, 24.

CHAPTER XXVIII.

1825.

CAMBRIDGE.

Meet Madden of the 43rd—Enter a fellow-commoner at Queen's College, Cambridge—Rub up Latin and Greek—Hyde Abbey School—Story of Dean Milner—Lecture-room—Mr. Simeon's parties—Religious reading parties—Origin of Jesus Lane Sunday School—Friend from New Brunswick.

At the end of 1824, when I determined to leave the army, I did not think of doing so with the view of taking orders; but after some little time I felt convinced that I should have greater opportunities of serving God and doing good if I became a clergyman, than would be the case if I remained unemployed; and this consideration, added to the strong recommendations, and persuasions I may say, of that good man, the late Rev. Wyndham Madden, who had served with credit in the 43rd Light Infantry during the greater part of the Peninsular War, and had retired and taken orders, induced me to decide on entering myself as a fellow-commoner of Queen's College, Cambridge, which was the college Madden himself had been at.

I considered it rather a formidable undertaking to set to work to rub up my Latin and Greek eleven years after I had left school, although that school, Richards's of Winchester, (Hyde Abbey,) was one of the best schools in the kingdom for grounding boys in what they learnt, and though I had got into its first class; but I determined to set to work, with the assistance of a neighbouring clergyman, who came to me, I think, two or three times a week. I was quite astonished to find how quickly the things I had never thought of for eleven years were recalled to and impressed again on my memory, so that when I went up to Cambridge in the Easter term of 1825, the whole thing appeared far less formidable to me than I could possibly have expected a few months before.

I have heard the following story of Dean Milner, who was the president of Queen's College, Cambridge, some ten years before I went there ; I think it is mentioned in his life :—When he first went up to Cambridge, as the coach came within a mile or two of the town, they at intervals met several of the undergraduates, taking their afternoon walk in their caps and gowns, which academical costume had such an imposing effect upon his mind, that he exclaimed, in his Yorkshire dialect, " Can't them " there fellows construe Greek and Latin ! " Afterwards, when he heard some of them attempting to construe Latin or Greek in the lecture room, he said to himself, " Coom, Coom ! "

I also was somewhat relieved when I heard the performances of many of the men of the freshmen's class, and was inclined to feel, if not to say, " Come, Come ! "

I found my university course much less irksome to me than I had expected. As a fellow-commoner I dined at the fellows' table, and associated with them a good deal, and with the other fellow-commoners, though several of my intimate friends were pensioners and sizars. I think there were more truly religious men at Queen's, than at any other of the seventeen colleges, in proportion to the number of men on the books.

Immediately after I got to Cambridge I became acquainted with about ten or twelve men, most of them of my own age, who were in the habit of meeting at each others' rooms to take tea, and to read the Scriptures together. This was a great comfort and advantage to me ; and once a week I usually attended Mr. Simeon's tea-parties, to which he invited all the young men with whom he was acquainted. We remained only an hour, and he sat ready to answer the questions which any of his seventy or eighty visitors might propose to him. They were often on some difficult passage of Scripture or on some interesting point of religion. Perhaps there would be time for some twelve or fifteen questions, and thus by means of these parties and his sermon-parties, at which he instructed the young men as to the best method of composing sermons, and also by his own public ministrations, did this good man confer, by God's blessing, in the course of years, incalculable benefits on hundreds of young men who were preparing themselves for the ministerial office.

During the long vacation of 1823, I had a pleasant trip round the Land's End, from Portsmouth to the Clyde, in the Herald, my brother's ship, which was ordered there to embark Lord Dalhousie for Canada. I saw something of the lake and mountain scenery; and, after visiting Edinburgh, returned home by land.

I do not think there was much variation in my course each term at Cambridge. In the beginning of 1827 it occurred to me one day, as I was walking along Trumpington Street, near my lodgings, that there were numbers of children in Cambridge, and especially in Barnwell, who went to no Sunday school, and that there were many undergraduates who would, if the subject was mentioned to them, be glad to teach the children on that day.

The following letter, which I wrote some years ago, gives the account of the origin of the Jesus Lane, or Cambridge Gownsmen's, Sunday School :—

"From the REV. W. LEEKE to the REV. C. A. JONES.

"Holbrooke, near Derby, February, 1859.

"DEAR SIR,—Your printed circular of the 1st of December "only reached me a day or two ago, owing partly perhaps to its "having been sent first of all to Holbrooke in Suffolk. I will "endeavour to give in detail what I recollect with regard to the "'foundation and early history of the Jesus Lane Sunday "'School.'

"After I had been some time at Cambridge, I think it was in "1826,* it occurred to me that as there were numbers of children "in Barnwell who went to no Sunday school, and as there were "many of the members of the university who no doubt would "be glad to assist in instructing them, it would be most desirable "to form a gownsmen's Sunday school. I spoke to several of "my friends on the subject, who promised to become teachers;

* It was in 1827.

C 2

"and I also ascertained that there would be nothing in what we
"proposed to do contrary to the university regulations.

"The next point was to get a suitable school-room. I was
"informed that as the Society of Friends seldom used their
"meeting-house in Jesus Lane more than once a year, it was very
"probable that they would lend it to us for the proposed Sunday
"school. I immediately wrote on the subject to a gentleman,
"whose name I forget, who was mentioned as being one of the
"principal members of that society, who lived about eight or ten
"miles, I think, from Cambridge; and as I did not receive a
"reply to my letter, in about a week afterwards I drove over,
"accompanied by some friend, and called upon him, when he at
"once most kindly placed the meeting-house at our disposal. I
"then immediately requested my three much-valued friends, the
"late Rev. A. T. Carr, of Beverley, the Rev. James Mellor Brown,
"of Isham, and his brother, the Rev. Abner Brown, of Gretton, (we
"were all undergraduates of Queen's College,) to join me in visit-
"ing the whole of Barnwell, containing then about seven thou-
"sand inhabitants, for the purpose of inviting to our school all
"the children of a suitable age who attended no other Sunday
"school. We divided Barnwell into two parts; one of which
"was visited by the two Mr. Browns, the other by Mr. Carr and
"myself. There was much prayer for God's direction and bless-
"ing, and especially as we went from house to house. Mr. Carr
"and I took opposite sides of each street. My own plan was, to
"spend about four or five minutes in each house, to state our
"object in a few words, to speak most *seriously* and *earnestly* to
"the parents about their own state before God, and their care
"for the spiritual and eternal welfare of their children, and, after
"taking down the number of Sunday scholars they would send,
"to leave with them a religious tract or two.

"I was most kindly received everywhere, and found the in-
"habitants of Barnwell a very different set of people from what
"I had supposed them to be. There were many religious per-
"sons; and of those who had been neglecting the care of their
"souls, perhaps as many as twenty burst into tears when ear-
"nestly spoken to concerning their religious state. I thought
"that in two of the houses I visited, there were women of bad

" character; but they, on being seriously addressed, wished to
" appear respectable.

"The week in which we visited Barnwell was one of the most
" pleasing weeks of my life. On the following Sunday morning,
" 220 scholars of both sexes made their appearance at the ap-
" pointed time, in Jesus Lane. They were formed into classes,
" and the first class of girls was assigned to me. I afterwards
" had good reason to hope that three of them were, by God's
" mercy, savingly impressed by the instruction they received.
" Nearly all the children were at first from Barnwell; but I
" recollect one of my class, who died in a most happy state,
" came from quite the other side of Cambridge, beyond the
" grounds of St. John's College. The teachers were in the habit
" of visiting the parents of the children belonging to their classes.
" I forget who was the first superintendent of the school. The
" three friends above mentioned were teachers; I cannot be quite
" sure about any of the others. At the request of the teachers, I
" drew up the first rules for the school. One difficulty which we
" anticipated, but which was overcome, was that of getting
" friends who would take charge of the school out of term time.

" I have now stated every particular I can recollect relating
" to the first establishment of this Sunday school, and I fear at
" the risk of being considered very egotistical. I perhaps should
" mention that I had been ten years in the army before I went
" to Cambridge, and that I and the three friends above mentioned
" were older than most of those who joined us in the work; this
" will account to you for our undertaking to visit the houses in
" Barnwell, and for my undertaking the charge of the first class
" of girls. I have no objection to your printing my name on the
" List of Teachers.   Believe me, dear Sir,
            " Very faithfully yours,
                  " WM. LEEKE,
      " Incumbent of Holbrooke, Derbyshire, and
          " Rural Dean of Duffield."

This school has, in the course of nearly forty years, been of
great service, I believe, to numbers of the scholars and teachers,
many of the latter being distinguished for their talents and for
their piety. Most of them are mentioned in the list published

in the "History of the Jesus Lane Sunday School," by the Rev. C. A. Jones. Some of the particulars mentioned by him are most interesting, though he has been led to publish some very incorrect statements with regard to the first origin of the school. I am much pleased to think, that at the time I am writing this (February 6, 1866) my four sons are all teachers in the school, the eldest being the superintendent. I may be allowed to state here that he was Second Wrangler, Smith's Prizeman, and Second Class Classic in 1864, and that he is a Fellow and Assistant-Tutor of Trinity College; thus evidencing that the giving considerable attention to that which relates to the highest interests of his fellow creatures, does not preclude a young man from exercising talents of a very high order in following out the studies of the university to which he belongs.

When speaking of St. Andrew's, I mentioned that one of our friends, who did not at all like my proposing to him to join us in studying the Scriptures at each other's houses once a week, afterwards became a very serious man, and I think I have stated that he came to see me at Cambridge. It was a great pleasure to me to meet him again under all the circumstances which had taken place; and, being anxious that he should derive some benefit during his very short stay at the place, I invited some of my most intimate and religious friends to meet him at my rooms. Our custom at our weekly meeting was to drink tea together, and afterwards to read some portion of Scripture and to discuss it, and I thought the best thing we could do, particularly as regarded my friend's benefit, was to pursue the same plan on the occasion of his being of the party. It happened, however, that during our tea-drinking a number of droll stories were told by one and another, so that we got into roars of laughter. Everyone appeared to vie with his neighbour in recollecting and relating the most ridiculous anecdotes imaginable; and this was so kept up, that although I was on the watch to bring out my Bible, and really anxious that we should endeavour to spend our time more profitably, it was quite impossible to do so, no one being in a state to commence reading or praying from the fear that he and the others might be convulsed with laughter; and we separated at our usual hour, nine o'clock, without being able to do that which, I believe, we all longed to do. I fear some of my readers will scarcely understand how this could possibly happen. I only recollect one of the ridiculous stories, which there was no harm in, and I have been thinking I would relate it for the amusement of my readers; but the bare thought of the roars of laughter which each reader must necessarily give way to, as he reads the anecdote, has led me, even when I am sitting writing by myself, to indulge in such merriment, that, although I shall no doubt be considered very tantalizing and unkind, I feel bound to withhold it, lest it should recur to the minds of my readers at serious times, as it is highly calculated to do, and thus occasion them much trouble and perhaps sorrow. Some people are much more addicted to joking and to relating silly anecdotes than others, and I do not mean to say that it is sinful to do so to a certain extent, but I have often known it to be unduly indulged in, and thus, to say the least of it, to take the place of that which might be more profitable to those engaged in it. The remembrance of that evening at Cambridge has sometimes checked me when inclined to give way to *too much* mirth. How far does the passage in James v, 13, "Is any afflicted? let him pray: Is any merry? "let him sing psalms," apply to the subject?

I felt deeply humbled before God and grieved as I started from my lodgings to walk with my New Brunswick friend to the hotel at which he was to sleep. I knew that probably we should not meet again in this world. But I look back with much thankfulness to what followed. As we walked along the streets we fell into conversation on those points which I had longed to speak to him about, and instead of our separating when we first reached the Eagle, we turned and walked up and down the streets for nearly, or quite, three hours, going into the various truths of Scripture connected with our salvation through the death and satisfaction of our Lord and Saviour, the way of holiness, and of present and everlasting happiness. I never enjoyed any conversation more, than that of which there seemed to be little prospect, when our party broke up. I think I have observed on many occasions in the course of my life, that great comfort and peace have followed almost immediately on a feeling of deep humility before God for "sins, negligences and

" ignorances." And further, although it does not particularly apply to what I have just related, that the *greatest* delight and joy I have ever experienced in the assurance of God's forgiveness, favour, and lovingkindness, I have felt in the midst of the very greatest trials and troubles which I have ever experienced in life : Psalm cxii, 4 ; Job xxii, 21, 29 ; Isaiah xxvi, 3, 4.

CHAPTER XXIX.

1826.

MALTA AND BACK.

Embark in the Herald—Violent gale—Ship in danger—Answer to prayer—Falmouth—Remarkable cure of a long standing cough—Lord Hastings and family on board—Gibraltar—General Don—Trip to the cork wood - Story of Spanish robbers—Magnificent view from the top of the rock of Gibraltar—43rd Regiment—Arrival at Malta—Invited to take up my quarters at the palace—Kindness of the family—Gozo—Ball at the palace—Spend the evening with Mr. Jowett—His remarkable saying on his death-bed—Four descendants of the author of "The Antiquities of the Christian Church"—Return to Gibraltar—The North Carolina—Man overboard.

ABOUT the beginning of March, 1826, I went to Portsmouth to see my brother before he sailed for Malta, whither he was to convey the governor, the Marquis of Hastings, and his family. I had at that time been suffering from a severe cough, from about the 20th of October, and I began to think it would never leave me. My brother and the surgeon of the ship thought that a sea voyage would probably be of great service to me, and I, taking into consideration my somewhat alarming illness a few years before, thought as they did, and made up my mind to go in the Herald to Malta. We had some very stormy weather in the Channel, and contrary winds. On the third day, when abreast of the bay in which Plymouth and Falmouth lie, we experienced the heaviest gale, the sailors said, and I suppose they often say it, they had ever been out in in their lives. There was some intention, I think, of putting into Falmouth when we were not far from the Lizard, but the weather proved very hazy near the land,

and the gale increased to a hurricane : it was considered, therefore, most dangerous to attempt to run for either of the above-
named ports, so the idea was given up, and the ship attempted
to beat off, the wind blowing right into the bay. The Herald
was a good sea-boat, but I think not very weatherly, as, I believe,
the sailors term it, so that, instead of beating out of the bay, she
went very rapidly to leeward. My brother came to me and said,
" I will tell you what I have not yet mentioned to anyone in the
" ship, and it is, that I consider we are in very great danger ; we
" are going to leeward at the rate of three miles an hour, and if
" the gale continues from the same point for three hours more,
" we must be driven on shore, and most likely every person on
" board will be lost. I dare not run for Falmouth or Plymouth
" in this hazy weather, for if we were to miss the entrance of the
" port, which it is most likely we should, the ship would be dashed
" to pieces." I proposed that we should go below to his cabin,
and offer up prayer to God to spare our lives, and the lives of the
crew, and of all on board, if it pleased Him to do so, and if not,
that He would fit and prepare us for the death which was so near
to us. My brother replied that it was what he was going to
suggest, and that afterwards, if the gale continued, he would call
the men together, and tell them of the great danger the ship was
in, and exhort them to prepare for the worst. We accordingly
went to his cabin, and earnestly prayed to our merciful God and
Father to the above effect. We spent about ten minutes or a
quarter of an hour in prayer, and then went on deck again.
When we had been about three minutes on deck, the officer of
the watch suddenly exclaimed, " The wind has changed, Sir ! "
And so it had : in the midst of a regular hurricane the wind had
chopped round four points of the compass, and the Herald stood
out to sea. My brother and I never speak of it to this day but
as a remarkable interposition of a God of mercy, in answer to the
humble and earnest prayers of us two poor, unworthy, sinful
creatures. Probably there were other persons on board who
trusted in God's mercy, and who also perceived or feared the
danger, and prayed for deliverance.

The next day the gale had considerably moderated, but the
wind being against us, we put into Falmouth. Strange to say,

my cough, which had lasted for more than four months, was *entirely gone*, notwithstanding that I had been on deck during almost the whole of every day, wet with the rain, and with the sea which occasionally beat over us. I preferred being on deck for two reasons; one was, that I was less inclined to be squeamish or sea-sick than I was when below, the other, that I was anxious to see the discipline of a man-of-war in a gale of wind. We were afterwards told that there was a report at Portsmouth that the Herald was lost, and that all on board had perished. My poor mother had a servant who was very fond of relating anything dreadful or marvellous, without having much consideration for the shock which he might thereby occasion to persons' feelings. Whilst this gale was at its height, or shortly afterwards, he came to her and said, "Have you heard the report, Ma'am?" She replied, "No, John, what is it?" He said, "It's reported that "the Herald is lost, and that all hands have perished!"

I took the opportunity of going down one of the mines in the neighbourhood of Falmouth; I think we were there for only one clear day. I recollect we experienced the hospitality and kindness of Captain King, the superintendent at Falmouth, and his family.

We had a pleasant voyage to Gibraltar, where the Herald remained several days, and this gave us an opportunity of exploring the rock, and its casemated batteries and other fortifications. We went with General Don, the governor, and the Marquis of Hastings and family, some few miles into Spain, to the cork wood; I was furnished with a horse, others went in carriages. One of the staff gave me an account of his having been attacked by robbers a few months before, when he had driven his wife over in a gig to the cork wood. It was not looked upon as a dangerous place at the time, but all at once he was called to stop, and on looking to see what was the matter, he observed four men at some distance advancing towards him, from different directions, with long guns to their shoulders pointed at him. He was unarmed, and very properly, under the circumstances, thought "the better part of valour was discretion;" he obeyed the summons to pull up, and, without inflicting any personal injury on him or his wife, they took their money and, what was worse, they took the horse, and left them to get back to Gibraltar as well as they could.

On our return from the cork wood we were to go to Sir George Don's, and dine there. I experienced what in those days we used to term " one of the miseries of human life :" by some mistake my proper things had not been sent on shore, and I was forced to appear at dinner in a portion of my riding costume. The governor and Lady Don were very kind. There were in the drawing-room the two largest and most beautiful dogs I have ever seen; I forget their exact breed, but I fancy they were Cuban or South American blood-hounds. They moved about at their pleasure, and took possession of the ottomans when it suited their inclination to do so, and went round to all the visitors to make their acquaintance. My brother and I dined with our old friends of the 43rd whilst we were at Gibraltar.

The splendid view from the top of the rock was what I admired and enjoyed more than anything else at Gibraltar. To look down, and away to the eastward, as far as the eye could reach, upon the blue waters of the Mediterranean, covered with the white and shining sails of countless vessels; and then to the north-east, on the long range of the coast of Spain, and of the mountains of Andalusia; and to the south and south-east, on Ceuta and the northern coast and mountains of Africa; and then turning about, to the north and north-west were to be seen the harbour of Gibraltar, and Algesiras, and Tarifa, and farther on, through the gut of Gibraltar, were the Atlantic Ocean and Cape Trafalgar, as famous in our naval annals as Waterloo is in those of our army; and not far to the northward was Cadiz, where my poor eldest brother lost his life. Altogether the panorama is the finest and most splendid, I should imagine, of any in the world; and then all the associations connected with that rock and view, and England's power and greatness as a nation—all helped to enhance the pleasure and wonder with which one contemplated the magnificent scene around.

I visited a battery on the top of the rock, from which I found that they occasionally fired at smuggling vessels. There was a serjeant's guard stationed there. I was told by the serjeant that there had been several cases of men losing their lives in getting down the scarped eastern side of the rock of Gibraltar, when wishing to desert. There were many monkeys on the western slope of the rock, but we did not see any of them.

Nothing remarkable happened on our voyage from Gibraltar to Malta. On our arrival at Valetta the Marquis of Hastings very kindly invited my brother and myself to take up our quarters at the palace whilst the Herald remained there. The Marquis and Marchioness and their four daughters made our visit to Malta most agreeable. All the officers of the ship received in turn invitations to dine at the palace; and what particularly struck me was, that if anyone appeared to be at all shy, both Lord and Lady Hastings had the very kindest way I ever saw of making them feel quite at their ease, without in the least appearing to take any notice of their shyness. I think I saw more of poor Lady Flora Hastings than of the rest of the family, as I usually sat next to her at dinner; and no one could be, even for a short time, in her company without perceiving how truly amiable and religiously disposed she was. The following stanzas, said to have been written by Lady Flora, who died in 1839, were sent to a member of my family not very long after that melancholy event took place :—

> " Still has my life new wonders seen
>   Repeated every year,
> Behold my days that still remain,
>   I trust them to thy care.
>
> Cast me not off now strength decays,
>   Now heavy hours arise,
> And round me let Thy glory shine,
>   Whene'er Thy servant dies."

I think it was the second day after our arrival at Malta, that Lord Falkland, who was on his way to join his regiment at Corfu, became a guest at the palace, and was in a way doubled up with me; that is, our bed-rooms were at each end of a sitting-room between them, which was common to us both. He was a nice young man, and made himself very agreeable during the few days that he remained at Malta.

The Herald was detained there nearly a fortnight, which gave us the opportunity of seeing something of the island, and also of Gozo, which is close to it. That I might go to the latter place in the most agreeable manner, Lord Hastings placed at my disposal a large boat and a boat's crew, and gave me a letter to the commandant of the island, who was to introduce me and my companion, my brother's brother-in-law, a midshipman of the Herald, to the prior of the monastery, at which we were to take up our quarters. We coasted the northern shore of the island, and passed the spot at which tradition says St. Paul was shipwrecked. There is the place where the two seas could meet; and the master of the Herald told me that the soundings off the island agree with those mentioned in the twenty-seventh of Acts, the 27th and 28th verses. We were kindly and hospitably taken care of by the commandant and the monks at Gozo. They have a fine garden attached to their monastery. I think it was from a terrace near it that I got a very distant view of Etna. We visited the Fungus Rock, which was one of the chief celebrities of Gozo. I forget whether we dined with the commandant or at the monastery, but what I remember best was, that I, as the principal guest at the monastery, had the best bed-room allotted to me, and my companion had to put up with an inferior one. I paid rather dearly for the honour, for I was devoured by fleas and could not get any sleep during the whole night, whilst my friend in the more humble apartments escaped molestation and slept soundly. I think we only remained one night at Gozo and then returned to Valetta.

Soon after his return from England Lord Hastings held a levée, which I attended. In the evening there was a grand ball at the palace: this I was not disposed to attend, and made an arrangement with that excellent man, the Rev. William Jowett, that I would drink tea with him, and pass the evening at his house. I spoke to Lady Flora on the subject, and she assured me that my preferring to pass the evening in that way instead of going to the ball (which, by the way, I had no intention of attending, although I was a guest at the palace) would not be annoying to Lord and Lady Hastings. Mr. Jowett was, I think, superintendent missionary of all the Church Missionary Society's missionaries and agents on the coasts of the Mediterranean, and a very able, diligent, methodical, and pious man he was. I always reckoned him amongst four of the most diligent Christians I had ever met with; and yet such a humble opinion had he of himself and of his own attainments, that when, many years after, the question was proposed to him on his dying bed, "Mr. Jowett, "are you afraid to die?" he replied, "No, I am not afraid to "die, but I am *ashamed* to die." By which, of course, he meant that although he knew he was pardoned and accepted through Christ, and sanctified by His Word and Spirit, yet he was but a poor, sinful, unworthy servant of his Lord and Master: Matthew v, 3.

He published a work, in four small volumes, called "The "Christian Visitor," which I have always considered a most useful work for ladies and others who visit the sick, or to lend to the poor. It contains short sermons, of about three pages, with a very short prayer at the end of each; there are two volumes on Old Testament and two on New Testament texts. Perhaps the following circumstances may help to recommend it to those of my readers who are not acquainted with the work, and who may wish to have some plain, simple volumes which they may read, or lend to their neighbours. Two of my parishioners made use of the same expressions with regard to one of the volumes; I think in both cases it was that which contained sermons on texts in the gospels. They told me that they "had reason to "thank God that that book had come into their hands." I was in London just at the time that one of my principal parishioners was leaving the parish, and wishing to give him some little remembrance, I sent him the four volumes of "The Christian "Visitor," and also one of the volumes for each of his servants. In writing to thank me for the books, he mentioned that the Primate of Ireland, (the late Lord John Beresford,) who was staying with them, had spent the greater part of the day before in reading one of the volumes, I think he said that on the epistles, and that he was so pleased with it, that he had written to London to desire several copies of the work to be sent to him in Ireland.

After passing a long and profitable evening with Mr. Jowett, and some missionary friends whom he invited to meet me, I returned to the palace, and, as I went along the corridor to my

room, of course found the ball going forward with great
vigour.

One day, during my stay at the palace, I came in rather too
late for dinner, and before I was nearly ready a servant came to
my room to tell me that the dinner was on the table; I took it
for granted that the party would go to dinner without me, but,
on my going down to the drawing-room, to my dismay I found
them still there; and, on my apologizing, and saying that I had
hoped they were not waiting for me, Lord Hastings, in his gentle
way, replied, "We could not think of going to dinner without
"you." This was a little lesson which I determined to profit by
for the future.

The captain and subaltern of the main-guard, which was opposite to the palace, always dined with the governor. One day I
found myself seated next to the captain of a Dutch frigate, which
had just arived at Valetta. He was a very agreeable man, and,
in the course of conversation, offered to give me a passage to
Smyrna. The offer was very tempting, but my plans would not
allow of my profiting by it.

I remember that Lord Hastings, one evening after dinner,
mentioned the following fact as having occurred when, as governor-
general of India, he was proceeding through the country with a
retinue consisting of a considerable body of troops and camp
followers, amounting altogether to some thousands of persons. I
do not recollect what part of India it was in, but they were encamped for the night on ground about a mile in width, and of
some considerable extent; and during the night a sort of pesti-
lential blast passed through the length of the encampment,
confining its effects, however, within the limit of about half a
mile, whilst those encamped on either side of that limit entirely
escaped it: vast numbers were seized with illness, and many
died. We heard little of cholera in those days in England, but
my impression is, that this sudden and fatal attack of pestilence
shews that it must have been the cholera-morbus. I think I
have given the account correctly, but I do not recollect that any
name was given to the pestilence.

We went with the family several times to a country-house
and garden which Lord Hastings had a few miles from Valetta.

It was just the time at which the oranges were becoming ripe, and I never tasted fruit of any kind more delicious than the blood oranges in that garden. My readers are aware that the oranges imported into England are gathered in a green state, and that they ripen on the voyage, and afterwards. To try the experiment, we took several of the ripe blood oranges with us when we left Malta: those that were not eaten were all rotten before the ship reached Gibraltar. Those which were gathered in a green or greenish state came into use at a later period of our voyage. No one, who has not tasted the ripe fruit gathered from the trees, can form any idea of the comparative insipidity of the best oranges which we eat in England.

I was only on horseback once whilst we were at Malta, and then it was to ride with a party to a place (I forget its name) about seven miles off, where was a famous library, which every one went to see. The only book I recollect was a Latin edition of my ancestor's, the Rev. Joseph Bingham's, "Antiquities of the "Christian Church." As I took down one of the volumes, I said to the priest, or monk, I forget which, who was shewing us through the rooms, "The author of that work was my great "great grandfather;" he very quickly replied, "Two English "officers, who were here a few weeks ago, said exactly the same "thing!" I was somewhat taken aback by the suddenness and manner of his reply; but I then recollected that there were two officers in the Mediterranean fleet who bore exactly the same relationship that I did to that great and learned man. I explained the thing to the priest, or monk, but he still appeared to be somewhat incredulous with regard to the author of the "Antiqui-"ties" having three great great grandsons (my brother was not there, or he would have made a fourth) who had visited the library within so short a space of time.

I have observed above that this was the only time I was on horseback whilst we were at Malta. My horse behaved very well during our ride out from Valetta, but not so on our return. Just as we were entering the fortifications he commenced some extraordinary pranks, which were certainly anything but pleasant. We were cantering or trotting quietly along, when, possibly at the sound of the clatter on the drawbridge, or from former associations, he tore away at the top of his speed, and then, when powerfully brought up, he performed, at a marvellously quick rate, a series of *girouettes* nothing like which I had ever known a horse to do before. Then off he started again furiously, running my leg up against and along the wall of a gateway, apparently with the intention of rubbing me off: then we had the *girouettes* again. Had I not been a tolerable rider, I must have been un-horsed by my Bucephalus; as it was, I was exceedingly pleased when I had safely dismounted from him. I was told afterwards that one of the officers of the garrison had, some time before, lost his life near the same place, when riding an unmanageable horse; and it was suspected that this was the same horse. I had not the opportunity of finding out whether it was or not.

It was with no ordinary feelings of gratitude for all the kind-ness and attention we had met with that we left Malta. Nothing very particular occurred on our voyage to Gibraltar: we came across a merchant-ship which had been partly dismasted by one of those sudden and partial squalls not uncommon in the Medi-terranean. We had experienced nothing but fine weather, and had come along only at the rate of eight or nine knots an hour; and it appeared strange to find a vessel so disabled, evidently only a very short time before, for when we passed her, she had not begun to clear away the wreck.

About three months ago, that is, nearly forty years after the circumstance occurred which I am about to mention, one of the old officers of the Herald fell in with my brother, and, in the course of conversation, enquired after me, and told him that he had great reason to be thankful to God that he ever became acquainted with me. That from having been very careless, he had become a religious man, and that he traced back his feelings of anxiety about his soul, and of desire to serve God, to a conver-sation he had with me on the quarter-deck of the Herald, when I had particularly called his attention to one of the chapters in Isaiah: I think it must have been the fifty-fifth chapter. This is another instance of the fulfilment of the promise contained in Ecclesiastes xi, 1, and should encourage all who fear God to attend diligently to the command given in the 6th verse of that chapter. I regret that I have not more regularly attended to it.

On our return to Gibraltar we found there the American 74, the North Carolina, Commodore Rogers or Porter, and, I think, the Hornet, sloop of war, forming part of their Mediterranean squadron. We went on board to call on the commodore, who received us with great cordiality; all hands were turned up on deck, and I never saw a finer set of fellows in my life. My brother's coxswain fell in with an old shipmate, who told him that three-fourths of the crew were English. Commodore Rogers spoke of his ship as being remarkably easy, and free from rolling and pitching, and, as a proof of this, pointed out to us a pair of ordinary candlesticks on the mantel-piece in his cabin, which had never been moved since the ship left America.

We had a pleasant passage to England. A few days, however, before we reached Spithead, one forenoon we were startled by the cry of "A man overboard!" The life-buoy was immediately let go from the stern, and nearly at the same moment Mr. Robbins, one of the midshipmen, jumped overboard. The man had fallen overboard amid-ships, and by the time the stern of the ship passed him the life-buoy and Mr. Robbins had both reached the water not very far from him. Had this young officer not gone overboard at the time he did, the man would have been drowned, as he could not swim a stroke. I forget now whether he got hold of the man and swam with him to the life-buoy, or whether he took the life-buoy to the man. Of course some time elapsed before the ship, which was going about seven knots an hour, rounded to, and before a boat was lowered, and reached those who were hanging on to the life-buoy. We were told afterwards that, only a few days before, Mr. Robbins had complained of this man for some neglect of duty, and that a slight punishment was awarded him. While they were in the water, and when the ship was at a considerable distance, the man referred to this, and after thanking his deliverer for jumping overboard to his rescue, told him that, whether they were picked up or not, he must remember that he bore him no ill-will for having reported him on the above-mentioned occasion.

CHAPTER XXX.

1827—1831.

CAMBRIDGE. WESTHAM.

Visiting Sunday school children—Lodging-houses—Severe illness—Friends and
clerical meeting near Chichester—Curacy of Westham—Hard work—
Services—Martello Towers—Coast-guard—Lord Cochrane's plan of blowing
up Martello Towers—Death of little boy—Curious case of want of memory
—Smuggling—Baby—Leave Westham.

AFTER the establishment of the Cambridge Gownsmen's Sunday
School in the beginning of 1826, I included amongst the persons
whom I visited the parents of the children who belonged to my
class; and this led me into visiting some of the sick in several
parts of Cambridge. I now forget the circumstances which led
me occasionally to visit two of the lodging-houses for beggars and
other poor travellers. It was, however, a very interesting part of
my work. They appeared to give great attention to all the
religious instruction which I endeavoured to give them, and expressed themselves as being very thankful for it. It was an
understood thing amongst them that they should never beg from
me; and I do not recollect that I ever gave them, when I visited
the houses, anything beyond tracts and small books, but I gave
the owners of the houses permission to make known to me any
peculiarly distressing case of destitution which might occur.

I only remember one instance in which this permission was
acted upon, and it very nearly cost me my life. A poor woman
was sent to me whose child was dying of the small-pox, not that
I might put her in the way of getting medical advice, but that I

might give her something towards burying the child. When I found that the child had not been seen by a surgeon, I desired the woman at once to come with me to Mr. Fawcett's. We met that gentleman not far from my lodging, and he very kindly went with us to the house. As it was only an infant, and I could be of no service to it, I remained below, in a rather large, airy room, with the door open, whilst he and the mother proceeded upstairs. I had no apprehension of taking the complaint, particularly as I had been inoculated for the small-pox as an infant. The child died, and on the fifteenth day from that on which the mother came to me, I was taken so seriously ill that my life was considered in great danger, and my mother was sent for. It turned out to be a very severe attack of small-pox. Whether I caught it at the lodging-house or from the smell of the woman's clothes I could not tell, but I recollected afterwards, that when she was telling me her case, and standing within a yard of me, I smelt the brimstone, which all the persons who lodged in those houses smelt of in those days, from the practice which prevailed of making the matches which they sold partly of brimstone. I presume that if persons can convey the smell of brimstone, of tobacco, or of a stable in their clothes, the clothes will just as readily convey infection. I have had to make many hundreds of visits to persons suffering from infectious disorders, but always endeavoured to change and air my clothes before going amongst my family or into other houses. I have sometimes omitted this precaution when the disease has been slight and I have been much in the air afterwards.

When I returned home, after recovering from my illness, I remember the surgeon told me I must not consider myself as free from the danger of taking the disease again because I had already had it twice, but rather take the view that I perhaps was particularly liable to it. When I went up to Cambridge again after the long vacation, in the very first house I went to visit, the people told me, after I had been there a few minutes, that there were two cases of small-pox in the house. Since then I have visited many persons suffering from this most dreadful of all diseases, but have been mercifully preserved from it, and from other infectious disorders, though I have frequently, but not always, felt unwell for a day or two after breathing the infected atmosphere.

I had the pleasure and advantage, sometimes in the vacations, of attending a very nice clerical meeting, composed of several of the clergy in the neighbourhood of Chichester. Amongst them were my much-valued friend the Rev. Stephen Barbut, Mr. Sargeant, the author of the Memoir of Henry Martyn, and Mr. Raikes, afterwards chancellor of Chester. At Cambridge I had a great number of kind Christian friends. Amongst them were two who afterwards became bishops; one of them, on my congratulating him, &c., on his elevation to the bench, wrote to me to say how much advantage he had derived from my example and kindness, &c., at Cambridge.

Although I passed my examination in January 1828, I did not take my degree till the October following, as I had some terms to keep. On the first of January, 1829, I was ordained by the Bishop of Chichester to the curacy of Westham, in Sussex. The vicar was my kind and esteemed friend the Rev. Henry T. Grace, Fellow of Emmanuel College, Cambridge. The village of Westham was on one side of the extensive ruins of Pevensey castle, and the village of Pevensey was on the other side. The sea had formerly come up to the castle walls, but now it had receded about a mile, and a plain of shingle lay between it and Westham church and parsonage. All along the coast were Martello Towers,* at the distance of about a third of a mile from

---

* The mentioning the Martello Towers puts me in mind of the following anecdote related to us by the late Admiral Sir Jahleel Brenton :—Lord Cochrane, afterwards Earl of Dundonald, when talking to him one day said to him in an off-hand way, " Brenton, how do you blow up Martello Towers?" Sir J. Brenton told him that he knew nothing at all about blowing up Martello Towers, never having been employed on any such service. Lord Cochrane, who, it must be remembered performed many services of this sort on the coast of Catalonia, then said that his plan was to land with a party of marines, whom he drew up sufficiently near to the tower to enable them to open fire upon any of the enemy shewing their heads over the parapet on the top, and that directly a head appeared, " bang " went two or three muskets at it ; by which means he managed to make them keep out of sight, whilst he and one of his men, carrying on his back a canvass bag with thirty-six pounds of powder in it, ran forward under the solid wall of the tower, and having laid the bag at the bottom of the wall, he held a parley with the enemy above, telling them that, unless they threw their gun over the top, he would blow their tower about their ears : in many cases the

each other; and in some of these were located the officers and men of the coast-guard. The population amounted to about 800, and I had the sole charge, as the vicar resided at his other living of Jevington, which was situated about six miles off on the other side of Eastbourne, amongst the south downs. I had become a married man in the October before, and as we had no very near neighbours we lived rather a retired life at Westham; our principal society being that of the clergy of the surrounding parishes and their families, who had established a nice clerical meeting which met at the different houses in turn. Indeed I found so much work to do in the parish, that there was no time for any other kind of visiting. There were the two services in the church every Sunday, and a gratuitous weekly service for the coast-guardsmen, one party collecting to the eastward one week and another to the westward on the alternate week. They now and then were marched to church; but that could not be done at all regularly, lest the smugglers should take advantage of it. There was a weekly lecture in the village of Westham, another at Handcomb, about a mile and a half to the northward, and another to the people in the alms-houses. I had altogether thirteen services in the fortnight; these, with my other parochial duties, kept me very hard at work. I always remember the pleasant feeling of lightness of heart and freedom from parochial care which I experienced when we got a mile or two from the

men above, probably having heard of his previous exploits against towers and signal stations on the coast, attended to his summons and sent the gun over. When they did not at once comply with his demand he lighted the match, and in a few seconds, as soon as they could arrive at a sufficient distance from the explosion, the fire reached the powder, and the massive wall came crumbling down. My recollection of the round Martello Towers on the coast of Sussex is, that the wall was from six to eight feet thick, and that they were entered by a ladder through a door on the land side, the bottom of which was about eight feet from the ground, and that from the door there was a passage through the masonry into the interior. During the Canadian rebellion, when I heard of the rebels making resistance in buildings, I thought the above account of sufficient importance to send it out to Lord Seaton through the adjutant-general's office. I may mention that a military friend, who was present when Sir Jahleel Brenton gave us the anecdote, afterwards maintained that Lord Cochrane's plan was to seek out some hole or gutter into which he thrust the bag of powder; but on my referring to Sir Jahleel Brenton on that point, he decidedly stated that the bag was laid against the bottom of the wall.

parish, on our leaving it on one occasion to take a holiday of a week or ten days in Hampshire.

We were not well off for teachers in the Sunday school; and I had about fifty boys, whom I instructed together. When we left the parish on the above-mentioned occasion, one of these boys, a child seven years old, was ill with rheumatic fever, a complaint which I did not consider dangerous; but on our return I found it had turned to scarlet fever, and that the poor little fellow was dead. I, of course, had known very little about him as regarded his knowledge of the simple truths of religion, as I chiefly taught him and the rest of the boys together. On my asking his mother, who did not know much about religion herself, what his feelings were, as far as she could judge, in the expectation of death, she told me that the day before he died, he inquired two or three times if she thought the Lord would have mercy on him; and that she had told him that He would if he prayed to Him. She added that she did not remember that he said anything more on the subject till just before his death, when she heard him exclaim in a loud voice, three times, "O Lord, *do* "have mercy upon me! O Lord, *do* have mercy upon me! O "Lord, *do* have mercy upon me!" And then he died. There was something so pleasing and so touching, and such simple faith in this, that I have thought it well to record it.

There was a rather remarkable case which I think it may be useful to mention. It was that of an old woman in the workhouse at Westham, whose memory was very defective with regard to the most simple truths of religion; and who yet appeared to receive them, and to rest upon them, and to take comfort from them, as they were spoken and explained to her from time to time. That she was a poor sinner in the sight of God she knew, and, every time it was mentioned to her, she received, and seemed to delight in, the great truth of all, that Jesus Christ, the Son of God, took our nature upon Him and died upon the cross to make satisfaction for our sins—to be punished in our stead. And when she was told that God had promised to give His Holy Spirit to those who ask Him, and that the Holy Spirit, by means of the Word, taught us our sinfulness and our need of a Saviour, and led us to trust in this Saviour, and to hate and strive against what was wrong, and to love what God commands, and to seek and find help to keep His commands—all this she would understand at the time, and would repeat after me simple sentences of prayer that God would give her those blessings; but the very next day, or even the next minute, I used to find that she had forgotten everything; and could not tell me who it was died to save sinners, or who it was that God sent to make us holy and to comfort us. To the very last day of her life it was the same; but though she had such a defective memory, yet was she enabled to receive the great truths of salvation when they were laid before her, and her soul appeared to be nourished by them.

Eastbourne was about three miles from Westham, and some of the visitors to that place used to come to our church on the Sunday. Smuggling was the great evil of that part of the country, and one that the minister had to contend against both in public and in private. One Sunday, after I had been preaching on the subject, one of the visitors told me of a clergyman in a distant part of the coast, who had been preaching one Sunday about the sin of smuggling, and that as the congregation were coming out of church one of them was heard to say, "Our minister does "very well till he gets to preaching upon *politics*, and there he "loses himself." The smugglers were very inveterate against any one whom they suspected of giving information of an expected run, as it was called. My predecessor, I was told, never ventured out at night without pistols in his pocket; and I heard that that good man, Dr. Fearon, of Oare, had in some way incurred their displeasure. I never had any opportunity of giving any information, but it was well known that I should think it right to do everything in my power to put a stop to their illegal and dangerous practices. The most of those who ran the blockade with the casks of spirits, lived, I think, more in the interior. We were returning one very dark night from the lecture at Handcomb, when we heard the measured tramp of a body of men coming towards us. We knew they must be smugglers. There was, perhaps, time at first for us to have got into the adjoining fields, or into the hedge. I did not wonder at my poor wife being considerably alarmed, but I did not think it good policy that there should be any appearance of our being afraid of them, and so we pursued our course on the road. We could distinguish figures, and that was all. I saw that they marched four abreast, and there must have been about seventy of them. They kept perfect silence, and took no notice of us, though they must have seen us, and probably knew, at least some of them, who we were. We were told afterwards that they had been expecting a vessel to land a cargo of brandy, but had been disappointed.

I was ordained priest by the Bishop of Chichester, on the 1st of January, 1830. I observed, and so did the other candidates, that the examination was much more prolonged, and what is termed stiffer, than it was the year before. I thought that for one question which had been proposed to me the year before there were at the least ten at this second ordination. It was mentioned afterwards that one of the candidates had travelled to Chichester with one of the bishop's examining chaplains, who had not assisted at the former examination, and was therefore unknown to the candidate; and the young clergyman had entertained him on the road with an account of the easy questions which had been given the year before, and of the little difficulty he had experienced in passing the examination. This incident was supposed to account for the more trying ordeal to which we were subjected on the following day.

Whilst I was at Chichester my wife, with her eldest child, then an infant three months old, was staying with some of our relatives at one of the hotels at Hastings. On my joining them there, I was, of course, received most cordially; and, after a short time, the baby was brought into the room, and I must say I was somewhat disappointed to find that my pretty child, as I had considered it, had become very much changed in appearance. At least I fancied it was not nearly so nice-looking as it was when I left it; however, I made no remark about it, nor did my friends. In a little time the nurse brought in another baby, and, on looking at it, I found that it was my own child, and that the infant child of the mistress of the hotel had been palmed off upon me instead of my own. My eldest daughter is now the wife of Mr. Horsfall, the member for Liverpool.

There are very extensive marshes in the neighbourhood of Westham, and after some time I found that, although the rest of our party seemed to enjoy good health, the place did not agree with me.   This led to my leaving the parish and my kind vicar, and many kind friends in and around it, when I had been there rather more than two years.

CHAPTER XXXI.

1831.

BRAILSFORD, DERBYSHIRE.

Derby riots—Address to the King on the sins of the nation—Lord Roden reads
it to the King—Several of the sins have been since given up.

PRINCIPALLY with the view of being near my wife's relations, I
looked out for a curacy in Derbyshire. Bishop Ryder, to whom
I had an introduction, was very kind about it, and, in the beginning of October, 1831, I was appointed to the curacy of Brailsford, a somewhat scattered parish of 800 inhabitants, lying about
half-way between Derby and Ashbourne, and being about six
miles and a half from each. Here I had plenty of work, and
enjoyed very good health. One of my chief works, besides those
connected with the parish, was the endeavouring to promote a
due observance of the Lord's Day, which was greatly profaned
throughout the land, and the divine authority and universal
obligation of which were boldly impugned in all directions.
Another work which I determined on was, to wage war with
and to oppose that system of pluralities which obtained in our
church, and which I considered to be a most disgraceful blot on
its escutcheon. There was also another work which employed
much of my time during my residence at Brailsford, and that
was, the trying to help to get the government to put a stop to
that abominable practice which prevailed, of requiring our officers
and soldiers to participate in the idolatrous ceremonies of the
Roman Catholic and Greek Churches. I think it may be useful
if I relate, to some extent, what course I pursued, and how far

God was pleased to prosper my poor but sincere efforts to remedy the evils I have enumerated. It was a habit with me, and I suppose it is also the practice of great numbers of earnest persons, that when I perceived anything which it was important should be done, and there appeared to be no one disposed to take it in hand, I, after duly considering it in all its bearings, generally ended by undertaking the matter myself; and thus I have been often engaged in all kinds of things which I have thought should be done, when there appeared to be no one else to do them.

I think it was on the very first Sunday on which I commenced my work at Brailsford that the Derby riots began. Two or three lives were lost; and they were put down chiefly, I think, through the energy of Mr. John Bell Crompton, one of the county magistrates. Having some business in Derby, and thinking that the riot was at an end, I went into the town on the Monday, and found that I had just come in for the chief part of it. A detachment from the 15th Hussars, at Nottingham, consisting of an officer and scarcely thirty men, charged the mob in the market-place very effectually, and then scoured the various streets leading from it. No lives were lost in the charge; many were tumbled over, but were apparently unhurt. I saw one man who was cut down by a sabre-cut down the side of his cheek. The mob were exceedingly cowed, and ran up the entries of the houses, and hid themselves in stables and pig-sties. When ordered out from the back premises of one of the houses, a serjeant and private of the 15th stood at the entrance of the passage, looking so formidable with their horses' fore feet on the pavement, and their swords uplifted, ready to make No. 7 cut, that I think there was not a single man out of more than a hundred of them who did not exceedingly tremble as he passed out, although they were told they should not be hurt if they went quietly home. One of a party of three, or four, who did not disperse immediately on being ordered to do so, was fired at and killed by one of the soldiers; but this I did not witness.

Some time after the Derby and Bristol, and other serious riots, I was led to draw up the following address to the King, and similar petitions to both Houses of Parliament. The idea of an address, and petitions, on the subject of our national sins,

will probably appear strange to many of my readers, but I think
they were not altogether without effect.

" *To His Most Excellent Majesty King William the Fourth.*

" The Humble and Loyal Address of the undersigned Inhabitants
"of the Parish of Brailsford, in the County of Derby.

" We, your Majesty's most dutiful and loyal subjects, beg
"leave in this time of trouble thus to approach your royal person,
"and to express our deep conviction that, on account of our many
"national sins, the favour of Almighty God is withdrawn from
"our land, and that He is visiting us with those most awful
"judgments, civil disorder and the noisome pestilence.

" We have read in the Word of God that whenever nations
"have departed awfully from the commands of the Lord, He has
"visited those nations with desolating and grievous judgments,
"and that when they have manifested a spirit of repentance and
"humiliation, He has been graciously pleased to avert His judg-
"ments from them :—

" And we therefore feel it our most bounden duty humbly to
"call the attention of your Majesty to some of the sins against
"Almighty God of which the rulers and people of this land are
"guilty, in the earnest hope that your Majesty may graciously
"see fit to take such steps on the occasion as may yet be the
"means of averting from us the heavy wrath of Him whom we
"have offended.

" We think it right to mention to your Majesty—

" First. The sin of holding six hundred thousand of our
"fellow-creatures in slavery, and the withholding from them
"proper religious privileges and instruction.

" Secondly. The sin of requiring our British Protestant sol-
"diers in foreign parts to participate in the idolatrous ceremonies
"of the Roman Catholic and Greek churches.

" Thirdly. The sin of levying the pilgrim-tax on the poor
"Hindoo idolators, by which we sanction and encourage their
"idolatry.

" Fourthly. The sin of affording supplies of the public money
"for the education of Roman Catholic priests, and to enable them
"to educate the Roman Catholic children in the religion of the

" church of Rome, whereby we virtually propagate doctrines
" which the Homilies of our Established Church declare to be
" hateful to God, and damnable to man.

"Fifthly. The sin of profaning the sabbath day, which most
" awfully prevails among rich and poor throughout the land, and
" which shews itself in a most glaring and public manner; in the
" vast concourse of equipages and people in your Majesty's parks;
" in the holding of cabinet dinners; in the unnecessary holding
" of cabinet councils; and in the travelling of coaches on that
" holy day, which last sin, may it please your Majesty, we espe-
" cially mourn over, as it leads many of your subjects in this
" parish to desecrate the Lord's Day.

" Believing that we should be partakers in the national sins
" did we not lift up our voices against them, and anxious that
" there may be a turning *from* them, that thus the judgments of
" the Most High God may be turned away from our unhappy
" country—

" We most humbly, but, at the same time, most earnestly,
" beseech your gracious Majesty to use every endeavour to put a
" stop to the sins and abominations above enumerated. May it
" please your Majesty, without delay, to appoint a day of national
" humiliation and fasting, and to restrict all persons belonging to
" your royal court and cabinet from profaning the Lord's Day in
" the manner above specified, or in any other way; that the ex-
" ample of keeping it 'holy to the Lord' coming from so high a
" quarter, the middle and poorer classes of this realm may also
" more strictly honour the Lord therein, and thereby increase in
" godly and holy fear, and bring back the blessing of Almighty
" God on their country.

" We would further humbly and *urgently* call the attention
" of your Majesty to the encroaching and alarming spirit mani-
" fested by the priests and leaders of the Roman Catholic party
" in Ireland. After having, by agitation, obtained the civil
" privileges which they stated would be perfectly satisfactory,
" and lead to peace and quietness; in violation of the most sacred
" assurances they have not ceased to agitate the minds of the
" people, and to urge them on to resistance to the laws, and to
" the pulling down of the Protestant institutions of the land.

"We most earnestly beseech your Majesty vigorously to up-
"hold, throughout the empire, the Protestant religion as it is by
"law established ; and further, to lend your sanction to the repeal
"of that law which accords to Roman Catholics, who are other-
"wise qualified, the privilege of being members of either House
"of Parliament ; a privilege which we conscientiously believe to
"be deeply injurious to the best interests of our country.

"With regard to agitation now on the subject of Reform—at
"the same time that we desire a moderate reform in the Commons
"House of Parliament, we beg to assure your Majesty that only
"the very lowest and most abandoned in this county are *agitators*,
"and that the *vast* majority of the inhabitants are peaceable and
"loyal men, well affected towards, and highly prizing, the noble
"and happy constitution under which, by the good providence
"of God, we live.

"We will not cease to pray that the God of heaven may bless
"your Majesty and this kingdom, and that in all your thoughts,
"words, and works, you may ever seek God's honour and glory,
"and study to preserve His people committed to your charge in
"wealth, peace, and godliness."

The address and petitions were signed by nearly all the men
of the parish, and were presented, I think, by Mr. Granville
Ryder in the House of Commons, and by Lord Roden in the
Lords. A rather singular fate awaited the address to the King.
I had sent both the address and the petitions to Mr. Granville
Ryder, with the request that he would place them in the proper
hands for presentation. I did not hear for some weeks, I believe,
what had become of the address, but at last I read a paragraph
in one of the papers to the following effect :—"The Earl of
"Roden, having obtained an audience of His Majesty, presented
"to him an address from the Protestants of Ireland so bulky, in
"consequence of the numerous signatures appended to it, that it
"was carried into the King's presence on a pole supported on the
"shoulders of two men. Lord Roden afterwards read to His
"Majesty an address from the inhabitants of Brailsford, in Der-
"byshire, on the subject of 'the sins of the nation.'"

I cannot now recollect the exact time when this address was

presented, but when the sudden dissolution of Lord Melbourne's Ministry took place, and the Duke of Wellington held so many of the offices of the state, until the arrival of Sir Robert Peel from the Continent, the thought passed through my mind that possibly the assurance of the loyalty of the subscribers to the address, and of the great mass of persons of the same class throughout the land, so clearly stated at the conclusion of it, may have been one cause of the King's decision of conduct in that remarkable transaction. Another circumstance occurred, not very long after, which most probably was connected with this address. There appeared a notice in the Gazette to the effect that noblemen wishing to present an address to the King were requested, on demanding an audience for that purpose, to state what the purport of the address was.

It is worthy of remark, that the three first national sins mentioned in the address and petitions, and the holding of cabinet councils and cabinet dinners on the Lord's Day, have long since been given up.

CHAPTER XXXII.

1832—1837.

BRAILSFORD. THE LORD'S DAY.

Anxious to promote sabbath observance—London Society—Sir Andrew Agnew's committee—Evidence taken—Mr. Bailey's work—Sir A. Agnew's Bills—Mr. Petre—My services mentioned—Mr. Hesketh Fleetwood—Mr. Poulter—Lord Wynford—Death of William IV.

BEING convinced that Sunday, or the Lord's Day, or Christian sabbath, is of divine authority, and that it is of universal and perpetual obligation, and having, as honorary secretary of the Derbyshire Lord's Day Society, spent a large portion of my life in endeavouring to promote its due observance, I am anxious to bring the subject and some account of the efforts made by myself and others prominently before my readers, in the hope that the Lord of the sabbath, in answer to my earnest prayer, may make what I write the means of leading many a one who may be as careless as I once was about observing God's holy day, to see that it is a blessing which God in His mercy has conferred on man, and to reverence and observe it, and also to use his efforts to extend the boon of a day of rest and of holy observance to the thousands of his fellow-countrymen and fellow-men who are now deprived of it. Surely every man in this professedly Christian country should, as far as works of necessity, mercy, and piety will permit, have the Sunday secured to him as a day of rest, so that he may have that opportunity, of which so many are now deprived, of worshipping and serving God according to the dictates of his conscience. We cannot make people religious by act of parliament, but we may, by wise laws and regulations, prevent the sabbath day from being publicly profaned; and we may strive to prevent persons from interfering with the religious liberty of others, and from depriving them of that day of rest which a merciful God has appointed for them.

The following is taken from the "Primary Address of the "London Society for Promoting the Due Observance of the Lord's "Day * :—

"London, Feb. 14, 1831.

"At a meeting held on Tuesday, January 25th, and by ad-"journment on Tuesday, February 8th, 1831, for the purpose of "considering what means could be properly adopted for lessen-"ing the great evil of Sabbath-breaking, and for restoring, under "the blessing of God, a due reverence for the divine authority "and practical duties of the Lord's Day, it was resolved unani-"mously :—'That this meeting is firmly persuaded, that the "'dedication of one day in every seven to religious rest and the "'worship of Almighty God, is of divine authority and perpetual "'obligation, as a characteristic of Revealed Religion during all "'its successive periods; having been enjoined upon man at the "'Creation—recognized and confirmed in the most solemn man-"'ner in the Ten Commandments—urged by the prophets as an "'essential duty, about to form a part of the institutions of the "'Messiah's kingdom—vindicated by our Divine Lord from the "'unauthorized additions and impositions of the Jewish teachers "'—transferred by Him and His Apostles, upon the abrogation "'of the ceremonies of the Mosaic law, to the first day of the "'week, in commemoration of the resurrection of Christ, and on "'that account called "The Lord's Day"—and finally established "'in more than all its primitive glory as an ordinance of the "'spiritual universal church of the New Testament, and a stand-"'ing pledge and foretaste of the eternal rest of heaven. And "'that this meeting believes that every person in a Christian "'country is bound in conscience to devote this seventh portion

* The committee of this society is composed of clergymen and lay members of the Church of England. Its offices are at 20, John Street, Adelphi. The Rev. Henry Stevens, M.A., is the clerical, and the Rev. W. Allen, M.A., the travelling secretary. They will be glad to hear from any person or persons who are disposed to help forward the good cause in which they are engaged.

" ' of his time to the honour of God, by resting from the business
" ' of his calling; by abstaining altogether from the pursuit of
" ' gain, and from ordinary pastimes and recreations; by guarding
" ' against every worldly avocation and interruption; and by
" ' spending the entire day in the public and private duties of
" ' religion; with the exception of such works of necessity and
" ' charity as our Saviour by His example was pleased to allow
" ' and commend; so as to designate this one day of rest and
" ' divine service, after six days of labour, as a more distinguished
" ' privilege of the Christian than it was of the Patriarchal and
" ' Jewish dispensations.' "

Some little time after the formation of the London society,
Sir Andrew Agnew moved for a select committee of the House
of Commons on the observance of the Lord's Day.   The report
of this committee and the evidence taken by it were ordered to
be printed in August, 1832.   Both the report and evidence may
be obtained from the London society, and will be found to be
most interesting.   The late Bishop of London and Dr. Farre, the
magistrates, the superintendents of police, different classes of
tradesmen, persons connected with public travelling, chaplains
of prisons, and other clergymen were examined.

After this Sir Andrew Agnew was induced to bring a bill
into parliament, the object of which was, as far as possible, to
secure to all classes of persons the Lord's Day as a day of rest.
The Rev. Henry Raikes, the late chancellor of the diocese of
Chester, wrote a most able pamphlet upon it, which may be
obtained at the London society's offices.   His bill occasioned no
inconsiderable sensation and discussion in the House of Commons,
almost all the members having received petitions to present
praying that it might pass into a law, and also private letters
from their constituents, begging that they would support the
measure.

I copy the following account of Sir Andrew's proceedings in
parliament from the "History of the Sabbath, or Day of Holy
" Rest," by the Rev. John T. Baylee, for some years the able
secretary of the London Society for Promoting the Observance of
the Lord's Day.   This work was printed by C. F. Hodgson, 1,
Gough Square, Fleet Street, and should be read by everybody

who wishes to help forward the sabbath cause in this country :—

" Sir Andrew Agnew's own opinions as to the importance of
" the subject and the necessity of the amendment of the law
" were doubtless strengthened by the information he had received.
" In the month of march, 1833, he moved for leave to bring in a
" bill 'to promote the better observance of the Lord's Day.' The
" bill was drawn up by Mr. George Rochfort Clarke, barrister,
" who was distinguished for his faithful and unflinching assertion
" of the divine authority and perpetual obligation of the Lord's
" Day as a truth of the Word of God, and as the only safe and
" secure basis on which exertions to promote its observance can
" be made. After full consideration, on the part of Sir Andrew,
" the committee of the Lord's Day Observance Society, and other
" friends, as to the character of the bill, it was finally decided
" that it should be based on the principle of the fourth command,
" and should prohibit all work not required by piety, charity, or
" necessity. The bill was rejected on the motion for the second
" reading on the 16th of May, 1833, by a majority of 79 to 73.
" Mr. Shaw, member for the University of Dublin, seconded the
" motion for leave to bring in the bill ; and Mr. Plumptre, one of
" the members for Kent, the motion for the second reading ; the
" minority was, all the circumstances considered, encouragingly
" large. The subject was distasteful to many even of those who
" professed a regard for the Lord's Day. Some thought that Sir
" Andrew Agnew attempted too much in presenting to the House
" a bill based on the full principle of the Lord's Day ; but Sir
" Andrew had in view to raise public Christian opinion to the
" standard held up in the Word of God, and this opinion he felt
" would be lowered still more by presenting a bill short of that
" standard, even if, on other and higher grounds, he did not
" object to such a course. The effects of the discussion that
" took place on the bill were very satisfactory. Many were led
" to consider the subject, and they soon perceived that they had,
" without thought, been in the habit of doing things not com-
" patible with the requirements of God's law.

" This improved state of feeling extended to all classes, in-
" cluding persons in the highest station. Orders were given at

" the royal palace that all provisions required for the Lord's Day
" should be purchased and delivered on Saturday. Cabinet
" dinners on the Lord's Day were discontinued, and labour was
" diminished or wholly suspended in many establishments.

"On the 11th of June, 1833, Sir Andrew Agnew, with
" characteristic perseverance, moved for leave to bring in a bill
" to amend the laws relating to Scotland. The introduction of
" the bill was opposed, but it was carried by a majority of thirteen;
" it was, however, subsequently withdrawn.

" Sir Andrew Agnew also brought in a bill for the removal,
" in certain cases, of Saturday and Monday fairs and markets to
" other days of the week, as local and relative circumstances
" might require. This bill was withdrawn, on the understanding
" that it was to be introduced as a clause in a bill to be brought
" in by Mr. Petre, member for Bodmin.

" A bill was brought in by Sir Andrew Agnew to enable the
" election of officers of corporations and public companies, then
" required to be held on the Lord's Day, to be held on the Satur-
" day next preceding, or on the Monday next ensuing. It re-
" ceived the royal assent on the 24th of July, 1833, and is the
" Act 3 and 4, William IV, c. 31.

" This bill, which was prepared by Mr. George Rochfort
" Clarke, is deserving of special notice, because the preamble
" asserts that it is the duty of the legislature to remove hind-
" rances to the observance of the Lord's Day; a principle of
" which it was important thus to secure the acknowledgment.

" Mr. Petre brought in a bill on the 10th of June, 1833, to
" consolidate and amend the laws relating to the Lord's Day. It
" was opposed by the Lord's Day Observance Society, as not
" recognising the authority of God, either impliedly or avowedly;
" as proposing to repeal ancient laws which, though not effective,
" acknowledge the divine authority of the Lord's Day; also as
" containing provisions at variance with God's Word, and the
" provisions of those very statutes which the bill professed to
" consolidate. The second reading came on for consideration on
" the 9th of July, when the debate was adjourned. Mr. Petre,
" however, ultimately withdrew the bill, owing to the opposition
" given to it by the friends as well as the opponents of measures

" based on the divine authority of the Lord's Day. The result of
" this attempt of Mr. Petre to conciliate the support of the House
" by what was called a moderate measure, still more confirmed
" Sir Andrew Agnew in the opinion that the course he had
" adopted, of framing his bills on the command of God, was the
" right and proper one. Sir Andrew Agnew received consider-
" able support by petitions to the House of Commons in favour
" of his bills—1061 such petitions, with 261,706 signatures, were
" presented, during the session, in favour of laws for the observ-
" ance of the Lord's Day.

" The committee of the Lord's Day Observance Society, dur-
" ing these efforts of Sir Andrew Agnew, actively assisted him,
" both in parliament and in the country. They aided him in
" drawing up his bills, and in promoting petitions in their favour.
" They widely circulated ' An Abstract of the Laws regarding
" ' the Lord's Day,' which was given in the evidence of Mr.
" Alexander Gordon before the select committee. They circu-
" lated ' Reasons for an Alteration of the Law,' an ' Address to
" ' the Clergy by the Bishop of Calcutta,' and ' Observations on
" ' the Bill now pending,' which were forwarded to members of
" both Houses of Parliament. They also inserted in the news-
" papers an analysis of Sir Andrew Agnew's bill. Deputations
" from the society likewise waited on members of the House of
" Commons, to secure their advocacy of Sir Andrew Agnew's
" bill or to disarm their hostility to it. The exertions of the
" Rev. William Leeke, to promote the observance of the Lord's
" Day, are deserving of special notice. He was instrumental in
" founding a society in Derby having that object in view, in
" December, 1833. He subsequently was the means of forming
" as many as ninety associations in different parts of that county;
" and he travelled into various parts of England in order to
" diffuse information, and create an interest in the object. Mr.
" Leeke's services were wholly gratuitous, and proved of great
" importance at this juncture, in aiding to secure support to the
" measures of Sir Andrew Agnew.

" Sir Andrew Agnew again renewed his exertions in the ses-
" sion of 1834. In the month of March he obtained leave to
" bring in a bill for the observance of the Lord's Day, similar in

"all respects to his former bill : only that the clause was omitted
"which excepted from the operation of the measure the trans-
"mission of the royal mail. The opinion now began to gain
"ground that there was no sufficient plea of necessity or mercy
"for the transaction of postal business on the Lord's Day ; and,
"indeed, the suspension of all such business in the metropolis on
"that day was a sufficient and practical proof that not only might
"it be dispensed with, without inconvenience to the public, but
"much to their satisfaction. Besides, it was felt that the trans-
"mission of the mail on the Lord's Day was an incentive to
"travelling, and was a sin in which the whole nation, with the
"exception of those who protested against it, participated, because
"it derived a revenue from it, and was a party to a system of
"traffic as public carriers on the Lord's Day. Some difficulty
"was at first felt by the friends of the Lord's Day as to the ex-
"pediency of omitting this clause ; but the more the subject was
"brought under consideration, the more clear appeared to them
"the duty of doing so—a conviction now almost unanimously
"entertained by them. Mr. G. Rochfort Clarke, who drew up
"the bill, strongly advocated the omission of the exception, and
"he had ultimately the gratification of seeing nearly the whole
"Christian community of his opinion.

   "The motion for the second reading was considered on the
"30th April, 1834. The debate on the occasion was very ani-
"mated, and a strong feeling of hostility was exhibited by the
"opponents of the measure, seven of whom in succession were
"allowed to speak against it. On a division, the motion for the
"second reading was rejected by a majority of 161 to 125.

   "Sir Andrew Agnew again introduced a bill to enable local
"authorities to change Saturday and Monday fairs and markets
"to other days of the week : the bill was, however, rejected by a
"majority of 50.

   "Nor were efforts for legislation in regard to the Lord's Day,
"in the session of 1834, limited to those of Sir Andrew Agnew.
"An impression prevailed, both in parliament and in the country,
"that the failure of his bills was attributable to their insisting
"upon the observance of the command of God, with only those
"exceptions required by piety, charity, and necessity : it was

" thought that there ought to be some accommodation to popular
" feelings and infirmities, and that it would be better, in the first
" instance, to seek for a small portion of what was due, and when
" once it was obtained, to proceed gradually towards the attain-
" ment of all that was required, with increased prospects of
" success, owing to the additional vantage-ground which would
" be thus obtained; but experience has thoroughly proved the
" fallacy of such reasoning.

" Mr. Hesketh Fleetwood brought in a bill of this description
" on the 21st of May, 1834, 'to facilitate and promote the better
" 'and more regular observance of the Lord's Day.' The bill
" proposed some valuable amendments in the existing laws; but
" whilst it proposed the repeal of some old statutes, it did not re-
" enact the substance of their provisions, and, in some respects,
" it sanctioned proceedings at variance with the due observance
" of the Lord's Day. The bill was rejected by a majority of 32
" on the second reading.

" Mr. Poulter, M. P. for Shaftesbury, at the same time brought
" in a bill, 'to render more effectual an act of 29th Charles II,
" 'for the better observance of the Lord's Day.' On the 4th of
" June, 1834, the bill passed through a committee *pro formâ*, on
" the understanding that the debate should be taken on bringing
" up the report. On the 2nd of July the details were considered,
" when clauses were omitted, and amendments introduced, which
" entirely altered the original object of the bill. One amend-
" ment, adopted on the motion of Mr. Cayley, was to the effect
" that nothing contained in the act should extend to prevent
" games of chance, exercise, or other recreations in the open air,
" which should not take place during the hours of divine service,
" or be played for money, or on the premises of a public-house.
" It passed as amended in the report. Further alterations of the
" same objectionable character being proposed, it was opposed by
" the friends of the Lord's Day, and, happily, rejected on the
" third reading.

" The subject was also brought under the attention of the
" House of Lords. On the 15th of May, 1834, Lord Wynford
" brought in a bill, in that House, 'for the better observance of
" 'the Lord's Day, and the more effectual prevention of drunken-

"'ness;' it passed a second reading, but, encountering great
"opposition from all quarters, his lordship withdrew it. The
"provisions of the bill virtually sanctioned travelling, baking,
"and the keeping open public-houses on the Lord's Day, not
"justified on the ground of piety, charity, or necessity.

   " These efforts made in parliament were regarded with great
"interest by the country; the debates were read with avidity,
"and in this way men were led to study and think on a subject
"which otherwise would have had little or none of their attention.
"The consequence was, that many consciences were awakened
"to the importance of the observance of the Lord's Day, and to
"its merciful bearings on the temporal and spiritual interests of
"man.   The favourable feeling of the public towards the measures
"of Sir Andrew Agnew were evinced by the number of petitions
"presented in the House of Commons in their favour, which in
"this session amounted to 1076, with 204,413 signatures.

   "Parliament having been dissolved, Sir Andrew Agnew was
"again elected : but he determined not to bring in a bill in the
"session of 1835, that the advocates of what were termed more
"moderate measures might try their plan—his various bills, which
"comprehended the whole subject, and which were based on the
"divine authority of the Lord's Day, having been rejected. Mr.
"Poulter again introduced his bill, which was looked upon as a
"moderate measure: it passed the second reading, but was ulti-
"mately lost. It was supported by the friends of Sir Andrew
"Agnew, but opposed by the advocates of moderate measures on
"the ground of its limited character.

   "Sir Andrew Agnew, on the 21st of April, 1836, moved for
"leave to bring in a bill for extending to all classes of His
"Majesty's subjects the protection of the Sabbath. The motion
"was seconded by Sir Oswald Moseley, Bart., and, on a division,
"was carried by a majority of 118; there being 200 for, and 82
"against it. The motion for the second reading was rejected on
"the 18th of May, by a majority of 32.

   "On the 4th of May, 1837, Sir Andrew Agnew brought for-
"ward his bill for the fourth time. Like his other bills it pro-
"ceeded on the ground of the Divine authority of the Sabbath,
"and the right of all classes to protection in the enjoyment of

" its privileges. The first reading was carried by a majority of
" 146. It was read a second time on Wednesday, the 7th of
" June, by a majority of 44.

" Thus this indefatigable advocate of the observance of the
" Lord's Day had at length the satisfaction of having the great
" principle of his bill acknowledged by the House of Commons.
" The majority would have been greater had the nonconformists,
" in the country and in the House, rendered the measure the
" support they had heretofore given ; but at this time the dis-
" senting denominations put forward with unusual prominence,
" as a fundamental principle, that it was wrong to legislate in
" regard to religion—not considering that the legislation sought
" for in this case was eminently protective of the well disposed,
" and compulsory on the unprincipled and unscrupulous. The
" 21st of June was appointed for the consideration of the bill in
" committee.

" The death of King William the Fourth, and the consequent
" dissolution of parliament before the day appointed for the con-
" sideration in committee of Sir Andrew Agnew's bill, prevented
" its further progress, and likewise terminated his honourable
" and distinguished career as a Christian legislator. He did not,
" it is true, succeed in carrying his bill, but by keeping the sub-
" ject constantly before the public, and by means of the discus-
" sions of it, that in consequence took place both in parliament
" and the country, he caused the reflecting and religious portion
" of the community to see the great importance of the Sabbath,
" in a light in which they had not seen it before. After he ceased
" to be a member of parliament, he exerted himself unremittingly
" till his death, (which took place in 1849,) in opposing the
" desecration of the Lord's Day in Scotland ; and became a rail-
" way shareholder that he might exercise the right, at the meet-
" ings of the proprietors, of opposing railway traffic on the Lord's
" Day.

" In the year 1837, 886 petitions, signed by 106,722 persons,
" were presented in the House of Commons, in favour of a law
" for the observance of the Lord's Day. In the session of 1838,
" Sir Andrew Agnew having failed in securing his election in the
" new parliament, Mr. Plumptree brought in a bill, on the 22nd

"of February, for the suppression of trading on the Lord's Day.
"It passed a second reading by a majority of 139 to 68, but it
"was so altered and curtailed in committee, and also in bringing
"up the report, that it was opposed by the friends of the Lord's
"Day on the motion for the third reading, and thrown out. It
"was, however, discussed with an amount of forbearance and
"moderation which clearly showed how greatly the previous
"discussion of the subject, whilst Sir Andrew Agnew was in
"parliament, had tended to improve the public feeling.

"The postmaster-general was invested with power, by an act
"passed this year, to require railway companies to transmit the
"mail every day of the week.

"In the session of 1838, on the motion of Mr. William Law
"Hodges, certain formal proceedings of the House of Commons
"were changed from Monday to other days, with a view of
"enabling the clerks and officers of the House to avoid attend-
"ance on their duties on the Lord's Day."

CHAPTER XXXIII.

1833—1849.

SIR ANDREW AGNEW.

Account of Mr. Leeke's acquaintance with Sir A. Agnew—Meeting with committee of Derbyshire society—Sir A. Agnew's correspondence with Mr. Leeke, taken from his " Life "—His bills—Loses his seat in parliament—His continued exertions—His death.

In the foregoing chapter, Mr. Baylee has spoken of my exertions in forming associations in Derbyshire, and in several of the other counties in England, and of the aid thus rendered by us to Sir Andrew Agnew in his parliamentary work.

The following pages of this chapter are copied from the interesting " Memoir of Sir Andrew Agnew, of Locknaw, Bart., by " Thomas McCrie, D.D., L.L.D.," published in 1850 :—

" The Rev. William Leeke, the honorary secretary of the " Derbyshire society, has favoured us with the following com- " munication, which cannot fail to prove interesting to our " readers :—

" ' Holbrooke, near Derby, August 23rd, 1850.

" ' I think my correspondence with my late much respected " friend, Sir Andrew Agnew, commenced in April, 1833, soon " after he had brought forward, in the House of Commons, his " bill for the protection of all classes of persons in the enjoyment " of the rest of the Lord's Day. I had explained the nature and " intention of the bill to the people of my parish, and had in- " vited them to sign a petition in support of it, which the whole " of the male population who were applied to did, with the

" exception of one individual. I shortly after wrote to Sir Andrew
" Agnew on the subject of the duties which excisemen were re-
" quired to perform on the Lord's Day, and, at the same time,
" mentioned the feeling with regard to his bill in my parish and
" neighbourhood. To this communication, Sir Andrew—who, I
" believe, never neglected to answer any letter on the subject of
" the observance of the sabbath—replied at length, explaining
" various points in his bill. From this period, for thirteen years,
" until I was induced from ill health to relinquish my office of
" honorary secretary to the Derbyshire Lord's Day Society, I was
" in very frequent correspondence with him, especially during
" the sessions of parliament. I made a rule of mentioning to
" him every project for the advancement of the cause he had
" so much at heart, which entered into my own mind ; and he,
" in return, never hesitated to communicate his own views and
" plans, and to urge me, or our society, to take any steps which
" he thought would assist in promoting them. His labours, in
" the way of correspondence, must have been very great. I re-
" member at one time that his own franks were so engaged, that
" my letters to several correspondents, which I had been in the
" habit of sending daily through him, were transferred to another
" member, who kindly volunteered to receive and forward them.
" I well recollect my first interview and conversation with Sir
" Andrew, when I called on him at one of the hotels in Derby,
" preparatory to his meeting our committee on the 29th of
" January, 1834. In the course of conversation, I remarked,
" that it was a considerable trial to me, and quite contrary to my
" natural inclination, and to the *beau ideal* I had formed of com-
" fort, that I should be drawn forth, by my desire to aid in pro-
" moting the due observance of the Lord's Day, from the quiet of
" my parish, to become a sort of public character, as one of the
" secretaries of an active society. Sir Andrew replied that his
" feeling had been precisely similar—that his inclination would
" have led him to prefer the life of a private country gentleman ;
" but that he had been brought by a sense of duty into his pre-
" sent position ; that, with regard to his taking up the cause of
" the observance of the Lord's Day, as a Member of the House of
" Commons, he felt the trial of becoming thus conspicuous, and

" so much exposed to the ridicule of the careless and thoughtless ;
" and that, when he at first turned his attention to the subject,
" he had no idea of becoming the champion of the cause in the
" House of Commons ; but, that he found no other member wil-
" ling to take it up, and, therefore, was impelled by a sense of
" duty not to shrink from doing so himself. He said that he had
" not thought at first of bringing forward so comprehensive a bill ;
" but he found that to be consistent he must endeavour to pro-
" tect all classes in the enjoyment of the rest of the Lord's Day
" as far as it was possible to do so, without interfering with cases
" of necessity and mercy, and with the privacy and religious
" liberty of individuals and families. He often remarked in his
" subsequent correspondence and conversations, that he felt it to
" be his duty to act upon the above principles in framing his
" bill, and that he must leave it to parliament to cut it down as
" they in their wisdom might judge proper. He said he was as-
" sailed by members on all sides to bring in a more moderate
" measure ; but that none could agree as to what that moderate
" measure should be. When thus pressed, he was in the habit of
" referring to the petitions from the several classes who were de-
" prived of the Lord's Day as a day of rest, and of asking the
" members which of these classes he was to exclude from the
" benefits which his bill was intended to procure for them. At
" this our first meeting he also remarked, that we must not shrink
" from the work, either from a dislike of publicity, or from any
" false modesty—that the affairs of the world were chiefly
" managed by persons of about our age. Sir Andrew was then
" about forty, and I a few years younger."

" ' Sir Andrew's first interview with the committee of the
" Derbyshire society, and the view then taken in this county of
" his principles of legislation, may be gathered from an account
" of the proceedings of the society, published on the 11th of
" February, 1834, seven weeks after its formation. *

* " The great object was further favoured in Derby, yesterday, by Sir Andrew
" Agnew passing through the town on his way to attend his parliamentary duties
" in London. He kindly permitted himself to be introduced to the committee, with
" mutual pleasure. Encouragement on both sides was the result, to endeavour to
" raise public opinion to legislation for the sabbath upon Christian principles,
" rather than to have legislation lowered to the prevailing tone of principles—or

"'This pamphlet was sent to each member of parliament, and
"Sir Andrew often referred to it in his conversations with in-
"dividual members, to show the feeling of the country in favour
"of his comprehensive measure. He told me that it served him
"as a "pocket pistol" on such occasions.

"'I have no occasion to trouble you with the details of the
"measures we took, in conjunction with the other societies, to
"support Sir Andrew's bills in the sessions of 1835 and 1836.
"At the close of the latter year, he did me the honour to address
"to me a letter, which he printed. In this letter he particularly
"spoke of the increasing support and encouragement he had re-
"ceived in the House of Commons in each succeeding session,
"although his bill had always been thrown out on the second
"reading; and he requested that in our communications with
"members we would urge them, in the ensuing session of 1837,
"to vote the bill into a committee of the whole House, "wherein
""the merits of each separate detail might be freely discussed, re-
""tained, amended or rejected, as might seem meet." He also
"spoke of the fact, that when several bills of a more limited ex-
"tent than his own were introduced by other members friendly
"to the cause, "they were all treated by the House worse than
""his."'

"To give our readers some idea of the correspondence in
"which Sir Andrew engaged, and on which he relied as his right
"arm in conducting the Sabbath conflict, we may here give a few
"extracts from his letters to the Rev. William Leeke. These
"letters alone, it may be observed, amount to nearly one hundred
"and fifty!

"rather no principles—of a more unworthy character. And while the committee
"seemed fully to depend upon the blessing of God for the success of the Sabbath
"Society, in connection with other means, in order to the desired elevation of national
"feeling, Sir Andrew appeared fully prepared to pursue his honest and honourable
"course, whatever the House of Commons might please to do with his measures.
"However they might be pared down or defeated, no legislation appeared to be
"really satisfactory, or permanently successful, but that which, first or last,
"amounted substantially to the system propounded in his bill. Several enquiries
"and details were mutually entered into; and the meeting separated with
"prayer."—*Some account of the proceedings of the Derby and Derbyshire
Auxiliary Society for promoting the Due Observance of the Lord's Day.*
(Page 9.) *Derby,* 1834.

"'March 8th, 1834. All looks well at present. Lord " Wynford, in the most courteous manner, apologized for his " seeming discourtesy. He knew nothing of my notice, until " Lord Bexley wrote to tell him of it. The incident will, I trust, " do good, being overruled. I must now proceed on Tuesday, " after a weary week. I rejoice to think that to-morrow is the " day that the Lord hath made. May he enable me and mine, " and you and yours, to rejoice and be glad in it! Confiding " that on Tuesday your prayers will be with me, faithfully yours.

"'March 15th, 1834. Many thanks for your congratulations, " and accept my felicitations on the success which has been " vouchsafed to your own cause, or rather to that cause which is " neither yours nor mine.

"'The change produced within the House, by the pressure " from out-of-doors, was most obvious during the last ten days ; " therefore, I say, take heart and proceed in the same course as " hitherto, and talk not of "taking too much upon you," unless " you mean to taunt a humble individual from a remote corner " of Scotland, who hesitates not to disturb the so-called peace " of civilized society.

"'April 3rd, 1834. There are some men who advised the " bringing in of a partial measure, without reference to the great " principle. To such we have already refused to listen. Mr. " Petre exemplified, last year, that the enemy could not be won " over by concession. But some of our best friends advised, at " the beginning of this session, that principle should be respected " by bringing forward the whole question, dividing the different " provisions into several bills. To me it always appeared that " such a course of proceeding would have, in effect, been an " invitation to a lukewarm House to make a show of complying " with the wishes of the country by supporting some one bill ; " and while each member supported some one bill, it requires " very little arithmetic to show that all the bills might at the " same time be rejected.

"'Our object is to bring both the House and the country to " the consideration of the principle—the object of the enemy is " to divert attention by dwelling on exceptions. His first " observation is, " You go too far ;"—his second is, " Why do you

"except domestic servants?" What I now wish to call your
"attention to, is the fact, that I did so far comply with the
"wishes of our best friends, as to make the fairs and markets,
"which occupied a clause last year, a distinct bill in this session;
"and it has been thrown out! Now mark the consequence—
"look to the evidence of the coach proprietors, and to the para-
"graph in the House of Commons' Report regarding travelling,
"and it will be found that it was never thought possible to put a
"stop to Sunday travelling without the removal of Monday
"markets. The coach proprietors still say—remove the markets,
"and the coaches will be unnecessary. Now, how are we to
"proceed with the travelling clause?

"'May 10th, 1834. It was with regret that I let yesterday
"pass away without thanking you for your kind letter of the 8th,
"and also for the Derby papers. Do not be distressed about the
"remarks of the editor; for I am so habituated to abuse that
"even faint praise has lost its sting. . . . . We surely have
"reason to be content with our progress, seeing in how few
"instances the influence of the press has been with us, and
"almost universally its mighty power directed against us.
"Although a Mightier has led us hitherto, yet we should not
"despise the means, when within our reach, of furthering our
""moral" cause; and I should be very glad if your former sug-
"gestions could be carried into effect. . . . . With our
"progress I am well content. An M.P., lately returned from the
"north of England, told me yesterday of the anxiety of his con-
"stituents, saying, with much gravity, "This House has no idea
""of the interest which people in the country take in the Sabbath
""question." He had just received petitions expressing regret on
"the rejection of my bill. It is most amusing and satisfactory
"to see the desire of many to originate bills. To-day I send you
"Lord Wynford's bill. I have many fears about Mr. H. Fleet-
"wood's bill. I am still endeavouring to get him to limit him-
"self to such points as we are agreed upon. If he persists in
"going against any principle, it will be my painful duty to point
"out such points for the opposition of our friends.

"'July 24th, 1834. For myself I can only say, that when a
"member, in private conversation, expressed the hope that I was

"not displeased with an observation which had fallen from him
" in the heat of debate, my reply was an assurance that nothing
" which could be said or done in the House of Commons could
" affect the opinion which I had formed, nor the merits of the
" question for which I contended."

" 'February 4th, 1835. Only stand to your colours, and fight
" every inch of the ground. If you give a point to the enemy, he
" will fling it back at your own head. Recollect, last year you
" endeavoured to raise the moral standard in every parish in
" England. A short time since, the Chelsea auxiliary recom-
" mended half measures. A deputation from the parent society
" went to argue the point. The result has been two donations ;
" and this day has come " a resolution," declaring that they " are
" " quite convinced that it is only by standing on Scripture ground
" " that the cause can be advocated." Let us not trouble ourselves
" about the result, but resolve to " endure all things." Every
" member of the Lord's Day Society I look upon as a school-
" master, appointed to bring his friends and neighbours to the Lord
" of the sabbath. It must be confessed that some of their pupils
" are very slow of understanding.

" 'February 12th, 1835. It is delightful to see that you are
" still true to your principles, unshaken by the assaults of the
" enemy. You have made the discovery, that " it is when we
" " refine that we differ, and this the Bible never does." We once
" thought that by limiting our demands on the legislature we
" should diminish our difficulties ; but experience has taught us
" that the greatest difficulties are to define limitation, and that it
" is in vain that we strive to frame an act of parliament more
" judicious than the written Word. We attained this knowledge
" step by step, and so probably must all others. While our
" friends and neighbours are in a state of pupilage, many will
" despise, but they will find in the end that they cannot improve
" upon, divine truth. In the mean time, we must endure patiently
" the imputation of bigotry.

" ' May 12th, 1836. In reply to your question, I should not
" be sorry if any unavoidable expedient within the House were to
" prevent my bringing on the question of second reading on
" Wednesday next. But I fear to show, or seem to show, an un-

"willingness to continue the contest. Hitherto, both victories
" and defeats have alike served our cause.   Mr. Haldane Stewart,
" with much animation, remarked some months since, "a few
" "more such defeats, and we are made !"

" 'May 20th, 1836.   Pardon me for not having written yester-
" day to congratulate you on the accomplishment of your wish,
" that no Lord's Day Bill should pass this session.   If it has been
" your object hitherto to convince the country that the members
" of the honourable House are ignorant of that which is experi-
" mentally known to all the coachmen, horsekeepers, canal-men,
" and hucksters in the kingdom, you have had much done to bring
" out that ignorance in its full extent.   But do not flatter your-
" self that Othello's occupation is gone.   The extent of the ignor-
" ance that is *within-doors* may be ascertained ; but *there* it will
" remain intact until through it your policy has made a breach.

" 'May 23rd, 1836.   In reply to Mr. Wilson's letter, I have
" told him how much I regret having brought the sabbath ques-
" tion to a close so soon ; not that there was any probability of suc-
" cess in the present session, but, by keeping it open, more en-
" couragement might have been given to the formation of country
" societies with a view to future campaigns.   Many such repulses
" we must look to.   Many members had gone out of town to eke
" out the length of the holidays, which were near at hand.   The
" Epsom races and the Derby took many away, &c., &c.   As
" regards the House, I could not have done better with any
" certainty ; but, as regards the country, I do regret what has
" happened.   My errors will, I trust, be overruled by the good
" providence of God ; and may I alone bear the chastisement,
" while the cause prospers!

" 'P.S.—More petitions come in every day to scourge me.

" 'May 27th, 1836.   "Go the ant, thou sluggard," as you well
" observe, implies that we all need to learn wisdom from that
" scriptural schoolmaster.   To your ant-like suggestions, I hope
" to be sufficiently awake to make a reply in a day or two.

" 'May 28th, 1836.   A few letters enclosed may help to show
" that, as regards the country, our parliamentary weakness
" maketh His strength perfect.   The subject has, I trust, been
" permitted to take a strong hold of the public mind.

"'September 8th, 1836. I have much pleasure in sending "Mr. Radford's reply, as a pocket pistol to be presented at every "coach proprietor on your line of road; and should the first "shot not take effect, the heavy metal of Mr. Bianconi's ex- "perience must silence all gainsayers.'

"On the 8th of March, 1837, a public breakfast was given to "Sir Andrew, at Derby, 'as a testimony of their high estimation "'of his unceasing and valuable exertions, both in and out of "'Parliament, to promote the due observance of the Lord's Day, "'and particularly to secure that day as a day of rest to the "'British community.' Upwards of a hundred gentleman, in- "cluding many clergymen, assembled, and the meeting was "presided over by the Mayor, W. L. Newton, Esq. The company "sat down at ten, and did not break up till two o'clock. On this "occasion Sir Andrew delivered one of his characteristic "speeches."

"He could assure the meeting, with perfect simplicity, that "no one could more truly feel his own inadequacy than he did, "to speak to a great public question like the present. One ex- "pression in the resolution gave thanks to the Almighty for "having raised him up as a humble instrument to carry on the "work which they were then met to advocate. All men were "answerable to God for the use of their influence or talent; but "the only talent for which he felt he was responsible was, that "he possessed the power to *stand up* in the House of Commons. "In defiance of prejudice and sarcasm, he would propose the "measure with which they were well acquainted. Adequately "to do justice to that measure, which had fallen into his un- "worthy hands, was beyond his capacity. He was thankful "that for five years he had been enabled to brave obloquy, and "had stood up in parliament in its defence. It had been his "prayer to be enabled to do this. It was for him to stand, and "for them to come to the rescue. After some further remarks on "the claims of the sabbath, and of the working classes, Sir "Andrew begged to thank a coach proprietor who, he under- "stood, was present, who had refused to run his coach on the "Sunday. [Some one informed the speaker that he had only "*objected* to it.] Well, that was good. It was an old expression

" in his country amongst those who had put down Popery, that
" if they could do nothing more they could testify.   His
" friend had testified against the running of the coach, and
" this was the first step to the suppression of the practice.
" But they must not place too heavy a blame on coach proprie-
" tors; it was not they only, but those who travelled, that were
" to blame.   One of the greatest coach proprietors in London,
" who had given up the Sunday stages, said to him, ' Do not give
" ' us too much credit; it is for want of passengers that we have
" ' abandoned the stages.' And he was convinced if every gentle-
" man in that company would persuade a friend to abandon
' Sunday travelling, it would almost stop the practice.   Without
" a radical change (he was quite content to be thought a radical
" here) in the habits of society their object could not be secured.
" Let all plans be formed during the week, with an eye to the
" sabbath as a day of rest.   No man wished to lead a life of
" perpetual labour; but this was never thought of by many per-
" sons who employ others.   He knew a lady who was asked by
" a tradesman on the Saturday, if she wanted any fish; she
" replied ' I will let you know to-morrow;' and when he ex-
" plained that he was anxious to avoid business on the Lord's
" Day, she frankly confessed it had never occurred to her, that
" when she was eating her usual dinner, she was the cause of
" the desecration of the sabbath.   Some persons said that they
" did not like the coercive character of his bill, but they did not
" reflect that the upper classes never gave an order without
" affecting many grades of society. He that received the order
" coerced those under him, down to the lowest class; and it was
" to protect that class, which was an act of true benevolence,
" that his bill was framed.

   " We continue our extract from his correspondence with the
" Rev. Mr. Leeke :—

   " ' March 14th, 1837. All your kindness, and that of so many
" good friends in Derbyshire, is more to be feared than the daily
" bread of frowns of the last few years; more likely to turn the
" head and delude into the idea that there is some merit in the in-
" strument. But you may also give the antidote, and pray that
" it may never, for a moment, be forgotten that the talisman

" is with "the Word" itself, whosesoever be the feeble hands in
" which, for the time being, it is found.

"'March 24th, 1837. The Carlisle address is milk for babes,
" nevertheless I wish that every town had such an infant
" school, that, by reason of use, their stomachs may in time be
" brought to digest strong meat. Enclosed is a letter from Mr.
" Garret, a Chancery barrister. Can you not follow up his sug-
" gestion of making a vehement appeal to the clergy, calling
" upon them to address the *rich* of all classes to assist, and not to
" thwart, by their example ?

"'April 19th, 1837. Your account of the correspondence with
" the boat-owners and wharfingers is very satisfactory. We were
" told, a few years since, that the flatmen were at the bottom of
" the scale of demoralization. They bid fair, in some districts at
" least, to ascend rapidly. The interval of the 4th of May grows
" rapidly shorter. I hope there may be no misunderstanding
" either with the boat-owners or their men ; but that they are
" taking care, with all others, to let their efforts point to the
" *committee of the whole House* for a general measure, which will
" bring every branch of the subject under discussion. Any mis-
" understanding on this point might at this moment be fatal to
" all our plans. It is thus that we hope to bring members to the
" test, who have hitherto shown *less* willingness to discuss a
" limited measure than to discuss my general measure, thus
" evading both.

"'May 3rd, 1837. The minds of men are scattered over many
" societies, and the religious public have not yet been enlight-
" ened to see that the observance of the Lord's Day is essential
" to the working out of all their benevolent schemes. This point
" was well argued by Sir Thomas Deanes, an Irish gentleman, at
" the breakfast.

"'May 29th,1837. We shall want all manner of letters from
" all manner of persons, to all the members with whom they
" have any acquaintance, asking all to be *in their places on the 7th
" of June*, to support the second reading of the Lord's Day Bill.
" Try the experiment of getting respectable men, in a humble
" walk of life, to address their representatives as above.

"'June 1st, 1837. My chief anxiety now is to get a good

" House on Wednesday next, therefore, letters, letters, letters.'

" The second reading of the bill was carried by 110 against 66,
" so that there was a majority of 44.

" The announcement of the division diffused sincere joy
" amongst all the friends of the sabbath. ' We return thanks,'
" says ' The Record' of June 8th, ' to Him who ruleth in the king-
" ' dom of men—to Him who is emphatically the Lord of the
" ' sabbath—to Him who governs the unruly wills of sinful
" ' mortals—that it has pleased Him so to order events, that the
" ' second reading of Sir Andrew Agnew's Lord's Day Bill has
" ' passed by a majority of 110 to 66. The House is to go into
" ' committee on the bill, on Wednesday, the 28th of June. This
" ' is *the first time* the bill has ever passed the second reading.'
" The Lord's Day Society issued a circular, calling upon all the
" friends of the sabbath to return thanks to Almighty God for
" this advance in the good cause. ' Most sincerely do I con-
" ' gratulate you,' writes Mr. Leeke, ' on the result of the second
" ' reading. Many prayers were offered up on Wednesday—many
" ' *praises* to-day.'

" In the inscrutable providence of God the bill was never
" destined to reach the next stage, that of being considered in a
" committee of the whole House. On the 20th of June, 1837,
" William IV died ; this led to a dissolution of Parliament, and
" to a new election, when Sir Andrew failed in his attempt to
" secure his return to parliament."

A few days after Sir Andrew Agnew's defeat at the election
for the Wigtoun Burghs, I received the following letter from
him :—

" Lochnaw Castle, July 31st, 1837.

" MY DEAR SIR,—My race is run. I had started for this
" county, and was opposed by a Ministerial candidate. But
" thereafter a conservative, powerfully supported, came into the
" field. I felt it a duty to withdraw and offer my support to the
" latter, with the hope of securing the defeat of the whig-
" radical. Whether I judged wisely the present week will
" determine. For myself I contested our boroughs, and on
" Friday I was defeated by a majority of 34. After seven years
" of parliamentary labour, my military service is over—my

" sword become a ploughshare! Doubtless 'rest' is wisely
" ordered, but there are many friends in the United Kingdom
" with whom, in mind, I have been in constant contact. This
" total separation is somewhat abrupt, nor can I yet imagine the
" extent of the privation. But many duties, domestic and pro-
" vincial, surround me, and I believe, in the simplicity of sin-
" cerity, that 'it is the Lord; let Him do what seemeth to Him
" 'good!'"

Although Sir Andrew Agnew's parliamentary course was
thus singularly brought to a close just at the very moment when
he had reached that point of legislation on the sabbath which
he had so earnestly desired, yet had his labours to promote
amongst his fellow countrymen a conviction of its divine
authority, and of the obligation to observe it, by no means come
to an end.

In the winter of 1838 he removed with his family to Edinburgh, and in January, 1839, he attended a crowded public
meeting, at which was formed the Scottish Society for Promoting
the Due Observance of the Lord's Day, of which society he
became the president.

It must have been after this, and I suppose after a meeting
at Chesterfield, to promote sabbath observance, that Sir Andrew
and I were to sleep at the house of Mr. Hill, then the Vicar of
Chesterfield, and now the venerable and indefatigable Archdeacon of Derby. After all the rest of the party had retired to
rest, we two sat up for two or three hours, and drew up the outline of a paper to be signed by presidents, secretaries, and other
office-bearers in sabbath societies, with a view to stir up the
friends of sabbath observance throughout the country, to make
a decided onslaught on all railway desecration of the sabbath
day, and especially on desecrations of it on railways in their
several neighbourhoods. This paper was afterwards printed and
circulated extensively by the Derbyshire society. Sir Andrew
Agnew headed the signatures to this document, as " President
of the Scottish Society for Promoting the Due Observance of the
Lord's Day," and the next name, I believe, was that of the late
Bishop Shirley, then the also indefatigable Archdeacon of Derby.
as a vice-president of the Derbyshire society. The appeal was

altogether signed by between twenty and thirty officers of sabbath societies.

Sir Andrew was occasionally our visitor both at Brailsford, when he was in Parliament, and afterwards at Holbrooke. On his getting out of the London mail at Brailsford, on one occasion, I was rather amused at his introducing me to a member, with whom he had travelled down, who was one of the most determined opponents of his sabbath bill. He was with us in 1843, when I was drawing up our lengthy and important address to railway proprietors, preparatory to my bringing forward, at the half-yearly meeting of the Midland Company, in the summer of that year, a resolution to stop all Sunday traffic on the Midland lines.* On that occasion Sir Andrew gave me the exact information which I required with regard to the sabbath lines.

The year after this Sir Andrew was mainly instrumental in stopping the running of trains on the Edinburgh and Glasgow Railway. He was always anxious that the sabbath societies throughout the kingdom should keep the whole subject of sabbath desecration, and of the injustice and hardship inflicted on those employed, before Parliament and the nation, by means of regular petitions to both Houses every session, whether there were any sabbath bill brought forward or not. He thought, and the Derbyshire committee thought, that thus the mind of the nation would be kept informed, and the people generally be benefited. The London committee were, many of them, at one time of a somewhat different opinion in the matter, and were not inclined to petition for a general measure of relief to those employed on the Sunday, in the absence from parliament of some such decided champion of the cause as Sir Andrew himself.

The consequence of this was that many of the societies, after trying what they could do by their own efforts to keep the whole subject alive before the country, and their own counties or neighbourhood, found that their efforts, after a time, did not tell on the country and the Parliament, as they had done at the first, and by degrees the friends of sabbath observance, being

---

* See Chapter XXXVIII for this address, and for the account of the meeting of the Midland proprietors, with Mr. Hudson in the chair, in July, 1845.

only called upon occasionally to withstand some fresh innovation on the sanctity of the Lord's Day, by degrees slackened in their energies, and numbers of the associations became either extinct, or in a very drooping condition. This was the case with regard to the numerous associations in Derbyshire, including ninety-one of our parishes. The efforts of the London society, in opposing these isolated points of desecration, were always well directed, and most important and valuable, and were supported by the strenuous exertions of the Derbyshire and other societies, but in some cases, as in that of endeavouring to put a stop to the conveyance of the mails and the delivery of letters on the Lord's Day, when the attempt, made in 1850, was, although successful at first, eventually defeated,* the friends of the cause in Derbyshire were greatly disappointed to find that it was not renewed in the following year by the London Lord's Day Society in conjunction with a newly formed and active society called the Metropolitan Committee. They felt that it was only by the renewed, continued, united, and, at the same time, prayerful efforts of all the friends of sabbath observance, that the victory could be won ; and that such continued efforts were also necessary in order to keep up the zealous exertions of the increasing numbers of persons who were anxious to see the Lord's Day preserved from public profanation, and secured as a day of rest to all classes of persons in the country. Whenever the efforts to put down all postal labour on the Lord's Day are renewed, I trust they will never be relinquished till that great national sin be abolished.

* On the 30th of May, 1850, the present Lord Shaftesbury, then Lord Ashley, moved, in the House of Commons, an address to Her Majesty to direct that the collection and delivery of letters should in future cease in all parts of the kingdom on the Lord's Day, and that an inquiry should be made whether the transmission of the mail could be suspended without injury to the public service. His motion was carried by a majority of 93 to 68, being supported by the presentation of 4475 petitions ; signed by 656,919 persons. The collection and delivery of letters were, in consequence, suspended in the United Kingdom on Sunday, the 23rd of June, 1850, and so continued until the 1st of September of the same year, when, in accordance with the recommendation of a commission, of which, I think, Mr. Berkeley was appointed the chairman, the collection and delivery were resumed. See *Mr. Bailee's History of the Sabbath. Printed by Hodgson, Gough Square, Fleet Street.*

I accompanied Sir Andrew Agnew, some few years after he had retired from Parliament, I think it must have been about 1848, to a meeting of the committee of the London society, for the express purpose of urging upon them the views above stated, which we thought had not been sufficiently followed out in their practice. There were several of the old and respected members present. Mr. Rochfort Clarke was there, the eminent barrister, who had drawn up Sir Andrew Agnew's bill, and who had, day by day, when there was anything to be done, most materially helped forward the good cause, by suggesting to those at the office of the society the course which should be taken. He was the life and soul of the London society, especially in the above kind of work. Mr. Wilson, the founder and honorary secretary of the London society, who helped us so much when our Derbyshire society was first formed, and who conducted, with so much energy and tact, many of the operations of the society in London and throughout the country, was also there. They very kindly listened first of all to Sir Andrew Agnew, and then to me. It was stated amongst other difficulties to the plan of petitioning each session, that people got tired of petitioning, and I remember saying, in reply, that when we had attended meetings we had often found persons averse to the trouble of getting up petitions, but that we had never left them so. After we had stated our opinion, and there had been some discussion, Mr. Wilson said to Mr. Clarke, "Mr. Clarke, what do you think "about it?" Mr. Clarke answered, "Well, I think we are all "twenty years older than we were twenty years ago!" They all, however, decided on acting upon our view of the matter, and a circular was promised, and was forwarded to all the friends of the cause thoughout the country, but the thing was not followed up, and nothing effectual was done.

After rendering the most valuable services to his country for nearly twenty years, in connexion with the cause of sabbath observance, Sir Andrew Agnew was rather unexpectedly called to his rest on the 12th of April, 1849. I wish all my readers could see the most interesting account of his last illness drawn up by the late Lady Agnew, and attached to his memoir. Sir Andrew's last signature was attached to a paper inviting the Lord Provost of Edinburgh to call a meeting to petition against Mr. Locke's bill to compel railway companies to carry passengers on the Lord's day by those trains which convey the mail. (This bill was defeated, on the second reading, by 131 to 122.) Having overheard the message about the requisition, he raised himself in bed, called for a pen and ink, and appended his signature, observing, with a smile, how firmly it was written for a sick man. It was the last he was ever to write. Immediately he felt an oppression in his breathing, and the sensation was as if something had "given way at his heart." The result of a post-mortem examination shewed that the immediate cause of Sir Andrew's death was disease of the heart.

CHAPTER XXXIV.

1838, 1839.

THE ABOLITION OF PLURALITIES.

Pluralities a disgrace to the Church—Pamphlet to members of both Houses—
Promotion of petitions from clergy and others—Bishop Butler disapproves
—Archdeacon Hodgson's letter—Memorial from clergy of Derbyshire to
the archbishop—Print it and send it to both Houses—Used as a brief by
members in· committee of the whole House--Circulate it through the
country—When Archdeacon Shirley was made bishop, the fate of his
pluralities—Pluralities now almost abolished.

TOWARDS the close of my residence at Brailsford, in the year
1838, when the Plurality Bill was first brought before parliament,
having a very strong feeling that the system of holding livings
in plurality, which then obtained, was a disgrace to the Established Church, I felt constrained to prepare and publish, and to
send to each member of both Houses of Parliament a pamphlet
with the following title, which, together with its two first and two
last paragraphs, will perhaps sufficiently explain its objects :—

"*A few Suggestions for Increasing the Incomes of many of the
"Smaller Livings, for the almost total Abolition of Pluralities, and
"for promoting the Residence of Ministers in the several Parishes ;
"more particularly addressed to the Members of both Houses of
"Parliament, by the Rev. William Leeke, M.A.*

"Although the real friends of our venerable Establishment
"have naturally shewn themselves disinclined to leave the
"matter of reforming the Church to those who are the avowed
"enemies of an established religion, yet are they most anxious
"that every real abuse should be abolished, and that every effort

" and sacrifice should be made to render the Church of England
" as efficient as possible.

" It is acknowledged on all hands that, in order to this
" efficiency, there should be a resident minister in every parish
" or district, and two full services in every place of worship be-
" longing to the Establishment. It is also universally ackow-
" ledged, that the system of holding sinecure incumbencies, or,
" in other words, the receiving money set apart for the payment
" of those who labour in the Gospel, without performing any
" part of that labour, is calculated, to say the least, to bring dis-
" credit not only on many of the pluralists themselves, but also
" on the Church, which continues to tolerate such an unworthy
" practice.

.   .   .   .

" The writer is deeply convinced that the present system of
" pluralities is a sad stain upon the Established Church, and that
" nothing would be hailed with greater pleasure by the great
" mass of intelligent persons of all parties in the country, than
" the adoption of this or any other plan, which would entirely,
" or almost entirely, abolish them. It may not be impertinent to
" state, that he has just joined in a petition to parliament, for the
" abolition of pluralities, with several clergymen, all of whom,
" with one exception, are of conservative principles.

" His earnest desire and prayer are that the storms which are
" now assailing the Established Church, may be the means of
" carrying away from its atmosphere those noxious exhalations
" which arise from the plurality and non-residence system."

I thought it very important to make an effort at this time to
promote petitions to parliament, praying for the total abolition
of pluralities, " except in certain cases of adjacent parishes hav-
" ing very small populations and incomes." These petitions were
very readily signed by the inhabitants of the parishes in Derby
and of the surrounding neighbourhood. The clergy in my own
neighbourhood joined in a petition, as has been before stated.
Some time afterwards, my kind friend and neighbour Mr. Shirley,
afterwards Archdeacon of Derby, and Bishop of Sodor and Man,
who had succeeded to the rectory of Brailsford-cum-Osmaston,
(the first presentation to it having been made over to him,) in

writing to me on another subject, mentioned that he thought it scarcely kind that his immediate neighbours, knowing how he was circumstanced with regard to his holding Brailsford-cum-Osmaston in plurality with Shirley-cum-Yeaveley, should have forwarded such a petition to parliament. I think he was quite reconciled to our proceedings on my assuring him that the petition was not levelled against him particularly, but against the system. The Bishop of Lichfield, Dr. Butler, in acknowledging the receipt of my pamphlet, merely mentioned that he did not agree with the views contained in it, but that he would not then state his objections to it, as he should have an opportunity of doing so when the bill reached the House of Lords. I found out, however, afterwards, in a curious way, which I intend to relate, that the bishop was annoyed at my interference in the matter. The Plurality Bill, it appears, though introduced in the Commons, had been sanctioned by the Archbishop of Canterbury; indeed, if my recollection be correct, it was called, "The Arch-"bishop of Canterbury's Plurality Bill." I should state that, although it was for the limitation of pluralities, it still permitted livings to be held in plurality which were within the distance of ten miles from each other.

The Archdeacon of Derby, Dr. Hodgson, (not Hodson, he was Archdeacon of Stafford,) sent me a very long letter, which I thought he should not have sent, appealing to me as to whether it was right that I should thus oppose the wishes of the bishop and, I think he added, of the archbishop? This was the first I heard of my pamphlet being obnoxious to either of them. The archdeacon was a kind and clever man, and afterwards became Provost of Eton; but I could not allow what he stated to have any weight in deterring me from pursuing the course which a sense of duty imposed upon me.

Almost immediately after this I was attending a most useful clerical meeting, which took place twice a year at Matlock Bath, and had the opportunity of bringing the whole subject of pluralities and of the Plurality Bill before the members. I think there were about six-and-twenty present. They all felt as I did as to the plurality system being a great evil; and when I proposed that we should send a memorial to the Archbishop of

Canterbury, containing a statement of our views and feelings, it was unanimously agreed to, and I was requested to draw it up. By sitting up late that night and getting up early the next morning, I was enabled to prepare and to write out ready for signature the following memorial:—

"ABOLITION OF PLURALITIES.

" To His Grace the Archbishop of Canterbury.

" The respectful Memorial of the undersigned Clergymen of the " County of Derby.

" We, your Memorialists, beg leave to address your Grace on " the subject of *the Abolition of Church Pluralities*—a matter " which we conceive to be of very considerable importance not " only to the Clergy of the Establishment, but to the Community " at large.

" We would respectfully offer the following observations :—

" It is almost universally admitted that the system of Plu- " ralities, which has grown up in the Church, most materially " interferes with its efficiency. There are at present about *five* " *thousand* Benefices held in Plurality.

" Although the smallness of the incomes of many of the " parishes constitutes one great difficulty in the way of the " Abolition of Pluralities, yet about two-thirds of these five " thousand Benefices are of a sufficient income to maintain a " resident Incumbent ; so that great numbers of Livings are " clearly held in Plurality for no other purpose than that of " individual advantage.

" In a vast number of instances the Plurality system has led " to there being no resident Clergyman, and only one service on " the Sunday, in the several parishes, and thus a wide field has " been opened for the spread of dissent from the Establishment, " which is much to be deplored.

" A most sad result also of the present system is, that the " Clergy as a body, and particularly those who are Pluralists, " are suffering thereby in the opinion of persons of all ranks " throughout the land ; and it is to be feared that the cases are " by no means uncommon, in which not only Laymen, but

" Ministers, have been so stumbled by it, as to have been induced
" thereby to secede from the Established Church.

" Some of the Bishops have shewn their strong disapproval
" of Pluralities, by never having given a Living in Plurality—
" others have not done so for several years past.

" Many of the leading Statesmen, of both parties in politics,
" have declared their conviction that the interests of the Church
" and of the Country require that Pluralities should be abolished,
" and that a resident Minister should be established in every
" parish and district.

" The plan proposed in the Plurality Bill now before Parlia-
" ment, of not allowing Livings to be held in Plurality which are
" more than ten miles distant from each other, *will leave the tre-*
" *mendous evil almost untouched :* of the Livings at present held
" in Plurality, nearly 3000 are within *ten* miles, and about 2000
" within *five* miles of each other ; it is evident also that the
" *exchanging* of Livings, and the supposed necessity of the smaller
" Livings being still given in Plurality, would most materially
" add to these numbers.

" The smallness of the incomes of many of the Livings being
" the chief difficulty in the way of the extinction of Pluralities,
" it is most earnestly to be desired that every effort should be
" made to raise them to an adequate amount.

" We should much rejoice to see a large grant made by Par-
" liament for the purpose of meeting the difficulty, but when we
" reflect on the more favourable opinion which must have gene-
" rally prevailed with regard to a proper provision for the Clergy
" in by-gone years since the Reformation, and consider that no
" effectual augmentation of small Livings has taken place, we
" have little hope of any large Parliamentary Grant being made
" to the Church in these days of such extensive separation from it.

" We are of opinion, under the circumstances in which we are
" placed, that the Church, (in which term we include the Laity,)
" would act judiciously, and in a manner pleasing to Almighty
" God, if it were to shew itself contented with its present scanty
" revenues, and if from those revenues it should endeavour to
" augment every small Living, with a view to the entire abolition
" of Pluralities.

"It appears from a small Pamphlet on the subject, which
" has been recently forwarded to your Grace, and to every Mem-
" ber of both Houses of Parliament, that there are 4861 Livings
" in England and Wales under £200 per annum, and that in
" order to raise them all to that amount the yearly sum of
" £407,275 would be required.

"To meet this demand there will be an available sum, on the
" reduction of the Cathedral establishments, of about £100,000,
" and possibly nearly an equal sum may be raised by an improved
" mode of leasing the Episcopal and Cathedral property : but
" still there would be a deficiency for the desired purpose of more
" than £200,000 per annum.

"We would particularly intreat your Grace's attention to,
" and support of, a plan proposed in the pamphlet referred to,
" (which was submitted to Sir Robert Peel some years ago, and
" which has been recommended for adoption in the 4th Report,
" and in the Draft of the 5th Report, of the Ecclesiastical Com-
" missioners, although it has not been embodied in the present Plu-
" rality Bill)—the plan of permitting Patrons to take a portion
" from the incomes of their richer Livings for the augmentation
" of the poorer ones to the sum of £200 a year.   This plan might
" be most readily acted upon in the case of the Livings in the
" Patronage of the Crown, the Archbishops and Bishops, the
" Deans and Chapters, the Colleges, and of other persons possess-
" ing the patronage of more Livings than one.

"We cannot conceive that there is anything *unjust* in thus
" taking from the clerical income raised in one parish for the
" augmentation of that of another.   Under the *present* system
" non-resident Incumbents, who hold more than one Living, draw
" from one of their parishes a large proportion of its clerical in-
" come which they spend in another.   The Patron stands, in some
" degree at least, in the place of the original donor.   The circum-
" stances of the different parishes, which were endowed by the
" person whom he represents, have greatly altered perhaps with
" regard to population or income, and we humbly submit that
" there is no invasion of the rights of property in the Country
" giving permission to the Patron to make an alteration, with
" which, it is to be fairly presumed, the original Endower's con-

"duct would have been in accordance, had the circumstances of
"the population, &c., been the same, when the grant was made,
"as they are now. The funds devoted to *charitable* objects, in
"ancient times, have continually been re-appropriated by the
" Court of Chancery, or by Parliament, so as to meet the altered
"circumstances of the charity, and such re-appropriation has
" never been considered as an invasion of the rights of property.

" We consider another suggestion, contained in the pamphlet
" to which we refer, to be of the very greatest importance in this
" matter:—it is that, in the case of poor Vicarages, Perpetual
" Curacies, and Donatives, (and nine-tenths of the poor Livings
" are of this description,) a grant should be made from the funds
"at the disposal of the Commissioners towards making up an
"income of £200 a year, to be met by a sum to be paid by the
" Patron, in proportion to the *increased value of the advowson* of
" the Living so augmented.

" We have no desire that Livings should be *equalized :* or that
" any diminution of the income of a Living should take place
" without the consent of the Patron ; or that there should be any
" interference with the rights of present Incumbents.

"The difficulty in the way of the utter extinction of Plu-
" ralities, which arises from some of the Livings having very
" small populations, not amounting to 100 persons, we think might
" be met, in some cases, by annexing a portion of another parish ;
" in others, by incorporating the parish with some adjacent and
more populous parish.

" We would take the liberty of mentioning our strong objec-
" tion to a plan, which has been much mooted, of a graduated tax
" of 5, 7, 10, and 15 per cent. respectively on Livings above the
" yearly value of £400, £500, £800, and £1200 ; the sum thus
" raised would only amount to about £100,000 per annum, whilst
" four hundred Livings would be taxed in sums varying from £80
" to £1080 a year ; which would not only be exceedingly unpala-
" table, but also a manifest injustice, to many private Patrons,
" inasmuch as the value of the advowsons in their patronage
" would thereby be greatly deteriorated.

" We, your Memorialists, venture to submit these views to
" your Grace, in the earnest hope that they may meet with the

" approval and support of your Grace, and of the other Digni-
" taries of our Church.

"We beg leave to assure your Grace, that our sole desire in
" this matter is to improve the efficiency of our beloved and
" venerated Church, by removing from it the odium and the other
" evils attaching to the Plurality system.

"With much prayer that the Great Head of the Church may
" purify and make our Zion a praise in the earth, and that He
" may bless your Grace and every Member of the same with all
" spiritual blessings in Christ Jesus,

"We remain, your Grace's humble Memorialists,

"And faithful Servants."

It was very gratifying to me to find, when I read the memorial over to my assembled brethren, that all the paragraphs were
approved of, except by one clergyman, who objected to one of the
latter paragraphs, I forget which it was, and declared that he
could not sign the memorial if that paragraph were retained. It
was put to the meeting whether we could part with it or not, and it
was retained by the unanimous decision of all but the one objector ;
not one word was altered. I well recollect, when it was settled
that the memorial should be adopted, that I handed it over to
that truly pious and devoted clergyman, the Rev. Walter Shirley,
(the father of Walter Augustus Shirley, who was some little time
afterwards Archdeacon of Derby, and then Bishop of Sodor and
Man,) who was sitting opposite to me at the table, saying, " Now
" Mr. Shirley, as you are our senior, will you kindly put your
" name first to the memorial ?" He replied in that gentle and
quiet way for which he was so remarkable, merely saying, " Well,
" you see, there's my son," referring to the fact of his son having
lately become a pluralist, and intimating that he could not well
sign the memorial, lest his doing so might have the appearance
to his son of his casting a reflection upon him. Of course I did
not press the matter for an instant, but handed the memorial for
signature to that good man, the late Rev. Samuel Hey, Vicar of
Ockbrook, who was the next eldest clergyman present.

The memorial was immediately printed, with the signatures
obtained at Matlock, and sent to every clergyman in Derbyshire,
with the request that he would allow his name to be appended

to it, and thus between forty and fifty signatures were added. Altogether there were seventy-two—a goodly number, considering that there were many pluralists, and many curates of pluralists, amongst the remaining clergymen of Derbyshire, who, whatever their opinions on the subject might be, would feel considerable difficulty in joining in such a memorial. The printed copies of the memorial, with the names, reached all the members of both Houses of Parliament by the same post which conveyed the memorial itself to the archbishop.

These papers came into the hands of the members of the House of Commons very opportunely, only a day or two before the Plurality Bill was to be considered in a committee of the whole House. I was told by one of the members that when the subject was brought forward, a rather remarkable scene was witnessed. Almost every member brought out a large printed document, which he unfolded and consulted as a lawyer would a brief: these were the printed copies of our memorial. No wonder they were referred to as so many briefs, for if the subject was not unknown to the several members, the details of it were.

Sir Harry Verney moved a clause in the committee to the effect that none but adjacent livings should be held in plurality, and only lost his motion by a majority of four. The bill, however, passed both Houses, without any material alteration having been made in it.

It is remarkable that almost all the recommendations contained in the memorial have since become the law of the land. Pluralities appear to be almost entirely abolished by the 13th and 14th Vic., c. 98, which enacts that no spiritual person shall hold together any two benefices, except in the case of two benefices the churches of which are within *three miles* of each other by the nearest road, unless the population of one of them, or both, (I cannot quite make out which,) shall exceed 2000. A dispensation is also necessary from the Archbishop of Canterbury. Probably public opinion will help to render it very difficult that livings should be improperly given in plurality for the future.

All the expense of sending the copies of the memorial to all the members of both Houses of Parliament, and to friends for distribution in the various counties of England, came out of my own not very well-stored pocket, though I believe that was entirely my own fault. I think the exertions made at that time were the means of dealing a deadly blow to the plurality system; and I have ever since felt thankful that I had so much to do with them.

A curious circumstance, which I have before alluded to, occurred in connexion with my plurality proceedings. When I was about to leave Brailsford, circumstances which I need not enter into led Archdeacon Hodson, of Stafford, to press me to become the curate of All Saints, the principal church in Derby, with the understanding that, on the death of the incumbent, I should succeed to the living, the advowson of which had some time before been purchased by Mr. Simeon. Archdeacon Hodson was one of his trustees, and had the whole arrangement of the disposal of the incumbency whenever it might become vacant. Bishop Butler, knowing this, placed the vacant curacy of All Saints also at his disposal, that he might appoint to it the person whom he wished to succeed eventually to the living. The archdeacon having received my consent to accept the curacy, and, eventually, the incumbency, provided he had any considerable difficulty in finding some other person equally suitable, (for I was very unwilling to undertake the charge of this large and important town parish,) mentioned my name to the bishop for the curacy, who, I was told, immediately replied that he would have nothing to do with Mr. Leeke, on account of the part he had taken in the matter of the Plurality Bill! Of course, under the circumstances, this did not give me one moment's uneasiness; on the contrary, I always considered that the being rejected on such grounds was a regular feather in my cap, and I believe I was as proud of it as I was of the honour of having stood in the forefront of the British troops at Waterloo, with the 52nd and Lord Seaton, and the Duke of Wellington, Lord Anglesea and Sir Colin Campbell a few paces in my rear, when the Imperial Grenadiers of France were making their last ineffectual stand, and the Emperor Napoleon and the Duke are supposed to have been nearer to each other than at any other moment of their lives. My readers must endeavour to bear with what must appear to them to be, and which perhaps are, sadly vain-glorious boastings.

I must not omit to mention, in connexion with my plurality work, that when Archdeacon Shirley became Bishop of Sodor and Man, and the first appointment to his livings of Brailsford-cum-Osmaston, and Shirley-cum-Yeaveley, became vested according to custom, in the Crown, it was currently reported that they were about to be bestowed on the brother-in-law of one of the ministers of the Crown. I thought it right, under all the circumstances, to write to the minister, and to state the strong feeling which had been displayed in the county of Derby, and especially in the neighbourhood of Brailsford, against the system of holding livings in plurality, and pointing out to him that although not a great deal had been thought of Mr. Shirley's holding these livings in plurality, because it was in consequence of a family arrangement which had been made many years before, yet if a minister of the Crown should, after all the stir which had been made on the subject, venture to present his relative to them, it would probably create a feeling of disgust in the neighbourhood which would not be readily allayed. Whether it was in consequence of this representation or not, I cannot say, but it was stated that the clergyman for whom the appointment was intended, after having come down to see the several parishes, declined to accept it. The living of Brailsford-cum-Osmaston, but not that of Shirley-cum-Yeaveley also, was given to the relative of another of the ministers of the Crown. After some months this clergyman was presented to another living, and old Mr. Shirley, father of the bishop, became rector of Brailsford, to the great gratification of many of his friends. Osmaston has now been long separated altogether from Brailsford.

CHAPTER XXXV.

1833, 1834.

SABBATH PROCEEDINGS IN DERBYSHIRE.

Meeting at Derby—County society formed—Bishop Ryder—Eighty meetings—School-rooms and churches crowded—Amusing incidents.

It was whilst I was at Brailsford that the chief part of my very laborious work in promoting a better observance of the Lord's Day was engaged in. Our Derbyshire society was formed on the 24th of December, 1833, at a meeting at Derby at which Bishop Ryder presided, and which eighty clergymen attended; and my friend, the late Rev. A. T. Carr, and myself, as honorary secretaries of the society, accompanied Mr. Wilson, the founder and honorary secretary of the London society, to meetings held at six or seven of the largest towns in the county.

Before the meeting took place at Derby, I wrote—for I was to be the corresponding and managing secretary—to all the clergy of the county, asking them if they were disposed to have meetings in their parishes, and offering our assistance. To this appeal I only received one favourable reply, and that was from the late lamented Rev. Henry Crewe, the rector of Breadsall, who said that he did not see the use of a meeting on the subject in his parish; but that if we would like to come there he should be happy to receive us. This untoward commencement was certainly highly calculated to damp one's ardour; I, however, learnt the lesson then more decidedly than I had ever learnt it before, that we must not allow even great difficulties at once to deter us from pursuing anything which we feel sure we have been led to engage in by the providence of God. We had commenced our work, and afterwards carried it on with much prayer to God. To a second appeal, made to the clergymen of the large towns, we received very favourable replies. Both then, and subsequently when Mr. Carr and I attended, either together or more frequently separately, about eighty meetings throughout the county, we found that a very great and growing interest was created among the people by thus calling their attention to the divine authority and obligation of the Lord's Day, and by going into various details and anecdotes connected with its observance. I think we had our meetings almost as frequently in the churches as in the school-rooms, the latter not being considered sufficiently large to contain the expected crowds of people. The fine old churches, and also the modern ones, were frequently crowded to the very walls. It was very gratifying to see the interest that was created, and the desire which was everywhere manifested that such a bill as Sir Andrew Agnew's might pass into a law, to secure to all persons, as far as possible, the Lord's Day as a day of rest.

In all directions, people determined to give up many things which they saw were contrary to the divine command; and in farmers' service and in private houses, more of the Sunday was rescued from work than had before been the case, by persons doing many things on the Saturday and putting off others to the Monday which they had been in the habit of doing on the Sunday. At the end of the Derbyshire society's address to railway proprietors, several instances are mentioned of the great desire of various classes of persons to be relieved from their Sunday labours, and of their petitioning the Legislature for this relief.

We met with scarcely a word of opposition to our views and proceedings, and with nothing really unpleasant, except on one occasion, and that was in another county, and did not arise from any apparent dislike to our wishing to promote a proper observance of the Lord's Day, but, I think, from a party and political spirit.

At one of our earliest Derbyshire meetings, our friend, Mr. Wilson, had preceded us, and on our arrival at the principal inn in the place about five o'clock, we found that he had been engaged for an hour and a half with the elderly clergyman of the town in a fruitless attempt to draw up three or four resolutions to be proposed to the meeting. The clergyman, it appeared, had not been very conversant with meetings and resolutions, and yet he had very determinedly opposed every endeavour on the part of Mr. Wilson to draw up suitable resolutions. It turned out that he did not consider Mr. Wilson to be—as he really was—the chief person in the deputation. Mr. Wilson was somewhat advanced in years, a gentleman of extensive fortune; he was either then, or had been just before, High Sheriff of Oxfordshire. He was brother-in-law to the Rev. Daniel Wilson, Bishop of Calcutta; and above all, he was the founder of the London Lord's Day Society, and the originator of the great movement which was then being made to promote a due observance of that holy day throughout the land.

When Mr. Carr and I made our appearance in the room, Mr. Wilson exclaimed, "I am so glad to see you," and said that there was a difficulty about the resolutions which Mr. ———— had been trying to draw out. On my looking at that part of the *first* resolution which he had written out, I found the following commencement, referring to the meeting at Derby at which the county society had been formed, and which had taken place ten days or a fortnight before :—"That the thanks of this meeting be given to my Lord Bishop for his kindness in taking the chair." I understood that they had argued about this resolution for a good hour; Mr. Wilson saying it was not at all the way to commence a series of resolutions connected with the formation of an association in the place, and the clergyman not giving way in the slightest degree. On my reading what he had written, I said at once, "This won't do at all," when our new friend immediately gave way, and proper resolutions were at once drawn out. I should not relate this little occurrence, did I not know that it cannot now possibly annoy any person, except perhaps some of my readers who may fail, from my want of power of description, to appreciate and enjoy the richness of the scene, including Mr. Wilson's impatience and the clergyman's quiet pertinacity, at all in the same degree that I was amused by it myself.

At one large meeting we had a slight attempt at interruption from a small knot of persons in one corner of the room, which was put a stop to in a rather laughable way. The first speaker had not spoken long, when one party stood up and said, "Mr. "Chairman!" The churchwarden immediately got up in another part of the room and appealed to the person by name not to interrupt the proceedings, but to allow the business of the meeting to go on quietly, He listened to this appeal and sat down; but towards the end of the meeting, when the last speaker was bringing his observations to a conclusion, our friend got up again, and seemed determined to obtain a hearing; interrupting the speaker, he called out, "Mr. Chairman! When I was in America," and, not having fully gained the attention of the meeting by the first sentence, he repeated it as follows, in a louder tone :—"I say, "when I was in America," and then, before he could utter another word, up started the churchwarden and said, "And *I* say, when "ye was there, why did'nt ye *stay* there." This produced such an outburst of laughter from the whole meeting that our friend sat down and gave up the contest. When the noise ceased, the chairman very judiciously at once gave out the Doxology, and the meeting came to an end. I never saw an interrupter so regularly and cleverly put down as in this instance.

At a meeting held in one of the churches in the south of Derbyshire, the proceedings began with a hymn, which was commenced by the clergyman in the reading desk and his wife in one of the pews, each starting at the same instant different tunes, which were proceeded with by each to the end of the first verse, the congregation endeavouring to sing with them, and not quite understanding what was the matter. Probably each of the leaders of the tunes was only aware that there was something wrong, without knowing what it proceeded from.

The immense quantity of work one got through at that period for several years in attending meetings, attending to one's parish, and in correspondence on the subject of the promotion of the observance of the Lord's Day and other matters, appears now very surprising when I come to look back upon it after the lapse of more than five-and-twenty or thirty years. I believe I tried my strength more than I should have done; but sometimes I am inclined to take a different view of those exertions, and to think the strength was well expended in helping to draw the attention of the country to the subject of the divine authority of the Christian Sabbath, and to "the blessings, temporal, spiritual, and "eternal, which God has been pleased in His mercy to connect with "its religious observance."

I always returned home after the meeting of the night if the distance rendered it at all practicable. I had a very excellent old black horse which I rode or drove on these occasions, and he travelled, from first to last, so many hundreds of miles in further- ance of the cause I was so much interested in, that some person playfully (not profanely) observed, that "Mr. Leeke's old black "horse knew more about the question of the authority and "observance of the Sabbath than half the people in the county."

The only very imprudent thing I recollect doing, was the going to a meeting at Ashbourne, and after my return home at a late hour, sitting up till six o'clock in the morning to write the report which was to be read at the annual meeting of the county society on the same day at twelve o'clock ; but this was, under the circumstances, unavoidable, if there was to be any report at all.

Sir Andrew Agnew, after I had been staying with him a couple of days at Leamington, wrote the following very hurried note to Mrs. Leeke, in her album, whilst the coach was waiting for me. It will be seen that in it he speaks most kindly of the hard work above referred to, which I had so long engaged in whilst trying, in various directions, to promote a due observance of the Lord's Day :—

"Leamington, 21st January, 1841.

"MY DEAR MRS. LEEKE,

"Accept my best thanks for the great pleasure of Mr. "Leeke's very kind visit to this place. You will not, I am sure, "find any cause to repent for having spared him to us for two days, "any more than you will sorrow for the many other sacrifices "which you have made for the good cause in which your honoured "partner is a chosen champion. When 'thou shalt delight thy- "self in the Lord' with all who, through your instrumentality, "have been brought to call the Sabbath a delight,—when feeding "with them 'on the heritage of Jacob thy father,' it will enhance "your joy to remember your having disregarded your own domestic

"comfort while sending your beloved husband through many a
"county beyond your own well-watered district.   Nor will you
"lament for long days and sleepless nights, given from love to God
"and man, calling upon all to remember the day of the Lord to
"keep it holy, in a correspondence which even now is transcribed
"in heaven.

"Praying that your dear children may be partakers of your
"blessedness,

"Believe me to be, my dear Mrs. Leeke,

"Your faithful and affectionate Servant,

"ANDREW AGNEW."

For a considerable time we employed a man at Derby to distribute papers, calculated to give useful information on the Sabbath question, amongst the passengers belonging to the coaches
which passed through Derby.   In the course of several months,
he circulated in this way 17,000 papers, which were almost universally well received.   He was called "Sir Andrew" by many
of the people.   On one of the few occasions on which Sir Andrew
Agnew was at Derby, when we were walking along the street I
saw our friend at a distance, and, before we came up to
him, told Sir Andrew about him, and by what name he was
frequently called.   On my making him known as our distributor
of papers, which I believe were chiefly the London society's
papers addressed to various classes of the community, Sir Andrew
told him he heard that some of the people turned him into
ridicule by applying his (Sir Andrew's) name to him; on which,
he replied, "I consider it quite an honour, Sir Andrew."

CHAPTER XXXVI.

1831—1839.

MINISTERIAL WORK AT BRAILSFORD.

Brailsford-cum-Osmaston—Interesting cases at Osmaston—Deaf gentleman—Put
Osmaston into other hands—Large classes of young men at Brailsford—
Dying publican—Relatives at Brailsford—Sudden death of a medical man
—War against public-houses—Sad end of a drunkard—Sleeping in church
at Shirley, curious scene—Baptism of a gipsy's child—Clerical meetings—
Subject of baptism—Archdeacon Shirley succeeds to the living—Leaving
Brailsford—Testimonial.

My ministerial work at Brailsford, though apparently much interrupted by my labours in connexion with our Lord's Day
Observance Society, was not so in reality. The fact was that I
was enabled to do a great deal of work at that time of my life,
though perhaps I overworked myself, and my health suffered
from it afterwards. I look back to my ministry at Brailsford
and to my residence amongst the people of Brailsford, with feelings of much gratitude for all the kindness I experienced from
all classes of persons, and of thankfulness that God was pleased,
as I believe, to make use of me, a poor, weak instrument,
(2 Cor. iv, 7,) to lead many of them to think and care about the
salvation of their souls, and to attend seriously to "the things
" which belonged to their peace."

The curacy of Brailsford-cum-Osmaston was the charge which
I entered upon, and this only necessarily involved a service at
Brailsford in the morning, and an afternoon service at Osmaston,
which was four miles distant, and contained then about 460 inhabitants. The having two churches at that distance from each

other did not really lead to much more labour than two services in the same church would demand, as there was, as a general rule, only one sermon to be prepared for the two, but, as soon as the arrangement could be made, I placed Osmaston in other hands, with half the curate's salary of £100 a year, that I might have two full services at Brailsford. I, however, had time at first and when there was a change of curates there, to become acquainted with all the people of Osmaston. I well remember that when I had visited rather more than half the families by house row, they told me that there was, in a house I had not yet come to, a very old woman of ninety-seven, who was not very well. I immediately went to the house and found her sitting in a chair in the parlour. She appeared glad to see me, but I found that she had very imperfect and confused ideas of the way of salvation. She shewed great intelligence for a person so advanced in years, and listened to me with the greatest attention and earnestness as I spoke to her of our state as sinners, and explained to her the way of salvation, to all who received Him as their Saviour, through the death and merits of Jesus Christ both God and man, and also the way of holiness and comfort. I was afraid I should fatigue her, but she appeared to drink in so greedily the great truths I declared to her, and which I had reason to think she had never understood before, that I continued with her for nearly an hour; her bright and intelligent eye being fixed upon me the whole time. I promised to see her again the next time I went to the village, which was three days afterwards, but her spirit had fled when I arrived. Her grave is the first to the left as you enter the Osmaston churchyard by the first gate you come to on the road through the village from Osmaston manor. I expect to see this poor creature amongst the saints in heaven, though I believe hers was a receiving the Saviour as *her* Saviour, and a turning of the heart to God at the very close of her life. But how sad it is that the great mass of the people of this professedly Christian country are contented to put off, to the close of life, any serious consideration about the salvation of their souls and the turning of their hearts from sin and worldliness to serve their God. I was led to say, a few Sundays ago, when speaking on this subject, and warning the careless of the congregation against such delusion, that I only *knew* of *one* instance of true repentance at the close of life, and that was in the case of the thief upon the cross.

Osmaston manor house, belonging to Mr. Francis Wright, a beautifully-situated and splendid mansion, where the great object of the owner is, that he and all his family and household may honour God, was not built or thought of at the time of which I am writing. But in a nice cottage, not very far from the spot on which the house stands, there lived an aged couple, who afterwards moved into the village of Osmaston, and of whom I wish to mention the following particulars :—They were, perhaps, the most regular attendants at church in the parish. There was a custom at Osmaston, but I never heard of it except in one other parish, the parish of Tickenhall, in Derbyshire, that on the entrance of the clergyman into the church, all the people who had already arrived stood up to receive him. The old man and woman sat in a pew directly opposite to the principal door, and I can see them now, after four-and-thirty years have passed away, rising up, Sunday after Sunday, and the old man bowing his head and stroking down his grey hair with his hand as a token of respect for my office, though it always made me feel all the more ashamed of my own unworthiness and sinfulness. After a time the old man fell sick and died, and although there was nothing particular in his case, I remember I thought that he was a truly Christian man. About three years after, when I was taking the afternoon duty at Osmaston on account of the illness of the clergyman, on my inquiring if there were any sick persons whom it was desirable I should visit, I was told that the old woman was ill, and would be glad to see me. I had not seen her for a long time, and found her in a very deplorable state of sickness; she was suffering from a cancer which extended down her cheek and neck and breast, but she was in a most happy state of mind. She gave me a very clear account of her trust in Christ's death as a satisfaction for sin, and of all the simple and main truths of religion. She told me that she was quite happy, and was enabled to leave herself entirely in God's hands; that if it pleased Him to take her at once she should be glad to go, or that if He was pleased to keep her in life a few weeks longer she should feel equally glad to remain, being assured that her heavenly Father knew and would do what was best for her. I thought I had never met with an instance of more simple and, at the same time, stronger faith than in the case of this poor woman. I asked her how she had acquired her clear knowledge of the great and saving truths of religion, and her answer was, " I picked it " up, Sir, a little at one time and a little at another, in the house " of God." And then I thought of the regular attendance of this aged couple at church, and of the beautiful passage in the ninety-second Psalm : "Those that be planted in the house of the Lord " shall flourish in the courts of our God. They shall bring forth "fruit in old age ; they shall be fat and flourishing."

The instance of strong and simple faith which I have just mentioned, brings to my recollection a short statement respecting real faith and strong faith, which I heard a year or two ago from a speaker at a public meeting. It was as follows, and may give instruction and comfort to some of my readers :—"The comfort " of the Christian belongs to strong faith, his salvation to real " faith."

At Osmaston there was a very elderly gentleman who was deaf, and he came frequently to church, and sat about three seats from the reading-desk. During the sermon or lecture he stood up, and leaning over the back of the pew before him, with his hands behind his ears, listened with great earnestness to see if he could hear some portion of my discourse. By speaking nearly at the top of my voice, I frequently managed to make him hear some of the most important points in it, for which he was very thankful. The services of our church afford great advantages to deaf people who can read ; for with the occasional assistance of some friend near them they can join in every part of the service except the sermon. I have, however, found it very difficult to induce persons, who had made deafness an excuse for staying away from church, to break through the sinful habit which they had indulged in.

When first I went to Brailsford I had a class of young men who met on the Sunday evening for religious reading and in-struction, and on the Monday evening to be taught reading, writing, and arithmetic ; and I allowed none to come on the

Monday who had not been on the Sunday. The numbers varied very much. At one time I recollect we had upwards of forty young men attending regularly, and then, as the days grew longer, they gradually decreased, so that the Monday evening class was given up in the summer and commenced again about the beginning of October. Although some were not regular in their attendance, I think this class was very useful in the parish, and that there was scarcely a young man in the parish, during the whole time I was there, who did not by means of it come more or less under my own personal instruction. Some four years ago, when I was riding one day on the Derby road, a man, whom I met, accosted me by name, and on my not knowing him, told me who he was, and mentioned the great religious benefit he had derived from attending those Sunday evening parties for reading the Scriptures. He said that he had there first received those religious impressions which led to his walking in a Christian course of life; that he used to go home from them and lie awake for a considerable time, anxiously thinking of his great danger on account of his sins, and of how he could escape the punishment hanging over him. I have since heard from those who live near him that he is one who, for many years, has been a truly religious and consistent character.

Either during one or two summers I arranged to have the second service at Brailsford in the evening instead of the afternoon; and the consequence was, that I had applications from friends in all directions to take their afternoon services for them, when they were forced from any cause to be away from their parishes on the Sunday. During the whole summer there was scarcely a single Sunday afternoon on which I was not thus employed. It was so great a convenience for my friends, that I could not refuse to take the duty when by a little extra exertion I could manage it.

A curious circumstance happened on one, or I should rather say, two of these excursions. The parish was ten miles from Brailsford. After the service on the first afternoon I inquired if there were any persons seriously ill whom I could visit, and was directed to a beer-house, in which I found a man of thirty or rather more, who appeared to be far advanced in consumption.

After speaking to him for some little time he told me, amongst other things, that he was very happy, and not at all afraid to die. Knowing that a man who kept a beer-house was very likely to be in the continual practice of sin by allowing drinking on the sabbath day, and by frequently permitting drunkenness in his house on other days, I spoke to him about sin generally, and the need of seeking pardon through the Saviour; and that change of heart, that true penitence, which always accompanies a humble trust in the death of Christ for pardon. All at once, somewhat to my surprise, he exclaimed very peevishly, "Why don't you "come to the point? Why do you go on teazing a poor fellow?" I immediately replied, "I will come to the point. You say that "you are happy and not afraid to die. But let me ask you, "Have you not, up to this very time, been sinning against God "by frequently permitting persons to get drunk in your house; "and have you not allowed drinking to be going on even on the "holy sabbath day? If this be the case, how can you be happy?" And then I explained to him such verses as 2 Cor. 5, 17, and exhorted him to seek mercy and true repentance whilst he had yet the opportunity. The moment I mentioned the sins connected with his beer-shop, I observed that his countenance fell, and he appeared all at once to see how he had been deceiving himself. He then received very thankfully what I said to him. I could not remain with him more than about a quarter of an hour; but I saw him again on the following Sunday, when he was evidently much nearer his end, and apparently in a very humble, penitent state, looking for mercy through the only Saviour of sinners. After speaking to him seriously on the great truths of religion, I said to him, "Now you are about to die, and you are leaving "your young wife and her two little children in the midst of all "the temptation to which you know she will be exposed in carry-"ing on this beer-house: let me urge you to give it up at once; "give it up from this very moment." In order to make it more easy for him I promised to take from him, and to pay the retail price for the ale which he had in the cellar, which I sent a cart for the next day. There was no other person in the house during this interview; but, with his permission, I made the man, who had brought up my horse for me, take down the sign over the door, which I destroyed by breaking it into small fragments, so that it could not be used again. My opinion about late repentances I will give in a subsequent chapter, when I mention the severe fever with which God was pleased to visit us at Holbrooke, about twenty years ago.

Our great attraction to Brailsford was that some of Mrs. Leeke's near relatives lived there; her uncle and his nice family, who lived at Brailsford Hall, and her aunt, who lived at Culland Hall. They all helped us much in the parish. Miss Mary Cox was a lady of exemplary piety, and was one of the most diligent and devoted Christians whom I ever met with. Her example was most beneficial. In every kind of weather was she to be found in her place at the church and at the school-room weekly lecture, when she would listen in all humility to me, as her appointed minister, to feed her soul from the Word of Life, (1 Peter ii, 2,) although I was nearly thirty years her junior; and although from her knowledge of Scripture she was ten times more able to give me instruction than I was to impart it to her. It was a great pleasure to her to come and see us at the parsonage; but I often observed that she refused herself this gratification when there was some superior duty, although it might appear to us a thing of small importance, which called her away. It was a great grief to her when she found that we should have to leave Brailsford on the appointment of Mr. Shirley to the living, and so much did she feel it that she made up her mind to leave the parish also; and at one time there was a hope that she would come and reside with us wherever we might be in the country. One evening, some months before we left Brailsford, when I was driving her home from my house, I spoke to her on the subject of her leaving the place, and spoke of old Mr. Shirley, who was to be his son's curate there, as he deserved to be spoken of, as a truly pious and devoted minister, whose ministrations would, I had no doubt, be a comfort to her; and I rather urged her to reconsider her determination. She immediately burst into tears, and declared that it could not be, she could not remain. I found she had made up her mind to avoid the pain which the being present when Mr. Shirley, junior, should read in would occasion her. The way in which her intention was, in God's pro-

vidence, carried out, was very remarkable. At the close of the
month of January, 1839, her valuable life was suddenly terminated
by apoplexy ; and on the Sunday on which Mr. Shirley had been
expected to read in, she was lying dead, and on the next Sunday,
when he did read himself in, her body was lying in the family
vault within a few yards of that church in which she had worshipped nearly all her life.

The following was written by her, several years before her
death, in Mrs. Leeke's album:

"Whit-Sunday, May 26th, 1833. Evening.

"Father of mercies, hear my prayer for him whom Thou hast
"appointed our pastor in this parish. May the Spirit of the
"Lord rest upon him—the spirit of wisdom and understanding
"—the spirit of counsel and might—the spirit of knowledge, and
"of the fear of the Lord. O grant him the comfort of seeing
"Thy work prosper in his hands, the effects of the Holy Ghost
"manifested, and the dear Redeemer glorified amongst us.
"Heavenly Father, bless my dear niece with all spiritual
"blessings in Christ Jesus. May she experience the substan-
"tial presence of the Holy Spirit, and more and more testify that
"she is born again, to the praise and glory of Him who hath
"called her out of darkness into marvellous light. May they
"both walk in all Thy commandments blameless, and bring up
"their children unto Thee. O bless their offspring; in their
"early years may Thy converting grace be apparent in them :
"blessed Jesus, carry them in Thy bosom, and save them from
"the devouring wolves *sin* has let loose upon the earth.

"Monday, May 27th. For unnumbered blessings I would
"praise the Lord ; amongst them I esteem (not least) my dear
"Christian friends at the rectory. May our communications be
"'subservient to each other's good,' and

"'When this poor lisping, stammering tongue,
Lies silent in the grave,'

"may they have a well-grounded confidence that aunt Mary was
"a monument of the wonderful sovereign mercy of redeeming
"love !   "MARY COX,

"Culland Hall."

Mrs. Leeke has added the following in her album :—

" My beloved aunt died January 30th, 1839."

In a paper intended to be read after her death, which was found in a small packet directed to her sister,* she thus writes :
" I know not how to speak of the wonders of redeeming love *now.*

> " ' Then in a nobler, loftier strain,
> I'll sing Thy power to save,
> When this poor lisping, stammering tongue
> Lies silent in the grave.' "

" It is all sovereign love and mercy. The Lord hath magni-
" fied His mercy in the pardon of my sins, for they are great !
" His mercies towards me are truly countless as the sands.

" My parting text is, ' The things that are seen are temporal,
" ' but the things that are not seen are eternal ': 2 Cor. iv, 18.

" Oh eternity, eternity ! Who can tell the length of eternity ?
" Hallelujah. Amen."

When first I went to Brailsford we had a very respectable and clever medical man there, but he scarcely ever attended church or any other place of worship; and I felt it to be my duty to speak to him on the subject several times. On one occasion he told me he had had a bad example set him in his youth in this respect; that he had been apprenticed to Sir Richard Crofts, who, when he settled as a surgeon at ———, on the first Sunday had desired this young man, after he had been in church a certain time, to come to his pew and tell him quietly that he was wanted. This occurred several times, and his master would go from the church, mount his horse and gallop off, and not return home for a couple of hours or more. He thus led the people to think that his services were in great demand, and succeeded in getting into good practice. It will be remembered that poor Sir Richard Crofts attended the Princess Charlotte, of Wales, at the time of her death, nearly fifty years ago, and im-mediately after destroyed himself. Mr. ——— confessed that he had got into a bad habit, and that he would try and act

---

* Her younger sister, Miss Maria Cox, who still lives, and is in her 87th year, has been as remarkably endued, as was her sister, with faith, and holiness, and peace, and devotedness of purpose. There was an evident distinction of manner in the holiness of their walk with God, though both were equally humble, which led me to designate the elder as " stern piety," and the younger as " mild piety." But I never ventured to *say* this to either of them.

differently. The habit, however, was not broken through. I had called on him two or three times and had not found him at home, and one day as I was walking down the village I saw him coming towards me on horseback, and, as he was walking his horse and did not appear to be in a hurry, I determined not to lose the opportunity of speaking to him. I accordingly stopped him for a minute or two, and told him that I again wished to remind him of the sad way in which he was neglecting those public means of grace which God had appointed, and the neglect of which must be highly offensive to Him, and endanger the salvation of our souls. For the first time he manifested, though very civilly, some little feeling of dislike to be spoken to on the subject, saying, " I think, Mr. Leeke, these kind of things should " be left to a man's own conscience." I immediately replied, " Mr. ———, if you saw a blind man walking straight towards " a deep precipice, and in danger of being dashed to pieces, would " you not knock him down if that was the only way in which " you could stop him, rather than let him walk on and destroy " himself." The only answer he made, as he put his horse in motion again was, " You are quite right, Mr. Leeke, quite right." This was the last time I ever spoke to him. I saw him once afterwards as he passed me in the village on horseback, on a very dark night, when I could only distinguish the outline of his figure. His end was very sudden. One of the neighbours told me that the night before his death, he called at her house to pay her husband half-a-crown for some work he had done for him, when she said, " I would rather not receive it on the Sunday, if " you please, Sir." In a little joking way he replied, " Oh, you " respect the Sunday, do you, Molly?" and she said, " Yes, Sir, I " hope you do." The next morning, in going to visit a patient in the village, he turned into one of the cottages to say a few words to the inmates, for he was very kind to the people, and much liked by them, when he was taken suddenly ill and died in a few minutes. Oh may we constantly remember that " in the " midst of life we are in death."

Whilst I was at Brailsford I waged a regular war with some of the public-house keepers, who permitted drunkenness on their premises, but, although I had them several times before the magistrates, I did not once succeed in obtaining a conviction: I think they were twice let off with paying the expenses. But some benefit arose to the parish, notwithstanding my want of success in these prosecutions; some of the drinking people resorted to public-houses in the neighbouring parishes, where they could drink without molestation, and the publicans became much more cautious about permitting drunkenness in their houses. Since I came to my present parish, twenty-six years ago, I have only once taken any steps against a public-house keeper, and that was when a woman complained to me that they had been harbouring her husband during the afternoon of Sunday, and had treated her uncivilly when she went to look for him. In this case I was rather astonished when thirty shillings, the moiety of the fine, were handed over to me as the informer: I had forgotten that this would form a part of the proceedings. I did not think it well to give it to the wife, but I soon disposed of it amongst six of the poorest people. I thought on coming to this parish (Holbrooke) that I would leave the duty of watching the public-houses to the constables and to the police, and not lose so much time as I had done, and place myself in a position with regard to the publicans which would probably so stir up their feelings against me, as to make it almost impossible for me to be of use to them in my ministerial capacity afterwards. I am inclined to think, however, that the police do not effect so much in the way of diminishing drinking and drunkenness as I effected under my system of supervision and prosecution at Brailsford. I have no doubt but that it was a sad mistake to do away with the law which made it penal for a publican to permit tippling in his house. The clergyman, churchwardens, and police had much in their power, under the old system, which would be of immense benefit, even if it were only exerted in preventing young lads from frequenting public-houses, where they soon learn to become regular drunkards.

I have seen the sin of drunkenness continued, and handed down in families, to the third and fourth generation. The one-half of the sin of drunkenness, and its attendant crimes, would be stopped if the legislature would only consent to close public-houses during the whole of the Lord's Day, in accordance with the petitions of multitudes of the poor drunkards themselves, and of their suffering families. There were several drunken men at Brailsford, whose career and end were most dreadful. I will only mention one of them. His was rather a remarkable case; he was often drunk, and when he left the public-houses, instead of making his way home, he was in the habit of lying down to sleep, often in the middle of the road, thereby exposing himself to the danger of being run over. I nearly drove over him twice in returning at night from some of my meetings about the observance of the Sabbath: indeed, on both occasions, the wheels of my carriage would have gone over him if my horse had not started at him. On the second occasion, on my getting out of the carriage to wake him up, and to see who it was, he swore very badly at me, not having the sense to discover, from my voice, who was speaking. I thought it right this time to summon him before the magistrates for swearing and, I think also, for drunkenness: he was convicted and fined for the swearing.

Some time after this occurrence, on visiting his sick wife, who was a pious woman, I one day found him at home, and had a great deal of religious conversation with him: he told me he had lately been reading "Baxter's Saints' Everlasting Rest," and had enjoyed it very much. We spoke about his drunkenness, and the danger that he was frequently exposed to by his habit of laying himself down to sleep in the middle of the road: he told me that he had a great fear of a fast coach, which then ran the distance between Manchester and London in eighteen hours. On its way from Derby to Manchester it passed along the road between Langley and Brailsford between nine and ten o'clock at night: he told me that when he was drunk, and saw it coming behind him, his practice was to get out of its way by running and throwing himself into the hedge by the side of the road. The night before Christmas Day, I think in the year 1838, they came to tell me that the poor old man had been run over and killed by this very coach. I immediately went down to the inn to which the body had been brought by some neighbours in a light cart, which was just behind the coach when it passed over his body: after staying there a few minutes, I proceeded with a party to examine the place at which he had been killed. He had come from a public-house at Langley, about a third of a mile off; there had been a very slight fall of snow a little time before the coach had passed along, so that we could see the mark of his body on the snow, and the track of the horses and wheels, and ascertained that he had not been knocked down by the horses, but that he had been lying asleep in the middle of the road when the off-wheels passed over his head, and crushed out his brains.

I twice took the duty at Shirley whilst I was curate of Brailsford, and on both occasions met with an adventure, though I am not quite sure that both the circumstances did not occur on the same afternoon. The afternoon was exceedingly warm, and in the middle of my sermon I observed that at least thirty of the congregation were very soundly asleep; as it was neither pleasant nor desirable to proceed under this difficulty I stopped, and turning my sermon, which on that occasion was a written one, down on the cushion, I said that I observed several of the congregation were asleep, and that I should be obliged if those sitting near them would awaken them. I was not at all prepared for the scene which followed : I saw more particularly what took place in the gallery before me, in which were a number of farmers' servants, many of them fast asleep, with their arms on the front of the gallery, and their heads on their arms. Directly I requested that they might be wakened, those next to them set to work in good earnest, digging their elbows most unmercifully into their ribs, and, although all those aroused from sleep, in different parts of the church, were not thus roughly treated, yet each individual, as he awoke, could only understand that *he* had been asleep, and that the clergyman was stopping in the midst of his sermon until he became more attentive. The great difficulty was for me to go on with my sermon at all, after witnessing such a ludicrous scene, in the midst of my address to them on the most solemn subjects connected with the salvation of their immortal souls.

The other event occurred after the sermon was ended, either on that afternoon, or on the other to which I have alluded. I found that, instead of leaving the church, by far the greater portion of the congregation remained, and it turned out that it was to witness the baptism of a gipsy's child. I may observe that I have always, in my own church, baptized children after the second lesson, according to the rubric, and have not admitted any to be sponsors unless they were communicants, according to the canon, considering that this is a considerable safeguard against our having unfit persons brought forward as sponsors ; but, in the church of another clergyman, I have always conformed to his practice, whatever it might be, in these particulars. In my own church I have often, when there has been a difficulty in obtaining spon- sors, only required one; and I believe we should be justified in doing without any sponsors, calling upon the members of the church who were present to be the sponsors, and to make the responses, rather than allow ourselves to be driven to receive as sponsors, and trainers of children in the ways of God, those who were so careless and negligent about their own souls as to live in the habitual neglect of the dying command of our Lord and Saviour. I shall, perhaps, slightly revert to this subject again.

It was very pleasing to see a party of gipsies assembled in the church for such a purpose, especially to myself, who have occa- sionally had a good deal to do with that class of persons in the course of my life. Everything went on very correctly until I took the infant in my arms and said, " Name this child !" Then a man, who appeared to be the eldest of the party, answered, "Dellareiffey, your honour!" I could not christen the child without making inquiry as to whether they were not making a mistake in the name, but they assured me there was no mistake, and told me I pronounced it correctly when I pronounced it as I have written it above ; they added, that the name was in the Bible, and then I was fully convinced that there was some mis- take. I inquired if they meant " Delilah," which was the nearest Scripture name I could think of, but that was not it. At last, on my telling them I thought they had better take some other name, the man said, " Let it be Amelia, your honour," and so the child was baptized by the name of " Amelia." They told me afterwards that Dellareiffey was an old family name, and I felt sorry to have disappointed them.

We had a very nice clerical meeting in the neighbourhood of Brailsford, which was attended by many of the clergy living a few miles to the right and left of that part of the main road from

Derby to Ashbourne which lies between the latter place and Langley. We met at each other's houses every month: Mr. Shirley (afterwards archdeacon, and bishop) was one of the members, as was also Mr. Shipley, the aged vicar of Ashbourne. I remember inviting Mr. Shipley to come to Brailsford on some occasion, and sleep there, and in his reply he said, "I shall be "very glad to lie in the bed you offer me, but I never *sleep* in a "strange bed." He had a dog which certainly shewed some amount of sagacity: when his master went out of his house on any week-day, the dog always prepared to go with him, but he never did so on the Sunday. Again, when he went to visit the sick the dog always lay down quietly in some part of the room until he came towards the close of his prayer, but his invariable practice was to get up the moment Mr. Shipley commenced saying, "The grace of our Lord Jesus Christ, &c."

Although our clerical meeting was usually very well attended, it once happened that there were only three members present. The subject was "baptism," especially in connexion with the catechism, and baptismal services of our church; and each of us took a very decidedly different view of it from those views taken by the other two. Shirley thought the expressions used at the commencement of the catechism, and in several places in the baptismal service for infants, were to be taken in an ecclesiastical sense, and referred principally to the advantages arising to the infant from its formal admission into the visible church of Christ. Our other friend held, what has been called, the "opus operatum" view of the subject, that every child baptized by a lawful minister receives grace, which he may either improve or neglect. And I argued that the compilers of the prayer-book intended much more than all this; that our services were not intended for unconverted men, but for true believers, who were justified when they brought their children to God, and presented them, with believing prayer, in His own appointed ordinance of baptism, in expecting the fullest blessings which the words in the catechism and in the baptismal service can possibly be understood to mean, to be poured out upon their offspring, in connexion with the ordinance. I believe that, in very many cases, perhaps in almost all, the children of real believers are sanctified from their birth;

of course I do not mean that they are without remaining sin, but I mean that they are regenerate, born again, born of the Spirit, and they are to be trained up by their parents in the nurture and admonition of the Lord: Eph. vi, 4: Proverbs xxii, 6. I look upon baptism as a declaratory ordinance, and consider that the baptism by the Holy Ghost often takes place, as I have said above, at the birth of the infant, sometimes whilst the administration of the ordinance is going forward, and also frequently in after life. When I say, in the words of the Nicene creed, " I "believe in one baptism for the remission of sins," I do not mean to say that the outward baptism with water washed away the guilt of my sin, nor do I mean to say that the baptism of the Holy Spirit, which water baptism represents, cleansed me from the guilt of sin, for the death of Christ as a satisfaction for sin has effected that, if I am a true believer, if I humbly trust in Him; but I mean that I believe in the baptism of the Holy Ghost, in that change wrought in the heart by the Holy Ghost, as *shewing* that the sins of those in whom this change is wrought are remitted, forgiven, blotted out: Romans viii, 14, &c.

When an *adult* comes to receive baptism, he is already born again, he has already faith in Christ and true repentance, and unless he was considered to be a true believer, and a truly converted person, the minister would not baptize him. Now our Church Catechism, which is intended for the instruction of the adult as well as for that of children, teaches him to say that in *baptism* he "was made a member of Christ, a child of God, and "an inheritor of the kingdom of heaven:" but he was a believer in, and a member of Christ, a child of God, and an inheritor of heaven, before he was received into the visible church by outward baptism. It therefore follows, I maintain, that our church does not mean to teach us to believe in a regeneration which necessarily first takes place at the outward administration of the rite of baptism. I may observe that a greater or less distance of time intervening between the work of the Holy Spirit and the administration of the outward rite does not appear to me to affect the question, whether that space be a few seconds, a few minutes, a few days, months, or years. In baptism, where there is not only the outward sign but also the inward grace, our article on baptism states that "the promises of forgiveness of sin, and of "our adoption to be the sons of God by the Holy Ghost, are "visibly signed and sealed; faith is confirmed, and grace increased "by virtue of prayer unto God."

No blessing is expected to be given to the mere formal worshipper; we cannot expect for one moment that God will bless the person who comes to the Lord's Table, unless he be a humble, penitent believer in Christ. How then can we believe that a blessing is invariably poured out upon children in baptism, however careless, worldly, and ungodly their parents may be?

We were very sorry to leave Brailsford, and all our kind and dear friends there. The leave-taking throughout the parish was very painful to us; indeed, I was forced to defer it, as regarded one portion of the houses, until my return to Derbyshire in the beginning of the following year. One farmer who I thought would not care much about our leaving the parish, particularly as I had found it necessary to speak to him very seriously respecting a particular part of his conduct, burst into tears on my giving him a parting shake by the hand. The people have kindly maintained, during the twenty-six years which have since elapsed, a very affectionate regard for me and my family, and we have always felt the same for them. I trust great numbers of us will, by God's mercy, meet around His throne hereafter. Of many I think I may hope that I was the humble instrument of leading them to seek and find mercy and holiness in Christ; and I think God also made use of me, a poor unworthy sinner, in building up many others in the faith, and holiness, and comfort of the gospel. But I feel ashamed to write this.

It was a great comfort to me also to think that my leaving Brailsford was not an event of my own seeking, but that it occurred in the wise and gracious providence of God, who, notwithstanding all their unworthiness and vileness, ordereth all the footsteps of those who have a sincere desire to serve Him in all things. Poor Mrs. Shirley, (the wife of old Mr. Shirley, who became curate of Brailsford, according to an old-standing arrangement with their son,) on meeting me one day in Derby, about the beginning of 1840, when they had been nearly six months at Brailsford, said to me, "Oh! I am so happy; I seem to have "only one drawback to my happiness, and that is, the knowing "that we have been the means of displacing you." She hoped I should soon be settled again in some suitable sphere, and this wish of hers was realized not very long afterwards.

For some months before we left Brailsford our friends employed themselves in having prepared for us a very handsome silver inkstand, and an elegant table on which it was to stand: these testimonials of their kind feeling cost them fifty-three pounds. The inkstand had the following inscription on it, and also the date of our departure from the parish :—

"Presented to the Rev. William Leeke, M. A., by the inhabi-"tants of the parish of Brailsford, in testimony of their grateful "remembrance of his unwearied and efficient ministerial labours "during his residence amongst them ; and to Mrs. Leeke as a "token of respect and esteem due to her uniform kindness and "benevolence.

    "20th July, 1839."

CHAPTER XXXVII.

1840—1843.

HOLBROOKE.

Appointed to Holbrooke—New church and school-room—Liberality of Patron and his son—Character of population—Chartism—Anecdote—Special constables – Chartist meeting at Holbrooke – Dragoon Guards and Yeomanry—Row in the village—Injury from stone-throwing—Black eyes on the Sunday—Illness.

In March, 1840, I became the incumbent of Holbrooke, a living of £57 10s. a-year without a parsonage house; but the patron (the late Mr. W. Evans, M.P. for South Derbyshire) offered it to me with the income made up to £100, and with Holbrooke Hall—one of the best clergyman's residences in the county—at a nominal rent. I was informed, by almost everybody I met, that the population was about the roughest population in Derbyshire. A large number were stocking and glove makers, who had the character also of being imbued, to a considerable extent, with chartist principles; so that I came to labour amongst the people of Holbrooke with some expectation of now and then having a door slammed in my face, and of meeting perhaps with other rudeness; but, of course, I knew that I should meet with persons of various characters in any parish I might go into, and if the parish had been really as bad as, or much worse than, it was represented to be, I should not on that account have refused it. Some of the events I shall think it right to mention will help to show how far the above expectation was correctly formed. Mr. Evans told me that he had been talking for some time of rebuilding and enlarging the church, and that he was ready to do so whenever I might think it desirable. I told him I thought there was "no time like the present," as we had the spring and summer before us. It was at once determined on; and a very commodious church, capable of holding four hundred persons— more than half the population at that time—was opened on Whit-Sunday, 1841. In the mean time we managed very well in the school-rooms, and in the open air in the park, when the weather would permit. This church cost altogether £2000. The first time he came to Holbrooke, Mr. Evans inquired if there was anything else wanted besides the enlargement of the church, and I mentioned an infant school at a particular spot at Holbrooke moor, which he immediately caused to be built, and which has been a great blessing to the parish. I have felt bound to mention the great kindness and liberality of the late Mr. Evans in laying out money for the benefit of the parish, the annual value of which, £500, exceeds the rental of his Holbrooke estate. His son, (one of the present members for South Derbyshire,) I must take leave to mention, treads in his father's steps in such matters, both here and in all directions. He has made over a house as a parsonage, which I do not, however, live in, and has given £1000 to the living; and these two gifts have been met on the part of the Ecclesiastical Commissioners by a grant of £2000; so that now Holbrooke has a parsonage house, and an income for the clergy-man of £157 10s.

When first I went about the parish I did not meet with any rudeness, but I met many persons, who appeared to be inhabit-ants, but who took no notice of me, although the most of them must have known me to be the new clergyman. I made it a rule, however, not to pass any persons in the parish without speaking as I went along, and in a little time I came to have everybody, who did not show me greater attention, at least as a nodding ac-quaintance. And now, although the great mass of the population (amounting to 1000) appear to be very little concerned about religion, we should feel it to be as great a trial to leave the people of Holbrooke, as it was to us to leave all our kind friends at Brailsford.

The chartist feeling was very prevalent amongst the people

during the first two or three years of my residence at Holbrooke. They were mostly kind-hearted people, and some of them were always glad to get me into long conversations and arguments about the five points of the charter. After a few years the subject was scarcely ever adverted to, and when it was mentioned I found persons making use of the same arguments, on various points connected with the distinctions between rich and poor and other matters, which they had heard from me when they had formerly stated and argued about the real or assumed grievances of the working classes.

Many of the chartist lecturers were mere stirrers up of discontent, and lectured, I imagine, chiefly to make themselves of some importance in the eyes of the people, and for the sake also of the collections which were made for them after the chartist preachings, as they were often called. The following rather curious circumstance occurred at Belper one Sunday afternoon :— A chartist lecturer was preaching to a party which he had collected around him, and took for his text the last sentence of the 3rd verse of the 37th Psalm, "Verily thou shalt be fed." From this passage he showed the people that God himself had declared in His Word that they were to be fed, and that it was the rich who deprived them of that food which God intended for every man, and then enlarged upon the deprivations the poor were subject to, and laid the whole blame of such a state of things on their employers and the other wealthier classes of the community, omitting all mention of the drunkenness and improvidence on the part of so many of the working classes themselves, from which such a large amount of poverty and misery arises. A very intelligent and religious young man, who is now a clergyman, happened to be passing along, and, stopping to listen to the chartist preacher, after a time interrupted him, and said to the people, "This man is deceiving you ; he pretends to declare to you the "Word of God, but he has only, for his own purposes, read to "you a portion of the verse in the 37th Psalm ;" and, producing a pocket Bible, he added, "Let me read to you the whole verse ; "it is as follows : 'Trust in the Lord, and do good ; so shalt thou "'dwell in the land, and verily thou shalt be fed.' This man has "not told you of the conditions mentioned in the verse. You must

"trust in the Lord as your God and Saviour and Benefactor. The
"verse says you must 'do good,' that is you must lead holy lives.
"If you trust in God as your God and Saviour, and serve Him,
"then, but not otherwise, you may be assured of His care over
"you with regard to all your temporal wants." The assembly
listened to him whilst he spoke in this strain for a few minutes,
and then dispersed without the usual collection having been
made for the lecturer.

In the summer of 1842, it will be remembered, there was much
chartist excitement, and that it was thought necessary to swear in
special constables in several parts of the country. I think we had
about ninety in Holbrooke, who were placed by the magistrates
under my orders. A large gathering of chartists was announced to
take place on Monday, the 22nd of August, in that year, on Holbrooke moor. Large numbers of men had come down from
Manchester to the Staffordshire potteries, and had advanced even
beyond the town of Leek, without anything effectual having been
done to stop them; and they committed considerable damage to
a clergyman's house in the potteries. In the neighbourhood of
Holbrooke men were turned out of work, and some from whom
one would have expected better things, went about in rather
formidable bodies, asking for—which amounted to demanding—
assistance. I thought it right to warn and exhort the people of
my own parish, both from the pulpit and wherever I met with
them, not to attend the meeting, particularly as it was held contrary to the Queen's Proclamation, forbidding such meetings, in
consequence of which the meeting might be attacked and dispersed
without any previous notice. I believe the immense proportion
of the people of Holbrooke kept clear of the meeting; I only ascertained that four of them attended it, or rather joined one of
the parties, which had come from a distance, with a view of
swelling its numbers. I think none of the Manchester people
were there. The Holbrooke special constables were not called
out, nor had I received any notice as to the precautions which
the civil authorities had been taking to meet the difficulty,
when, as we were sitting at breakfast, we had the pleasure of
seeing the helmets of a troop of Dragoon Guards who were winding along the road at the bottom of the park, two hundred yards

off, on their way to the appointed place of meeting, about a mile further on. They were met by a well-appointed troop of Derbyshire Yeomanry, and a large force of special constables, who had come up from another direction. One of the principal chartist lecturers was in a cottage not very far from the spot near which the various groups of people who were to form the meeting were standing, and he, probably knowing what the law was, sent more than once to the magistrates to know if they would give him permission to address the people; they, however, gave him no answer; so the different bodies, after hanging about the place for some time, began to disperse. By some strange oversight the magistrates, and special constables, and troops, allowed one large body of about six hundred to slip away from them unperceived, and to take the lower road through the village of Holbrooke. I had a brother-in-law, an old sailor, who had seen some service, staying with me, and not knowing exactly how matters might turn out, we had, in the morning, loaded our arms, including a double-barrelled gun of his, with the determination to resist any attempt to enter the house.

When these six hundred men came through the village, I was looking over a wall from a plantation, and when I heard the word "halt" given opposite to our gate, I thought it was time that we should be at our posts; but, on our running up quickly to the house, we were surprised and amused to find that, in making it secure, the inmates had forgotten their principal defenders, and had so regularly fastened the doors, that we met with some delay in getting in, which would have been anything but pleasant if the party below had come straight to the house, as I, for one minute, thought they intended to do when they halted at the gate. They, however, took the road to Derby, and, owing to the difficulty which a messenger had in passing them, they had almost reached it before any troops could be assembled at that entrance of the town to stop them. They occasioned some alarm and confusion in the town; but I think they were by that time rather tired of their day's work, and alarmed at what would probably be the consequence, and were glad to disperse and get away in small parties.

We had a very unpleasant affair five or six weeks afterwards at our village wakes. They always commenced on the Sunday and on that Sunday there was more than the usual amount of drunkenness, and I gave two persons into custody. The next night the magistrates ordered all the public-houses to be closed at nine o'clock ; and in carrying this order out I was requested, as something had been stolen at one of the public-houses, to let two of the five special constables whom I had called out stand at the door of the house, that each person as he passed might be examined as to the article which was supposed to have been purloined. This led to a parcel of drunken fellows, as they came out, standing near me and the constables, and repeating all kinds of ribaldry, thinking, as it was "pitch dark," that they would not be known. One man advanced near to me several times, and repeated the verse, "Go to now, ye rich men, weep and howl for "your miseries that shall come upon you," and then, when I advanced to lay hold of him, he stepped back into the crowd. At last, without any body observing it, it being so very dark, I slipped away from the constables and got into the rear of the riotous party, and passed to their front just in time to seize the culprit when he was returning, as he thought, from addressing the obnoxious verse of Scripture to me. There was a partial light from a single candle in a house near, so that sometimes we could discern figures and sometimes not. When the riotous party found that I had got hold of the man, they immediately rushed to the rescue, and the five special constables also rushed down to prevent it, and were dragging him off in custody to see who he was, when one of the constables was tripped up, and, on getting on his legs again, struck one of the men heavily in the face with his staff; at that moment, the person who had applied for the two constables, came and told me who the man was, and we then let him go. We stood there for some little time, thinking the party would disperse, and I began to feel that I had allowed myself to be placed in a false position when I, the clergyman of the parish, was led to take charge of the constables, and had called a few of them out to keep order on that occasion. We six special constables could have knocked over, or have taken into custody, or put to flight, the whole party ; but I felt I was not authorized to take either of these steps, more particularly as many of those whom we should have attacked were probably not implicated in the row. To add to the pleasantness of the situation, I received a heavy blow from a stone under my right ear, which cut my stock, and I am not quite sure that it did not do me a permanent injury; it did not knock me over, but I thought it doubtful whether I was not going over. The person who had requested me at the first to send the two constables, standing near me, said, "One of your constables, Sir, has just hit me a very "heavy blow with his staff along the top of my head." I replied that I thought he was mistaken, that it probably was a stone, that they were flying about, and that I had just been struck heavily on the side of my head; just then I received a heavy blow from another stone on the nose, between the eyes, and a very large stone or furnace-cinder struck the wall behind us, and somebody exclaimed, "That would have killed a horse." All the stones were probably aimed at me, and I heard a long time afterwards who had thrown them; he was a person of bad character. The person who fancied he had been struck by the constable, said he thought if I would withdraw with the constables, he could manage to get the crowd to disperse. I have been somewhat ashamed to relate all this so circumstantially; but, not to speak of its having been the greatest fight I ever was in besides that of Waterloo, I have a reason for so doing, which will perhaps subsequently appear, so I hope my readers will forgive me. I am aware that they could, at any time, read a much more interesting account of a street fight in the police reports of the London papers.

It appeared to the magistrates that there was hardly any sufficient evidence to enable them to proceed against any of the parties connected with this drunken row. I believe the chartists had nothing to do with it, for from that time forward nothing could exceed their kindness to me, and the marked attention, respect, and civility, which they manifested towards me, as if they were anxious to prove that it was a mere drunken escapade, and had not its origin in any political feeling on their part. On the following Sunday, the people of Holbrooke had the honour of seeing their clergyman taking his duty in the church with a couple of regular black eyes and a bruised face. I did not choose to procure assistance and to be absent myself, for I thought if there was any disgrace in the exhibition of the proofs of my ill-treatment, it did not attach to me but to others.

In the spring of 1843, I became seriously unwell; the symptoms being a giddy or faint feeling at times, and particularly when I attempted to read or to preach in the church. Whether it had anything to do with the blows from the stones, or whether it proceeded from over-working myself, or from some other cause, I could not make out. I was told by some of the doctors that it might have arisen from blows on the head. I began to get somewhat better in about a year, and could take some duty, but to this day I feel it a comfort to have stools in the reading-desk and pulpit. I never sit when I am preaching extempore, but always do so when I have a written sermon.

CHAPTER XXXVIII.

1845.

ADDRESS TO RAILWAY PROPRIETORS ON THE DESECRATION OF THE LORD'S DAY.

Divine authority—Feeling of railway servants—Public danger—Cases of necessity—Cabinet councils—Running of the Mail—Not receiving letters—Medical men and solicitors—Bath—Liverpool—Derby—Attempt to open the London post-office—Efforts to stop Sunday trains—Scotch and Irish railways—Pecuniary loss—Present law—Paley—God's judgments—Continental habits—Strong feeling and efforts of those deprived of the Sabbath—Canal and coach proprietors—Railway meeting at Derby—Proposal to stop Sunday trains—Mr. Hudson.

THE following address which I drew up in 1845, and which was sent to all the proprietors of the Midland Railway, preparatory to their half-yearly meeting in the summer of that year, soliciting their support to a motion which I was about to bring forward, contains many useful and interesting particulars:—

"*Address of the Committee of the Derbyshire Society for Pro-*
"*moting the Due Observance of the Lord's Day, on the Desecration*
"*of that Day by the Running of Railway Trains.*

"*Patron.*—THE LORD BISHOP OF LICHFIELD.
Vice-Patrons.
SIR MATTHEW BLAKISTON, BART.
THE VENERABLE THE ARCHDEACON OF DERBY.
E. S. CHANDOS-POLE, ESQ.—WILLIAM EVANS, ESQ., M. P.
Treasurer.—W. L. NEWTON, ESQ.
Hon. Secretary.—REV. WILLIAM LEEKE, Holbrooke, near Derby.
Hon. Sec. for North Derbyshire.—REV. A. A. BARKER, Baslow, near Bakewell.

Committee.

Rev. E. H. Abney	Rev. H. J. Feilden	Peter Le Hunt, Esq.
Rev. Philip Browne	Rev. W. Fisher	Rev. John Latham
Rev. H. Buckley	John Flewker, Esq.	Rev. Edward Lillingston
Colonel Clowes	Rev. R. H. Frizell	Rev. R. Macklin
Rev. Richardson Cox	Rev. P. Gell	Rev. G. Pickering
Henry Cox, Esq.	Major Gell	Rev. E. Poole
Rev. H. Crewe	Rev. J. Hamilton	Rev. W. Shirley
Edmund Crewe, Esq.	Rev. S. Hey, Sen.	Rev. E. Unwin
Rev. James Dean	Rev. R. Hope	Rev. E. Wade
Rev. W. Dewe	Rev. J. G. Howard	Rev. T. W. Whitaker
Charles Dewe, Esq.	Rev. N. P. Johnson	Wm. Williamson, Esq."
Samuel Evans, Esq.	J. N. Kahrs, Esq.	

"Derby, March 1st, 1845.

"The Committee of the Derbyshire Society for Promoting "the Due Observance of the Lord's Day, are fully convinced that "that day is of Divine appointment,* and that the command to

* "The opponents of the doctrine of the *Divine Authority and Universal* "*Obligation* of the Lord's Day, (who, it may be observed, have been remarkably "few in number,) state that the Sabbath was first instituted immediately after "the departure of the Jews from Egypt, when the Ten Commandments were "delivered to Moses, and that consequently the command to observe it was only "binding on the Jews. It appears, however, according to the simple and plain "meaning of the three first verses of the second chapter of Genesis, that it was "instituted at the creation of the world, 2500 years before the giving of the Law "on Mount Sinai, and nearly 2000 years before the birth of Abraham, the first "of the Jewish race ; and, consequently, that its right observance is a duty in-"cumbent not only on the Jews, but on every descendant of Adam. The ob-"servance of the Sabbath is mentioned in the sixteenth chapter of Exodus, in "regard to the not gathering the manna on that day ; and this also is a proof "that the Sabbath had been instituted before the Ten Commandments were "delivered to Moses. Another objection has been that no mention is made of "the Sabbath in the Bible from the second chapter of Genesis to the sixteenth "of Exodus ; but this is not very extraordinary, as all the events of the first 2000 "years from the creation are compressed into the eleven first chapters of Genesis, "only three or four of which refer to general matters ; and *this* argument against "the observance of the Sabbath from the creation of the world to the time of "Moses, would equally well prove what is acknowledged to be the reverse of truth, "that there was no observance of the Sabbath amongst the Jews, from the time "of Moses till the latter end of David's reign, a period of nearly 450 years, "because no mention of the Sabbath occurs in the books of Joshua, Judges, Ruth, "in the 1st and 2nd books of Samuel, or in the 1st book of Kings. On turning "to the first part of the fifty-sixth chapter of Isaiah, and particularly from the "last clause of the seventh verse, it will be clearly seen that the whole passage "refers not merely to the Jewish, but also to the Christian dispensation, and "that a day of rest and spiritual observance is as binding on Christians as it was

' keep it holy is o perpetual and universal obligation: that
" the blessing of Almighty God rests on those individuals, and
" companies, and nations who observe it—His curse on those who
" desecrate it. They are also as fully convinced that works of
" necessity, piety, and mercy, and such works alone, ought to be
" performed on that holy day. They moreover feel assured that
" it is the bounden duty of Christian Governments and Legisla-
" tures, and of Companies and Individuals, to do all in their
" power to prevent the Lord's Day from being publicly profaned,
" and, if possible, to secure it as a day of rest to every member
" of the community, so that he may have the *opportunity* of wor-
" shipping God according to the dictates of his conscience.

" In accordance with these convictions the Committee feel
" bound to state that the traffic on Railways on the Lord's Day,
" (as also on Canals and by Steam Vessels, and other conveyances,)
" is a gross violation of God's holy commandment, entailing on
" the numerous servants of the several companies employments

" on the Jews, for God's house could not 'be called an house of prayer *for all*
" ' *nations*,' until the Jewish dispensation was at an end. The thirteenth and
" fourteenth verses of the fifty-eighth chapter of Isaiah, being in the midst of
" the prophecies which relate, or extend, to the Christian dispensation, confirm
" the proof that a Sabbath is to be observed by Christians, and, not only so, but
" they shew also, in what a strict and holy manner the day is to be passed by
" them; they are to 'honour God, not doing their own ways nor finding their
" ' own pleasure, nor speaking their own words.' If any are disposed to think
" that this passage refers only or principally to the Jews, they must at the same
" time feel constrained to make the following important admission : ' That, if the
" ' Jews, who were under a dispensation, one of the main features of which was
" ' the observance of many burdensome rites and ceremonies, if they were re-
" ' quired to keep the Sabbath in this *spiritual* manner, how incumbent must it
" ' be on *Christians*, supposing that day of holy rest is to be kept by them at all,
" ' to keep it in a holy and spiritual way, seeing that they are under a dispensa-
" ' tion which is almost altogether spiritual.' On looking to the New Testament
" it will be found (Mark, chap. ii) that our Lord states, ' that the Sabbath was
" ' made for man, and not man for the Sabbath.' It was instituted for the good
" of man, of every man, Christian as well as Jew. It was instituted not only
" that every man might have it as a day of rest for his body, but also as a day of
" spiritual instruction and comfort for his immortal soul. Man was not made for
" the Sabbath, so as to be required to adhere strictly to the letter of it, to his real
" detriment. Our Lord states most fully (Matt. chap. xii) that works of neces-
" sity, piety, and mercy, ought to be performed on the Sabbath Day, but he no-
" where sanctions the idea that the observance of one day in seven was not to be
" retained by His followers, or that the day of rest might be passed in dissipation

"which cannot be justified on the ground of necessity, and de-
"priving them of a great portion of that day which God has
"ordered to be wholly sanctified, or set apart for holy purposes.
"It is true that, on some Railways, Churches have been built for
"the accommodation of the Railway Servants, but how can they
"be expected to effect the benefit intended, if these same persons,
"for whom the Churches are erected, are continually required to
"'pollute the Sabbath' by a participation in the unhallowed
"traffic which almost everywhere prevails ?

"By their present course Railway Companies deprive them-
"selves of the services of great numbers of most efficient and
"trustworthy servants, whose conscientious feelings prevent them
"from accepting employment which involves what they conceive
"to be a direct violation of the command of their God. It is
"well known that the large majority of those now employed most
"earnestly desire to have the Lord's Day as a day of rest; whilst
"many of them, who have not sufficient strength of principle to

"or amusement. The day of rest and holy observance was changed, on the au-
"thority of the inspired Apostles, from the seventh to the first day of the week,
"in honour of our Lord's Resurrection on that day. It should be observed that,
"when St. Paul tells the Colossian Christians that 'no man was to judge them
"'in respect of an holy day, or of the new moon, or of the sabbath days,' and
"when in his Epistle to the Romans, he says, 'One man esteemeth one day
"'above another: another esteemeth every day alike ; let every man be fully
"'persuaded in his own mind,' he refers not to the Lord's Day, but to the
"seventh day, the Jewish Sabbath, and to their other sacred days, the observ-
"ance of which some of the Judaizing teachers very improperly wanted to im-
"pose on the Gentile converts to Christianity, and which some of the Jewish
"Christians, in addition to their observance of the Lord's Day, were still dis-
"posed to keep holy, although as the observance of these days was a part of the
"ceremonial law which was abolished, the doing so was no longer required of
"them. It must be remembered that the Christian Sabbath is nowhere in
"Scripture, nor in the early Christian writers, called the 'Sabbath,' or the
"'Sabbath Day,' but always the 'first day of the week,' and the 'Lord's Day.'
"(Rev. c. i, v. 10.)

"The command to keep holy one day in seven is considered by the vast body
"of Churchmen and Dissenters to be as binding on Christians as the other Com-
"mandments of the Decalogue. It is placed in the most conspicuous part of our
"churches, and is read, and also responded to by the congregations in prayer for
"God's mercy and assistance, the same as in the case of the other nine Com-
"mandments. And, it is evident, there is no more ground for singling out the
"fourth Commandment as not binding, than there is for saying that the second,
"third, or any other of the Commandments, is no longer of divine obligation."

" enable them, at all risks, to throw themselves out of employ,
" yet have their minds ill at ease under their present participation
" in Sunday railway traffic.   It is not improbable that the want
" of a regular day of rest, according to God's appointment, and
" the consequent overworking of the men, more especially of the
" Engine Drivers, may have been, in some cases, the cause of those
" fearful accidents which have frequently occurred.   Surely the
" Legislature, the country at large, the railway proprietors, are
" bound most seriously to consider the responsibility of thus
" forcing unhallowed employment on so many thousands of per-
" sons who long to be set free from it.

    " In some of the discussions which have taken place at the
" half-yearly railway meetings, on the proposition 'not to run
" ' trains on the Lord's Day, excepting so far as might be required
" ' by Act of Parliament,' one of the most specious arguments
" used for the continuance of these trains was the importance of
" providing for the convenience of the public in cases of necessity
" and mercy.   It is admitted that cases of necessity do sometimes
" arise in which persons are fully justified in travelling on the
" Lord's Day, but travellers in cases of necessity are very few in
" number compared with those irreligious persons who travel on
" that day for mere pleasure or worldly business, and no conscien-
" tious man can sanction that which, although affording to the
" *few* the means of travelling *in allowed cases of necessity and*
" *mercy*, proves a temptation to the *many* to break the express
" command of God.   In the matter of no letters being delivered
" in London or sent from London on the Lord's Day, cases of
" necessity are not permitted to interfere with general regulations
" for the moral and religious well-being of the community.   It
" may be a case of mercy that a person should hear in London on
" the Lord's Day of the illness of a friend at a distance, but the
" people of London are content, for the much higher benefit
" resulting from the general cessation of correspondence on that
" day, to do without such intelligence.   So it may be fairly main-
" tained that the proprietors of railways are not justified in
" providing the means of travelling to a few persons in cases of
" necessity, if it involve the employment on every Lord's Day of
" many thousands of railway servants, and at the same time holds

" out facilities to immense numbers of persons to spend in plea-
" sure and dissipation that sacred day which God in his mercy
" set apart not only as a day of rest from bodily labour, but also
" of instruction, edification, and comfort for their immortal souls.

" It has been often asked—' Would you prevent the poor man,
" ' who is shut up in some close street in a town during the six
" ' days of the week, from enjoying a little fresh air with his
" ' family on the Lord's Day?' By no means! But, supposing
" it to be otherwise lawful for him to travel on the Lord's Day, is
" it right that multitudes of railway servants are to be deprived
" of their Sabbath privileges on his account? Let occasional
" holidays be given to the working classes, and suitable recrea-
" tions be provided for them on the week-days; but let them not
" be encouraged to spend God's holy day, which was set apart
" for far higher purposes, either in dissipation or amusement.
" The fact is, that nine hundred and ninety-nine out of every
" thousand of the poor throughout the country do not at all use
" the railway on the Lord's Day; numbers of them being under
" the influence of religious principles which prevent them; and
" few comparatively, if they had no other objections, being
" inclined to make the necessary outlay.

" There are, no doubt, cases in which the use of railways and
" the employment of railway servants on the Lord's Day are per-
" fectly justifiable. For instance, Government should have the
" power, in cases of urgent necessity, of sending dispatches, and
" of requiring the conveyance of troops, and others; and some of
" the railway servants must by turns be employed in watching
" different parts of the several lines on that day. Public opinion
" would probably be sufficient to prevent the Government, were
" they so disposed, from abusing such power.

" The following will help to shew how seldom these expected
" cases of necessity may arise. In the year 1835, Sir Robert Peel,
" in deference to the opinions expressed in numerous petitions,
" decided on the discontinuance of Cabinet Councils and Minis-
" terial Dinners on the Lord's Day; and this rule was adhered
" to by his successors in office. It was expected that cases of
" very great emergency would occasionally arise, in which it would
" be perfectly right to call Cabinet Councils on the Sunday; such

" a case however has not yet occurred, and thus for nine years
" not one Cabinet Council has been held on that day.*

   " Many persons may be disposed to think that the *conveyance*
" *of the Mail* on the Lord's Day can also be justified on the ground
" of necessity.   The Committee so far from thinking so, are of
" opinion that this is the MONSTER EVIL, the GREAT NATIONAL SIN
" with regard to the Sabbath, inasmuch as the Legislature and
" Government not only sanction, but enforce this mode of dese-
" crating it.   It is a practice which, so far from being looked
" upon as necessary or inevitable, is one for the abolishing of
" which every effort should immediately be made.   The Com-
" mittee also consider it to be of all others that desecration of the
" Lord's Day which may the *most easily* be abolished.   And they
" are most thankful to learn that numerous and influential bodies
" of men in all parts of the country are about to address the
" Government on the subject.   With the view of shewing how
" easily men of business and others may satisfy themselves that
" the transmission of the Mails, and the delivery of letters are
" unnecessary on the Lord's Day, it may be mentioned that, in
" the beginning of 1839, about 1500 of the principal inhabitants
" of the Derby district sent a request to the Postmaster that their
" letters might not be forwarded to them, except in cases of
" emergency, on that day.   With the exception of a few, these
" persons have adhered to the good rule which they laid down for
" themselves in that year.   The request was signed by the three
" County Members residing within the district, by a very large
" portion of the Country Gentlemen, and of the Commercial men
" and Tradesmen of Derby, including the four Banking Companies,
" and the proprietors and editors of both the Derby Newspapers.
" All the Clergy, and eight Dissenting Ministers also signed it.
" About 30 of the medical men and solicitors (thinking that so
" long as their letters arrived in Derby on the Lord's Day the
" interests of others required that they should receive them)
" signed a statement that they would 'very willingly see the
" 'transmission of the Mails and the delivery of letters altogether

---

* March 9th, 1866.   Twenty-one years have elapsed since the above paragraph
was written, and still it has never been found necessary to hold a Cabinet Council
on the Lord's Day.   They have been discontinued now altogether for thirty years.

"' discontinued on that day.' A similar request has been signed
" in Bath by upwards of 2500 persons. Lest it should be sup-
" posed that the reservation with regard to ' cases of emergency'
" indicates an opinion on the part of those who signed the request
" to the Postmaster that the transmission of the Mails could not be
" entirely abolished, it should be stated, that it was merely in-
" tended to refer to letters conveying intelligence of sickness or
" death, or other urgent matters, which, so long as the Mails
" arrived, the parties wished to receive ; and that throughout the
" Town and County of Derby petitions have frequently been
" signed by several thousands of persons (including probably
" almost every one of the individuals who joined in the request)
" praying, amongst other things, that ' the transmission of Mails'
" might be discontinued on the Lord's Day. A Memorial has
" recently been transmitted to the Secretary of State, signed by
" 600 Merchants and 5000 of the other inhabitants of Liverpool,
" praying that the practice in their Post-office may be assimilated
" to that of London by the suspension of all business on the Lord's
" Day. At Belfast, in consequence of a Memorial from the in-
" habitants to the Postmaster-General, there is no longer any
" delivery by the Letter Carriers on that day. In Scotland letters
" are not delivered from door to door on the Lord's Day : and it
" has been ascertained that not more than one-fourth of the
" letters are inquired for at the Edinburgh Post-office. Very
" many of the most respectable men in business in that city do
" not send for their letters ; and, amongst others, ten out of the
" eleven Banking Companies, within the last few years, have mu-
" tually agreed not to hold any communication with the Post-
" office on the Lord's Day. In the early part of 1839 fifty-six of
" the leading Bankers of London, 1600 Solicitors' firms, upwards
" of 1000 Merchants, and several hundreds of the members of the
" Stock Exchange signed memorials to the Lords of the Treasury,
" praying that there might be no delivery of letters in London, or
" transmission of country letters through London, on the Lord's
" Day. If all the Inhabitants of London, if the Country Gentle-
" men, the Professional Men, the Bankers, the Commercial Men
" and Tradesmen of Edinburgh, Liverpool, Bath, Derby, and their
" neighbourhoods, and of other places, can do without their letters

"on the Lord's Day, what necessity can there be why the same
" classes, or any other class of persons, should receive them on
" that day in any part of the country? Why should not the
" Sabbath Day be a blank day, with regard to the running of
" Mail Trains and all other Post-office business, not only in Lon-
" don, but throughout the United Kingdom? Almost all incon-
" venience attending such an arrangement, even with regard to
" the most distant parts of the kingdom, may be obviated by the
" Mails being started from the different ends at the usual hours,
" and being made to arrive at some station about half-past eleven
" o'clock on the Saturday night, where the bags may be kept in
" safe custody until about half an hour before one on the Monday
" morning, when the Mails may be again forwarded to their
" destination.

" Many attempts have been made by Directors and Pro-
" prietors of Railways to have them closed on the Lord's Day.
" Clauses were originally introduced into some of the Bills to
" this effect, and actually passed the House of Commons, but did
" not pass the Lords. When the proposition to close the London
" and Birmingham Line on the Sabbath Day was first brought
" forward at a meeting of the Directors, it was only lost by a
" majority of one. It was afterwards rejected by a large majority
" at a General Meeting, 3621 votes having been recorded in its
" favour, and 7,486 against it. The Manchester and Leeds Rail-
" way was at first closed on that day by the Directors, but was
" afterwards opened by the decision of their General Meeting.
" Attempts have been made, but unsuccessfully, to close the fol-
" lowing lines, amongst others, on the Lord's Day; the Edin-
" burgh and Glasgow, the York and North Midland, the North
" Midland, the Midland Counties, and the Birmingham and
" Derby. In the attempt thus to close the three last-mentioned
" railways (which abut on Derby and are now consolidated, and
" called the Midland Railway) some of the Members of this Com-
" mittee were actively engaged; several of them being Proprietors
" of Railways, solely or chiefly with the view of using every
" effort in their power for the abolition of the Sunday traffic.
" The proposition was to close these railways altogether, so far
" as the power given to the Postmaster-General by Act of Parlia-

"ment would permit it, that is, that no trains or carriages should
"run on the Lord's Day, except such as could be enforced for
"the service of the Post-office. At the Midland Counties'
"General Meeting, there were 955 votes given in favour of the
"proposition, and 1773 against it; at the Birmingham and
"Derby Meeting 213 votes were in its favour, 1360 against it;
"and at the North Midland Meeting 3792 votes were for the
"resolution, and 5498 against it. This proposition was sup-
"ported by numerous Memorials to the several Railway Com-
"panies from Derby and its neighbourhood, signed by persons of
"all denominations. More than half the votes connected with
"these three railways were not given on either side. It should
"be stated that at some of these meetings the leading opponents
"of the proposal professed to have a respect for the Lord's Day,
"and appeared not to be without some strong doubts as to the
"propriety of their opposition to its strict observance. At one
"of them there appeared to be a very general feeling amongst
"the Shareholders that Parliament should be petitioned to pro-
"hibit all Sunday Travelling. The Committee trust that all
"Railway Proprietors will take the same view of the matter, and
"unite with the tens of thousands of their fellow-countrymen,
"who are so anxious on the subject, in soliciting the Legislature
"to put a stop not only to this, but to every public profanation
"of the Lord's Day. It should be mentioned that the Proprietors
"of the Birmingham and Gloucester Railway have, since the
"Line was opened, confined themselves to the running of the
"*Mail* Trains only on the Lord's Day, which trains convey pas-
"sengers; this is going a step farther than is required by the
"Act of Parliament. On several of the Scotch railways there is
"no Sunday traffic. At the end of the year 1840, on the repre-
"sentation of the Directors and Proprietors of the Greenock and
"Glasgow Railway to the London Post-office, 'that it was their
"'earnest desire that the railway should not be used for any
"'purpose, except on the six week-days,' the Postmaster-General
"consented not to use the power allowed to him by Act of Par-
"liament, and did not require them to convey the Mail on their
"Line on the Lord's Day. The Directors of the Glasgow and Ayr
"Railway, who had previously made an offer to Government for

" carrying the Mail, withdrew that offer as regards the Lord's
" Day, in compliance with the remonstrances of deputations from
" the Church of Scotland and other religious bodies. The Dundee
" and Arbroath Railways are required to carry the Mail, but
" decline passengers on the Lord's Day.   It should be here stated
" also that the several Presbyteries throughout Scotland have
" memorialized the Government that there may be no transmis-
" sion of the Mails on the Sabbath Day.

   " The Hon. Mr. Maxwell, the High-Sheriff for the County of
" Cavan, has altogether declined taking any part in the promo-
" tion of the projected railway from Dublin to Cavan, on the
" sole ground of the violation of the Lord's Day, by the running
" of trains on most of the lines already formed in the United
" Kingdom.

   " The Committee have thought it desirable to give these
" details in order to the better understanding of the state of feel-
" ing on the subject of Sunday Railway traffic, both amongst
" Proprietors and the Public in general in those quarters in which
" the subject has been much agitated.   It ought to be borne in
" mind that, notwithstanding the vast extension of railways,
" Railway Proprietors still form only a small minority of the in-
" telligent public ; and that multitudes of religious persons
" throughout the country have refused (the Committee think
" erroneously) to become Railway Proprietors from a fear of in-
" curring guilt on account of the Sabbath desecration which is
" permitted ; thus helping to swell the numbers, in the several
" companies, of those who desire-the continuance of the Sunday
" traffic, and giving them a temporary triumph.   On the other
" hand, (whilst probably in the aggregate not half the votes have
" been given,) whenever the question has been agitated, except
" in one instance, there has always been a large minority, among
" those who have voted, altogether opposed to any violation of
" the Lord's Day on their several railways.   Perhaps it is not
" too much to expect from those who have withheld their votes,
" and also from great numbers of those who have hitherto voted
" for the running of Sunday Trains, that, in deference to the
" feelings of so many of their Fellow-Proprietors, of the Bishops
" and Clergy, of the General Assembly and Presbyteries of Scot-

"land, of pious Dissenting Ministers, and of laymen of all
" denominations in every part of the land, they will yet unite in
" opposing the Sunday trains at the different half-yearly meet-
" ings; and also (and this appears to be at least of equal import-
" ance) in petitioning the Legislature to prohibit the running of
" all trains, (Mail trains as well as others,) and to put down every
" kind of traffic on God's holy day. Such a prohibition will
" indeed rejoice the hearts of hundreds of thousands, and espe-
" cially of many of those who, for the sake of employment, are
" now tempted to violate the command of their God. It may be
" hoped also that it will prove a blessing to many of those who
" are at present reckless of His commands. And when in the
" execution of their perilous duties, any of them shall from time
" to time be cut off by sudden death, surely it will be no small
" comfort to the Proprietors who employ them, and to the com-
" munity in general, to reflect that they have by their exertions
" assisted in securing to them one day in seven as a day of rest,
" and have thus given them at least the opportunity of preparing
" for death and eternity.

" Motives of a pecuniary nature, the Committee feel assured, do
" not weigh with great numbers of those who hitherto have not
" advocated the closing of the railways on the Lord's Day; but
" it may not be out of place to state, that some time ago one of
" the Directors of the London and Birmingham Railway proved
" most satisfactorily, that so far from the total prohibition of
" Sunday trains being productive of any loss, the contrary would
" rather be the effect. It is self-evident that if no trains run on
" the Sunday there must be a great saving of wear and tear, and
" on the other hand that (as far at least as passengers for any dis-
" tance are concerned) those who find they cannot travel on that
" day, will not altogether give up their journeys, but will travel
" on some other day instead.

" Proprietors of Railways are at present only forced to convey
" the Mails and the Post-office servants on the Lord's Day; the
" clause in the late Railway Bill relative to third-class passengers,
" only enforces conveyance for them on the Lord's Day in case the
" proprietors run any train for passengers on that day, and not
" otherwise.

"The opinions of Paley have sometimes been appealed to, in
"mistake, by those who advocate the propriety of Sunday traffic
"on railways, as sanctioning their view of the subject; it may
"be well, therefore, to say that there is not one word in his
"chapter on the Christian Sabbath which has the least
"appearance of giving such a sanction; but, on the contrary, he
"states, that 'the uses proposed by the institution are:—1st. To
"'facilitate attendance on public worship. 2nd. To meliorate
"'the condition of the laborious classes of mankind, by regular
"'and seasonable returns of rest. 3rd. *By a general suspension of*
"'*business and amusement to invite and enable persons of every de-*
"'*scription to apply their time and thoughts to subjects appertaining*
"'*to their salvation.*' He expressly states that 'the duty of the
"'day is violated *by the going of journeys.*'

"The Committee fear that if the present desecrations of the
"Lord's Day (and they especially refer to those on railways), are
"allowed to continue, the just judgments of the Almighty must be
"expected to be poured out upon this offending country, hitherto
"so highly honoured and blessed. On this ground, it concerns
"every member of the community to render every possible assist-
"ance in suppressing the evil. If it be permitted to proceed, the
"present generation will also incur the guilt of handing down to
"posterity a state of things with regard to the Sabbath very
"different from that orderly observance of it for which, notwith-
"standing many grievous desecrations, this country has hitherto
"been so pre-eminent. Many of the habits of the people of this
"land, with regard to the Lord's Day, are becoming more and more
"assimilated to those of our continental neighbours, amongst whom
"the 'holy Sabbath is polluted' by attendance at the theatres,
"and by dances and festivities, which prevail more on that day
"than on any other. One consequence of this profanation to the
"present inhabitants of this country and to their posterity, must
"surely be a similar increase amongst them of infidel or super-
"stitious opinions, and eventually a total abandonment of true
"and vital religion. Let the people of this land beware of giving
"up one of their dearest birthrights, one of the best inheritances
"which they can transmit to their children. May all who are in
"any way the promoters of Sabbath desecration reflect on the

" awful responsibility which they incur ; and may those who have
" hitherto been tempted by the thoughtlessness, wickedness, or
" avarice of others, to deprive themselves of that day of holy rest
" which a merciful God has accorded to them, be induced to ab-
" stain from that which is so evil in the sight of their God, and
" to confine themselves to works of necessity, piety, and mercy,
" on the Lord's Day.   May God of His great goodness send forth
" a spirit of repentance and reformation in this matter on all
" classes of persons throughout the length and breadth of the
" land!   May they 'turn every man from his evil way.'   May
" they 'hallow God's Sabbaths, and they shall be a sign between
" ' Him and them that he is the Lord their God.'   (Ezekiel xx., 20.)
" May they always remember that 'righteousness exalteth a
" ' nation; but sin is a reproach to any people.'

  " The following extract from a circular letter, sent to every
" member of both Houses of Parliament, in the year 1837, was
" appended to the foregoing address :—

  " ' Almost all the keepers of Posting-houses in Derbyshire and
" their Servants, to the number of 228, have petitioned Parliament
" against all posting and travelling on the Lord's Day ; the
" majority of the Coach Proprietors of Derby and their Servants
" against Coach Travelling ; 87 of the Canal-men of Derby, and
" others at Shardlow, &c., against all traffic on the Canals ; the
" vast majority of the Butchers, Bakers, Hairdressers, Grocers,
" and Hucksters of Derby, for some stricter enactment to prevent
" the exercise of their trades on the Lord's Day : 70 of the
" Publicans of Derby and its neighbourhood, 28 at Ashbourne,
" and 50 at Alfreton, have petitioned that Public Houses may be
" closed (with certain necessary exceptions) during the whole of
" the Lord's Day.—About 2500 of the Merchants, Captains, and
" Seamen of Liverpool, and upwards of 1200 of the same class
" belonging to the Port of London, have petitioned in favour of
" the clause which prohibits the Sailing of Ships from Port on the
" Lord's Day.   Nearly 800 of the Severn Boatmen, and 400 of
" those employed on the Trent, have prayed for the prohibition of
" all Sunday traffic on Canals and Navigable Rivers ;—7000 of
" the Journeymen Bakers, and 500 of the Master Bakers of Lon-
" don and the neighbourhood, have petitioned for the Abolition of

"Sunday Baking; some hundreds of the Newsmen and News-
"vendors that Sunday Newspapers may be prohibited, and 220
"of the Gin-Shopkeepers that Public Houses may be closed on
"the Lord's Day. The Journeymen Poulterers and the majority
"of the Journeymen Fishmongers have sought protection in the
"same way.

"'The Coach Proprietors state that if the Smithfield Market,
"and the London Corn, Lace, Silk, and other Markets were trans-
"ferred from the Monday to some other day, there would be
"scarcely any *occasion* for the running of Sunday Coaches.
"Great numbers of the Proprietors are anxious that *all* Sunday
"Travelling and Traffic should be prohibited, as it would not
"only set multitudes of Coachmen, Guards, and Horsekeepers at
"liberty to attend some place of worship; but would also be a
"positive saving to themselves of one-seventh part of the expense
"of Horses, Tolls, &c., &c. One extensive Proprietor on the
"Great North Road, who has stopped almost all his Coaches on the
"Lord's Day, mentions the unnecessary starting of the London
"and Edinburgh Steam-Packets from both ends *on the Saturday*,
"as one reason why the Proprietors are unwilling to stop their
"Sunday Coaches in those places. The fear of competition is the
"only thing which prevents vast numbers of Coach Proprietors,
"Boat Owners, Carriers, Public House-Keepers, and Tradesmen,
"from giving up, at once, the following of their several callings
"on the Lord's Day. Their almost universal language is, as
"stated also in the Report of the Select Committee of the House
"of Commons, 'Give us a law which shall restrain *all*, and we
"'shall be very much obliged to you; but you must not expect
"'even a large majority of us to give up our Sunday Traffic if
"'you permit others to carry it on, as they would thereby gain an
"'unfair advantage over us.' Somewhat of this feeling is stated in
"the following extract from a letter lately addressed to the
"Chairman of the Derbyshire Sabbath Committee:—'Your letter
"'of the 25th of March, together with the resolution of the
"'Sabbath Committee, at Derby, was laid before the General
"'Assembly of the Trent and Mersey Canal Company on the
"'29th, and I am directed respectfully to inform you, that they
"'were well disposed towards the object you have in view, viz.,

"'the putting a stop to the desecration of the Lord's Day; but
"'they are apprehensive that unless it be made a general practice
"'throughout the kingdom, not only as regards Canals, but like-
"'wise as affecting Roads, Public Works, &c., no good would
"'result.'

"Since the above document was forwarded to each Member
"of Parliament, no less than *two hundred and thirty-five* Coach
"Proprietors of England and Wales, and *all* the Proprietors of
"the Coaches and Omnibuses belonging to Richmond, Kew,
"Sheen, Mortlake, and Barnes, have petitioned that *all kinds* of
"travelling and traffic may be prohibited on the Lord's Day."

The following account of the proceedings relating to the Sunday trains, which took place at the half-yearly meeting of the
Midland Railway Company, at Derby, on the 25th day of July,
1845, is taken from " the Derby Mercury :"—

"SUNDAY TRAVELLING.

" Mr. Hudson, the chairman, said that notice had been given
" by the Rev. Mr. Leeke, to move a resolution relative to Sunday
" travelling. He thought it might be as well to mention, to avoid
" if possible a discussion on the subject, that the Directors of that
" Company were not desirous of promoting Sunday travelling,
" and that they only ran two trains beyond the Mails, which they
" were obliged to run by Act of Parliament. He therefore sug-
" gested to Mr. Leeke the propriety of not persisting in propos-
" ing his resolution. He would repeat, that they were anxious
" to do all they reasonably could not to induce travelling on the
" Sabbath Day. And he could assure the rev. gentleman that the
" Directors would again consider the subject. It should be re-
" membered that theirs was a long line, and on that account the
" difficulty was greater, and he did think it was fairly a question
" whether, in a country like this, all railways could be shut up
" on a Sunday. But it had better be left in the hands of the di-
" rectors.

" In answer to this appeal, Mr. Leeke said that if the directors
" were prepared to put a stop to the running of the two trains,
" which were not Mail trains, and which ran each way from
" Derby on the Sunday on each of the three lines (thus causing

" six trains to arrive at, and the same number to depart from the
" Derby Station, besides the Mail trains) the motion should not
" be persisted in.   He also spoke of the trains for the conveyance
" of goods and cattle on the lines on the Lord's Day.

    " The Chairman stated that this practice had been discon-
" tinued, and intimated that the directors could not accede to the
" proposal to stop all except the Mail trains.

    " Mr. Leeke then said, he felt bound to give the shareholders
" an opportunity of expressing their opinion on this important
" subject.   He would not, however, enter at any length upon a
" discussion of it, the more especially as every Midland proprie-
" tor had had forwarded to him papers which would put him in
" possession of the details connected with it, as applicable to
" Sunday railway travelling.   He presumed that all would admit
" that the Sabbath was of Divine authority, and that the rule of
" conduct in this matter should be the command of God rather
" than the convenience of the public.   Cases of necessity, in
" which persons were perfectly justified in travelling on the
" Sunday, not unfrequently occurred, but was it right that, to
" meet the wants of these few persons, hundreds of railway servants
" should be employed day after day all the year round, and be
" deprived of the privileges of the Sabbath Day ?   With regard to
" the Midland Railway, there were 439 proprietors who had signed
" a petition to do away with all Sunday travelling, and these
" gentlemen had expressed their willingness to send their proxies,
" in case a vote was taken on the subject.   They held £700,000
" of the Midland stock.   The rev. gentleman then mentioned, that
" the general principle of abstaining from desecrating the Lord's
" Day was becoming daily more acknowledged by the public at
" large, and he mentioned as regarded the supposed necessity for
" the Mail trains, that 600 merchants of Liverpool, and 5000 of
" the inhabitants of that town, had signed a memorial to the
" government praying that all post-office business might be dis-
" continued in that town on the Lord's Day, and that their post-
" office might be put on the same footing in that respect as the
" London Post-office.   He also stated that the Lord Mayor of
" York, and all the principal inhabitants, with scarcely any ex-
" ception, had memorialized that there might be no Sunday

" delivery of letters in that city ; and that most of the principal
" inhabitants of Derby, Bath, Edinburgh, and other places, did
" not receive their letters on the Lord's Day.   After several other
" remarks, Mr. Leeke moved :—

" 'That, after Sunday, the 3rd of August next, no Trains be-
" longing to this Company be permitted to run on the Lord's
" Day, excepting so far as may be compulsory on the Company
" by Act of Parliament, and excepting also in special cases of
" necessity.'

" Mr. Wright, of Lenton, seconded the motion.

" A short debate took place, in the course of which a Share-
" holder suggested that separate accounts should be kept of the
" Sundays' traffic, and the portion derived therefrom be deducted
" from the dividends of those who objected to it.

" A proprietor strongly censured the introduction of the
" subject, terming it an insult to the meeting.   They could not
" stop the great arteries of traffic in a country like ours.

" Mr. Leeke defended the motion, and said it surely could not
" be considered an insult to such a meeting to draw its attention
" to a subject which involved the observance of the Sabbath Day.
" (Cries of ' No, no.')   With regard to stopping the traffic he
" would contend that, if we did wrong and went in direct con-
" tradiction to the command of God, the country could not hope
" for permanent prosperity.

" On a show of hands the motion was negatived by about
" three to one, but many proprietors did not vote.

" Mr. Leeke then proposed the following resolution :—

" 'That copies of the following petition for the prohibition of
" all Sunday travelling and traffic on Railways be signed by the
" Chairman on behalf of the Company, that the Company's seal
" be affixed to them, and that they be forwarded for presentation
" to both Houses of Parliament.'

[The petition was not read, as every proprietor had received
" a copy of it.   It is the same as that already signed by so many
" of the proprietors.   As it is an important document we give it
" in the 3rd page of our paper.]

" After a short discussion the motion was refused by about
" the same majority as on the previous occasion.

"The following is the Petition against all Sunday travelling,
"referred to in our account of the Midland Railway Meeting:—

"'The humble petition of the Midland Railway Company,

"'Showeth—That your petitioners are of opinion that the
"running of Railway Trains on the Lord's Day, except in cases
"of urgent necessity, is a violation of the commands of God;
"that whilst it provides the means of travelling to a very few
"persons in allowed cases of necessity, it at the same time holds
"out a strong temptation to others to profane the Sabbath by
"travelling for mere pleasure or worldly business, and deprives
"several thousands of railway servants of a considerable portion
"of that day, which was set apart by Almighty God not only as
"a day of rest from bodily labour, but also for the more important
"purposes of religion.

"'Your petitioners are of opinion, particularly now that such
"increased rapidity of communication has been obtained by
"means of railways, that the prohibiting of all Sunday traffic on
"the several lines, will not be attended with any great difficulty
"or hardship either as regards the conveyance of the Mails or
"Passengers, whilst such prohibition (which they think should
"also be extended to canals and other modes of public conveyance)
"will give the Lord's Day as a day of rest to multitudes, who are
"now deprived of it, and will afford an example of obedience to
"the Divine Command on the part of the Nation, which may be
"of the most beneficial tendency, in a moral and religious point
"of view, not only to the present, but also to future generations.'

"'Your petitioners, therefore, humbly request your honourable
"house to use its efforts to put a stop to all Sunday traffic, ex-
"cept in cases of urgent necessity. And your petitioners will
"ever pray, &c.'"

CHAPTER XXXIX.

1845, 1846.

JOURNEY TO VEVAY AND BACK. HOLBROOKE.

Summons to Vevay—Sudden death—Incidents on journey—Return—Illness at
Dijon—French physician—French posting—Paris—French postilion—Return to Holbrooke—Severe fever at Holbrooke—One hundred and thirty
cases—Serious impressions in almost all the cases—Few seemed to be lasting—Wood smoke useful—Case of late repentance at Cambridge—Kindness
of the people of Holbrooke—Testimonial and touching address.

At the beginning of December, 1845, my poor brother-in-law,
who was with me at the time of the attempted Chartist meeting at Holbrooke Moor, died very suddenly in Switzerland,
and I had to go out to meet and bring home my sister. I went
through Flanders and up the Rhine, and through Basle and
Neufchâtel to the Lake of Geneva.

Somewhere between Basle and Neufchâtel, as I was posting
along on a beautiful moonlight evening, all at once there came
several stones through the front windows of the carriage. I was
out in a moment, and the postilion, who had pulled up on the
spot, was equally quick. We found three young men standing
upon a heap of stones, who made no attempt to run off, and had
evidently been drinking to some extent. They were sufficiently
sober, however, to understand that we did not intend to part
with them until they had satisfied the postilion's charge for the
damage done to the windows. When this was paid we left them
and drove on.

I recollect it was at the next posting-house that I consented
to take with me a traveller, who was anxious to get forward,

and was waiting for some later conveyance. He was an intelligent man, and we fell into a long conversation on religion, in which, of course, it was very difficult for us to understand each other, as he did not know two words of English, and as I had only once spoken on religious subjects in French, and never before in German. He professed to hold Socinian views, at least so far as to deny the atonement and divinity of the Lord Jesus Christ. On my inquiring how he was to obtain the pardon of his sins, if he disbelieved these two great doctrines, and compared his state with my own, he having nothing to rest upon, and I, having learnt from the Word of God to trust for pardon in the full and sufficient satisfaction made by Him who was both God and man, by His death upon the cross, he appeared to feel deeply what I said, and acknowledged that I, according to my views of salvation, had sure grounds to rest my expectation of pardon and acceptance on, which he, according to his system, had not.

I was scarcely fit to undertake so rapid a journey, and was very much disappointed, when I arrived at my destination, to find that my sister had been persuaded to start two days before, for fear the Jura should become impassable for a carriage. The following night I left Lausanne, which I had reached in the afternoon, with the mail courier for Besançon, hoping to overtake my sister's carriage if she should have been detained by the snow. I felt wretchedly ill the next afternoon towards the latter part of my journey to Besançon; but I got on as well as I could with post-horses and wretched vehicles to Dijon, and then I was so ill that I could not sleep at night, and began to think I should probably end my days there. This feeling was not at all lessened when the waiter told me that a young English gentleman, not long before, had been laid up there for several weeks with typhus fever. I was not alarmed at the idea of death, but I was for a time very melancholy and sorrowful at the thought of the sorrow which my death, under the circumstances, would occasion to so many dear relatives at home. It was necessary that I should send for a physician, and here I had an instance of the good that, I believe, is often done by medical men, when they speak cheerfully and encouragingly to their patients about their state. I

could speak French very tolerably at one time, but had got out
of the way of doing so; and I had never spoken in French on
the subject of my health or sickness, so that I was afraid I
should have much difficulty in making the physician understand
anything about my general state of health, or about my illness
at that time arising from over-fatigue in travelling. We, however, managed to understand each other pretty well, although he
did not know a word of English. After I had described, as well
as I could, what I had been doing and how I felt, he made
rather light of it, and said, " Ah ! you have a little feverish feel
" about you from over-fatiguing yourself, and must be quiet here
" for two or three days, till it has passed off." I took courage
from this, and told him I was most anxious to get on, as soon as
possible, to Paris. " Well, then," he said, in an off-hand way,
" You must rest a few days when you reach Paris." But this
did not satisfy the idea which, under his slighting treatment of
my illness was increasing every moment, that there was not very
much the matter with me, so I told him there were some very
urgent reasons why I should get to my home as quickly as possible : " Well, then," he rejoined, " You must keep quiet for a
" little when you reach home." He then wrote out a prescription for me, for a cordial which would, he said, do me good, and
told me to live well on the journey. He spent about half an
hour with me, and left me feeling almost well, at least, so much
better that I went out at once to hire a carriage to take on with
me to Paris. Had the physician been anything but the straight-
forward, honourable fellow he was, he might have kept me there
as a patient for weeks, for I really thought I was very seriously
ill. I am so sorry that I did not recollect his name, and I have
always felt very sorry that I lost his prescription, for the cordial
was the very nicest stuff, in the shape of medicine, I ever tasted ;
and the knowing I had something to fall back upon, if I felt ill,
helped me to keep up during the remainder of my journey to
Paris. Of course I slept well that night ; and I started the next
morning with a roast fowl and some bread, as eatables, and
with my large bottle of cordial in a pocket to the right of my
head, and a bottle of Burgundy in the opposite pocket of the
carriage.

As it was desirable that I should get along the road as fast as possible, and I had forgotten all about the proper rate of payment to the postilion, I consulted the *maitre de poste*, at Dijon, on the subject, and ascertained from him what was considered by the postilions themselves the best pay. On my mentioning a trifling addition to this sum for each post, he said that, if I gave that, I should be paying them "like a prince." It was necessary that I should have a courier. Before I started I told the postilion and courier that I wished to be driven as fast as they could go without doing injury to their horses, and that, if they drove me to my satisfaction, I would pay them at such a rate, mentioning the "princely" rate before referred to. We certainly did get over the ground in fine style, and I had no occasion to find fault with the driving between Dijon and Paris. The courier had much difficulty in keeping so far ahead of the carriage as to have the fresh horses ready to be put to at the end of each stage.

They have a curious custom with regard to their post-horses in France, which is, that before they are put to, they are brought out to drink as much water as they will, at the trough or tank in the yard. This appears strange to Englishmen, but it is the regular custom; and one of the postilions told me that he should have driven faster had it not been that the carriage had arrived so close upon the heels of the courier that he had not had time to let his horses drink before we started. I think I slept at Joigny the first night, and reached Paris before it was dark the next day. I found my sister, who had been anxiously expecting me for two days, at a hotel opposite to the Tuileries' gardens. She had one adventure, before I joined her, which was very disappointing. The people of the hotel knew that she was expecting her brother, and I think it was the day after her arrival, that the door of her room was thrown open by the waiter, who, as he ushered in a gentleman, exclaimed, " Voila monsieur votre frère, " Madame!" Both, of course, were disappointed, and the stranger, who was a foreigner, and had been enquiring for some lady at the hotel, beat a hasty retreat.

Nothing very particular happened on our way from Paris to Boulogne. According to the postal tariff we were required to take four horses to my sister's carriage, as in addition to ourselves there were her maid and man, who, by the way, had been an officer in the Swiss troops, when they had been called out some time before on the occasion of some troubles which had broken out in some of the cantons. I gave the same notice and the same payments to the postilions as I had done to those between Dijon and Paris, and they drove us, with the exception of one man, as well as the others had driven me. To this postilion I paid a less sum than I had paid to the others; it was a handsome sum, but not the payment "en prince," as the Dijon postmaster designated the sum per post which I gave to the others. This man was greatly affronted, and said, in an uncivil tone, that had he known he would have been so treated, he would not have driven so fast. The French regulations in France, with regard to the behaviour of the postilions and others connected with the service are very strict, and a book is kept at every post-house, in which travellers are requested to enter any complaints which they may wish to make. This book I demanded, and for some minutes there was a very evident disinclination on the part of the people to produce it. I was, however, quite determined that it should be brought to me, and at length they brought it out, and I was about to enter my complaint, when a very venerable and most neatly-dressed old lady, who appeared to be between eighty and ninety years of age, came into the room and very earnestly begged of me to forgive the man. She hoped I would take into consideration that it was a *jour de fête*, (it was the 1st of January, 1846,) and that probably he had taken rather more to drink than he was accustomed to take. It appeared that the whole establishment was in a state of great anxiety that the man's incivility should not be recorded. I felt it quite impossible to resist this kind old lady's appeal, and said I would excuse the man if he would express his sorrow for what had occurred, and promise to be of better behaviour for the future. The poor fellow came in, cap in hand, looking very much ashamed of himself, and made the required apology and promise.

On driving off from the post-house, I observed that our new postilion took the thing very quietly, and drove at a very slow trot for about two or three hundred yards, probably in order to manifest his *esprit de corps* to the postilions and others whom we had left behind us, but directly we had passed over a little rise in the road, he put his four horses into a good fair gallop, and continued it until he brought us up, all standing, at the door of the next post-house. The stage, I think, was a very short one; not more than six or seven miles.

We arrived safely in England, and I was very thankful to find myself, after all my illness at Dijon, not much the worse for my hurried journey to Switzerland and back.

In the autumn of 1846 it pleased God to visit Holbrooke with a severe affliction. Typhus fever was introduced into the parish from two different directions, and spread into nearly one third of the houses; 52 families and 132 persons were attacked by it in the course of four or five months, out of a population of about 800; only eleven of them died. My own family were spared the infliction. It was a time of great trouble and trial in the parish; but my own health had very much improved, and I was enabled to visit the sick very regularly. I did not make these typhus fever visits, which I think amounted to more than five hundred, every day, for I thought it would be less trying to one's health and spirits, and equally beneficial to the sick, to make a greater number of visits every other day than to make a less number every day, though that often happened. All the sick people who were of an understanding age, upwards a hundred of whom recovered, appeared to be deeply humbled and penitent for sin, and to be relying on the death of Christ as a satisfaction for their sins, and to be most anxious, if they should be restored to health, to lead a new and holy life; and had they died, I should not have been without considerable hope, that they had died in the faith of Christ and were gone to everlasting happiness. But I had to experience that which I believe has been experienced by every minister of the gospel almost without exception, that the most pleasing appearances, in what persons expect may prove fatal illnesses, constantly turn out to have been mere delusions. We have a right to insist upon it, that if these appearances of humility, faith, and newness of heart, had been the real work of the Holy Spirit of God, that work would have remained, and the persons manifesting these deep and serious impressions, though still poor helpless, sinful creatures, would not, immediately on their recovery, have cast off these feelings, and have returned again to their old, worldly, and sinful ways, and have been as careless about the salvation of their souls and the public and private means of grace, as they ever had been before. Of the hundred responsible persons who recovered from the fever at Holbrooke, and of whom I should have had considerable hope, had they died, that they were gone to heaven, only three, as far as I could judge, showed by their after lives that their hearts had been turned from careless and sinful ways to love, and fear, and serve God. This is a most melancholy state of things, and helps to cast some considerable doubt on the reality of a late repentance, however pleasing the attendant circumstances may appear to be. Oh that every one of my readers may lay such passages as the following to heart:—"Seek ye the "Lord while he may be found, &c.:" Isaiah lv, 6, 7; "Behold "now is the accepted time; behold now is the day of salvation."

In Trinity Church, Cambridge, (I believe I may have mentioned it before,) there used to be a monument on one of the pillars which, after recounting the name, &c., of some person, has a sentence to the following effect at the close of the inscription : "It is hoped that he found mercy at the last : he sought it dili- "gently, with many tears."

Why is it, it may be inquired, that an almighty and most merciful God permits such delusions ? Why is it that God appears to permit Satan thus frequently to put off persons, in a dangerous state of illness, with the mere appearance of true faith, and of a real change of heart, when there is no real work of God on their souls ? This is a question more easily asked than answered. I do not think I shall be able to answer it in a manner which will satisfy many of the readers of this book. The following ideas, however, occur to my mind. I assume it to be a fact that God does, in numberless instances, permit this delusion to exist on what appear to be dying beds, and therefore also, it is to be inferred, on what prove really to be dying beds ; and that the mere appearance of true faith and true repentance are often so exactly like the real things themselves, that not only the sick and apparently dying persons, but their friends and ministers, are unable to distinguish the difference, and therefore are not without considerable hope with regard to the salvation of persons dying under these appearances of a real though late repentance. I may add the following idea, which I have met with years ago, but I forget where :—That just as a forged five-pound note, or a bad sovereign, would not take people in unless they were made very much like sterling money, so the mere appearance of religion would be easily detected, if not by the persons themselves, yet by the ministers of religion, unless it also very closely resembled the true work of the Spirit of God on their souls. " Satan," in such cases, seems to be "transformed into an angel of light." These may be cases of persons who have withstood God, and whom He may have given over to hardness of heart, and final impenitence.

We read in Proverbs i, 23—26 :—" Turn you at my reproof : " behold I will pour out my Spirit unto you, I will make known " my words unto you. Because I have called and ye refused ; I " have stretched out my hand, and no man regarded ; but ye have " set at nought all my counsel, and would none of my reproof : I " also will laugh at your calamity, I will mock when your fear " cometh." The verses also which follow to the end of the chapter may throw some light on the subject.

May not Luke xiii, 24—27 have reference to such cases as those we have been considering ? " Strive to enter in at the " strait gate : for many, I say unto you, will seek to enter in, and " shall not be able," &c., &c.

In the case of such persons as those who recovered from the Holbrooke fever and who afterwards led careless, irreligious lives, their sad delusion and inconsistency may have been permitted as a merciful warning to others not to put off the turning to God to a future time, and to trust to a death-bed repentance. " God's " ways are not as our ways, &c." " Shall not the Judge of all the " earth do right ?"

There is one case in connexion with the Holbrooke fever which it may be of service to others that I should mention. A young married man had the fever severely, and appeared to be very anxious about his soul. Whilst he was confined to his bed, and in danger, his wife locked him into the house, and went away to the dance at the village wakes; probably she did not think him in danger, but everybody was astonished at her conduct. She shortly afterwards took the fever herself, and was very humble and penitent for sin, and appeared to look and pray for mercy through the atonement of Christ; she died—he recovered, and, after the lapse of twenty years, although he is a moral man, neglects the means of grace, and appears to be regardless of the safety of his soul.

There were still several cases of fever, particularly in two different places in the parish, when it had been amongst us between four and five months, and it occurred to me that it might be of service to endeavour to cause an alteration in the air by means of wood smoke: I therefore chose out two spots on which to have fires lighted, so that the smoke from each would be carried by the wind amongst, and into, the houses in which fever still existed. These fires were kept up for many hours, and the plan completely succeeded, for we scarcely had a case of fever afterwards.

The people of Holbrooke were very kind in expressing their gratitude to me for my kindness to them during the fever. I was not at all aware that they were intending to present to me an address and testimonial, when, the very day before I was leaving Holbrooke for some weeks, I was invited to meet the male portion of the parishioners at the school-room. It was most interesting to see the room filled with the stocking and glove makers, and others of the working men of the parish. I understood that none but the working classes were invited to subscribe towards the purchase of the testimonial. When we were all assembled, three of the party stepped forward, and one of them read to me the address, and presented the testimonial, as is described in the following paragraph, which they themselves sent for insertion to the Derby papers :—

" *Testimonial to the Rev. W. Leeke.*

"On the 1st instant the inhabitants of Holbrooke presented "their worthy minister, the Rev. Wm. Leeke, with a handsome "portable Communion Service, bearing a suitable inscription, "accompanied by an address expressive of the sentiments they

" entertain towards him for the truly Christian solicitude he has
" always evinced to promote their spiritual and temporal interests ;
" and particularly during the prevalence of a contagious fever,
" when his attentions were unremitting, visiting the sick at the
" hazard of his life to administer the consolations of religion to
" the afflicted, and at the same time contributing liberally to their
" physical necessities.

" The rev. gentleman accepted this testimony of their grati-
" tude with much feeling, and delivered an appropriate address.

" The cup, which was furnished by Messrs. Moseley and Co.,
" jewellers, Derby, bore the following inscription :—' Presented
" ' to the Rev. Wm. Leeke, by the inhabitants of Holbrooke, as a
" ' testimony of their gratitude for his pastoral kindness during
" ' the late fever.   June 1st, 1847.' "

The following is a copy of the address, which, I need hardly
say, was very gratifying to me, although I, at the same time, felt
how little my poor services deserved to be so acknowledged and
rewarded :—

" HONOURED SIR,

" We, your parishioners, are assembled for the purpose
" of presenting you with a small testimonial of our gratitude for
" the many instances of kindness you have manifested towards
" us since your appointment as our minister, and particularly
" during the late fever. The manner in which you performed
" your arduous duties throughout that terrible visitation has left
" an impression upon our hearts which will never be obliterated ;
" and, Sir, we hope you will accept this small present at our
" hands, and we think that you will esteem it no less because a
" portion of the subscribers, owing to misapprehension and pre-
" judice, have not justly appreciated your actions and motives ;
" but your persevering kindness, under many discouragements,
" has dissipated the mist which warped our judgment, and we
" take this opportunity to express our regret that we remained
" so long in ignorance of your true character, and humbly apolo-
" gize for all the undutiful and obstinate behaviour which you
" have experienced from us, and hope that you will accept this
" our apology."

In 1847 the following resolution was passed by the committee of the Derbyshire Society for Promoting the Due Observance of the Lord's Day:—

"Mr. Leeke having expressed his wish to retire from the "office of honorary secretary, it was resolved, on a motion of the "Rev. J. Dean, seconded by Wm. Newton, Esq.:—'That his "'resignation be accepted with a painful reluctance, and the "'deepest gratitude, on account of his long and effective services, "'(for a period of fourteen years,) and the committee beg him "'hereby to feel assured that he carries with him their best "'thanks for the benefits which have resulted to the community "'at large in an improved observance of the Sabbath, and also "'their best wishes for his welfare, and they hope for his valuable "'counsel in the future business of the committee.'

"Secondly. Moved by Mr. Newton, seconded by the Rev. T. W. "Whitaker:—'That Mr. Macklin be requested to act as secretary "'*pro tem.* Mr. Macklin accepts the office on the understanding "'that it is only a temporary appointment.'"

Mr. Macklin was the honorary secretary of the Lord's Day Society till January, 1857, when he wished to resign it, and I once more undertook the office.

CHAPTER XL.

1845. 1851.

WILLIAM SHAW AND JOSEPH STEVENS, OF HOLBROOKE.

God's loving-kindness and great comfort given to them in answer to prayer for
the Holy Spirit—No wish to live—J. S. taking leave of family—Message
to his father—Happy death—Contrast in the death of another person.

I THINK I may have observed before that if an angel were sent
round to see the happiest people in the world he would not go to
the rich, and powerful, and prosperous; not probably to persons
of this description, even should they be also the children of God,
and heirs of everlasting life, but He would, I believe, find the
greatest happiness to be possessed by those who were in poverty,
and sickness, and pain, and who were destitute of earthly comforts. Such persons look immediately to God for their happiness
in the assurance of His forgiveness, and loving-kindness, and
tender mercies; whereas those who fear, and love, and serve God,
and are surrounded by various earthly comforts, seek much of
their happiness in such comforts, and do not seek it altogether
and immediately in God's favour and love, so that any failure of
these earthly sources of happiness, (and failures are frequently
occurring,) will occasion them anxiety and sorrow to which those
who have not these earthly sources of comfort, are not so liable.
Certainly the happiest persons whom I have met with in the
world have been those who have been most afflicted.

I should mention also that I consider it to be a peculiar mercy
when God is pleased to manifest His grace and goodness, in any
remarkable manner, to the young. That He should wonderfully

fulfil His promises to them in giving them abundance of faith, and holiness, and peace, appears to arrest the attention of those who see it or hear of it more frequently than when the same blessings are granted to older persons, such as the poor woman at Osmaston, of whom I have before spoken.

Since 1 have been at Holbrooke I have had two instances of great faith, and peace, and joy, having been vouchsafed to young lads. The first, by the name of William Shaw, died in January, 1845, at the age of fourteen : I do not recollect so many particulars about him as I do of the other, who died some years afterwards. But I recollect he was of feeble health for a year or two before his death, and that he once told me, at the Sunday school, that when he was ill at one time he had taken *nothing but water* for nine days. In his last illness, which lasted for some months, he was enabled to give me a very clear account of his feeling himself to be a poor sinner, and of the necessity of trusting in the Lord Jesus Christ, who, being God and man, had suffered death upon the cross to make satisfaction for the sins of the whole world, and of the change of heart, and desire to walk in the ways of God, which he had experienced ; but he did not feel sure that his sins were forgiven, and that he was a child of God. I remember pointing out to him that the Holy Spirit of God was not only promised to us, in answer to prayer, to shew us our lost condition through sin, and our need of a Saviour, and to lead us to holiness, but that he was also promised to us as a Comforter. He then promised me that he would pray frequently to God each day to give him His Holy Spirit, not only to work every other needful work in him, but also to comfort him. It was not very long when, in answer to this prayer which he offered up many times a day, his gracious heavenly Father was pleased to give him sweet peace and joy in believing. May this account, by God's grace, lead all who may read it to attend to the directions of God's Word day by day, and to seek repentance, saving faith in Christ, holiness and comfort, in the way that this poor lad did ; and, 1 am sure, if they will do so, God will grant them all those blessings which he so abundantly received. One afternoon, when I was sitting by his bed-side, some boys were playing very merrily in the street close to the house, and I said to him,

"William, do you not sometimes wish that you were quite well
"again, and could play about with the boys, as you used to do?"
He at once replied, "Oh no, Sir, I have no wish to get well, I
"would rather die, and go to be with Jesus."

    Joseph Stevens, who died in May, 1851, at the age of sixteen,
had more intelligence than William Shaw, and that might be
partly accounted for from his being two years older than Shaw
was at the time of his death. When first I knew him, on his
coming to reside in Holbrooke, about two years before he died,
he was in a very deplorable state of health. He went on crutches,
and had extensive sores on various parts of his body. He was
enabled to get about, and at times to attend the Sunday school,
but he was a great sufferer all along to the time of his death, and
suffered particularly from the sores on his body after he became
confined to his bed. He was very attentive to the instruction he
received on religious subjects, and it was greatly blessed to him;
by degrees his knowledge of the way of salvation, holiness, and
eternal life became more and more clear; he felt his sins, and
had learnt to trust in the Lord Jesus Christ as his Saviour, who
had died to make satisfaction for his sins, and by the Spirit and
Word of God had been led to strive after holiness. He was certainly taught by the Holy Spirit to understand clearly the main
truths of our religion, and to rest upon them; he also, like poor
William Shaw six years before, prayed many times a day, as he
told me, that the Holy Spirit might be sent, not only to teach
him his sinfulness and helplessness, and to lead him to Christ for
righteousness and for strength, but also as a Comforter. I was
one day, about six weeks before his death, going to see him, when
I met his sister coming in great haste to request that I would
come to see him as soon as I could: she told me he was in great
alarm, and said "he could not face death." On my reaching his
bed-side I inquired what it was that alarmed him, and said, "Are
"you afraid that when you die you will be cast into hell on
"account of your sins?" He replied, "Oh nothing of that sort,
"Sir!" and then I gathered from him that it was a fear of some
great pain and agony which he would have to encounter at the
time of death. As I spoke to him of the 4th verse of the
twenty-third Psalm, and explained to him that God, who had

already done such great things for him, and had invited his children to cast all their care on Him, would, in answer to his prayer, be with him, and take care of him, and comfort him in the hour of death, and from that passed on to other points connected with his salvation; through God's mercy, he entirely lost sight of his fears, and he told me afterwards that he had never been troubled with them again. I think it was two or three weeks before his death that I put the same sort of question to him which I had before put to William Shaw : I inquired if he did not sometimes feel a desire to live, and to be restored to complete health, and I well remember the solemn and intelligent manner in which he replied to me, I believe exactly in the following words:—"I do assure you, Sir, that if I could get "entirely well, and have everything I can think of in the world, "I would rather die, and go to be with my Saviour."

And now the time of his death was drawing very near. I think it was on the day before he died that he told me he had a favour which he wished me to grant him, and it was that, when he was gone, I would speak to his father on one point, and tell him that I did so at his request. He said he thought his mother had more to do, with her large family and her work in the stocking-frame, than she could possibly manage, and he feared his father did not see it, and would often urge her to perform more work in the frame than her strength would permit. He shewed the greatest delicacy of feeling towards his father in making this request. I promised to attend to it, and his father received his child's dying message in a very nice spirit.

As I took leave of him, for what proved to be the last time, after I had shaken hands with him, and was passing his bed again when I had taken up my hat, he gave me his little parting salutation by taking hold of the front lock of his hair, and bowed his head forward. It was all very right that the poor dear lad should do this as a token of respect to his minister, but I felt most deeply humbled in reflecting that he, who was an heir of glory, and who would so soon be in the presence of the God of glory, should be shewing marks of respect to me, a poor sinful man, who, whilst he was a glorified spirit in heaven, would, very possibly for several years to come, have to make my daily confession, that I had "followed too much the devices and desires of my own heart, and had offended against God's holy laws; that I had left undone those things which I ought to have done, and had done those things which I ought not to have done." The next morning, although I thought it very probable that he would not live through the day, I did not go to see him, for I had what appeared to be a more important duty to perform in another part of the parish. As I returned, the passing bell announced to me that the happy soul of Joseph Stevens had "departed to be with "Christ." I find I have written against his name in the margin of the parish burial register, "A truly happy child of God. W. L."

The next day I called at the house, and his mother asked me if I would go up to his room and see him. I sat with her there for some considerable time, whilst she related to me several particulars connected with his death. He appeared to understand very clearly that he was about to die, and said to her, "What a mercy "it is that I am free from pain this morning!" "Yes," she replied, "we prayed, you know, that you might be free from "pain when you were about to die." He said, "Yes, we did." Just before his death he took leave, one by one, of the whole family; and, when he had done this with regard to all but the youngest, a little sister about six or seven months old, he said, "and now bring me my little baby." After he had taken leave of her, a kind neighbour and relative came in; but his sight had, in some degree, failed, and he did not recognize her till they told him who she was. After speaking to her he stretched forward his hands, and on their asking him what he wanted, he said, "I "want heaven, and I think I see heaven!" and then he instantly died.

His mother told me how he had, a day or two before, talked over with her all the arrangements about his funeral, and in what shirt, &c., his body should be dressed before it was put into his coffin; and who should carry him to the grave, and what others should be invited to attend. I recollect one thing she said with regard to their family affairs was, "He was always so "thoughtful; he was more like a father to us than a child."

Not very long after the death of Joseph Stevens, I went over to my old parish, to visit, in his last illness, Mr. Oastler, the surgeon, a good man who had succeeded to the practice there some years before we left Brailsford. On my giving him the above account of Joseph Stephens, he burst into tears, and said what a mercy it was that God had permitted him to hear it; that, in His Word he had promised to give His believing people such wonderful blessings; but to hear that he had really fulfilled these promises in giving perfect peace to such a youth, he considered to be a great mark of His loving-kindness to him, and one highly calculated to strengthen his faith in all the promises of God.

A very remarkable escape, as I have always considered it, from what might have been a most serious, if not fatal, injury, occurred to me two or three years after the death of Joseph Stevens, when I was just entering the room in which he died, to see a poor girl of another family who was dying of scarlet fever. There were no regular stairs to the room, but merely a step-ladder. I had reached the last step, and was just on the point of placing my foot on the floor within the room, when the stair-ladder, which it appeared was very old and decayed, broke into a thousand pieces, and precipitated me on my back and the back of my head, on to the stone floor eight feet below. I had nothing to lay hold of, and so suddenly did the stairs go to pieces just as I was stepping from the upper one in a forward direction into the room, that I thought I must receive serious injury; but, to my great surprise, when my back first struck the stone floor rather heavily, I was not in the least hurt, and then, as the back of my head came to the ground, the blow was so slight, that, as I expressed myself at the time, it would not have killed a fly. Are we not justified, under such circumstances, in applying to ourselves the passage in Psalm xci, 11, 12 ? The accident alarmed the poor dying girl very much for some minutes, until she found that I was not in the least hurt.

Twenty years ago the father of this young girl, after having led an irregular and careless life, became seriously and dangerously ill. I saw a good deal of him, and he appeared to be much impressed by the solemn truths of God's Word, and to seek mercy through the Saviour, and holiness of heart and life; but he recovered, and immediately returned to his former ways, and,

I believe, scarcely ever entered the church or any other place of worship, from the time of his recovery down to the time of his death, which has only recently occurred. I scarcely ever met him during the last twenty years of his life, without speaking to him, and warning and exhorting him. He was always very civil, and said what I said was quite right, but he went on in his old sins, till a few months ago, when I was told that he was most seriously ill. I found him very ill and very anxious about his soul. It was determined that he should go into the infirmary, but he had not been there long before, thinking he should not get better, he determined to come home. At the infirmary the physician, who attended him, spoke to him several times on religious subjects, and he seemed to be much impressed by what he said to him. He offered up often, after his return home, two lines of a hymn which he had learnt there :—

> "Make me to know my sins forgiven,
> And fit me for the joys of heaven."

During the short time he had to live, he seemed to be very much in earnest about his everlasting state. We spoke of his former illness and serious feelings, and how, afterwards, he had made God to bear with his sinful and careless life for twenty years, and he seemed to feel it all very acutely, and to seek earnestly for pardon through the atoning blood (death) of the Son of God, and to pray earnestly also for the work of the Holy Spirit upon his heart. The day before his death, I talked to him for some time, and he spoke with such strength of voice and so clearly, that I could hardly imagine that his end was very near at hand. I recollect that I was telling him that in order to his having a real and saving faith in Christ, and real repentance, it must be God's work upon his soul, and that he must ask God to work this work in him ; and I put him in mind of the way in which he had been deceived with regard to himself in his former illness. In some way he a little misunderstood something which I said, and asked me if I meant to say that, after what had happened, "it was impossible for him to be saved?" Of course I told him that I did not mean that, but that I was anxious he should feel his own weakness and the deceitfulness of our hearts, and should be led earnestly to pray that he might not deceive

himself, as he had done in his former illness, but that God Himself would give him a real and saving trust in Christ's death, as
a satisfaction for his sins, and really give him a change of heart.
Poor fellow! he passed much of that night in prayer : he made
his daughter-in-law and another woman frequently pray with
him.   He pointed out those three beautiful prayers which I had
shewn him, and used with him, at the end of the Visitation of
the Sick, and made his daughter-in-law read them to him, as
also a prayer and a tract which I had given him when he was
going to the infirmary.   Some time before his death, he called
his daughter-in-law to pray with him, saying, " I am going to
" die, and I know not whether I shall wake up in heaven or
" hell."   And later on in the morning, (it was Sunday morning,
and a quarter before eight when he died,) he said, " I am going to
" die, and I hope I shall go to heaven."   I have given this account, hoping and praying that God will bless it to the benefit
of the souls of many of my readers : Deut. xxxii, 29.

What a contrast between the death of this poor fellow and
the deaths of those youths mentioned above.   I hope he may
" have found mercy at the last."

CHAPTER XLI.

1847.

SIR HENRY LEEKE'S SERVICES.

H. M. ship Queen—Arrival at Spithead—Meeting Admiral Sir Charles Napier—
The Prince Consort and the Prince of Prussia on board the Queen— Order
and comfort in the Queen—The command handed over to Captain Bruce—
Addresses of Sir Henry Leeke and Captain Bruce on the occasion—Some
statement of Sir Henry Leeke's services, &c.

I DO not wish to intrude my family affairs on my readers, but
I may mention that in 1847 I experienced the greatest sorrow I
have ever met with, in the death of my dear mother. It was a
very deep affliction, although God, in his mercy to her family,
spared her to them till she had reached the advanced age of
eighty-five, and left with them a bright hope that she was gone
to eternal glory. All her sons served their country, the eldest
losing his life in its service.* Her three daughters also married
sailors.

In June, 1847, some weeks after the above event, I went with
my family to Ryde, in the expectation of the assembling, at
Spithead, of the channel squadron under Admiral Sir Charles
Napier, as the Queen, which was then the largest ship in the
navy, and was commanded by my brother, was to form part of
the squadron.

After we had been at Ryde about three weeks, we, one forenoon, were told that the Caledonia and Queen were rounding St.
Helen's point. I immediately went over to Portsmouth by the

* See Appendix No. 1.

packet, and on landing found the admiral's barge just starting for Spithead, and the midshipman in charge, on my telling him who I was, and that I wanted to get on board the Queen as soon as she anchored, told me he could take me on board the St. Vincent, the flag-ship, and that I could easily get from her to the Queen. We reached the St. Vincent some little time before the two ships had arrived at Spithead, and I very much enjoyed seeing those two noble ships stand into their anchorage, which they did in very fine style, and to the admiration of the officers of the St. Vincent. As they were watching the Queen through their glasses from the poop of the St. Vincent, I heard one of them say, amongst other observations, "Commander Schomberg's a *sailor*;" and another added, "Yes, and Sir Henry's a *sailor*." I believe this is about the greatest compliment that one sailor can pay to another. Captain Milne was very civil and kind to me. On getting on board the Queen, I found my brother on the point of starting in his gig to the St. Vincent to pay his respects to the admiral. And this he did, as a matter of etiquette, though the admiral was on shore. Afterwards, on our way to Portsmouth, we met Sir Charles Napier pulling out to Spithead in the same barge which had taken me out a couple of hours before. I never before witnessed the ceremony practised on the occasion of a captain of a man-of-war in his gig meeting the barge of the admiral commanding the squadron, when the captain wished to speak to the admiral. When we were within about eighty yards of the barge and nearly right ahead of her, the crew of the gig tossed up their oars by word of command, and we awaited the admiral's approach. When he had come near us, my brother took off his hat, which salutation the admiral returned, and, on finding that he wished to speak with him, invited him to come on board the barge, which he did, at the same time introducing me. The admiral asked if I would not come on board also ; but this I declined, knowing my brother would only be on board for three or four minutes, as both boats pulled out towards Spithead. My brother had learnt from Captain Milne that no person was allowed to sleep out of the squadron without the admiral's leave, and as he wished to accompany me to Ryde for the night, he intercepted him on his way to Spithead to obtain the requisite permission. When my brother was about to leave the admiral's boat, I was terribly afraid of showing off my bad seamanship as steersman when we pulled alongside to take him on board, and I certainly did give the barge a very tolerable bump on her quarter. After the usual salutations the admiral pursued his course to Spithead, and we turned back towards Portsmouth. Some of the officers of the Queen told me that she was such a superior sailer, that on coming round from Plymouth she had spared three-and-twenty sails to the Caledonia, in order to enable the latter ship to keep up.

We were forced to return home before the Queen had been long at Spithead, but we had several opportunities of seeing her. One day, when the Prince Consort came to see the squadron with the Prince of Prussia, after visiting the St. Vincent they came on board the Queen, when the Prussian standard was hoisted, and accompanied by Sir Charles Napier, the Chevalier Bunsen, and a number of Prussian officers, they spent some considerable time in going over the whole of the ship, and were highly pleased with all they saw.

The squadron sailed, shortly after the ships were all assembled, for Lisbon, and at the end of November, Sir Henry Leeke, who was to have the command of the St. Josef, Admiral Sir John West's flag-ship, at Plymouth, was superseded in the command of the Queen by Captain Bruce.

The following is from the pen of one of the newspaper correspondents, and will give some idea of the fine state of order and discipline in which the Queen was handed over to Captain Bruce :—

"November 29th, 1847.

"To-day Captain William H. Bruce, who came out in the "Comet, has superseded Sir Henry Leeke in the command of the "Queen : the latter officer has commanded this fine ship for more "than two years, and under almost every circumstance and situa-"tion in which a man-of-war can be placed—and some of these the "most trying—with great credit and zeal. His successor, Captain "Bruce, who is an excellent officer, receives from him a ship in "the most perfect order, and smart at everything; and the gal-"lant captain leaves us, taking with him the best wishes and

"kindest feeling of every captain, officer, and man in the fleet.
"It is rather an extraordinary fact, that during the two years that
"Sir Henry Leeke has commanded the Queen, although she has
"been in the heaviest gales of wind, and has with other ships of
"the trial squadron been under a heavy press of sail, and has
"been worked off a lee shore, she has never carried away a spar
"of any description, and during this cruise she has not lost one
"man from accident—this alone speaks volumes for the discipline
"and management of the ship!

"We will here quote Sir Henry Leeke's short but pithy
"speech to his ship's company, on reading Captain Bruce's com-
"mission :—

"'Captain Bruce, I congratulate you upon being appointed to
"command the Queen and the young men we have assembled
"now before us. I have had the pleasure and boast to command
"them and this noble ship for upwards of two years, in almost
"every situation, some of these the most trying, and a finer set of
"young fellows are scarcely to be met with; and when I tell you
"that punishment is scarcely known here, and that I have given a
"certificate of "very good" and "good" to every seaman, marine,
"and boy in the ship, (excepting two,) you will, I am sure, give
"them all credit for having done their duty. Three times I have
"had the satisfaction and gratification of expressing the approba-
"tion of the Lords of the Admiralty, and their Admiral, for their
"zeal, smartness, and seamanlike conduct; and yesterday I re-
"ceived a letter from Sir Charles Napier, expressing his approba-
"tion of her great improvements and efficiency in her gunnery,
"and I know this ship's company so well, that I am sure they
"will continue to be smart, active, and orderly, and keep up the
"name and the fame of the Queen, as being one of the smartest
"ships in the service; for it is confessed by all that she is in
"perfect order.

"'I now recommend them to your care, feeling that, as
"they deserve it, they will find in you a kind friend and captain.

"' I will now say a few words of the boys; I cannot speak
"more strongly in their favour, or better recommend them to you,
"than by saying that in the 200 I have had under my command
"only one has been punished, and that was for stealing a sove-
"reign from his messmate's bag.

"'My lads, I thank you, seamen, marines, and boys, for your "willingness, for your smartness, and general good and steady "conduct. You have thoroughly done your duty, and I have put "that faith and confidence in you, that if a war had broken out, "and it had been my good fortune to place you alongside of an "enemy's ship of your own size, you would have shown your pluck "and the good stuff you are made of. I now bid you each and all "good bye, and willingly would I take you all to my new ship, if "it were possible. I may yet be placed in the proud situation of "commanding such another ship as the Queen, when I shall feel "a pleasure in having such a crew with me again; and be as- "sured that the man who produces one of my certificates with "'good' upon it, will never fail to find in me a friend. Now, re- "member, that I hope to see the Queen what we have always "known her, "The Cock of the Roost."'

"Captain Bruce then said:—'My lads, I can only say that I "am proud to command such a set of young men; and when I "tell you that your ship is so well spoken of by the Lords of the "Admiralty, and by your friends at home, and that I now bear "witness, and have myself seen her beautiful order, there is not "one thing I could have altered. I intend everything to go on, "and the same arrangements to be kept up as have been hereto- "fore by your excellent captain. Wherever I have gone I have "heard of the Queen as being one of the smartest and best- "regulated ships in the service, and I am quite sure, from all I "hear of you, that you will assist me in not allowing her to fall "back. Since I have seen the crew of the Queen, and heard of "her great efficiency in gunnery, I feel satisfied that if, unhappily, "our country should again be involved war, and it should be my "good fortune to lead you to battle, we need not fear the result, "for I believe the Queen would be one of the foremost, and would "play her part well. The commander, (Little,) whose commis- "sion Sir Henry Leeke has just read, I have known for years. "He will carry on the duty as it has been done before, and in "him as well as myself you will find those who will promote "your welfare, as long as the duty of the ship is carried on with "the same spirit and good-will, and in the same marked and "smart way.'"

I think it may be interesting to some of my readers to read
the following statement of some of my brother's services, which
was sent in to the Admiralty when, on his return from the capture of Bushire, and from his command of the Indian Navy, he
applied to be placed on the active list of British admirals. One
of my daughters copied it out for him, and retained a copy for
herself, which I now venture to publish :—

Sir Henry Leeke's Statement.

"In the year 1845 Admiral Sir John West was appointed
"Commander-in-Chief at Devonport, and he offered me the posi-
"tion of flag-captain. I waited upon Sir George Cockburn, the
"First Sea-Lord, upon the subject; he said 'Yes; but what are
"'we to do with Captain Martin ?' (whose admiral had died at
"Sheerness.) I urged that all admirals were allowed to name
"their own captains, his answer was, 'Well, Sir, you will be
"'appointed to command the Queen, or whatever ship is to be
"'the flag-ship.'

"I called at the Admiralty the next day. Sir George Cock-
"burn said, 'By the bye, Sir William Symonds wishes his friend
"'Sir B. Walker to sail his ship, the Queen, for two or three
"'weeks. I suppose it will make but little difference to you.'
"I replied, 'Every day, Sir, is of the utmost consequence to me,
"'but of course I must do as I am ordered.' A month or six
"weeks passed away, and I was without my ship, and became
"very uneasy about my time. I waited again upon Sir George
"Cockburn, and urged him to give me a ship, saying that I
"never could regain the time I had lost. He replied, 'You
"'make a great fuss about a few weeks' loss of time ; if _you_ do
"'not like it, there are plenty in that Blue Book, Sir, who will
"'be glad to stand in your shoes.' I said, 'Yes, Sir George ;
"'but that is nothing to me; it is my only chance to enable me
"'to serve my time, and pray let me urge upon you to give me
"'a ship.' He said, 'Well, a small frigate is coming forward
"'for commission, and you shall have her ;' and I was appointed
"to the Calliope. She was fitted and ready for sea in a month,
"and I was superseded, and again I was without a ship: I

"urged in vain that I might have another command, but no
" vessel was ready. In October, my own ship, the Queen, arrived,
" and I took the command, having lost nearly six months of my
" time ; but having done the duty of flag-captain during the
" whole period without time or pay.

" The First Lord of the Admiralty and Sir George Cockburn
" both said mine had been a very hard, as well as a very peculiar
" case, and both promised that it should be made up to me at
" the end, and that I should lose nothing by it. I commanded
" the Queen, San Josef, and Calliope for two years and nearly
" eight months. Soon after quitting my command, I waited
" upon Lord Auckland, and mentioned what had passed to him,
" and asked for the command of the Ordinary at Devonport.
" His reply was, 'There is no officer, Sir, who stands before
" ' you upon that list. I shall be glad to meet your wishes, and
" ' I shall hope to meet you at Devonport in the autumn.'

" Lord Auckland died, and my hope vanished. I was
" anxious for a command, and really importuned the First Lord
" to such a degree that I was almost ashamed of myself for
" doing so.

" I was told by Admiral Dundas, at the end of the year
" 1849, that if I had a ship, it would be putting me to a very
" useless expense and trouble ; it had been talked over, and it
" was found to be impossible that I could serve my time, for, I
" must be an admiral in two years. (I was *not* an *admiral*
" until nearly five years afterwards.) I still urged for a com-
" mand until I was nearly heart-broken.

" When I found all my applications useless, I, at the end of
" 1851, was offered the command of the Indian navy, and an
" official request was made by the Court of Directors to the
" Board of Admiralty that I might be allowed to command their
" naval forces in India. The Burmah war commenced, and my
" Broad Pendant as Commodore and Commander-in-Chief was
" flying the whole time. I fitted out our men of war ; sent con-
" stant supplies to them, as well as officers and men, and all
" reports and despatches were sent to me.

" Again : During the Crimean war I fitted out men-of-war
" and transports, and sent two regiments of cavalry, with 14,000

"horses, to Suez and overland to Alexandria on to Lord Raglan;
"and so good were the arrangements that only eight horses were
"lost in the hot months of the Red Sea. For this I received the
"thanks of the Government at home and in India.

"Again : The war with Persia broke out. Orders arrived
"from England to fit out an expedition ; this was done in a very
"short space of time. I sailed as Commander-in-Chief with
"fourteen men of war, six hired armed steam vessels, forty-eight
"transports, and eight gun boats. I landed, under fire, 6000
"fighting men, 5000 camp followers, and 100 horses, without
"the loss of a man, ship, or spar, and with only two horses
"drowned.

"I bombarded the fort of Reshire and supported the left of
"the army at the assault and capture on the 9th of December,
"and on the 10th of December took up my position off the
"town and forts of Bushire, and bombarded it for five hours,
"until their flag was hauled down in token of submission.

"It was said by the Persian Government and pilots, that no
"ship could get within 1900 yards of the ports. I sounded and
"ran my ships in at high water over very soft mud, and formed
"the line of battle within 800 yards of their *strongest position.*

"After the action I got them off in safety, and landed the
"whole of the camp equipage, stores, and provisions, and saw the
"troops sheltered and my fleet in safety. I received the sick,
"wounded, and prisoners on board, took the island of Karrack
"and garrisoned it before the gale came on.

"My orders from the Governor-General were to return to
"Bombay as soon as the above service was completed, as I
"should be of more use there in forwarding the objects of the
"expedition than I could be by remaining any longer in the
"Persian Gulf. On my return in my flag-ship I fell in, on the
"18th December, with the Persian army, (off Larg and Linghar,)
"5000 strong, advancing to attack (with the other portion of
"the Shah's troops) our forces at Bushire. I hauled my ship to
"within 700 yards of their entrenchments, engaged them for
"one hour and thirty minutes, destroyed their guns, burned a
"great number of their tents and stores, killed and wounded a
"great many men, horses and camels, and dispersed the army.

" The result of the battles of Reshire, of Bushire, and the
"above, is known to the Government and my country. The
" Shah of Persia was brought to terms. Peace was concluded,
"and it enabled all the European troops to be recalled from
" Persia. I was then called upon to assist Government by
" sending two regiments to Calcutta; the fearful mutiny had
" broken out. The 64th and 78th arrived at Bombay at nine in
"the morning of Saturday.

" I had the vessels coaled, stored, watered and provisioned,
"and the 64th sailed at four in the afternoon of the same day ;
"and the 78th steamed out of the harbour on Monday morn-
"ing at 9 o'clock. 'The opportune arrival of these two
"'regiments in ten days, saved Calcutta from bloodshed, and
"'destruction of property, and put an end to the panic that was
"'then raging.' I have letter upon letter from the Governor-
"General of India, from the Governor and Government of
" Bombay, from the Home Government and from Her Majesty's
" Government, acknowledging and thanking me for my various
"services ; but it would be useless to take up time in their
" perusal. The public despatches likewise shew that I have
"performed my duty. I am very averse to making comparisons
"or quoting precedents, but in this instance I trust it may not
" be wrong. I do so in the hope of shewing that my case and
"that of a gallant brother officer, Sir Baldwin Walker, are nearly
"parallel, and I hope to be admitted to the same privilege with
" regard to my position on the active list of admirals, and I feel
"confident there is not an officer in the service who would not
" rejoice that such an honour had been bestowed upon me.

" The following is a copy of the order in council relating to
" Sir Baldwin Walker's time in the Turkish service, having been
"counted as sea service in H.M. navy to enable him to be
" placed on the active list of admirals :—

" ' Whereas, by a letter bearing date 1st September, 1838,
" your Majesty's Secretary of State for Foreign Affairs communi-
"cated to the Admiralty your Majesty's commands that the
" naval officers of rank and ability should be sent to serve in
" the Turkish navy for the purpose of rendering the ships of
" that nation more effective for acting in conjunction with your

"Majesty's squadron, and whereas Captain Sir Baldwin W
" Walker was the senior officer who volunteered to serve on such
" duty, and was placed by the Sultan in the high station of a
" flag-officer, and in that capacity co-operated with your
" Majesty's fleet under the command of Admiral Sir Robert
" Stopford, your Majesty's Commander-in-Chief in the Mediter-
" ranean, and bore a conspicuous and gallant part in the attack
" of St. Jean d'Acre and in other operations, and having thereby
" obtained great experience in command in war operations, and
" having made application that the time he so served should be
" reckoned as time served in your Majesty's navy, we beg with
" all humility to state that under the peculiar circumstances of
" the case as aforesaid of Sir B. Walker's appointment to the
" Turkish navy, we are of opinion no inconvenient precedent
" could be established by acceding to this request, and that the
" distinguished manner in which he performed the duties in
" question merit very favourable consideration and reward.

" ' We therefore humbly recommend that your Majesty would
" be graciously pleased to direct by your Majesty's order in
" council that the time during which Sir B. W. Walker's flag
" was flying in the Turkish service, namely, from the 26th
" March, 1839, to the 30th December, 1843, should reckon as
" sea time served by a captain in your Majesty's navy.

" ' Dated 23rd December, 1845.'

" Annexed is a statement of the time during which both Sir
" Baldwin Walker and myself actually commanded ships in
" the Royal Navy, as commander or second captain, and as
" captain.

" It is mentioned in the memorial from the Lords of the
" Admiralty to Her Majesty, in behalf of Sir Baldwin Walker,
" that he has gained great experience in command in war
" operations, and that he co-operated while in command of the
" Turkish fleet with Her Majesty's fleet under the command of
" Admiral Sir Robert Stopford; that the distinguished manner
" in which he performed the duties in question merits very
" favourable consideration and reward.

" I may be permitted here to say in my own behalf that
" I have gained much experience of the management and

" manœuvering of large fleets, having served for some years in a
" line of battle ship in the fleets under Lord Collingwood and
" Lord Exmouth, and having commanded the largest line of
" battle ship in the Royal Navy, (The Queen,) in the fleets under
" the command of Admiral Sir William Parker, and Vice-
" Admiral Sir Charles Napier, and in the squadron of evolution
" under Sir Francis Collier. That I commanded the fleet of the
" Indian navy during the Burmah war; that I was engaged in
" sending troops to the Crimea; that I commanded the fleet of
" men of war and transports, amounting to seventy-eight sail,
" during the Persian war.

" In thus advocating my own cause, and requesting to be
" placed on the active list of admirals, I beg to add that as the
" Indian service will now probably be under Her Majesty's
" Government, no inconvenient precedent can be established, for
" it is scarcely within possibility that such a case as mine can
" again occur.

" At the creation of the reserved list it was mentioned in
" Parliament and fully understood, that, if for *any reason*, Her
" Majesty's Government should wish to take any admiral from
" that list to place him on the active list, there would be no
" difficulty in doing so. I humbly submit that the prompt
" manner in which the capture of Bushire was effected may
" constitute a claim for the favourable consideration of my
" wishes, even if my service as Commander-in-Chief of the
" Indian navy for upwards of five years would not have that
" effect; especially when it is borne in mind that, had there
" been any hesitation or failure in the capture of Bushire, the
" consequences might have been most disastrous as regards the
" termination of the Persian war, the evacuation of Herat, the
" conduct of the Affghans, and the consequent state of the
" Punjab, the *quiet condition* of which has so evidently conduced
" to our success at Delhi, and to the present favourable state of
" affairs in India.

" The Services of

REAR ADMIRAL Sir Baldwin Walker, Bart, K.C.B.	Yrs.	Mo.	Dys.	REAR ADMIRAL Sir Henry Leeke, Kt., K.H.C.B.	Yrs.	Mo.	Dys.
As Second Captain or Commander of H.M.S. Vanguard (84.)	2	0	0	As Commander in Command of H. M. Sloop Alert (18.) ...	0	5	0
				As Commander in Command of H. M. Sloop Myrmidon (20)—3½ years on the Coast of Africa, during a part of which time he was Senior Officer, and fought a successful action in Command of a squadron	3	6	0
				In Command of H.M. Yacht Herald.........	2	2	0
Total as Commander . .	2	0	0	Total as Commander .	6	1	0

As Captain.

	Yrs.	Mo.	Dys.		Yrs.	Mo.	Dys.
In Command of H.M.S. Queen (112)	0	6	12	In Command of H.M.S. Queen (112)............	2	1	7
In Command of H.M.S. Constance (52).........	1	4	0	In Command of H.M.S. San Josef (112)	0	5	7
				In Command of H.M.S. Calliope (26)	0	1	0
Total service as Captain	1	10	12	Total service as Capt. in the Royal Navy...	2	7	14
In Command of Turkish Fleet, as Admiral	4	9	0	In Command of Indian Navy as Commander in Chief	5	7	25
Total service in the Royal and Turkish Navy	6	7	12	Total service in the Royal, and Indian Navy	8	3	8"

The result of the consideration of his services by the Admiralty, will be seen in the following notice, which appeared in the London Gazette :—

"Admiralty, August 14, 1858.

"Her Majesty having been pleased, by Her Order in Council "of the 31st of July, 1858, to approve of Rear-Admiral Sir Henry "John Leeke, C.B., K.H., being transferred in his proper seni- "ority from the Reserved to the Active List of Flag-Officers of "Her Majesty's Fleet, the name of Sir Henry John Leeke, C.B., "K.H., has this day been placed on the List of Rear-Admirals of "the Red Squadron of Her Majesty's Fleet, with seniority of the "15th of April, 1854, accordingly."

Sir Henry Leeke was soon afterwards made a K.C.B. for his Indian and Persian services, and became a lord of the admiralty and member of parliament for Dover.

I think that, when in command of the Queen, my brother had prayers read by the chaplain to the ship's company every morning ; and the same practice was kept up on board his flagship, on his voyage from Bombay to Bushire ; General Stalker, who commanded the troops, and his staff, always attending. I trust the same observance of reading each morning a few of the prayers of our excellent liturgy, by the chaplain or one of the officers, will soon become the rule in Her Majesty's navy. Surely God has not said in vain, "Them that honour me, I will "honour."

I subjoin some few extracts from O'Byrne's "Naval Biography" of 1849, which give an account of my brother's earlier services :—

"Sir Henry John Leeke is son of Sam. Leeke, Esq., a Magis- "trate and Deputy-Lieutenant for co. Hants, and brother-in-law "of Rear-Admiral Sir Edw. Tucker, K.C.B., and of Capt. W. B. "Bigland, R.N., K.H.

"This officer entered the Navy, 28 Sept., 1803, as Fst.-cl. Vol., "on board the Royal William, Capt. John Wainwright, bearing "the flag of Admiral Montagu at Spithead. In the course of "1806 he successively joined the Iris 32, Capt. John Tower, "Ville de Paris and Royal Sovereign, both commanded by Capt. "Henry Garrett, and Terrible 74, Capt. Lord Henry Paulet ; as "Midshipman of which latter ship, and the Volontaire 38, Capt.

" Chas. Bullen, we find him continuously employed off Cadiz and
" in the Mediterranean until January, 1810. Previously to leav-
" ing the Volontaire, he had an opportunity, besides commanding
" one of her boats at the destruction of a French vessel near
" Marseilles, of serving with those of a squadron which, on the
" night of 31 Oct., 1813, captured and destroyed, after a fearful
" struggle and a loss to the British of 15 men killed and 55
" wounded, the French store-ship *Lamproie,* of 16 guns and 116
" men, bombards *Victoire* and *Grondeur,* and armed xebec *Nor-*
" *mande,* with a convoy of seven merchant-vessels, lying under
" the protection of numerous strong batteries in the Bay of Rosas.*
" Between the period of his advancement to the rank of Lieu-
" tenant, which took place while he was serving with Capt. Sam.
" Martin Colquitt on board the Persian sloop, 24 Nov., 1810, and
" the receipt of his second promotal commission, bearing date 15
" June, 1814, he was again employed in the Mediterranean, and
" also at the Cape of Good Hope, in the Volontaire and Cambrian
" frigates, each under the orders of Capt. Chas. Bullen, Lion 64,
" flag-ship of the late Sir Chas. Tyler, Harpy Sloop, Capt. Allen,
" and Medway 74, bearing the flag of Sir C. Tyler. On one
" occasion, while the Persian, with a host of French prisoners on
" board, was off Cape Trafalgar on her passage home, the latter,
" availing themselves of the absence of the crew, (who, worn out
" by fatigue, had all, with the exception of Mr. Leeke, the Quar-
" termaster, and two men, gone below,) assembled on the deck,
" and were in the act of making a rush aft, when Mr. Leeke
" seized a cutlass, threw another to the Quartermaster, and with
" much gallantry succeeded in keeping them off until the alarm
" had brought the ship's company to his assistance. On 26
" March, 1819, after he had had the command for about six
" months of the Alert sloop, and had served as the senior officer
" of a small squadron ordered to escort the Grand Duke Michael
" to Calais, Capt. Leeke was appointed to the Myrmidon 20, on
" the Western coast of Africa, where he cruized with great ac-
" tivity against the slave-trade, and either liberated, or con-
" tributed to the release of, upwards of 3000 human beings. In
" May, 1820, having the command at the time of H.M. ships

* *Vide* Gaz. 1809, p. 1908.

" Myrmidon, Morgiana, Thistle, and Snapper, he landed at the
" Pongas, in the neighbourhood of Sierra Leone, and, at the head
" of only 170 seamen and marines, added to 180 black soldiers of
" the 2nd West India Regt., contrived to burn eight towns, to
" demolish a battery, and to effect the utter defeat of a barbarian
" force of 5000 men, commanded by King Munga-Brama, a
" ruffian who had murdered an officer and several men belonging
" to the Thistle, and had retained three others as prisoners. The
" combination, indeed, of skill, perseverance, prudence, and
" bravery, exhibited by Capt. Leeke, proved the means of not
" only recovering the captives, but of saving the colony itself
" from much anarchy and bloodshed. Correspondent, therefore,
" with the importance of the exploit, were the terms of gratitude
" on the one hand, and of admiration on the other, with which
" its achievement was hailed by Brigadier-General Sir Chas.
" M'Carthy, the Governor of Sierra Leone, and Sir Geo. Ralph
" Collier, the Commodore of the squadron employed on that sta-
" tion. In Sept., 1820, Capt. Leeke suppressed a mutiny which
" had broken out on board a Brazilian sloop-of-war, *Les Trois*
" *Royaumes Unis*, and then restored the vessel to her Commander.
" He next succeeded by his exertions in saving a Portuguese
" schooner from being wrecked in the Sierra Leone river; and on
" a subsequent occasion he carried the Myrmidon over the fear-
" ful bar of the river Bonny for the purpose of attacking two
" slave-vessels who had beaten off his boats and had wounded
" two officers and several men. After he had accomplished their
" capture, he compelled the King of that part of the country to
" enter into a treaty fixing the duty to be paid by British mer-
" chants trading to the river for palm-oil—an arrangement which
" in particular saved many thousands per annum to the importers
" of Liverpool. During the three years that he remained on the
" African station, Capt. Leeke surveyed the coast to the extent of
" 600 miles. He attained his present rank 27 May, 1826; and,
" on 18 Oct., 1845, after having held for a short period the com-
" mand of the Calliope 26, was appointed to the Queen 110, in
" which ship, now bearing the flag of Sir John West, Commander-
" in-Chief at Devonport, he has repeatedly cruized with experi-
" mental squadrons.

" Sir H. J. Leeke, a Magistrate for cos. Hants and Sussex,
"and a Deputy-Lieutenant for the former, received the honour
"of Knighthood, as a reward for his eminent services on the
"coast of Africa, 1 April, 1835, and was nominated a K.H. 25
"Jan. 1836. In acknowledgment of some good offices he had
"the fortune to render the King of the French when a Midship-
"man, he has been presented by that monarch with a gold
"medal; as he has also been by the King of Prussia.

CHAPTER XLII.

1860.

LORD'S DAY CONFERENCE MEETING AT DERBY.

Sir Matthew Blakiston and Archdeacon Hill preside—Fundamental resolutions—
Order of discussion—Subjects under the following heads:—Travelling,
Trading, Amusements, Miscellaneous—Resolutions—Sunday movements of
the King of Saxony and Marshal Soult—Letter from the French ambassador—Sunday bands, news-rooms, &c., &c.

I THINK I shall bring the main part of the subject of the due
observance of the Lord's Day usefully before my readers, and
certainly with much saving of time to myself, if I insert at length,
in the following pages of this work, an account which I drew up,
with much labour, from the verbatim report by a London reporter,
extending to 695 folios, of the speeches which were made, and of
the conversation which took place at the conference at Derby, in
November, 1860, on the subject of the abounding desecrations of
the Lord's Day, and of the best plan of providing some effectual
remedy for them :—

"*Lord's Day Conference Meeting, held at Derby, on the 27th
and 28th of November, 1860.*

"Derby, March, 1861.

"The Committee of the Derbyshire Society for Promoting the
Due Observance of the Lord's Day, in publishing some account
of the late Conference at Derby, desire to express their sense of
the great mercy and loving-kindness of the Lord of the Sabbath,
as manifested in permitting so successful a commencement of
their attempt to make a fresh start and a combined effort

against all the abounding desecrations of the Lord's Day. They are most thankful also for the unanimity of sentiment and feeling which prevailed on the occasion.

"They would now entreat all the friends of this most holy cause to unite with them in a prayerful, united, immediate, and continued effort to grapple, in every way which may approve itself to them, with every desecration of the Sabbath in their respective neighbourhoods, assured, if the religious and well-disposed public can be aroused to such action, that, through the Divine blessing, immense benefit will arise from their labours to their respective neighbourhoods, to the whole country, and even to distant regions of the earth. Many of the difficulties in the way do seem to be almost insurmountable, but the Committee and all the friends of the cause must engage in the work in simple dependence upon Him whose is the Power, and the Kingdom, and the Glory, and they may fully expect that, in His own best time, this mountain of difficulties shall 'become 'a plain:' Zech iv, 6, 7.

"The Conference was attended by many friends from a considerable distance, a list of whose names and addresses will be found in Chapter XLIII. Numerous letters were received from every part of the country, containing the most encouraging promises of co-operation in the movement. Sir Matthew Blakiston, Bart., and the Ven. the Archdeacon of Derby were Co-Presidents of the Meeting.

"After singing and prayer, the following Resolutions of the Derbyshire Committee of the 2nd of November were read :—

"'The following Plan having met with the approval of the London Lord's Day Society,

"'It is Resolved,

"'I. That a Conference be held at Derby, it being a central point, on Tuesday, the 27th of November, at Twelve o'Clock, at the Athenaeum Room, which friends from the Northern and Midland Towns shall be invited to attend, for the purpose of considering the best means of making a fresh start and a combined effort against the abounding desecrations of the Lord's Day.

"'II. That the Secretary be empowered to invite members of the Church of England, holding the Divine authority of the Lord's Day, to attend the Conference Meeting, especially those who are Secretaries or members of the Parent Society, or of Auxiliary Societies for Promoting the Due Observance of the Lord's Day.

"'III. That this Committee especially desire the assistance, at this Conference, of the members of the Clerical and Lay Association of the Midland District.

"'IV. That it is all-important that this effort should be commenced and carried on by all who take part in it, in humble dependence on, and prayer for, the Divine blessing.

"'V. That the Meeting, at Twelve, on Tuesday, the 27th, last till Three o'clock, when there shall be an adjournment for two hours; that the Second Meeting shall be from Five to Eight o'clock, and that there shall be a further Meeting on Wednesday, at Ten o'clock.'

"Then the two following fundamental Resolutions of the Parent Society were read, as a basis of action :—

"'I. That this Meeting desires to record its firm belief of the Divine authority and perpetual obligation of the Christian Sabbath; and of the blessings, temporal, spiritual, and eternal, which God has been pleased in His mercy to connect with its religious observance.

"'II. That this Meeting is persuaded that it is the paramount duty, both of private Christians and Christian rulers, to confess their allegiance to Almighty God, and their faith in the Divine Redeemer, by exerting their influence to promote the due observance of the Lord's Day.'

"In order to preserve some method in the deliberations, and also to economise time, it was thought desirable to arrange the various desecrations under the four following heads :—Travelling, Trading, Amusements, Miscellaneous.

"1. Travelling, under which the following desecrations were taken :—
Railway Travelling—Excursion, Goods, and Cattle Trains, the transmission of the Mails, and in connection with *that* all Post Office Work; Cabs, Carriages, and other Conveyances, &c.; Riding and Driving in the Parks; Steam, Canal, Fishing, and Pleasure Boats, Wherries, Shipping.

"2. *Trading*—Including Shops, Public Houses, Hawking, and Crying Goods; Markets, the changing of Saturday and Monday Fairs and Markets to some other day; Printing, Selling Newspapers.

"3. *Amusements*—Crystal Palace, &c., Tea and Public Gardens, Bands, Wakes or Revels, &c., &c.

"4. *Miscellaneous*—Neglect of Public Worship, Sunday Funerals, any other violations of the Lord's Day not included in any of the above items; Desecrations by persons of high rank, and by foreigners; Cheese-making; Farm Labourers; the improper employment of others in any way.'

"After these preliminary steps had been taken, the meeting was addressed by the Presidents, and by the Secretaries of the London and Derbyshire Societies ; and the various Members, who wished to do so, spoke on the several points, precedence being given to those who had come from a distance, and could only remain for the morning meeting. At the evening meeting, and at that of the following morning, many of the ideas which had been expressed were gathered up into the following Eleven Resolutions, and were passed unanimously. There were, however, many other very important points which were mentioned, and favourably received by the Conference, and which the Derbyshire Committee are of opinion would have been adopted, in the shape of resolutions, had the time and the difficulty of framing and accurately considering a series of resolutions in a large meeting permitted it. The Committee have therefore thought it right to append them, as resolutions, to those passed at the Conference.

RESOLUTIONS.

"'I. Resolved that the Conference would recommend the immediate formation throughout the land of Associations of the London Society for Promoting the Due Observance of the Lord's Day (local Associations having the entire control of their own funds, and independent liberty of action upon every question, but adopting the Parent Society's fundamental rules.)

"'II. That such local Associations should endeavour to obtain for the Post-office employés their rightful Sabbath rest by inducing inhabitants to agree not to receive letters and newspapers on the Lord's Day.

"'III. That a combined effort should forthwith be made throughout the land, to stop all travelling on the Lord's Day that is not called for by necessity or mercy, by petitioning Parliament, by memorializing Railway Directors, and by other measures that may be found desirable.

"'IV. That this Conference would call upon Christian ministers of all denominations throughout the Christian world, as far as this invitation shall reach, to bring before their people, on the fourth Sunday in March, (Easter Sunday next,) the subject of the nature, duties, and privileges of the Lord's Day, pointing out the present desecration of it.

"'V. That this Conference also calls upon all Christians in this country to make the preservation of the Sabbath a subject of prayer at all times, and especially in the second week of January next.

"'VI. That this Conference looks upon the sale of intoxicating drinks on the Lord's Day as one of the most uncalled-for and demoralizing desecrations of that day; and therefore would urge upon Parliament the necessity of extending to this country such provisions of the Act for the better regulation of public-houses in Scotland, (16 & 17 Vic., c. 67,) commonly called the Forbes Mackenzie Act, as relate to the sale and giving out of liquors, and the opening of houses and premises for the sale thereof, on the Lord's Day.

" 'VII. That the late Meeting at Birmingham clearly shows that the majority of traders, and of the inhabitants generally, are willing to combine for the suppression of Sunday trading, and that, in cases where such majority call upon the local authorities to protect the rest of the many against the selfishness of the few, it is possible to put in force the present law against Sunday trading, and therefore, that similar movements in other towns should be originated.

" 'VIII. That this Conference would recommend the formation, wherever it may be possible, of Working Men's Sabbath Defence Committees, as Auxiliaries of local Associations.

" 'IX. That this Conference is of opinion that it is of the greatest importance that friends throughout the country should endeavour to furnish the London Secretary with information as to the various kinds of labour in their respective neighbourhoods prevalent on the Lord's Day, in order that correct information relative to Sabbath desecration may be circulated as widely as possible.

" 'X. That this Conference would solemnly protest against the admission of shareholders to the Crystal Palace on the Lord's Day as being a violation of the spirit, if not of the letter, of the charter of the company; while working men, among others, are thus enticed from Christian worship, giving rise to the employment of labour at those places.

" 'XI. That this Conference would strenuously promote the movement for obtaining the earlier payment of wages, the earlier closing of shops, and a general Saturday half-holiday, in order to procure for the people time for all lawful secular enjoyment without encroaching upon the rest of the Lord's Day.'

" Additional Resolutions mentioned in the Preceding Page.

" 'XII. That it should be most distinctly understood that the Lord's Day Society and its Auxiliaries have always repudiated the idea of what may be termed 'making men religious by Act of Parliament;' and that all they seek from the Government and from the Legislature is, that all public violations of the Lord's Day by which Almighty God is dishonoured, should be put down, and that every subject of the realm should, as far as is possible, have it secured to him as a day of rest, in order that he may have the *opportunity* of serving his God according to the dictates of his conscience; and further that works of necessity, mercy, and piety ought freely to be performed on that day; the Sabbath, according to the Divine authority, being 'made for man, and not man for the Sabbath.'

"'XIII. That it is most desirable that *every* desecration of the Lord's Day should in some way or other be met, and contended with, as by such a course Almighty God will be most honoured in the sight of all men, and the exertions which are made to suppress each will have a most beneficial effect in helping forward similar exertions, with regard to other desecrations.

"'XIV. That it is of the greatest importance to the success of the movement that Addresses be presented to the Queen, and Petitions from all classes be forwarded *every Session* to *both* Houses of Parliament, praying Her Majesty and the Legislature to use their influence to promote the due observance of the Lord's Day; and particularly that distinct petitions, &c., be promoted from all classes of tradesmen and others who, under the present system, are deprived either wholly or in part of the rest and other privileges of that holy day, that by the publicity given to the presentation of these Petitions in *both* Houses, the public mind may be informed, and the friends of Sabbath Observance be stimulated to fresh and continued efforts when they thus become acquainted with the feelings of others in every part of the country.

"'XV. That those who take part in this movement be requested, from time to time, whenever occasion may require it, to communicate with their own representatives and such other members of the Legislature as they may be acquainted with, begging them to use all their influence, both in and out of Parliament, in endeavouring to withstand the torrent of Sabbath Profanation, which is setting in on the land.

"'XVI. That the holding of Annual Meetings in all the Towns and Parishes of the Country, be strongly recommended as one great mean of diffusing information as to the objects and proceedings of the Lord's Day Society, and of exciting and keeping up an interest in them.

"'XVII. That it is very important to make constant use of the Public Press by getting articles and paragraphs inserted in the local and other papers.

"'XVIII. That it be suggested to the friends of this movement that it is desirable there should be sound books and tracts on the subject of the Christian Sabbath at the Booksellers' shops in the various towns throughout the country, so that they may be easily procured by all who may feel a desire for such publications.

"'XIX. That it may be desirable at times for County Associations to send copies of important papers, not only to the Secretaries of other Associations, but also to the Members of the Government and of both Houses of Parliament.'

" It having been found unadvisable, and indeed impracticable, to give a condensation of the very long verbatim Report * of the Speeches which were made, and of the conversation which took

* Extending to 695 folios.

place at the Conference, with regard to the desecrations of the Lord's Day, and the various ways in which attempts might be made to lessen and suppress them, the Derbyshire Committee have thought it well to collect, from the Report, all the most important observations which were made, and to place them as notes under the several Resolutions with which they appear to be connected.

" ' 1. Resolved that the Conference would recommend the immediate formation, throughout the Land, of Associations of the London Society for Promoting the Due Observance of the Lord's Day (local Associations having the entire control of their own funds, and independent liberty of action upon every question, but adopting the Parent Society's fundamental rules.) '

" A combined effort against all the profanations of the Lord's Day, in order to be successful, requires the regular organizing of County and other Associations, throughout the Country, which will extend their ramifications into every Town and Village around them.

" It is better that all should be in connexion with the London Society, with the full liberty of action, &c., mentioned in the resolution, so that whenever any important and perhaps immediate action is required, that Society can at once recommend it. It was thought that no part of the Country, and, if possible, no Parish, should be without its organization for helping forward the great movement. At present there are multitudes of persons, in every direction, most anxious to promote the proper observance of the Lord's Day, but without such an organization as that proposed, there can be no concerted action.

" The London Lord's Day Society, and almost all its auxiliaries, are Church of England Societies. It was mentioned at the Conference that whilst those Dissenters, who are opposed to Legislation, will not unite with Churchmen in appealing to the Legislature to protect the working men and others who are now deprived of their Sabbath rest, they will in other ways heartily withstand every attack made on the Sabbath, but that Churchmen and Dissenters get on better in this matter also in separate Societies; and that they have thus worked most cordially together in resisting several of the attempted inroads on the sanctity of the day. The Wesleyans are not opposed to Legislation, and have always been ready to join in any movement recommended by the Lord's Day Society, still they have their own machinery, and they prefer working in connexion with that. They would rather take their own independent course.

"As the Derbyshire Lord's Day Society was the first County Society formed, it may be well to mention that it was commenced by getting two Laymen and two Clergymen to append their names to a short circular, which was sent to about thirty of the Clergy and Laity, inviting them to a preliminary meeting to consider the best plan to be adopted in order to the formation, &c., of a County Society. It was determined to call a meeting of those in the County who were favourable to the object, and to invite the Bishop to preside. Bishop Ryder presided at this meeting, on the 24th of December, 1833, the only day he could fix on, and although it was such an inconvenient day for the Clergy, 80 of them attended. The Bishop became the President of the Society, and a Committee of 36 Clergymen and Laymen, and two Secretaries, were appointed. Mr. Joseph Wilson, the Founder and Secretary of the London Society, accompanied the Derbyshire Secretaries to six or seven of the large Towns of the County, at which meetings were held, and the Secretaries, having had this advantage, found themselves prepared to attend meetings, either together and singly, in large numbers of the Parishes throughout the County.

"'II. That such local Associations should endeavour to obtain for the Post-office employés their rightful Sabbath rest by inducing inhabitants to agree not to receive letters and newspapers on the Lord's Day.'

"The following was the request to the Postmaster, signed, in 1839, by about 1500 of the principal letter-receiving inhabitants of Derby, and its neighbourhood:—

"'We the undersigned request you not to forward our letters 'to us on the Lord's Day, unless they are especially required in 'cases of emergency.'

"It was at first signed by about thirty heads of families, and then sent with those names to each member of the Committee, that he might add to them; and thus the number rose to about

1500, and eventually to 2000. 2500 persons signed a similar request at Bath. The Postmaster-General now sanctions the retaining these letters at the office.

"The Conference also considered that efforts should forthwith be made to prevent the Rural Postmen from being employed on the Lord's Day. It was stated, that out of 404 Rural Postmen, in the large Midland District of the General Post-office department, having its centre at Derby, only 75 now travel on the Lord's Day; and that in any rural district in which a sufficient proportion of the letter-receiving inhabitants should state to the Postmaster-General that they were willing to do without their letters, the Postman of such district would be relieved from his Sunday labour. Such efforts will not only relieve the Letter-carriers and Postmen, but, when another great attempt is made to put a stop to the transmission of the mails and the delivery of letters on the Lord's Day, they will help to prove to the Government, and to the Legislature, that all Sunday labour, connected with the Post-office, may easily be dispensed with. Of the above-mentioned 329 Rural Posts, which do not go out on the Sunday, nearly one half are new Posts, and for several years no *newly* established Post has been made, or allowed to travel on that day. The old Rural Posts have been stopped on the Lord's Day in consequence of applications from the inhabitants of the several districts. Of the sixteen Rural Messengers which are despatched from the Derby office and its sub-offices, three only travel on the Lord's Day. An Address, requesting the inhabitants not to receive their letters on the Lord's Day, was left by the letter carriers at every house in Manchester and Derby.

"In connexion with the point sometimes argued, that the Mails should be forwarded on the Lord's Day, in order that persons might receive early intelligence of the dangerous illness, &c., of their relations, and that railway trains should run for the purpose of conveying them to their sick and dying beds, it was suggested that, even in such cases in which persons' feelings were the most deeply touched, and which were most decided cases of mercy, Christian men might feel it right to forego their liberty, rather than by their example appear to countenance a system which involves the regular employment of many thousands of their fellow-creatures on that holy day, and which tends to the destruction of their immortal souls.

"Because a few persons in various parts of the country may be placed in such circumstances every Sabbath Day, should tens of thousands be deprived regularly of the privileges of that day? Would any reasonable Christian man desire that all these persons should be deprived, and regularly deprived, of one of the greatest blessings which God has bestowed on man, because it might, once or twice in his life, possibly happen in God's providence that a dear friend was lying dangerously ill at a distance on the Lord's Day? Might he not rather, even in such an anxious state of trial, leave himself, as in all other times, to the care of his Heavenly Father? It was mentioned in support of this view, that when Mr. Hume proposed to open the London Post-office on the Lord's Day, 56 of the leading Bankers of London, 1600 Solicitors' Firms, upwards of 1000 Merchants, and several hundreds of the members of the Stock Exchange, signed memorials praying that there might be no Sunday delivery of letters in the Metropolis. Each would be as anxious as any other persons in the country could be, to have the earliest intelligence of the serious illness of a near relative at a distance, but he is content, for the very great benefit resulting to thousands from the general cessation of correspondence on that day, to do without such intelligence.

"'III. That a combined effort should forthwith be made throughout the land, to stop all travelling on the Lord's Day that is not called for by necessity or mercy, by petitioning Parliament, by memoralizing Railway Directors, and by other measures that may be found desirable.'

"The conference considered that the whole system of railway travelling on the Lord's Day, including the regular trains, the goods trains, and the excursion trains, was a most gross and grievous violation of the Divine command. Although the Sunday excursion trains are now attracting so much attention, as they are the means of inundating many of the Towns, and otherwise quiet Villages of the land, with hundreds and thousands of Sabbath-breakers, it was thought better not to specify them as the most glaring evil, lest it might lead the public generally to think more lightly of the grievous sin of those Companies who do not run excursion trains, but passenger, and goods or cattle trains on the Lord's Day. Throughout the length and breadth of the land, many thousands of Clerks, Guards, Engine Drivers, Pointsmen, Porters, &c., are tempted to labour on the Lord's Day, whilst the inducement is held out to multitudes of persons, to spend in travelling, sinful amusements, and dissipation, that day which Almighty God has set apart as a day of rest from labour, and also for higher and holier purposes.

" It was well stated, that it was a painful and mournful thing that the public bodies should seek to enrich themselves out of the sins of the people, and that all Railway Companies who throw these temptations in the way of their own servants, and of the people, have a grave sin to answer for, and that if they cannot be made amenable to human tribunals, the day will come when every man who has made a shilling by the sins of his fellow-men, will incur a grave responsibility indeed in the sight of God.

" It was stated that on a recent occasion, one of the railways conveyed vast numbers of persons to an infidel open air meeting, at which they were harangued by several notorious infidels. It appears that the great proportion of persons who make use of these Sunday excursion trains, immediately on the arrival of the trains at their destination, usually fill all the public-houses in the neighbourhood, and spend much of their time in drinking, whilst they of course employ great numbers of persons in attending upon them. These trains also, as well as the regular trains, lead to the employment at each end of the line, of great numbers of omnibus and cab drivers; and at one of the watering-places, soon after the arrival of a train, 40 or 50 boats have been observed to put to sea, eighty or a hundred men being employed to manage them. The parties who avail themselves of the Sunday excursion trains, are generally of those classes who can afford to make such excursions on other days. Almost all persons employed on the railways; in connexion with Post-office work; and in the conducting of public conveyances of every kind; on roads, canals, and navigable rivers, are most anxious to escape from their Sabbath thraldom, and many who are religiously disposed feel most acutely the difficulty of their position, although they have not that confidence in God which would enable them at once to renounce their profanation of His day, and trust Him with the consequences.

"Amongst the REMEDIES recommended to be tried with regard to railway desecration of the Lord's Day, were the following,—several of which apply also to other desecrations : Sermons, and the distribution of publications on the subject of the due observance of the day ; the presentation of petitions to parliament from those employed, and perhaps even from the directors, praying that a general legislative measure may be passed to put a stop to all railway traffic and travelling on the Lord's Day, excepting in cases of necessity and mercy ; that the Directors of each Company should be requested to receive a deputation on the subject of the Sunday traffic on their line. This deputation should consist of a goodly number of influential persons resident in the neighbourhood of the line. Amongst other proposals made to them, might be those mentioned above ; the joining in a petition themselves ; and the permitting those employed in connexion with the railway, to petition for the prohibition, except in necessary cases, of all travelling, &c., on the Lord's Day. It is thought that directors would not think of withholding such permission, and yet that the men might feel an awkwardness in petitioning without it. They may also be induced to invite the body of their proprietors, assembled at the half-yearly meeting of the Company, to consent to a similar petition.

"A general petitioning for the putting down of all railway travelling on the Lord's Day, was mentioned at the Midland Counties' meeting, in 1839, by some of those who on that occasion were opposed to the proposition to close their own line on that day. In cases in which Railway Bills have passed the Commons, with a clause in them prohibiting the use of such railways on the Lord's Day, on their being taken to the House of Lords, the chairman of the Lords' Committee has invariably run his pen through such clause, declaring that if railways are to be closed on the Lord's Day, it must be done by a general act.

"These statements are made on good authority, and may be mentioned as facts to the directors. This plan of a deputation to wait upon the directors is about to be adopted at Derby, and it is hoped that it may be adopted also in all parts of the kingdom. The waiting of such a deputation on a body of directors, may appear to some to be almost useless, yet who can tell but that the great Lord of the Sabbath, who regards with favour the prayers and efforts of his people, may be pleased to bless this attempt, and incline the hearts of influential men in this way to forward this holy cause. If the directors of some of the leading railways can be brought to act in the matter, as it is hoped they may, a most important step will have been made. From time to time resolutions have been proposed at the half-yearly meetings of several Companies, to put an end to all Sunday traffic on their railways, but, although there have been in some cases large minorities, the resolutions have almost always been negatived.

" Colonel Young has for many years most nobly stood up, and protested, almost single-handed, against the sad desecrations of the Sabbath Day, which are permitted by the directors of the London, Brighton, and South Coast Railway. It was thought that these attempts had done much good. A very excellent letter, written by Colonel Young, will be found in the next chapter.

" The plan of getting persons to purchase largely into some particular line or lines, with a view to the closing them on the Lord's Day, was mentioned at the Conference, and it was stated that if those, who could conveniently purchase only one or two shares, would attend the half-yearly Meetings, they would have it in their power to render very great assistance in the effort which will be made to promote Sabbath Observance on Railways, and also at the Crystal Palace. It was stated that in the year 1845, a proposition to close the Midland Railway, as far as the Post-office Act would permit, was brought forward and negatived, although supported by the promise of the proxies of 439 proprietors, holding £700,000 of the Midland Stock ; that the stock of the Midland Company then amounted to about £6,000,000 ; and that since then it had increased to £21,000,000.

" With regard to *Memorials* to the directors, signed by persons of the greatest influence in various parts of the country, it appears that the answer is nearly always to the following effect :—'That the Company would be most willing to attend to

'the Memorial that had been laid before them so far as the ac-
'commodation of the public permitted.' This was the reply to
the Memorial from Worcester, with regard to Sunday Excursion
Trains on the newly-opened line from that place to Malvern.
The station at Worcester is close to one of the churches, and
numbers of omnibuses and cabs assemble at it to meet the
hundreds of excursionists from the large manufacturing districts
around Birmingham who have arrived just before the commencement of Divine service, and who are also encountered by the
teachers and scholars of the Sunday school on their way to church.
The Conference considered that it would be right to continue to
present memorials to the directors, as well as to petition Parliament. Such memorials may be presented by deputations or
otherwise. It may be well here to state that the Lord's Day
Societies have acted upon the rule, in the matter of petitions,
memorials, and resolutions, of contending for *all* that the law of
God requires, lest they should seem to sanction anything that is
sinful, but with regard to railway and other desecrations of the
Sabbath, they are thankful to see any step taken in the right
direction.

One of the speakers urged the desirableness of a sub-com-
mittee of the London Lord's Day Committee to promote Sabbath
observance on railways, with power to associate with itself corresponding members. The Conference did not enter into the
matter, but the London Secretary undertook to mention it to the
London Committee.

"With reference to other conveyances, it was stated that there
was a very great improvement in London and in the country
with regard to the higher classes of society not using their carriages and horses on the Lord's Day, and that a very large amount
of those throughout the country, who used their own or public
conveyances on the Lord's Day, would be found to be of the class
of small innkeepers, small shopkeepers, and small farmers; that
it had been the custom in the petitions from Derbyshire to pray
that a humble address might be presented to the Queen, 'praying
'that the *carriage* gates of the parks might be closed on the Lord's
'Day, so as to prevent in them that concourse of the Higher
'Classes with their Horses and Carriages, which not only consti-

'tutes one of the most glaring profanations of the Sabbath Day,
'and deprives so many Servants of their Sabbath privileges, but
'which also has so pernicious a tendency, in the way of example,
'on all ranks of her Majesty's subjects.' This practice and the
following statement will help to show how undeserved is the ac-
cusation, made by some against those who are anxious to secure
the Lord's Day as a day of rest for the thousands of working men
who are now deprived of it, that they wish to prevent them from
getting a little fresh air on the Sunday, whilst they leave the
rich to do as they please.

"It was mentioned that some years ago, the King of Saxony,
when in this country, travelled about a good deal on the Lord's
Day, and that other foreigners of distinction often made it their
day of arrival or departure, thereby occasioning unnecessary employment to the naval and military officers and men, and to
other persons, on the Lord's Day. The departure of Marshal
Soult on the Lord's Day, on which occasion there was a great
deal of saluting, as he passed down the river, was particularly
mentioned. This led the Committee of the Derbyshire Lord's
Day Society, when the King of the French was about to visit
England, to send the address to the Queen, which will be found
in the next chapter. Printed copies of this address were sent to
the principal Ministers of State, to Prince Albert, the Queen
Dowager, the Duchess of Kent, and also to all the foreign Ambassadors, &c., with a request that it might be brought under the
notice of their several courts. One of the private secretaries wrote
from Windsor, mentioning that the King's visit had been beforehand
so arranged that he would neither arrive nor depart on the Lord's
Day. The French Ambassador in his reply, just before the arrival
of the King, said that he would take care that the document should
be placed in the hands of the proper person to lay it before his
majesty immediately on his landing in this country. (See Chapter
LVII.) Another Ambassador stated his intention of sending
the address to his own court. There was reason to hope that the
address helped to do good in high quarters. The preface to a
sermon entitled "The Queen's Sunday Visit to Guernsey," and
preached August 5th, 1860, by the Rev. William Brock, M.A.,
Rector of Bishop's Waltham, Hants., contains a faithful remon-

strance, which was mentioned at the Conference, against Sabbath desecration on the part of several persons of high position in this country. [A portion of this preface is given in the next chapter.]

"With regard to SUNDAY TRAFFIC ON CANALS AND RIVERS, it was stated that it has entirely ceased on the Weaver, and almost entirely on the Mersey and Irwell navigations, much to the advantage of proprietors, and boatmen. This was effected principally by the exertions of one individual. Nearly 800 of the Severn Boatmen, and 400 of those employed on the Trent, and and many at Derby and other places have petitioned Parliament to prohibit all Sunday traffic on canals and navigable rivers.

"Through the exertions which have been made in former times, many of the foreign steamers which used to start on the Lord's Day, have had their day of departure changed. Many merchants never allow their ships to sail on the Sunday, and have never traced any loss to themselves from that practice. About 2500 merchants, captains, and seaman of Liverpool, and about 1200 of the same class belonging to the Port of London, and others at Bristol, petitioned that ships might not be allowed to sail from port on the Lord's Day.

"The improper use of fishing boats, wherries and other boats, may be met by private remonstrance, and by the circulation of suitable books and tracts amongst the offenders, and where the desecration is still persisted in, recourse may be had to the magistrates. On a late occasion, at Derby, when pleasure boats were begining to occasion much unseemly desecration of the Lord's Day, a meeting was convened through the active exertions of one of the clergy of the town, and on the mayor's attention being drawn to the case, the profanation of the Sabbath was immediately put down, and the boats were sold.

"Much was said at the Conference on the subject of omnibuses and cabs being used on the Sunday. Many of the men themselves feel this Sunday employment to be a heavy burden. In London alone there are 24,000 employed in connexion with these conveyances.

"A letter was read to the Conference from the late mayor of Southampton, in which he states that their Local Act had enabled them to put an end to all buying and selling on the Lord's

Day : and that the Commissioners unanimously agreed upon a regulation, prohibiting cabs from appearing on the public stands, or plying for hire on the Lord's Day:—'This regulation has 'been of most immense importance, as it gives the poor cab-'driver an opportunity of attending public worship, relieves over-'worked and jaded horses, and produces a quiet in our streets 'which would not be otherwise obtained. Nor is this the only 'good. It removes, from the idle and thoughtless, the tempta-'tion to employ cabs on that day for pleasure excursions, and is 'a testimony against the desecration of that holy day by such 'practices. If at Southampton, the principal packet port of ' England, where there are constant arrivals of large numbers of ' passengers, these regulations can be carried out, it is fair to infer ' that the like could be effected in other large towns, if an attempt ' were made to that end.'

" An interesting account was given of a cabman, in London, who had written a tract, on the observance of the Lord's Day, which had gained a prize, offered by a committee of noblemen and gentlemen, and which, he said, had been chiefly written as he sat on the box of his cab, waiting for fares. Some of the London cabmen have established clubs and reading rooms. 1800 of the cabmen in London do not work on the Lord's Day. All the cabs which have numbers higher than No. 10,000 are only week-day cabs. At Derby no cabs are allowed to be on the stands, even on the railway stand, on the Lord's Day ; this is an arrangement made by the cab proprietors. The following is taken from a late London paper:—

" ' A Public Meeting was held on Thursday, at the Boys' Refuge, 8, Great Queen Street, Lincoln's-inn-fields, to which cab proprietors were especially invited, to consider the expediency of taking out six-day licences for the ensuing year. Mr. Powell, cab proprietor, occupied the chair, and was supported by Messrs. Girdleston, Bennett, Allen, Shaen, Langley, Hill, Smith, and Maxwell. Several speakers addressed the Meeting in support of the movement, and ultimately it was resolved " That it is the opinion of this Meeting, it would be advantageous both " to masters and men if cabs discontinue working on Sundays." '

" A remarkable meeting of cabmen was mentioned as having taken place at Manchester, when 450 cabmen took tea together, and heard addresses on the subject of the Divine authority and sanctity of the Lord's Day, from twelve o'clock at night till three in the morning. All the cabmen appeared exceedingly anxious to have every alternate Sabbath to themselves, and almost every cab proprietor is willing to consent to this arrangement. It was stated that the prejudice of the omnibus drivers and cabmen against religious people was very great, because they used these conveyances very much on Sunday, to go and hear celebrated preachers ; and because ministers themselves continually made use of them, when they were going to preach charity sermons, and thus helped to keep up a system most injurious to the best interests of those whom they thus employed.

"An omnibus driver, some three or four years ago, spoke in the following strong terms to a clergyman who was riding by his side on a week day, and conversing with him on this subject : ' Sir, there is not a man living that would delight to spend his 'Sabbath with his family more than I should, and go to God's 'house on Sunday, but it is you religious people that prevent me. 'Upon this line my master finds the omnibus pays better on the 'Sunday than on any other day of the week. And why is it ? 'Simply, because people make use of me to drive them to their 'churches and chapels.'

"It was strongly argued that this was not right, and that in order to remedy it, the parochial clergy should more and more seek to extend their personal ministerial influence simply over a given area. The following letter on this subject from a clergyman in Suffolk, was read to the meeting :—

"'There is one point connected with the Sabbath, which has 'long been upon my mind, and as I have not seen it referred to 'in any of the publications of the Lord's Day Societies, I venture 'to suggest some consideration of the point, if your own feelings 'on it should agree with mine. This is with reference to the 'Sunday journeys, so often taken by the deputations of our Mis- 'sionary and other Religious Societies.

"'Where a minister resides some distance from his church, or 'where in the case of occasional absence, or illness, a Clergyman 'undertakes the service in a neighbouring church, it seems to me 'quite justifiable to ride or drive, the alternative probably being 'that the Clergyman should use his horse, or that a congregation

'should be without a service ; but it seems to me a very different
'case, when it is only one of comparison between the attractive-
'ness of some stranger, and the regular ministration of the
'ordinary minister—between the pecuniary productiveness of the
'one as greater than that of the other, and the necessity of a
'Sunday journey instead of the maintaining the honour of that
'day by no work for the horse and the groom.

"'The arrangements made by our deputations too often in-
'volve the being driven from one church to another, either by
'hiring or by the clergyman's conveyance ; and when we remem-
'ber that it is not money alone that we want, but a divine bless-
'ing on all the work, is it well, in the hope of a larger collection,
'to do that which by example seems to sanction the principle,
'that for the sake of gain work may be done on the Lord's Day ?

"'I have been in my present living now sixteen years, and I
'have various societies supported in my Parish ; but I have always
'acted on the plan, that no one preaches for a Society in my
'church, unless he can come to my house on the Saturday, and
'spend the Sunday here, so as to require no fetching or forward-
'ing, or taking to another parish on that day. If such an
'arrangement cannot conveniently be made, I preach for the
'society myself, giving the cause my own inferior advocacy, but
'trusting that the blessing of that God, who honoureth them that
'honour Him and His day, will more than compensate for this
'disadvantage. And I cannot but think that if clergymen would
'more frequently preach for our religious societies in their own
'pulpits, there would be, in addition to various other advantages,
'this also, of quieter and more hallowed Sabbaths, and of our
'being able with clearer consciences to urge upon the world
'to avoid all unnecessary work and journeying on the Lord's
'Day.'"

"Since the Conference one clergyman has acted upon the
suggestion contained in this letter, and it is but right to insert
the views which the Association Secretary of one of the religious
Societies stated in his reply :—'I feel assured that it is no sin to
'travel on that day to do the Lord's work, and that the work for-
'bidden in the Fourth Commandment is secular work and for
'secular ends.'

" 'IV. That this Conference would call upon Christian ministers of all denominations throughout the Christian world, as far as this invitation shall reach, to bring before their people, on the fifth Sunday in March, (Easter Sunday next,) the subject of the nature, duties, and privileges of the Lord's Day, pointing out the present desecration of it. Where the suggestion cannot be acted upon on the day mentioned, it is hoped that some other early day will be fixed on.'

" It was suggested at the Conference that it might not be inconvenient in some places to make a collection after the sermon.

" When an active County or District Association shall be formed, it will require, in order to carry on and extend its operations, considerable funds. Each Association should also endeavour to aid the funds of the London Society, which, if the contemplated movement go forward, will have an immense work before it, greatly increasing its expenses.

" 'V. That this Conference also calls upon all Christians in this country to make the preservation of the Sabbath a subject of prayer at all times, and especially in the second week of January next.'

" It is feared that this account of the Conference cannot be very widely circulated by the second week in January. It is however suggested that the cause of the preservation of the Sabbath and its due observance in every part of the world, should continually be made a subject of special prayer on every Sunday morning, at some time between the hours of seven and nine. This was the time, forty years ago, at which numbers of people were in the habit of praying for the outpouring of the Holy Spirit on the whole world; and it appears to be a particularly appropriate time and hour for prayer for the continuance of, and a blessing on, the ordinance of the Lord's Day.

" 'VI. That this Conference looks upon the sale of intoxicating drinks on the Lord's Day as one of the most uncalled-for and demoralizing desecrations of that day; and, therefore, would urge upon Parliament the necessity of extending to this country such provisions of the Act for the better regulation of public-houses in Scotland (16 & 17 Vic. c. 67.) commonly called the Forbes Mackenzie Act, as relate to the sale and giving out of liquors, and the opening of houses and premises for the sale thereof on the Lord's Day.'

" Distinct petitions on this subject, to both Houses, were recommended in addition to the general parochial petitions.

"It was thought that the most frightful source of Sabbath desecration, in the present day, was the peculiar state of the law about beer-shops and public-houses, and that it was most remarkable that whilst shops are required to be closed where they sell beef and bread, those might be open during a considerable part of the day, in which beer and brandy are sold. The amount of drunkenness on the Lord's Day was considered as most appalling, and the number of public-houses altogether out of all proportion to the reasonable wants of the population of the Country.

"In one small parish in Derbyshire, with 470 Inhabitants, there are six public houses and beer shops, or one to every sixteen families.

"It was stated that drunkenness and crime had everywhere diminished in proportion to the restraint which the Legislature had placed on the sale of intoxicating drinks on the Lord's Day. In seventeen of the chief Towns of Scotland, containing together about a million of Inhabitants, the number of cases of drunkenness alone, or of drunkenness and crime combined, on Sundays, amounted, during the three years before the Forbes Mackenzie Act came into operation, to 11,471; whilst, during the first three years in which public-houses were closed on Sundays, cases of the same description amounted, in the aggregate, only to 4299.

"It was thought that whilst the Churchwardens and police might do something towards mitigating the evil, the only proper and effectual remedy would be the closing the public-houses during the whole of the Lord's Day; and the Conference was most sanguine, that, if all who value that day would unite in the proposed effort, a law for that purpose would be enacted by the Legislature.

"The difficulty of ascertaining who was a *bona fide* traveller was discussed. It was considered that the evil of public-houses being kept open on the Lord's Day, whereby misery is inflicted on thousands, ought not to be tolerated for the sake of those who were violating the command of God, by using Sunday excursion trains, and moreover, when such trains and all Sunday railway and other travelling, unconnected with cases of necessity and mercy, should be put down, that very few would claim to be travellers. It was also maintained that the expansive character of British Christianity should be such, that in order to do away with so frightful a source of evil, the *bona fide* traveller should allow his convenience to be curtailed ; and that if men must really travel, in cases of necessity, on the Lord's Day, they can at least, by taking provision with them, do without the public-house at that time, unless they are going to lodge there. It was believed that all the dissenters, even those who generally object to Legislation in matters of religion, would join heartily in pressing upon their representatives the immense importance of closing public-houses on the Sabbath Day.

" It was urged that numbers of the poor drunkards themselves, when they become sober, bewail the temptations to which they are exposed under the present system, and would gladly join with their wives and neighbours, in praying for more stringent regulations with regard to public-houses on every day of the week, and especially that they should be closed during the whole of Sunday. When mention was made of petitions to the same effect from the innkeepers, public-house, and beer-shop keepers themselves, it was thought by some that the attempt would be perfectly useless ; but it was stated that in several parishes of Derbyshire, and in other places, many of them had signed such petitions, being anxious, if all were forced to close their houses, to have the Lord's Day as a day of rest, &c., 70 of the publicans of Derby and its neighbourhood, 28 at Ashbourne, 50 at Alfreton, and 220 of the gin-shop keepers of London petitioned Parliament some years ago, that all houses for the sale of spirits, wine, and beer, might be closed during the whole of the Sabbath. The speaking to these persons on the subject of the petition, had given to the clergymen, and others, an opportunity of having useful conversation with a class of men with whom they but seldom came into close contact on religious matters. It was mentioned that the number of licenses granted in 1859 was 137,804, and supposing that only two persons were engaged in each case, there were 275,608 persons deprived of the advantages of the Sabbath Day, by their unhallowed employment.

"'VII. That the late Meeting at Birmingham clearly shows that the majority of traders, and of the inhabitants generally, are willing to combine for the suppression of Sunday trading, and that, in cases where such majority call upon the local authorities to protect the rest of the many against the selfishness of the few, it is possible to put in force the present law against Sunday trading; and, therefore, that similar movements in other towns should be originated.'

"It was considered particularly important that the petitions to Parliament should mention an address to the Queen for the enforcement by the London and country authorities of the present law against Sunday Trading. There is an almost universal feeling amongst tradesmen of all descriptions that they should be protected from the unfair competition of others, and that where the present law is defective it should be amended, so as to secure to all the opportunity of enjoying the rest and other privileges of the Lord's Day.

"The case of Birmingham is as follows:—In September last out of 7000 shops, 1689 were opened on the Lord's Day. The Watch Committee of the Town Council thought it right to endeavour to put a stop to this desecration. Some conversation took place in that committee which was reported in the public papers. A few friends combined together, and in the course of two or three days 2500 shopkeepers, many of whom were Sunday traders, memorialized the Watch Committee to enforce the law, they being supported by a similar memorial signed by about 1500 Sunday School Teachers. The Watch Committee published a respectful request, signed by the Superintendents of Police, to the shopkeepers, to keep their shops closed on the Sunday. This was the first note of warning: 800 shopkeepers at once complied. A second placard was issued, warning those who persevered in opening of the consequences of doing so, and one-half of the remainder also complied. Up to this time nothing was done in the way of issuing summonses, or laying informations against tradesmen. The result was that the chief Superintendent of Police reported to the Watch Committee that in one Sunday in April last there were not fifty shops open in Birmingham. There was a memorial from 200 butchers, praying the Watch Committee to enforce the law, and assuring them that their own trade was almost unanimous in favour of its enforcement.

"It was stated at the Conference that the London Society had used every effort to prevent the passing of Lord Chelmsford's bill against Sunday trading, which, although well intended by that justly respected nobleman, would, if it had passed, have rendered legal the doing of several things on Sunday which it is now illegal to do. It would have legalized the sale of newspapers, periodicals, provisions, &c., &c., during certain hours of the Sabbath Day. If the bill should be again brought forward in its objectionable shape, which there is some fear of, the London Committee rely on their friends throughout the country uniting with them in opposing it by all means in their power. The petitions to Parliament and the letters to Members were of the greatest use in defeating it in the Commons, after it had passed the House of Lords.

"At Derby the Municipal Authorities have frequently, when applied to, interfered on behalf of the observance of the Lord's Day; and the different traders have sent distinct petitions to Parliament for the prohibition of all Sunday Trading.

"In London the keeping open of shops, and the hawking and crying of goods on the Lord's Day prevail to a very great extent. Whole streets of shops are open, and some markets, and hundreds of people are buying and selling as on other days. The voice of the nation should be brought to bear on the authorities, to arouse them to put a stop to these sinful and demoralizing proceedings.

"Monday and Saturday Fairs and Markets lead to much Sabbath desecration in many parts of the country, and it was suggested that power might be given to the Municipal Authorities, or to the Magistrates assembled in Quarter Sessions, to alter such Fair and Market days, whenever they might think it necessary to do so. The lateness of the Saturday Markets in some Towns was particularly spoken of, as leading to much profanation of the Lord's Day.

"'VIII. That this Conference would recommend the formation, wherever it may be possible, of Working Men's Sabbath Defence Committees, as Auxiliaries of local Associations.'

"It was stated that there is a deep conviction in the minds of a large mass of the working classes of this country, of the great advantages to them of the Sabbath Day. At Leeds, ten

years ago, the fight against the delivery of letters on the Lord's
Day was chiefly conducted by the working classes, and it was
mentioned at the conference, that the feeling of great bodies of
the working men of this country is exceedingly favourable towards
the attempting the formation of such Societies as those recommended in the Resolution.

"'IX. That this Conference is of opinion that it is of the greatest
importance that friends throughout the country should endeavour to
furnish the London Secretary with information as to the various kinds
of labour in their respective neighbourhoods prevalent on the Lord's Day,
in order that correct information relative to Sabbath desecration may be
circulated as widely as possible.'

"Amongst other objects of this Resolution, one appeared to
be that some correct idea might be arrived at as to what were,
or were not, works of necessity or mercy. There was a question
as to whether there was any part of the process of malting, which
ought to be done, as a work of necessity, on the Lord's Day.

"'X. That this Conference would solemnly protest against the admission of shareholders to the Crystal Palace on the Lord's Day, as being
a violation of the spirit, if not of the letter, of the charter of the company; while working men, among others, are thus enticed from Christian
worship, giving rise to the employment of labour at those places.'

"In the charter given by Government it was intended to be
very distinctly stated that the Crystal Palace was not to be
opened on the Lord's Day. The special object was to prevent
its being a temptation to working men to profane that day. But
great efforts have been made by the Sunday League and others
to turn to account the decision of the Vice-Chancellor that the
shareholders have a right to visit their own property on that day.
The £5 shares now sell for about thirty shillings, and they have
formed clubs amongst working men by means of which, when a
man has subscribed a few shillings, and is successful in drawing
a ticket, he may go at once, as a shareholder, to the Crystal Palace
on the Lord's Day. Very great efforts have been made by the
London Society to oppose the various attempts made to desecrate
the day. They have urged shareholders throughout the country
to oppose *all* opening on the Lord's Day which employs numbers
of men at the Palace and on the railways. It is clear that the
Company loses by this system, but their evident view is to work

for the opening of the Crystal Palace to the public generally on the Lord's Day.

"The Parent Society in London are most anxious that their friends throughout the country should use every effort to counteract the insidious efforts of the opponents of Sabbath Observance : some by purchasing shares and attending the half-yearly meetings of the Company, and all by petitioning Parliament, and by urging their members to assist in passing a measure which shall keep the Company to the spirit, as well as to the letter of their charter. On the first occasion that a proposition was made at the half-yearly meeting to close the Crystal Palace on the Lord's Day, out of 64,000 votes polled, about 24,000 were in favour of it. The next year, when 170,000 votes were recorded, the opponents had a majority of 17,000.

"There were presented during the session of 1853, chiefly from working men, 764 petitions, with 165,757 signatures against the opening of the Crystal Palace on the Lord's Day: in favour of it only 119 petitions, with 23,081 signatures. Amongst the most remarkable of the former was one signed exclusively by those connected with cabs and omnibuses, which had nearly 2000 signatures attached to it. Seventy chaplains of prisons, and 640 medical men of London, petitioned against the opening.

"'XI. That this Conference would strenuously promote the movement for obtaining the earlier payment of wages, the earlier closing of shops, and a general Saturday half-holiday, in order to procure for the people time for all lawful secular enjoyment without encroaching upon the rest of the Lord's Day.'

"This Resolution was considered by the Conference to be one of the very greatest importance, in connexion with the proper observance of the Lord's Day, and it was recommended that all employers of labour should be urged never to pay wages at the public-house, which is not an uncommon practice, particularly in large towns, and that they should also be solicited to pay their workmen on some earlier day of the week than Saturday. In many parts of the kingdom, where wages are paid on the Saturday evening, it often leads to the husband taking his wages home at a very late hour, which is the occasion of the wives going to the shops, and to the Butchers' Market as late as Twelve o'Clock on the Saturday night, so that some of the tradespeople do not get to rest till Two o'Clock or later on the Sunday morning, and the late payment of wages also leads to the buying and selling of bread, meat, and vegetables on the Sunday. It was mentioned that, in most places in Derby, wages are paid earlier than they used to be, few of the mill owners paying their hands later than Two o'clock on Saturday; the Railway men are paid on Thursday. Some years ago the Derbyshire Lord's Day Society invited the Clergy and Churchwardens of every parish in Derby to a Conference on this very subject, when it was determined to ask the Mayor to summon a meeting to consider it, and although the meeting was not attended by a great many persons, a paper was agreed upon, which many of the leading firms afterwards signed, expressing the intention of paying wages, for the future, on an earlier day than Saturday. With regard to early closing, and a weekly half-holiday, and now and then a whole holiday, it was argued that the working men must see that those were their best friends who sought to gain these advantages for them, and also to secure to them the whole of the Sabbath Day.

" It was stated that the Saturday half-holiday prevails in the large Manufacturing Towns, as the Factories are under the Factory Act, and all the Mills must be closed at Two o'Clock on the Saturday. It was thought that the provisions of that Act might well be extended to other branches of trade; a commission has just been appointed to see if it cannot be extended to Nottingham.

" The printers and others employed at the Art Journal Office used to work till Seven o'clock on the Saturday evening, and they got up a request to their employer to allow them to leave off work at Four, and they would make the time up. This was acceded to; the men became more regular in their attendance on the Monday, and the arrangement turned out so much to the advantage of the employer, that of his own accord he closed the establishment at Two o'clock on Saturdays, and from that time to this (it is four years ago) the practice has been continued without asking the men to make up the two hours. There has been a very great increase of temperance amongst the men of the establishment; their wives often meet them when they leave work at Two o'clock, and they go away together, and the money which used to be spent at the public-house is spent in a much better manner. Price's Candle Works are closed all the year round at Half-past Twelve on Saturday Afternoon.

"'XII. That it should be most distinctly understood that the Lord's Day Society and its Auxiliaries have always repudiated the idea of what has been termed the "making men religious by Act of Parliament:" and that all they seek from the Government and from the Legislature is, that all public violation of the Lord's Day by which Almighty God is dishonoured, should be put down, and that every subject of the realm should, as far as is possible, have it secured to him as a day of rest, in order that he may have the *opportunity* of serving his God according to the dictates of his conscience: and further that works of necessity, mercy, and piety ought freely to be performed on that day; the Sabbath, according to the Divine authority, being "made for man and not man for the Sabbath."'

"There are vast numbers of conscientious or well-disposed butchers, bakers, greengrocers, and other tradesmen who are most anxious to be protected against the unfair competition of their less scrupulous neighbours, and it was strongly urged that opportunities should be afforded to them of making their wants known to the Government and Parliament in distinct petitions and memorials.

"'XIII. That it is most desirable that *every* desecration of the Lord's Day should, in some way or other, be met and contended with, as by such a course Almighty God will be most honoured in the sight of all men, and the exertions which are made to suppress each will have a most beneficial effect in helping forward similar exertions with regard to other desecrations.'

"When the Conference Meeting was first proposed and arranged it was with a view to *every* desecration of the Lord's Day being constantly grappled with, either by private advice and remonstrance, or by books, or sermons, &c., and, in some cases, by petitions and memorials. At the Conference one of the speakers observed—'I feel very thankful with regard to this Meeting, that it is convened for the purpose of considering how we can bring to light and try to remedy *all* the various desecrations of the Lord's Day.' It had been the opinion of many, that for some time ground had been lost by only or chiefly contending against the fresh aggressions on the sanctity of the day, and that had there been continuous and combined action against all Sabbath desecration on the part of those who value the Sabbath,

some of the dreadful profanations of the day which now exist
would hardly have been attempted, or, if they had been attempted,
would, with God's blessing, have been speedily put down.

"'XIV. That it is of the greatest importance to the success of the
movement that addresses be presented to the Queen, and petitions from
all classes be forwarded *every Session* to *both* Houses of Parliament, praying her Majesty and the Legislature to use their influence to promote
the due observance of the Lord's Day, and particularly that distinct petitions, &c., be promoted from all classes of tradesmen, and others who,
under the present system, are deprived either wholly or in part of the
rest and other privileges of that Holy Day; that by the publicity given
to the presentation of these petitions in *both* Houses the public mind may
be informed, and the friends of Sabbath Observance be stimulated to
fresh and continued efforts, when they thus become acquainted with the
feelings of others in every part of the country.'

" It was mentioned at the Conference that petitioning Parliament, each session, was considered by many of those who had
worked hard to promote a better observance of the Lord's Day,
as one of the indispensable means of stirring up and keeping
alive, throughout the Country, an active interest in the combined
and continued effort which the Conference desired to promote.
It was stated also that the late Sir Andrew Agnew had declared,
when he was no longer a member of Parliament, that the friends
of the Sabbath cause should *load* the tables of both Houses with
petitions *every year*, though they might have no one prepared to
propose any measure in either of them. The pressure would
have a most beneficial effect upon the members and upon the
Government. It is obvious that if petitions are only addressed
to the Commons, one half of the publicity which might be gained
would be lost. Addresses to the Queen, if sent up in large
numbers, will also have their effect upon the Government. Important addresses may be read to her Majesty by any Peer, who
can demand a private audience for that purpose. There was one
instance in which this was done in the late reign, in connexion
with the profanation of the Lord's Day.

" In this combined effort, the friends of the cause should seek
earnestly to promote petitions, &c., from every parish around
them ; if all will try and exert their influence in this and in other
ways, and make a long pull and a strong pull, and a pull al-

together, as one of the letters mentioned, then great results may, through God's blessing the effort, be fully expected.

" ' XV. That those who take part in this movement be requested, from time to time whenever occasion may require it, to communicate with their own representatives and such other members of the Legislature as they may be acquainted with, begging them to use all their influence, both in and out of Parliament, in endeavouring to withstand the torrent of Sabbath profanation, which is setting in on the land.'

" The importance of thus writing to members, and of getting friends to do the same, is very great. Separate and not joint letters should be addressed to them. Even the letter of one individual has been known to lead his representative to interest himself about the measure mentioned to him. A member thinks much of a friendly communication from any individual constituent, and will take much trouble to comply with his wishes, if he can do so conscientiously. It often happens that, owing to the multiplicity of parliamentary and other printed papers which he receives, a member would overlook or forget a particular measure which was coming on, were he not reminded of it by the letter of his constituent.

" ' XVI. That the holding of annual Meetings in all the Towns and Parishes of the Country, be strongly recommended as one great mean of diffusing information as to the objects and proceedings of the Lord's Day Society; and of exciting and keeping up an interest in them.'

" It was found in Derbyshire in the year 1833, and in the two following years, that these meetings in the towns and villages were every were numerously attended, and excited general interest. In this way much information on the Divine authority and obligations of the Lord's Day was diffused, and petitions were sent to Parliament on the subject of its due observance from several thousands of persons. Many who did not at first see the use of petitions readily joined in them after the meetings. Many of the meetings were held in the churches because the school-rooms were not large enough to hold the numbers who were expected. Associations may be formed and funds collected at these meetings. The facts related at them on the subject of the profanation and observance of the Lord's Day were known in several instances to have a beneficial effect on those who were present.

"'XVII. That it is very important to make constant use of the Public Press by getting Articles and Paragraphs inserted in the local and other papers.'

"It was considered that much information may be thus diffused throughout each neighbourhood, and that it may be spread still more widely, by sending papers, or slips from them to correspondents, who would be likely to get them inserted in their Country Newspapers.

"'XVIII. That it be suggested to the friends of this movement, that it is desirable there should be sound books and tracts on the subject of the Christian Sabbath at the booksellers' shops in the various towns throughout the country, so that they may be easily procured by all who feel a desire for such publications.'

"This was mentioned as having been proposed by one of the friends, who could not attend in person; according to his suggestion the names and prices of several works on Sabbath observance are here given:—The late Bishop of Calcutta's "Seven Sermons on the Lord's Day," 3s. 6d., Seeley. Hill's "Essay on the Sabbath," 8s.; with Marginal References, 10s. 6d. (both strongly recommended at the Conference.) The Publications of the London Lord's Day Society. "The Week Complete," 1s. 6d.; all in boards. There appear to be several tracts on the subject, on the lists of the Society for Promoting Christian Knowledge, and of the Religious Tract Society. At one time, the Derbyshire Society employed a man, who circulated in the course of some months 17,000 tracts on the subject of Sabbath observance, to Coach Passengers, thus spreading information. "History of the Sabbath," by the Rev. John Baylee, late Secretary of the London Lord's Day Society; published by subscription, and printed for the Author by C. F. Hogdson, 1, Gough Square, Fleet Street; a very valuable work in connexion with the present movement. "The Pearl of Days," and other prize works on the Lord's Day.

"'XIX. That it may be desirable at times for Country Associations to send copies of important papers not only to the Secretaries of other Associations, but also to the Members of the Government and of both Houses of Parliament.'

"The Derbyshire Society have expended a large proportion of their funds in this way, and feel assured that much benefit has arisen from their having thus endeavoured to diffuse information. The London Society should be supplied with interesting facts connected with Sabbath observance, that they may be inserted in their quarterly paper.

Several subjects, more or less considered by the Conference, appear not to be properly connected with any of the above resolutions. It is therefore thought better to take them separately.

"SUNDAY BANDS are considered a very great evil. They draw numbers of young persons away from the schools and public worship to congregate in the parks, or in the barrack yards. The regimental bands have been withdrawn from the parks, consequent upon a memorial to her Majesty's Government, supported by various representations from the country; and now there are in the parks only bands paid for by public subscription, the Sunday League taking an interest in the matter. The Government have refused to interfere with them, and even permit them, contrary to the law, to sell bills containing the programme of the performance. One thing, the Commissioners of Works have yielded after opposing it for a long time. They appear to have been somewhat ashamed of its being said of them that they allowed crowds to gather in the parks round political demagogues, and to gather round musicians playing secular tunes, but not to collect round the preachers of the Gospel, and the police received orders before the last summer, no longer to interfere with the open air preaching. Missionaries from the City Mission and others had been listened to with great attention. The commanding officer of a regiment quartered in York on being applied to not to permit the Sunday band playing, said the Queen allowed her band to play at Windsor on the Sunday, and he did not see why the band of his regiment should not play also on Sunday.

"The Volunteer Bands play through the streets, on their way to church, and draw a great rabble after them; it was hoped that in many cases private representation might prevent this, and the playing also of the Regimental Bands; in the event of that not succeeding, application might be made to the Secretary for War. It was urged that the Sunday Bands at Windsor, and in the Parks, &c., should be continually mentioned in the petitions sent to the Legislature, and in the letters sent to Members.

"THE CLOSING OF PUBLIC LIBRARIES AND NEWS ROOMS— At Sheffield, about two years ago, an attempt was made to open the Free Library on the Lord's Day; the Clergy were alarmed, and took the matter up warmly, a Sermon was preached in the Parish Church, a Memorial was sent to the Town Council, and there was a good deal of excitement in the town on the subject; the result was, that the proposition was withdrawn.

"At Derby, several years ago, when a Town and County Library and News-rooms were set on foot, it was proposed at a meeting of about 90 Subscribers, that they should be closed during the whole of the Lord's Day. There was much opposition to this, and speech after speech was made against the proposal, and those who were anxious for the due observance of the day, began to fear that they would be left in a minority. On a division taking place, there were eighty in favour of the proposition, and nine only against it.

"PRINTING on the Lord's Day is supposed to prevail to a very considerable extent in London, and in the larger Towns, Newspapers and Periodicals being regularly prepared and printed on that day. It was hoped by the Conference that some plan might be adopted, by which the Publishers might be induced to honour Almighty God, in this matter, and set those whom they employ at liberty from their sinful occupations.

"SUNDAY FUNERALS—When this subject was introduced at the Conference, it created some alarm in the minds of several of the members, and it was agreed to let it drop, but since then the following paragraph has appeared in the newspapers, and the Derbyshire committee think, that had the members of the Conference been aware of the state of things mentioned in the paragraph, they would have dealt differently with the subject.

"*Sunday Funerals*—A letter in the *Patriot* says—'The discontinuance of Sunday funerals in the metropolis has for a long time been attempted, and not without considerable success—the Directors of all the principal incorporated Cemetery Companies having resolved that no interment shall take place in their respective cemeteries on the Sabbath-day. The Burial Board of Camberwell have signified, during the present year, their readiness to co-operate with other Parochial Boards in a general arrangement to close; and it is believed that in some other parishes a similar desire exists. In the parish of St. Mary, Islington, it is pleaded by the Burial Board that they have not the power to refuse the application of a parishioner to bury his relative on the Sunday; and yet, strange to say, they have that power (if the exercise of it is any proof) in the case of Good Friday and Christmas Day, when no interments are allowed. In the parish where I lived, the Clerk of the Burial Board has refused to receive from me an order for interment on Good Friday, and at the same time accepted it for Easter Sunday.'

" It was stated that the Clergy were bound by law to bury on the Sunday, if required to do so; but that, all over the Country, Sunday Funerals led to the loss of the whole or a considerable portion of the privileges of the day, by the Undertakers and others : and that, having all due and tender regard for the feelings of relatives, there could be no harm in trying to lead the public to consider the subject. An anecdote was related of an Undertaker who, at the close of a meeting in London to promote Sabbath observance, got up and said, 'Pray, gentlemen, do not forget the Undertakers in this matter.'

"It was mentioned by a clergyman, that on coming to his present parish, many years ago, the first Funeral was to have been on a Sunday, that he went to the relatives, and told them he was quite ready to perform the Service on the Sunday, if they felt strongly on the subject, but that he should feel obliged if they could with comfort change the day. This request was immediately acceded to, and it being known that he would prefer not having funerals on the Sunday, he had only had one, and that in a case of necessity, in the course of twenty years.

"The COUNTRY WAKES OR REVELS, which in many places commence on the Lord's Day, were mentioned as leading to very disgraceful scenes at the public houses, to which men and women, most of them of loose habits, resort on that day from the surrounding parishes. Public-house keepers had entered into agreements to close their houses on the Wake Sunday, and had broken through them. It was thought that if private remonstrance was of no avail, the magistrates in petty session, or at the quarter sessions, would possibly be enabled to check the evil, and might be led to act when they became acquainted with the sad profanation of the Lord's Day which prevailed on such occasions.

"The assembling of boys and lads on the outskirts of towns for PIGEON FLYING, PITCH AND TOSS, DOG FIGHTING, COCK FIGHTING, &c., would be put down by the magistrates and police, if they were applied to.

"With regard to SUNDAY CHEESE MAKING it was stated that in Cheshire many persons had given up that practice, that Mr. Storr had published a very useful pamphlet on the subject, and that one large landed proprietor had a clause introduced into every new lease, binding the tenant not to make cheese on the Lord's Day. It was thought by some that cheese making was a work of necessity in Derbyshire, as the cheeses were thinner than the Cheshire cheeses. But one of the speakers mentioned a case within his own knowledge, in which at a Derbyshire dairy farm, of upwards of 20 cows, no cheese-making had been allowed on the Lord's Day, and the cheese of that dairy had been sold at a very high price; the Sunday morning's milk having been only twice set up for butter during the season. Another similar case was mentioned, after the Meeting, in which the cheese had been also sold at a high price. It was hoped that the plan of not making cheese on the Lord's Day would at least meet with a fair trial from the Derbyshire farmers. (See the next chapter.)

"The practice of many Farmers was spoken of, who start their servant lads away to their homes, many miles distant, in the forenoon of the Lord's Day, to get their clean things, which generally ends in their going to no place of worship. It was thought that the Clergy might in many cases induce masters to make some different arrangement.

"The ATTENDANCE ON PUBLIC WORSHIP in Towns and Villages was said to be wholly neglected by numbers of the people. In a regular visiting of the Town of Derby, some years ago, there was found a large court in which none of the inhabitants attended any place of worship, and in another court only one family in ten professed to do so. Good has been effected in many places, by persons visiting, both on the Lord's Day, and on other days, and leaving tracts, on this, and other subjects. The holding of Week-day Cottage Lectures at different houses in the same locality, has brought people to the House of God.

"The Conference did not, of course, go into the subject of the

Divine authority, and the perpetual obligation of the Lord's Day, but more than one speaker expressed a feeling which was responded to by the whole meeting; a feeling of great thankfulness to God, that the Fourth Commandment is interwoven with the other Commandments, and forms a part of the service of the Church. One clergyman had received a pamphlet from London, through the post, gravely proposing to abolish the reading of the Decalogue in all the churches of the Land. It stated, that as long as the Commandments were read Sabbath after Sabbath in our churches, it would be in vain to hope that the people would fall into their notions of Sunday.

"Every point of any importance brought forward at the Conference is, it is believed, mentioned in this account. It has been found impossible to preserve any very regular order in drawing it up. The Derbyshire Committee would urge every one into whose hands it may come to endeavour at once to help forward this movement, in prayerful dependence upon God for a blessing on their efforts. As they have stated in a former paper, 'they fear that if the present desecrations of the Lord's Day are 'allowed to continue, the just judgments of the Almighty must be 'expected to be poured out upon this offending country, hitherto 'so highly honoured and blessed. On this ground it concerns 'every member of the community to render every possible assist- 'ance in suppressing the evil. If it be permitted to proceed, the 'present generation will also incur the guilt of handing down to 'their posterity a state of things with regard to the Sabbath very 'different from that orderly observance of it, for which, notwith- 'standing many grievous desecrations, this country has hitherto 'been so pre-eminent. Many of the habits of the people of this 'land with regard to the Lord's Day are becoming more and more 'assimilated to those of our continental neighbours, amongst 'whom the "holy Sabbath is polluted" by attendance at the 'theatres, and by dances and festivities, which prevail more on 'that day than on any other. One consequence of this profana- 'tion to the present inhabitants of this country and to their pos- 'terity, must surely be a similar increase amongst them of infidel 'or superstitious opinions, and eventually a total abandonment of 'true and vital religion. Let the people of this land beware of

'giving up one of their dearest birthrights, one of the best in-
'heritances which they can transmit to their children. May all
'who are in any way the promoters of Sabbath desecration reflect
'upon the awful responsibility which they incur; and may those
'who have hitherto been tempted, by the thoughtlessness, wicked-
'ness, or avarice of others, to deprive themselves of that day of
'holy rest which a merciful God has accorded to them, be induced
'to abstain from that which is so evil in the sight of their God,
'and to confine themselves to works of necessity, piety, and mercy,
'on the Lord's Day. May God of his great goodness send forth a
'spirit of repentance and reformation in this matter, on all classes
'of persons throughout the length and breadth of the land! May
'"they turn every man from his evil way." May they "hallow
'"God's Sabbaths, and they shall be a sign between Him and them,
'"that he is the Lord their God:" Ezekiel xx. 20. May they
'always remember that "righteousness exalteth a nation: but sin
'"is a reproach to any people."'"

CHAPTER XLIII.

1860.

FROM THE APPENDIX TO THE CONFERENCE REPORT.

Persons who attended the Conference—Address to the Queen on the Desecration of the Lord's Day by Foreign Princes and Statesmen—The Queen's Sunday Visit to Guernsey and Aldershot—Colonel Young on Sunday Railway Travelling—Sunday Cheese-making not a work of necessity—Address to the Queen—Petition for the Sunday closing of Public-houses—Females' Memorial to the Queen—Sunday School Teachers.

THE following portions of the Appendix to the foregoing account are here inserted in the hope that they may be interesting and instructive to many of the readers of these volumes, and may help to induce them to do what in them lies to help forward the observance of the Lord's Day, not only in their own neighbourhood, but in every direction throughout the country. A few forms of petition are inserted in the hope that some of them will be useful to those who may have it in their power to join, from time to time, in calling the attention of the Legislature to the importance of endeavouring to secure, as far as may be, the Lord's Day as a day of rest to every member of the community.

"*Names and Addresses of those who attended the Conference :—*

"Sir M. Blakiston, Bart., Ashbourne ; the Ven, the Archdeacon of Derby, Hasland, near Chesterfield ; William T. Cox, Esq., of Spondon, Mayor of Derby ; Rev. Henry Stevens, Secretary of the London Lord's Day Society ; Rev. Wm. Leeke, R. D., Holbrooke, near Derby, Hon. Secretary of the Derbyshire Lord's Day Society ;

Rev. Thomas W. Whitaker, R. D., Stanton-by-Bridge, Derby; Rev. R. Chandos Pole, Radbourne, Derby; Rev. R. Cox, Tickenhall; Rev. David Metcalf, Derby; Rev. C. Cameron, Trusley, Derbyshire; Rev. Thomas Sale, D. D., Vicar of Sheffield; Rev. Thomas Lund, Morton; Charles F. Dewe, Esq., Derby; Rev. Henry Gamble, Clifton, Ashbourne; Rev. James Brook, Helme, Huddersfield; Rev. John Hull, Poulton-le-Fylde; Rev. F. Parry, (late Incumbent of St. Clement's, Liverpool,) Derby; Rev. J. Garton Howard, Stanton-by-Dale Abbey, Derby; John Rand, Esq., Wheatley Hill, Bradford, Yorkshire; Rev. R. E. Roberts, Incumbent of St. George's, Barnsley; William Rand, Esq., Bradford, Yorkshire; Edw. Radford, Esq., Tansley Wood, near Matlock; Rev. F. C. Morton, Incumbent of Wadsley, Sheffield; John Borough, Esq., Derby; Robert Green, Esq., Milford House, Derby; Rev. John M. Webb, Swarkeston, near Derby; Rev. E. S. Greville, Bonsall; Rev. W. Findley, Willington; Rev. Henry M. Mosse, Heage; Rev. M. H. Etches, Hamstall, Rugeley; Rev. J. Magens Mello, Grove Bank, Derby; Rev. Henry Moore, Chaplain of the County Gaol, Derby; Rev. Warden Stubbs, Incumbent of Rocester; I. Clarke Sowter, Esq., Castle Donnington; Rev. Henry Linton, M. A., St. Paul's, Nottingham; Rev. C. J. Hamilton, Kimberworth, near Rotherham; Rev. H. R. Crewe, Breadsall; Rev. W. H. Barlow, Secretary of the Bristol and Clifton Lord's Day Association; Rev. J. Catchpole, Clifton, Ashbourne; T. P. Bainbrigge, Esq., Derby; Rev. J. G. Croker, Brailsford; Colonel Robert Holden, Nuttall, Nottingham; Captain H. Young, Bedford; L. E. Mann, Esq., Hazlebrow, Belper; R. C. Hankinson, Esq., Derby; Rowland Smith, Esq., Duffield Hall, Derby; Rev. John Denton, Ashby-de-la-Zouch; Rev. C. E. L. Wightman, Shrewsbury; Rev. R. Macklin, Derby; John Cockayne, Abbey Cottage, Derby; Rev. John N. Worsfold, Wellington Parsonage, Hanley, Staffordshire; Rev. A. Slight, Alkmonton Parsonage, Derby; William Briddon, Esq., Uttoxeter-road, Derby; William Ogle, Esq., M. D., Derby; J. B. Miller, Esq., Liverpool; Richard Sale, Esq., Normanton, near Derby; Rev. James Bardsley, Manchester; Rev. William H. Bathurst, Darley-dale; Geo. Beaumont, Esq., Bridgeford Hill, near Nottingham; Rev. John Connington, Southwell, Notts.; Rev. Josh. J. Miller, Blore, Ashbourne; Rev. Richard

Mosley, Rotherham; Rev. F. I. Jones, Darley Abbey, Derby; Rev. John G. Bourne, Castle Donnington; Rev. Henry Cheetham, Quarndon; Rev. Philip Gell, Duffield-bank, Derby; Rev. Gerard Smith, Osmaston-by-Ashbourne; Rev. T. Green, R. D., Rector of of Cubley, Derbyshire; Rev. James Chancellor, St. John's, Derby; Rev. Wm. Morris Colles, Curate of Melton Mowbray; Rev. G. F. Williamson, Longnor, Buxton; Rev. Wm. Jones, Burton-upon-Trent; Rev. Melville Holmes, Tansley, Matlock; S. H. Evans, Esq., Derby; Rev. E. W. Foley, Derby; Rev. Charles Evans, Worcester; Rev. A. A. Holden, Spondon, Derby.

" Desecration of the Lord's Day in this Country by Foreign Princes and Statesmen.

"The following address was forwarded for presentation to her Majesty, in 1844, from the Committee of the Derbyshire Society for Promoting the Due Observance of the Lord's Day:—

"'We, your Majesty's loyal and dutiful subjects, beg leave thus 'humbly to approach your Majesty, with the expression of our anx-'iety in a matter which compromises, in no small degree, that ob-'servance of the Lord's Day for which this nation, notwithstanding 'many grievous desecrations, is still so pre-eminent. We allude 'to the habit of many distinguished Foreign Princes and Statesmen, 'who, on visiting this country, have made that holy day their day 'of arrival or departure, or of travelling about, thereby occasion-'ing, at times, much unnecessary employment to your Majesty's 'Military and Naval Officers, and others; and setting an example 'of evil tendency to all classes in this land, in regard to the com-'mand of our God, to " keep holy the Sabbath Day." We have 'seen with gratitude, that for several years past, in accordance 'with the petitions of your loyal subjects, your Majesty's Minis-'ters have altogether abstained from the holding of Cabinet 'Councils, and the giving of Public Dinners on the Lord's Day; 'and we now humbly pray your Majesty to use your Royal influ-'ence for the prevention of that desecration of the day to which 'we have ventured to solicit your attention, and also of all other 'infringements on that due observance of it which so much pro-'motes that righteousness which alone exalteth a nation. We 'earnestly pray that He who is King of kings, and Lord of lords,

' may vouchsafe to your Majesty all spiritual and temporal hap-
' piness.

'J. G. HOWARD, Chairman.'"

*Extract from the Preface to the Rev. W. Brock's Sermon on the
Queen's Sunday Visit to Guernsey.*

"Christianity is part and parcel of the law of the land. It
is the basis on which our Protestant Constitution in Church and
State rests. The Throne itself is founded upon it, and
it can only be established in righteousness, when our gracious
Sovereign, and all who are in authority under her, are observant
of its sacred obligations. Happily, by the good hand of our God
upon us, and by His blessing upon our land, we are favoured in
this country with the high and inestimable privilege of a virtuous
Court ; and we can boast of a Sovereign who, in her public duties,
as well as in her domestic life, has presented a pattern which all
her subjects would do well to imitate. But in proportion to the
exemplary life, and the generous and confiding nature of our
gracious Queen, it will be held to be undutiful and unmanly for
her responsible advisers, or her representatives in any place, to
press upon her adoption a course which would be alike at variance
with the laws of God and the established religion of the country.

" It is generally supposed that on the occasion to which reference is made in the following pages, the Queen was induced to
forego her resolution *not* to visit Guernsey on the Lord's Day, by
the urgent representations of ———. There can be no question
that the first thoughts of her Majesty, under the circumstances
of the case, were right : and had she been permitted to act up to
her own convictions, she would not have landed during the hours
of divine service ; nor would she have sanctioned the act of ———
in calling the militia of the island from the worship of the King
of kings, to do honour to their earthly Sovereign. It is a melancholy fact that the worship of Almighty God was neglected, the
churches during the afternoon and evening services were deserted,
the Sunday-schools were empty, and the mass of the inhabitants
of the island were kept in a ferment of excitement, and in many
cases exposed to toil and labour during the hallowed hours of the
Sabbath, in consequence of the visit of her Majesty. Surely

every Christian patriot must deplore this. All the forms of British government, whether Civil, Military, or Ecclesiastical, are connected with the worship of Almighty God and the solemn observances of the Christian religion. In the royal proclamations which are periodically issued for the encouragement of piety and virtue, the Sovereign acknowledges that she 'cannot 'expect the blessing and goodness of Almighty God, by whom 'kings and queens reign, and on which she entirely relies to make 'her reign happy and prosperous to herself and her people, with- 'out a religious observance of God's holy laws.' She proclaims to all her loving subjects 'that for the encouragement of religion 'and morality she will, upon all occasions, distinguish persons of 'piety and virtue by marks of her royal favour; and that she 'expects and requires that all persons of honour, or in place of 'authority, will give good example by their own virtue and piety.' She 'commands them, and every one of them, decently and 'reverently to attend the worship of God on every Lord's Day, on 'pain of her highest displeasure:' and she further 'strictly charges 'all her judges, mayors, sheriffs, justices of the peace, and all her 'officers and ministers, both ecclesiastical and civil, and all other 'her subjects whom it may concern, to be very vigilant and strict 'in the discovery, and in the effectual prosecution and punish- 'ment of all persons who shall be guilty of profanation of the 'Lord's Day, or other dissolute, immoral, or disorderly practices.' Nor are the religious duties of her military and naval servants overlooked by her Majesty in her proclamations. Her last words are addressed to all her 'Commanders and Officers whatsoever, 'that they take care to avoid all profaneness, and that they set 'good examples to all such as are under their authority.'

"The author respectfully recommends the salutary counsels of the royal proclamation to the attention of —— at Guernsey, and to —— at Aldershot, by whose pressing solicitations it is understood that her Majesty was induced to visit the camp on the Lord's Day, contrary to her own inclination. He may also be permitted to remark, that if some of her Majesty's Judges of Assize were to have their notice called to the terms of this proclamation, they might possibly deem it expedient for the future, if not out of regard to their Almighty Judge, at least out of respect to her

Majesty, whose commission they hold, and whose laws they are pledged to execute, 'decently and reverently to attend the worship 'of God on the Lord's Day' whilst they are on circuit, according to the commands of their Sovereign, instead of setting an example of its profanation, by going out fishing, or pleasuring in the Lake Districts, on Sunday morning, while the Sheriffs and her Majesty's loyal and dutiful subjects are at church. It is the author's painful conviction that the state is endangered, and the throne of these realms is being undermined, by the spread of popish and infidel principles, which weaken the bands of our national piety and virtue, and place in jeopardy our national prosperity, by striking at the sanctity of our national Sabbath; and, therefore, as a loyal subject of 'our religious and gracious Queen,' and as an ardent patriot, no less than as a Christian and a minister of the Gospel, he has thought it his duty to raise his feeble voice on this occasion."

Accidents on Railways, and the Lord's Day.

"SIR,—In your number of December 3rd, you have called attention in a leading article to a letter in *The Times* by Mr. Thomas Wrigley, on the subject of railway accidents. The suggestions of Mr. W. deserve the serious attention of Railway Companies. It can scarcely be doubted, that 'a code of railway 'laws, made binding by Government on every line in the king-'dom,' would, 'if duly observed,' be a great boon to travellers; but I take the liberty of demurring to your statement, that it would 'make next to impossible the occurrence of catastrophes' similar to the late Trent Valley disaster. The wisest code of laws which human ingenuity can devise, enforced by the most stringent regulations, must fail to ensure that amount of security from avoidable catastrophes which the public have a right to expect, as long as the servants of the Company are deprived of their Sabbath rest. I say this, not merely on the ground—true though it is—that a continued and open defiance of God's commandment must bring with it retributive penalties even in this world, but on the lower ground of the physical nature of man requiring a seventh day's release from continuous toil; which boon cannot be denied him without serious detriment to his usefulness as a living machine, possessed of reason and con-

science, as well as of bone and muscle, nor without guilt as well
as folly on the part of the employer.   But the avaricious master
knows of no responsibility beyond the commercial code; he has
made the utmost of his machine, while it could work to profit,
and when it is worn out, and is no longer of use as an instrument of mammon, he throws it aside and procures another, to
be treated in the same way.   Thus, in many departments of
business, mammon has its victims prematurely cut off by the
hard bondage of Sabbathless toil; but these murders—for such
they are in the eyes of the Great Heart-searcher—excite no
public attention, they do not disturb our social self-complacency.
But the case is very different with railway delinquencies; when
the overtasked powers of muscles or brain of the guard, or
driver, or other servant, fail him at the critical moment, a fearful
collision is the consequence, society is alarmed, the shrieks of
mangled victims seem to strike upon its ear, and to awaken the
consciousness of individual danger;   inquests are held, and heavy
penalties are imposed upon all who can be proved to share, however remotely, in the blame.   But I hesitate not to say, that
under the present system of Sunday trains, no considerable
diminution of what are called accidents can be reasonably looked
for, whatever rules be adopted.   If clearness of head, steadiness
of eye and hand, in short, perfect bodily and mental integrity,
together with, let me add, a clear conscience, be requisite in any
employment, it is emphatically so in the railway service; where
the lives of hundreds may be sacrificed through the negligence
or recklessness of one man.

"It must be borne in mind, that the want of the seventh
day's rest may tell upon the poor servant on any day of the
week, as well as on the Sabbath; thus, the entire community,
those who have a conscience in relation to Sunday trains, as
well as those who have none, are exposed to the dangers resulting from the cupidity of shareholders seeking larger dividends
by holding out inducements for Sunday pleasure trips.   When,
to the moral and physical deterioration of the servants by this
systematic defiance of the judgments of God, be added the
temptations placed in their way, by the facility with which they
can procure intoxicating drinks, which Directors, with an in-

fatuation almost amounting to suicidal folly, permit to be sold at every refreshment-room on their line, the wonder rather is, that a single day passes without the occurrence of some appalling calamity. Truly our God is long-suffering.

"I venture to recommend to Christians the practice of a venerable servant of God, who, on entering a railway carriage, used silently to commend himself and fellow-travellers to the special protection of the Lord. "Faithfully yours,

"Bedford, December 7th, 1860. "H. Young."

"Soon after the Conference, the Derbyshire Lord's Day Society passed the following Resolution:—

"'That this Society do present to the Derbyshire Agricultural Society Ten Guineas, to be offered by them as a prize for the best dairy of cheese from any farm on which none is made on the Sunday, to be competed for by persons not keeping less than twenty cows for the purpose of cheese-making; much preference being given to those, who during the season use in their cheese the largest number of Sunday meals or milkings.'

"Some of the Committee and other friends of Sabbath Observance have subscribed funds for additional prizes, and the prize list about to be issued by the Derbyshire Agricultural Society, will include the following, for the best Cheese not made on Sundays:—

"'Large dairy of 20 cows and upwards—1st prize, £10 10s.; dairymaid £1. Given by the Derbyshire Society for Promoting the Due Observance of the Lord's Day. 2nd, £5; dairy-maid, 10s. By subscription.

"'Under 20 cows, and not less than 10—1st, £5; dairy-maid. £1. Given by Wm. Thos. Cox, Esq., of Spondon, High Sheriff. 2nd, £3; dairy-maid, 10s. By subscription.

"'Under 10 cows—1st, £3; dairy-maid, £1. By subscription. 2nd, £2; dairy maid, 10s. By subscription.'

"The following Prize has been offered by a few friends of the Derbyshire Society for Promoting the Observance of the Lord's Day, at the Agricultural Show in September, 1866:—

"'Cheese of not less than 1 cwt., made by the Exhibitor in 1866, to be competed for only by those persons, who being Members of the Derbyshire Agricultural Society, shall not have made any Cheese on the Sunday after the 17th of June, 1866, £5. To the Dairy-maid who makes the Cheese, £1. None of the Cheese to be bored or tasted previous to Exhibition.'

"The following is from the Derby papers of September, 1865 :—

"'SUNDAY CHEESE-MAKING.—The following fact will be interesting to those who maintain that the making of cheese on Sunday is not a work of necessity. At the late Derbyshire Agricultural Show, the terms of competition for the prize given for cheese from farms on which no cheese-making takes place on Sunday, were such this year as to allow of cheese competing which had not the Sunday's milk in it. The Rev. W. Leeke, of Holbrooke, sent in from the same dairy two batches of cheese of 1 cwt. each, the one being made on Mondays, and having the Sundays' milk in it, the other being made from the milk of some of the other days of the week. The judges, without knowing anything about the cheese, after some deliberation, awarded the prize to that batch which contained the Sundays' milk. It was thought that the cheese, which was made from the milk of 25 cows, was very good. The prize-money (£5, with £1 for the dairy-woman) will be given back to the society to be competed for another year.

"'Mr. Leeke has only ordinary dairy accommodation.'

"The Derbyshire Committee think the following Forms of Petition, &c., or portions of them, may be found useful by some of their friends at a distance, when preparing their own petitions. They therefore venture to add them to this document :—

"'*To the Queen's Most Excellent Majesty.*

"'The humble and loyal Address of the undersigned Clergy 'of the Archdeaconry of Derby.

"'We, your Majesty's most dutiful and loyal Subjects, beg 'leave thus to approach your Royal Person, with the assurance 'of our unfeigned loyalty and affection, desiring to express to 'your Majesty the grief and alarm with which we view the sys- 'tematic and extended desecration of the Lord's Day by all 'classes of your Majesty's Subjects.

"'We desire to avow to your Majesty our solemn conviction, 'formed on the unerring Word of God, of the Divine appoint- 'ment of that day from the era of the Creation, when the Lord 'rested on the seventh day from all His work which He had 'made, and blessed the seventh day and sanctified it; that we 'are also persuaded of its universal and perpetual obligation, 'from the circumstance of its forming a part of the moral law, 'afterwards delivered by Jehovah himself; and also more subse-

'quently from the Divine Lawgiver, our Lord Jesus Christ, who
'is over all God blessed for ever, expounding that law, and
'asserting, as Lord of the Sabbath, that works of necessity and
'mercy should be performed on that day, by which assertion he
'did enforce the moral part of the commandment, implicitly pro-
'hibit all other works, and clearly show that the Sabbath was
'made for man and not man for the Sabbath. And lastly, from
'the example and practice of the early disciples of the Lord
'Jesus, who, when the day of rest was changed to the first day
'of the week in honour of the Saviour's Resurrection, and on the
'authority of the divinely inspired Apostles, always kept that
'day "holy to the Lord."

"'We can by no means consent to the opinions stated by
'some, that the observation of the Lord's Day, whether in whole
'or in part, is a matter of expediency, thereby subjecting the
'observance of that day to the caprice, or convenience, or will of
'man. We conceive, to use the words of that Church of which
'we are ministers, that "no Christian man whatsoever is free
'"from the obedience of the Commandments which are moral,"
'and we claim for the Fourth Commandment an equal sanction
'with every other in the Decalogue; and for the Lord, His use
'and service, one whole and entire day in seven.

"'We desire to express to your Majesty our opinion as
'ministers of the Word of God, that the devout observance of
'the Lord's Day tends greatly to promote the glory of God and
'the happiness of man; that therein provision is made for the
'propagation of true and undefiled religion, for the godly edifying
'in faith and love of Christ's Holy Catholic Church; that the
observance of this day from a principle of faith is a mark or
'sign of our love to Christ, and a part of that righteousness
'which exalteth a nation; and that the profanation of this day
'tends only to the increase of impiety, profligacy, and every kind of
'vice, and is an awful feature of the sin which is a reproach to
'any people.

"'We would humbly entreat your Majesty's gracious atten-
'tion to the following grievous desecrations of the Lord's Day:
'the circulation throughout the country of Sunday journals, the
'keeping open of shops and public-houses, the plying of boats

'and vessels on canals and rivers, and the running of railway
'trains for the purpose of traffic or pleasure, the transmission of
'the mails and the delivery of letters, by all of which desecra-
'tions multitudes of persons are deprived of the privileges of the
'Lord's Day, and the law of the Most High is trampled under
'foot.

"'We would also humbly solicit your Majesty's Royal inter-
'ference, to prevent the unhallowed assemblage of the Higher
'Classes with their equipages in your Majesty's Parks, on the
'Lord's Day, which is highly demoralizing not only to the per-
'sons themselves, and to their Servants, who are thus *forced* to
'desecrate the Sabbath, but highly injurious, in the way of ex-
'ample, to all classes of your Majesty's subjects.

"'We also respectfully entreat your Majesty to exercise your
'Royal influence and authority to put a stop to the playing of
'the Bands at Windsor, in the Kensington Gardens, and in other
'places on the Lord's Day, whereby those who are so employed
'are deprived of the rest and other privileges of the day, and
'large assemblages of the people are attracted, any of whom, but
'for this attraction, might be led to spend these sacred hours of
'the day in a manner tending to their own spiritual good, and to
'the honour of the Most High God.

"'We grieve to call your Majesty's attention to the fact, that
'whilst there has been an improvement in some respects in the
'observance of the Sabbath within the last few years, in others
'the desecration of it has greatly increased, and that systematic
'attempts are being made, from time to time, by the opponents
'of the due observance of the Lord's Day, to obtain the sanction
'of the Legislature to the opening of the Crystal Palace, of the
'British Museum, and other Public Institutions, on that holy
'day. We earnestly pray your Majesty to withhold your sanc-
'tion from, and to discountenance in every possible way, pro-
'positions of such evil tendency, which, if carried out, would
'probably lead to the opening of the Theatres and other places
'of public amusement, and by which great dishonour would be
'done to God's holy law, and great scandal and discouragement
'would be brought on the cause of true religion in the land.

"'We submit to your gracious Majesty, that at the present

'time, when Almighty God has been graciously pleased to give
'us some respite from those grievous judgments, war and mutiny,
'with which he has seen fit to visit us, it especially becomes us
'to examine our ways and to see wherein we have departed, as
'a people, from the laws of our God, to humble ourselves before
'Him, and to turn away from all our profanations of His holy
'day, and from every other sin, lest we provoke Him to visit us
'in His wrathful indignation, and perhaps even to deprive us of
'that Sabbath, which is one of the bulwarks of religion, and
'which is so grievously polluted amongst us.

"'We earnestly desire your Majesty's gracious consideration
'of this our humble and loyal Address, and we beg to assure
'your Majesty, that we will not cease to pray that the God of
'Heaven may bless your Majesty, and that in all your thoughts
'words, and works, you may ever seek His honour and glory, and
'study to preserve His people committed to your charge, in
'wealth, peace, and godliness.'"

This may be easily turned into petitions to both Houses of
Parliament, or parts of it can be transferred to parochial addresses
and petitions. The use of the same petitions, in various parts of
the country, does no harm to the cause, as it is well known that
the Society has widely extended ramifications.

"*Parochial Petition.*

"'*To the Right Honourable the Lords Spiritual and Temporal
'of the United Kingdom of Great Britain and Ireland, in Parlia-
'ment assembled.*

"'The humble Petition of the undersigned Inhabitants of the
'Parish of ——, in the County of Derby,

"'Sheweth—That your Petitioners are fully convinced, that
'the Lord's Day is of Divine appointment; that the command
'to keep it holy is of perpetual and universal obligation; that
'the blessing of Almighty God rests on those individuals and
'Nations who observe it—His curse on those who desecrate it;
'and that it is the bounden duty of a Christian Legislature, to
'prevent the Lord's Day from being publicly profaned, and also
'to secure it, as a day of rest, to every subject of the realm.

"'Your Petitioners are deeply concerned to find, that so
'widely extended is the system of Sabbath profanation in this

'country, in consequence of the travelling and traffic on Roads,
'Railroads, Rivers, and Canals, the keeping open of Gin-Shops,
'Public-houses, Shops, &c., &c., that some hundreds of thousands
'of their fellow-countrymen have thereby placed before them the
'cruel alternative, that they must continue to break the express
'command of the Most High God, and thereby bring down His
'judgments upon them, or deprive themselves of their means of
'subsistence.

"'Your Petitioners have good reason to believe, that upwards
'of twenty thousand persons in this kingdom are deprived, either
'of the whole or a considerable portion of their Sabbath rest, by
'the transmission of the Mails and the delivery of letters on that
'Holy Day. Your Petitioners believe, that no *necessity* exists
'for the infliction of such a grievous hardship on these persons.
'And they beg leave to state, that great numbers of men of busi-
'ness and of extensive correspondence, both in the county in
'which your Petitioners reside, and also in other parts of the
'country, have discontinued to receive their letters on the Lord's
'Day. Your Petitioners humbly pray your Right Honourable
'House to take steps for the early abolition of this great national
'Act of Sabbath profanation.

"'Your Petitioners would also *most particularly* call the at-
'tention of your Right Honourable House to the awful *increase*
'of the profanation of the Lord's Day by Railway Companies.

"'Your Petitioners would earnestly entreat your Right Hon-
'ourable House to oppose the opening of the Crystal Palace, of
'the British Museum, and other Public Institutions on the Lord's
'Day, and to present an Address to Her Majesty the Queen,
'requesting her to prevent the playing of Bands at Windsor
'and in the Kensington Gardens, and in Barrack Yards,
'and other places, and to cause the *Carriage* Gates of the Park
'to be shut on the Sunday, so as to prevent in them that con-
'course of the Higher Classes with their Horses and Carriages,
'which not only constitutes one of the most glaring profanations
'of the Sabbath Day, and deprives so many Servants of their
'Sabbath privileges, but which also has so pernicious a tendency,
'in the way of example, on all ranks of her Majesty's subjects.

"'Your Petitioners, whilst they earnestly desire the enforce-

'ment of the existing laws relative to the observance of the Lord's
'Day, pray your Right Honourable House, that wherever these
'laws are found to be defective, they may be amended; and
'generally, that such measures may be taken, that Almighty God
'may be publicly honoured by this Nation in regard to His Sab-
'baths; that the conscientious Trader may be protected against
'unfair competition; and that all classes of the community may
'have the opportunity of observing the Lord's Day as a day of
'rest, and also for the more important purposes of religious in-
'struction and devotion.

"'And your Petitioners will ever pray, that Almighty God
'may bless and direct all your deliberations.'

"Distinct Parochial Petition for the Closing of Public-Houses.

"'The humble Petition of the undersigned, &c.

"'Sheweth—That your Petitioners believe that the Lord's
'Day is of Divine authority, and of perpetual and universal obli-
'gation; that the blessing of Almighty God rests on those nations
'and individuals who observe it—His displeasure on those who
'profane it.

"'Your Petitioners are of opinion, that drunkenness is one of
'the chief prevailing vices of this country, and that it and Sab-
'bath-breaking are the fruitful sources of almost every crime
'which is committed; that it produces frightful misery in
'families, and that it leads to the yearly expenditure of very
'many millions of money, which, if laid out in the necessaries
'and comforts of life, would greatly increase the home trade of
'the country, and at the same time would be sufficient to com-
'fortably feed and clothe every really destitute person in the land.

"'Your Petitioners are informed that the cases of drunken-
'ness on the Lord's Day and crime combined, are very much in
'excess of those which are committed on any other day of the
'week.

"'Your Petitioners also find, that under the present system,
'two or three hundred thousand Public-House Keepers and their
'servants are tempted to deprive themselves of a considerable
'portion of their Sabbath privileges.

"'Your Petitioners, under the circumstances, pray your

'Honourable House to use its efforts to suppress the evils arising
'from Public-Houses and Beershops generally, and to close such
'Houses during the whole of the Lord's Day, except against
'lodgers and those who are travellers in cases of necessity and
'mercy.'

"*Females' Memorial.*

"'To the Queen's most excellent Majesty.

"'The memorial of the undersigned Female Inhabitants of
'the Parish (or District) of ———, in the County of ———,

"'Humbly sheweth—That your Majesty's Memorialists view-
'ing with deep anxiety the present public profanations of the
'Lord's Day, and the further desecration with which its sanctity
'is threatened, feel it an incumbent duty in our relation of wives,
'mothers, and daughters, to express to your Majesty, yourself a
'mother, the reality of those dangers which experience has taught
'us, have arisen and must arise from the Lord's Day, or any
'portion of it, being regarded as a time to be spent in mere scenes
'of pleasure or excitement; which is in direct opposition to the
'express command of the Most High God, which declares that
'we must "not be doing our own ways, nor finding our own
'"pleasure" on His Holy Day.

"'We would solicit your Majesty's gracious attention to the
'following statement, extracted from a work lately published by
'the Rev. Joseph Kingsmill, M.A., Chaplain of the Government
'Model Prison, at Pentonville, as more fully setting forth the
'view which your Memorialists take of the misery and evil
'arising to families from the increasing facilities and attraction
'afforded them for absenting themselves from their homes, and
'passing the Lord's Day in pursuit of worldly amusement. The
'tradesman, the mechanic, the day-labourer, alike are, by this
'means, *enticed away from their wives and their children, on the
'only day when they can thoroughly enjoy home.*

"'Earnings are squandered on one day's amusement in the
'week, by which the dwelling might be made more commodious
'and neat, the parents more respectable and happy, and the
'children better educated, better fed, better clad. Elder boys, as
'they grow up, soon follow their father's example, and break loose
'from a mother's feeble restraint. Yet they do not go with the

father even, but in the company of their own choosing.
'Daughters, at like critical age, accept invitations from thought-
'less and vicious youths, rapidly become immersed in the vortex
'of pleasure, and form foolish attachments, which end in a miser-
'able home, or in their irretrievable ruin.

"'It will not be affirmed, I think, by any one who has
'narrowly looked into the matter, that this sort of family disrup-
'tion is an infrequent appendage to our present Sunday excursion
'system. It is the common result, in my opinion, with those
'who have families. Few can afford to take their families with
'them on the Sunday excursion ; and fewer still entertain the idea
'at all, selfishly reasoning, that they alone are entitled to all the
'play, because they get all the earnings (though the hardest work,
'after all, may be the wife's lot in the house), and the temptation
'constantly occurring, the habit of family neglect, and of pleasure-
'taking in company with *strangers*, is effectually formed, and
'the home is dislocated and disorganized.

"'Your Memorialists humbly and earnestly entreat your
'Majesty to use your royal influence and authority to prevent
'the running of excursion and other trains, and the opening of
'public-houses on the Lord's Day, and to prohibit the playing of
'bands at Windsor, in Kensington Gardens, and in other places on
'the Lord's Day, and to resist every attempt which may be made
'to open on that day the Crystal Palace, the British Museum, the
'National Gallery, or other Public Institutions.

"'And your Memorialists will ever pray, that the blessing of
'the Most High may ever attend your Majesty and all your
'Royal Family.'

"*Address of Sunday School Teachers.*

"'To the Queen's Most Excellent Majesty.

"'The humble and loyal Address of the undersigned Sunday
'School Teachers of ——, in the County of ——.

"'We your Majesty's most dutiful and loyal Subjects, beg
'leave to approach your Majesty with the assurance of our un-
'feigned honour and affection, desiring to express to your Majesty
'our great grief and alarm, at the widely extended and increased
'profanation of the Lord's Day, the due observance of which, by
'persons of all ranks and ages, we believe to be most intimately

'connected with their own temporal and eternal good, and also
'with the well-being of the community.

"'We feel deeply concerned, in this matter, for the rising
'generation of our land, many of whom are led by the example
'of others, and by the facilities which are now afforded, to spend
'their Sabbath in scenes of pleasure and excitment most detri-
'mental to their best interests.

"'We have learnt with much concern, that attempts are
'about to be made to induce the Legislature to sanction the
'opening of the Crystal Palace, the British Museum, and the
'National Gallery, on the Lord's Day; we beseech your Majesty
'to discountenance and reject every such proposal; and also to
'prohibit the playing of Bands on the Lord's Day, as we know
'full well, that the attraction afforded by such proceedings, will
'not so much tend to draw persons away from public-houses, gin-
'shops, and other haunts of vice, as to lead many, especially the
'young, to neglect attendance at the Sunday School, or at the
'House of God.

"'We grieve to think of the many inducements which the
'present abounding profanations of God's holy day hold out to
'the young, to forsake Public Worship, and those means of in-
'struction which are calculated, with God's blessing, to lead them
'to honour and fear God, and to become dutiful and loyal
'subjects.

"'We would respectfully remind your Majesty of the awful
'fact, that the Chaplains of the various Gaols in the Metropolis
'and throughout the Country, all unite in the testimony, that the
'Gaols are filled with those who, by one allurement or another,
'have in their youth been tempted on the Sabbath Day, to turn
'their backs upon the House of God, and upon the Sunday
'School.

"'As Teachers of the young, and caring for their best interests,
'and bearing in mind, that the Word of God declares we must
'"not be doing our own ways, or finding our own pleasure on his
'"holy day;" we beseech your Majesty to use your Royal in-
'fluence, to put down every existing and every projected desecra-
'tion of the Lord's Day, as being calculated to induce the young,
'either for the sake of gain, or in the pursuit of amusement, to

'turn their backs upon God's Ordinances, to forsake the guide of
'their youth, and so in the end to fall into the most pernicious
'practices, destructive alike to their present and to their future
'happiness.

"'We will not cease to pray that the God of Heaven may
'bless your Majesty, and all your Royal Family, and that you
'may ever set forth God's glory, and endeavour to lead all com-
'mitted to your care, to wealth, peace, and *godliness.*'"

"The Address may be readily curtailed and converted into a Petition to either
House of Parliament.

"*Parochial Petition against Opening Places of Public Amusement, &c., on the Lord's Day.*

"'To the Honourable the Commons of the United Kingdom
'of Great Britain and Ireland, in Parliament assembled.

"'The humble Petition of the undersigned Inhabitants of the
'Parish of ———, in the County of ———,

"'Sheweth—That your Petitioners are fully convinced, that
'the Lord's Day is of Divine appointment; that the command to
'keep it holy is of perpetual and universal obligation; that the
'blessing of Almighty God rests on those individuals and
'nations who observe it—His curse on those who desecrate it.

"'Your Petitioners would urge your Honourable House to
'use the great influence which, under God, you possess, to en-
'deavour to counteract every desecration of God's Holy Day, and
'especially would they entreat your Honourable House, at the
'present moment, to resist the efforts which are about to be made
'to obtain the sanction of the Legislature to the opening of the
'Crystal Palace, the British Museum, and the National Gallery,
'on the Lord's Day; and they also beg your Honourable House
'to present an Address to her Majesty the Queen, requesting her
'to prohibit the playing of Bands at Windsor and in Kensington
'Gardens, and in other places, and to cause the *Carriage* Gates of
'the Parks to be shut on the Sunday, so as to prevent in them
'that concourse of the Higher Classes with their Horses and Car-
'riages, which not only constitutes one of the most glaring profa-
'nations of the Sabbath Day, and deprives so many servants of
'their Sabbath privileges, but which also has so pernicious a

'tendency, in the way of example, on all ranks of her Majesty's
'subjects.

"'And your Petitioners will ever pray, that Almighty God
'may bless and direct all your deliberations.'

"*Petition on the subject of changing Fair and Market days.*

"'The humble Petition of the Clergyman and undersigned
'Parish Officers of the Parish of ———, in the County of ———

"'Sheweth—That your Petitioners beg respectfully to suggest
'to your Right Honourable House that the present system of
'allowing Fairs and Markets to be held on the Saturday or the
'Monday often leads to a great profanation of the Lord's Day in
'various parts of the kingdom; that numbers of Salesmen,
'Butchers, Drovers, &c., are thereby induced to deprive them-
'selves of the privileges of the Sabbath; that the open desecra-
'tion of that holy day, by the driving of Cattle, and by the
'concourse of persons on the different roads, is exceedingly dis-
'tressing to all those who are assured that the Christian Sabbath
'is of Divine appointment, and of universal obligation; and that
'such scenes are calculated to be exceedingly injurious to the
'religious welfare of those, and particularly of the young, who
'witness them.

"'Your Petitioners would earnestly solicit the attention of
'your Right Honourable House to the prevention of the evil com-
'plained of. And they will not cease to implore the blessing of
'Almighty God on all your deliberations.'

"*Memorial to Railway Proprietors, to be presented at the Half-
Yearly Meeting.*

"'We, the undersigned, fully believing in the Divine authority
'of the Christian Sabbath, and that the blessing of Almighty
'God rests upon those Nations, and Companies, and Individuals,
'who keep it holy, and His wrath upon those who profane it,
'earnestly request you to come to the resolution not to run your
'Trains on that holy day; that thus the numerous servants
'employed on your Line of Railway may have the opportunity
'of observing the whole of the Sabbath Day in a religious man-
'ner; and that no temptation may be held out by you to thought-
'less and ignorant persons to spend that day in amusement and

'dissipation which a merciful God has set apart, not only as a
'day of rest from bodily labour, but also as a day of instruction,
'edification, and comfort for their immortal souls.

"'We beg leave to state, as has been recently stated by a very
'large proportion of the letter-receiving inhabitants of the Derby
'district, that we do not consider it at all necessary or desirable
'that the *Mails* should be forwarded on the Lord's Day.

"'In conclusion, we pray that your Company may be led to
'honour Almighty God in this matter, and that you may have
'His blessing resting upon you, who has said, "Them that honour
'me, I will honour."'

" *Forms of Petitions from Butchers, Bakers, &c.*

"'The humble Petition of the undersigned Butchers, Bakers,
'Greengrocers, and other Tradesmen of the Town of ——, in the
'County of ——

"'Sheweth—That your Petitioners are persuaded that the
'Lord's Day is of Divine appointment, and that all men ought to
'observe it as a day of rest, and also for the higher purposes of
'religion.

"'Your Petitioners pray your Honourable House to use its
'influence for the effectual closing of all shops and public-houses,
'and for the stopping all travelling, traffic, and business through-
'out the land on the Sabbath Day; that the hundreds of thousands
'who are tempted by the competition, or avarice, or thoughtless-
'ness of others, to deprive themselves of the privileges of that
'holy day, may be set at liberty from their present thraldom, for
'their proper and rightful enjoyment of it.

"'And your Petitioners will ever pray that the blessing of
'God may accompany all your deliberations.'

" This Petition can be made a separate Petition for each trade, if it is thought
more desirable.

" *Form of Petition from Public-house Keepers.*

"'The humble Petition of the undersigned Keepers of Inns,
Public-houses, and Beer-shops, in the Parish and Neighbourhood
'of ——, in the County of ——

"'Sheweth—That some of your Petitioners and their Families,
'as the law at present stands, are not only deprived of many of

'the comforts and blessings of the Sabbath, *but are required to*
'*profane* that sacred day.

"'Your Petitioners entreat your Honourable House to fur-
'ther the enactment of a law which shall close all Taverns,
'Public-houses, and Beer-shops, *during the whole of the Lord's*
'*Day*, so as to prevent in such Houses the sale of Spirits, Beer,
'and Wines, except to such persons as shall have slept in the
'House on the Saturday, or shall be travelling on the Sunday in
'cases of necessity or mercy.

"'And your Petitioners will ever pray that Almighty God
'may bless all your deliberations.'

"*Crystal Palace Petition or Clause.*

"'Your Petitioners are grieved to learn that by an evasion of
'the spirit if not of the letter of the Crystal Palace Charter, the
'Shareholders of that Company are admitted to the building and
'grounds on the Lord's Day, and that working men, who become
'shareholders by means of clubs, are, amongst others, enticed from
'Christian worship to secular sight-seeing ; all which gives rise
'to the employment of labour both on the Railway and at the
'Crystal Palace on the Lord's Day.

"'Your Petitioners entreat your Honourable House to use its
'utmost efforts to put a stop to a state of things alike dishonour-
'ing to Almighty God, and injurious to the best interests of those
'who are thus employed.'

"The above may be used as a separate Petition, or it may be embodied in a
general Petition.

"*The opinion of 'The Times' Newspaper on Mr. Hume's pro-*
posal to open the British Museum every Sunday, which applies
with at least equal force against opening the Crystal Palace on the
Lord's Day.

"'Every hour's reflection confirms us in the opinion we ad-
'vanced, that the success of Mr. Hume's scheme would speedily be
'attended with most serious mischief to those very classes whose
'condition it was meant to improve. There is already a strong
'disposition to grasp at the privileges of the Working Classes.
'As much food as will sustain, and as much rest as will preserve,
'that strength which is consumed for the gains of others, is less
'than would be left them by their Masters if no law intervened

'to curb their rapacity. Laws, custom, and opinion, at present
'too strong for the aggressions of avarice, protect the labourer in
'the enjoyment of his periodical relief from toil. The taskmaster
'dares not yet deny the pittance of time that is demanded in the
'name of religion, and for the purposes of rest. But already he
'grudges this abstraction from his means, and if the barrier which
'now restrains him is once broken down for another object, he
'will quickly seize the opportunity for effecting his own. Nor
'will his task be any longer difficult. The workman will have
'voluntarily forsaken the usages he could have pleaded in his own
'behalf. The necessity of excursions and sight-seeing can never
'be urged like the necessity for worship and rest. That griping
'spirit which has already encroached upon the years of infancy,
'and the hours of sleep, will hardly give way to the claims of a
'museum or a steam-boat. They who are so eager for jaunting
'will be not unreasonably presumed to be brisk enough for work-
'ing, and the Seventh Day will soon be swallowed, like the
'thirteenth hour, in the gorge of commercial cupidity.

"'These considerations are not over-strained. The unavoid-
'able necessities of competition soon turn an exception into a
'rule. We know that the persistence of a single tradesman in
'extreme or inconvenient hours of trade compels all his brethren
'to the same course. The opening of museums on the Sundays
'would preclude the possibility of closing exhibitions equally
'innocent and attractive. Why should private collectors be de-
'barred the license assumed by the nation? If Sunday visitors
'are able and willing to spend a shilling of their weekly earnings
'in the purchase of a harmless gratification, why should they not
'be as free to do so as to avail themselves of a gratuitous exhibi-
'tion? Why should not Madame Tussaud's be open? Why not
'Vauxhall? The line of demarcation would grow more and more
'difficult to draw. Under our present Institutions we can very
'justly close the Theatres on the Sunday, but after the proposed
'infraction of them we should be in a strange dilemma, even on
'this point. If scenic representations are abstractedly innocent,
'why proscribe them on a Sunday? If abstractedly otherwise,
'why encourage them on the other six days of the week? But
'each of these exhibitions would entail a proportionate extension

'of traffic and trade, till at last a closed shop on a Sunday would
'be a rarity, resulting from the circumstances of the district, or
'the position of the individual.'—*Times, September 3rd, 1846.*

" This might with advantage be reprinted and widely circulated .

" *Further Movements with regard to Sabbath Observance about to
be proceeded with by the Derbyshire Society in 1861.*

" Deputation to the Railway Directors on the Wednesday in
Easter week.

" The Society have ascertained from the Directors that those
employed on the Midland Line will not in any way incur their
displeasure by joining in Petitions to Parliament to put a stop to
all Railway Travelling and Traffic on *all* Lines on the Lord's Day,
except in cases of necessity or mercy ; but at the same time the
Directors object to Petitions being brought on to the Railway
premises for signature. The Derbyshire Society are therefore
about to promote meetings, and the signing of Petitions from
those employed by the Midland Company at the various large
Stations along the Line ; and they hope for the zealous co-operation, in this most important movement, of the friends of the
cause residing near the several localities.

" The Committee will endeavour at once to promote general
parochial Petitions from each Parish in the County, and, in addition, distinct parochial Petitions for the closing of Public-houses
on the Lord's Day ; also Petitions from the Clergy of the Archdeaconry ; also from the Public-house keepers, and various
tradesmen who, under the present system, are suffering from
unfair competition, &c.

" They are taking steps with regard to the closing of shops
on the Lord's Day.

" They also hold themselves in readiness to promote letters to
members, especially if called upon to do so by the London Society
in any case of importance.

" They will endeavour to promote Sermons, Meetings, the use
of the local Press, the circulation of Publications, and the inter-
change of papers, &c., conveying accounts of what is doing, with
Secretaries of Societies, and other friends of Sabbath observance
at a distance.

CHAPTER XLIV.

1863.

SUNDAY CLOSING OF PUBLIC-HOUSES.

Mr. Somes's Bill—Misery to families—Loss to the country—Forbes Mackenzie's Act—Decrease of drunkenness in Scotland—Increase in England—Feeling of publicans—Cab and omnibus men—In Liverpool 44,000 householders in favour of total closing—Birkenhead—Two hours' exception—Beer purchased on Saturday will keep—Feeling of the labouring classes and drunkards—Public-house keepers—Address to the Queen from one hundred and seventy-five Derbyshire clergymen—Roman Catholic bishops—Saturday half holiday—Clubs—Vast numbers deprived of their Sabbath—No efforts made by those in authority—God's judgments may be expected.

In May, 1863, I drew up, by the desire of the Committee of the Derbyshire Society for Promoting the Due Observance of the Lord's Day, an address to the public in favour of Mr. Somes's bill for closing public-houses during the whole of the Lord's Day. It was sent to every member of both Houses of Parliament, together with a copy of the address to the Queen from the clergy of Derbyshire, to which the document referred. The following is a copy of the document, with the omission of a paragraph at the commencement and of another at the end, and of a paper on the Divine Authority of the Lord's Day, all of which will be found in the " Address on the Desecration of the Lord's " Day by the running of Railway Trains." The various statistics contained in the following pages will be found extremely interesting :—

" The Committee are of opinion, that drunkenness is one of

the chief prevailing sins of this country, and that it and Sabbath-breaking are the fruitful sources of almost every crime which is committed; that it produces great misery in families, and that it leads to the yearly expenditure of very many millions of money, which, if laid out in the necessaries and comforts of life, would greatly increase the trade of the country, and at the same time would be sufficient to comfortably feed and clothe every really destitute person in the land. It is calculated that at least twenty millions sterling are thrown away in this country every year in drunken drink.

"The Committee consider that the state of the law with regard to the opening or closing of shops and public-houses on the Sunday is most peculiar; that whilst shops are required to be closed in which such articles as meat and bread are sold, those may be open during a considerable part of the day in which intoxicating liquors may be purchased. The amount of drunkenness on the Lord's Day is most appalling, and the number of public-houses altogether out of all proportion to the reasonable wants of the population of the country.

"In one small parish in Derbyshire, with 470 Inhabitants, there are six public-houses and beer-shops, or one to every sixteen families.

"It has been stated, that drunkenness and crime have everywhere diminished in proportion to the restraint which the Legislature has placed on the sale of intoxicating drinks on the Lord's Day. In seventeen of the chief Towns of Scotland, containing together about a million of inhabitants, the number of cases of drunkenness alone, or of drunkenness and crime combined, on Sundays, amounted, during the three years before the Forbes Mackenzie Act came into operation, to 11,471; whilst, during the three first years in which public-houses were closed on Sundays, cases of the same description amounted, in the aggregate, only to 4299.

"The daily average number of prisoners confined in the Edinburgh and Glasgow prisons during the three years before the passing of the Act was 1221, while the daily average number during the three years, subsequent to the passing of the Act, was 864.

"The total number of cases of drunkenness taken charge of by the Edinburgh police in 1853, the year before the passing of the Act, and in 1861, was as follows :—

In 1853	9730
In 1861	6656

Number of cases on Sundays—

In 1853	1305
In 1862	858

Number of cases on Saturdays, Sundays, and Mondays—

In 1853	4420
In 1861	2918

Number of cases between eight o'clock on the Sunday mornings and eight o'clock on the Monday mornings—

In 1853	648
In 1861	205

"'He is something more than a bold man who, with such 'facts before him, will dare to say that the Forbes Mackenzie 'Act has demoralized Scotland—has been else than a blessing to 'the country.'

"On the other hand, drunkenness seems to have greatly increased during the last few years in England, where drinking in public-houses is permitted for many hours on the Sunday. It appears from the police reports, that in 1856 there were apprehended in Manchester, from 10 a.m. on the Saturdays to 10 a.m. on the Mondays in the whole year, 417 drunken persons; in the year 1862 the aggregate number of drunken persons apprehended on those days was 1824. A larger proportion of these apprehensions occurred on the Sunday, and till 10 a.m. on Monday, than on the Saturday. The total number taken before the Manchester magistrates for drunkenness in 1862 was 3373; of these 1824 were for drunkenness on the Saturdays and Sundays, the remaining 1549 on the other five days of the week; so that the whole number for the Saturdays in the year may be taken at 912, that for the Sundays at 912, and the aggregate for each of the other days at 310.

The following is a table of public-house and beer-house offences for 1862 :—

	Number of Houses.	Total Reported.	Offences.	
			Week days.	Sundays.
Gross Total of Public-houses in Manchester	482	59	13	46
Gross Total of Beer-houses	1792	595	136	459

The number of licences granted in 1859 was 137,804, and supposing that only two persons were engaged in each house, 275,608 persons would be thereby deprived, either wholly or in part, of the advantages of the Sabbath Day!

"Great numbers of public-house keepers have, as opportunities have been afforded them, shown a desire to have a measure passed for the closing of all public-houses on the Lord's Day, except against travellers and lodgers. Nearly thirty years ago, 148 of the public-house keepers of Derby, Ashbourne, Alfreton, and their neighbourhoods, and 226 of the gin-shop keepers of London petitioned for the total closing. In 1857, the licensed victuallers of Liverpool were canvassed, and declared themselves in favour of Sunday closing by a very large majority.

"A Petition is about to be forwarded to Parliament, signed by upwards of five hundred cab and omnibus men of Manchester, in favour of Mr. Somes's bill.

"The following tables are taken from the account of a large and influential meeting of 4000 people, held in St. George's Hall at Liverpool, on Monday, the 18th of May. The Rev. Dr. White stated on the part of the canvassing committee, that they 'be-'lieve the figures to be a fair, honest, and impartial representa-'tion of the feelings of the householders of Liverpool on the 'subject of the Sunday closing of public-houses :—'

TABLE I.

GENERAL SUMMARY.

Number of houses in the borough, about .	72,350
Uninhabited	5,350
Inhabited	67,000

FORMS RETURNED.

No. 1. For total closing on Sundays 44,149
„ 2. Against Sunday closing 3,330
„ 3. For closing, except for two hours . . . 6,417
Neutral—" Don't care how it is " . . 6,339

Total returns . . 60,235

Double occupations, 2 per cent. 1,340
Houses shut and no return, 3 per cent. . . . 2,010
Hostile—refused to receive forms—1 per cent. . . 670
Lost by negligence of masters or servants, masters absent and
no instructions, 2½ per cent. . . . 1,675

65,930
Houses omitted or forms not collected . . . 1,070

Total . 67,000

TABLE II.

CLASSIFIED SUMMARY.

	No. 1.	No. 2.	No. 3.	Total.
Artisans	14,828	1,387	2,370	18,585
Labourers	15,092	734	1,602	17,428
Shopkeepers, &c.	5,145	298	738	6,181
Clerks, agents, &c.	3,479	246	543	4,268
Mariners	2,093	104	307	2,504
No business	1,481	119	353	1,953
Merchants	705	49	170	924
Professionals	683	62	177	922
Publicans	432	199	93	724
Beersellers	119	132	62	313
Scripture readers, &c.	92	0	0	92
Totals	44,149	3,330	6,417	53,896)
			Neutrals, 6,339)	60,235

" The next two tables show two districts in which the great mass of the inhabitants belong to the working classes.

TABLE III.

MARYBONE DISTRICT—Bounded by Moorfields, Tithebarn Street, Vauxhall Road, Paul Street, Bevington Bush, Scotland Road and Place, Byrom Street, and Dale Street to Moorfields.

	No. 1.	No. 2.	No. 3.	Total.
Artisans	352	55	56	463
Labourers	1687	159	131	1977
Shopkeepers	182	20	33	235
Clerks, agents, &c.	27	3	8	38
Mariners	19	3	0	22
No business	3	0	0	3
Merchants	1	3	3	4
Professionals	10	0	0	10
Publicans	11	18	3	32
Beer-sellers	5	10	2	17
Totals	2297	268	236	2801

TABLE IV.

SCOTLAND ROAD DISTRICT—Bounded by Bevington Bush, Paul Street, Vauxhall Road, Burlington Street, the Canal, Boundary Street, Scotland Road, New Street, Great Homer Street, Great Nelson Street, and Scotland Road to Bevington Bush.

	No. 1.	No. 2.	No. 3.	Total.
Artisans	1612	92	256	1960
Labourers	2638	80	266	2984
Shopkeepers	527	21	70	618
Clerks, agents, &c.	153	12	28	193
Mariners	180	9	21	210
No business	12	0	6	18
Merchants	6	0	2	8
Professionals	20	2	2	24
Publicans	25	19	18	62
Beer-sellers	22	14	11	47
Totals	5195	249	680	6224*

"At Birkenhead, a similar canvass to that at Liverpool has been instituted. Out of 5870 returns, which have been collected from householders, 4560 were in favour of Mr. Somes's bill; 3000 of these are from working men; 422 only are opposed to the bill; most of the publicans are in favour of it. A large

* An error of one.

and influential meeting was held in the Music Hall, on the 28th of April; W. Hind, Esq., Chairman to the Board of Commissioners, presided. Between one and two thousand persons were present, the majority of whom were working men. The meeting was most unanimous, all present, without one exception, being in favour of the Sunday closing.

"Some are of opinion, that it will be well to except two hours, in the middle of the day, from the operation of any bill for the Sunday closing of public-houses, during which persons may be permitted to purchase beer for their dinners. If this were in accordance with the Divine Law as a work of charity, all would most gladly promote such an exception; but there is really no necessity for any such provision. The persons who propose it have probably never tried the plan of putting the public-house ale into a common quart wine bottle, and corking it up to be used on the next day, or they would have ascertained that it is quite as fresh then as when it is drawn from the barrel. If the house is small and close, the bottle may be placed in cold water. One of these bottles can be purchased for a penny. A London publican who does a large business on Sunday, lately said, 'As for working men not being able to get their beer on 'Sundays (supposing Mr. Somes's bill to pass,) that's all a farce. 'They can provide for that as well as they can provide for having 'clean linen. Any respectable landlord would lend his cus- 'tomers bottles on the Saturday night.' There is no reason on this score for inflicting Sunday labour on the publicans and their families; and, if public-houses are to be kept open for the sale of beer for two hours on the Sunday noon, it may open the way for the purchasing of any quantity of intoxicating liquor, to be consumed in private houses, and so lead to a large amount of drunkenness and disorder.

"Under the present law, no licensed Victualler or Beer Seller can open his house for the sale of intoxicating liquors before half-past twelve o'clock in the afternoon of Sunday, Christmas Day, Good Friday, or any public fast or thanksgiving day. He must also keep it closed on those days between the hours of three and five o'clock in the afternoon, *and from eleven o'clock at night till four o'clock in the morning of the day following those days.* It may or may not be of importance that the restriction as to the not opening till four o'clock on the Monday morning should be extended to a later hour ; but the closing of all public-houses at eleven o'clock on the Saturday night is obviously a most important point, both as regards the comfort of the Publicans, and as some check upon excessive drinking ; and also on many other accounts.

"To ascertain who is really a traveller may be a great difficulty, but it is not a difficulty which should be allowed to prevent the passing of Mr. Somes's bill, calculated as it is to confer such immense benefit, not only on thousands of Publicans and their families, but also on the whole community. Under the existing law there is the same difficulty to some extent. In most of the country places it is not so difficult to distinguish who is or who is not a traveller, as it is in very large towns. In most cases it may not be difficult to distinguish between those who are merely using the public-house for refreshment, and those who are there for the purpose of indulging in drink.

"There is a very strong feeling amongst the great proportion of labouring men, many of them being regular drunkards, and especially amongst their wives and families, that the closing of public-houses on the Lord's Day will be a great boon to them. It will be seen in the Second Table of the Liverpool Statistics, that 30,000 householders, who are artisans and labourers of that place, are in favour of their being closed from eleven on the Saturday night, till six o'clock on the Monday morning. The Birkenhead returns also show a very remarkable state of feeling in this respect on the part of the great mass of the labouring householders.

"It has just been ascertained that 258 of the public-house keepers in 58 Derbyshire Parishes, will be glad to have all public-houses closed during the whole of the Sunday.

"In an address to the Queen, and in similar petitions to both Houses of Parliament, signed by the Archdeacon and 174 of the Clergy of the Archdeaconry of Derby, which set forth in detail the Divine authority and universal obligation of the Lord's Day, and which point out many of the grievous descerations of the day, and pray that they may be remedied, the keeping open of public-houses is expressly mentioned. The opinions of such a vast proportion of the Derbyshire Clergy, as stated in these documents, may be fairly assumed to be the opinions of the vast proportion of the Clergy of the Church of England, and also of the great body of the Dissenting Ministers of the country, and will of course carry due weight with them.

"It is very gratifying to find, from a correspondence which has lately been published, that many of the Irish Roman Catholic Bishops fully coincide in the opinion that the closing of Public-houses on the Lord's Day will be a great boon to the whole community.

"Those who are desirous of putting down the abounding desecrations of the Lord's Day, so that it may not be publicly profaned, and that tens of thousands of Publicans, Railway Men, Post-office Servants, and others who are now employed on that day, may have it as a day of rest, and may also have the opportunity of "keeping it holy to the Lord," are at the same time most anxious to promote the real welfare and legitimate pleasures of the working classes. The Parks, if closed against carriages and bands, that bandsmen and servants may also have their Sabbath, should be open both to the rich and the poor as on other days. Great numbers of the working classes now also enjoy the Saturday half-holiday, and an occasional whole holiday on other week days ; and there is every prospect that this boon may be more generally accorded ; then may the bands play, and railways convey their thousands of passengers, and persons may 'breathe 'the pure air of heaven,' without dishonouring the Lord of the Sabbath, by polluting His holy day, and depriving their fellow-men of its opportunities and advantages.

"With regard to the "closing of public-houses against the poor, and keeping open the Club-houses for the rich," it may be observed that Clubs are not like public-houses, which are principally open for the sale of intoxicating drink ; they are the homes of many of the members of the Clubs, when they are in London, though they do not sleep in them, but usually in some neighbouring house ; yet, if it appears that the opening of them is not a work of necessity, and that it inflicts labour contrary to the Divine command on those who are employed in them, then let proper restriction be put upon them also as regards the Sabbath Day.

"There is a strange and melancholy state of things in this professedly Christian country, even in the midst of a great increase of true and vital religion throughout the land. Hundreds of thousands of persons are trampling under-foot the command to keep holy the Sabbath Day, one of the most merciful institutions that the God of Heaven has vouchsafed to give for the recovery to His service of sinful man, and for his increase in the knowledge of God and in all holiness. Many thousands of these are the Public-house Keepers, to whom this paper chiefly refers, and the hundreds of thousands who are tempted by the opening of these houses to break the Sabbath of the Lord, and to commit the sin of drunkenness. Thousands of others, also, are led, under the present state of things, to forego their birthright, and to disregard the day of rest and religious observance. Great numbers of them are ill at ease, but have not the religious principle which will enable them to give up their ungodly employments at all risks. Indeed, they may begin to doubt whether the observance of the Sabbath is binding to them at all, if they see those in authority making no efforts to secure to them the Lord's Day as a day of rest from their worldly employments, so that they may have at least the opportunity of observing it in a right manner. There is no effort made to put down the most open and glaring profanations of the Sabbath, by which Almighty God is so greatly dishonoured; no attempt to prevent temptations from being held out to allure the young from the Sunday school and the House of God; no effort to enforce the present Law against various kinds of Sabbath-breaking, or, where it is insufficient for that purpose, to have it amended. Surely it is the duty of the Legislature and of a paternal Government to use all proper means to set free from their Sabbath thraldom the immense and increasing numbers of persons who are now led by the thoughtlessness, and competition, and avarice of others to deprive themselves of the rest and other blessings of that sacred day. Surely the opportunity which now presents itself of closing public-houses on the Lord's Day, and of thereby diminishing one great source of evil, will not be lost upon our statesmen.

·   ·   ·   ·   ·   ·   ·   ·   ·   ·   ·   ·

"If the Jews, the favoured people of God, did not escape His just and desolating judgments, when they provoked him by their idolatry and their pollution of His Sabbaths; if their judgments were all the more terrible because they were His people (Amos iii., 2); if God in our days has seen fit, notwithstanding our high privileges and advantages, to visit our nation with those sore though partial scourges of war and mutiny; if America is bathed in blood, notwithstanding the great amount of true godliness which is to be found there, should not God's professing Church in highly favoured England take warning, and should not every inhabitant of the land be humbled for our national sins, and by prayer and supplication seek the pardon of them, and that they may be given up, and that the most righteous anger and awful judgments of the Lord may be turned away from us."

CHAPTER XLV.

CAPTAIN ATCHISON AND LIEUT. DAWSON, AND THE ROMAN CATHOLIC CEREMONIES AT MALTA.

State of the defences of the Thames in 1852—Restoration of Captain Atchison to rank of captain on full pay—Colonel commandant of Lancashire Artillery—Sir Manly Power, Sir Thomas Maitland, the Marquis of Hastings—Shameful proceedings with regard to the Court-martial on Atchison and Dawson—These officers cashiered—Their difficulties—Their relatives at first angry with them—Concern of the King, George IV—Lord Denman and the King's Bench—The conduct of the captain of the main-guard at Valetta.

In the ninth chapter of this work I have mentioned the case of Captain Atchison and Mr. Dawson, of the Artillery, who were brought to a court-martial, and dismissed the service, for requesting to be relieved from the execution of an order which they had received to superintend the firing of a salute, and the tolling of a bell, in connexion with the procession of the image of a Roman Catholic saint. Several months ago, as I have stated at the end of Chapter IX, I wrote to my friend Colonel Atchison to request him to let me have the particulars of his restoration to the service, and of his having become colonel commandant of the Royal Lancashire Militia. The following letter, which I have received from him, furnishes those particulars, and I trust the whole country, with a feeling of indignation at the treatment he has received, will insist on his not being merely restored to the rank of (retired) captain on full pay, but that he shall now, in his advanced age, be restored to his original place in the Royal Artillery, by which he will be nearly at the head of the list, and, as I see by the

"Army List," become a colonel commandant of a battalion, and a lieutenant-general in the army. If he is restored, and his back pay and emoluments are made good to him, (and should not the country, in common honesty, do this?) he and his family will have many thousands of pounds to receive :—

"Old Charlton, Kent, November 28th, 1865,
"(with additions inserted September 20th, 1866.)

"VERY DEAR SIR,

"I cannot well express how my mind was affected by "your kind letter, so calling to mind the hearty and Christian "affection, and constant efforts of yourself and friends on behalf "of Mr. Dawson and myself, when we were dismissed the army "for objecting to comply with an idolatrous requisition of the "Romish church, though we acted strictly within the solemn "provisions of the Articles of War, providing for officers to make "their representations of wrong, and seek their redress; and our "requests to be exonerated from the idolatrous ceremonies, as "proved in the evidence, *were most fully complied with by our "superiors on the spot, without any censure whatever.* It also "most forcibly brought to my mind all the wonderful acts of our "Lord's providence over us both, and so many other things "respecting them, that, from being hurried with other affairs, and "suffering from much weak health when your note arrived on the "22nd instant, I could not find time or strength to sit down and "write to you the details which you wish to know, and so the "subject has been put off from day to day in a manner which "has grieved me. My step-daughter, however, has providentially "called to my recollection the enclosed printed paper, which "shows the measures taken in my behalf in January, 1853. From "want of time I can only add, on that part of the subject, that "when I was taking my *month's leave* from my situation as assist-"ant secretary of the Church Pastoral Aid Society, and, with my "invalid wife, staying at Gravesend in 1852, I was led in my "walks to study the amount of artillery defence which the then "batteries on the Thames afforded to London, and such results, "with regard to their insufficiency, were exhibited, as were dis-"tressing to contemplate. The fact was, Government, in old

"times, always trusted to their fleet at the Nore. A religious
"friend, and well-known able officer, the late Major-General
"Anderson, of the Royal Artillery, was so struck with my details
"on the river defences, that he presented them to Major-General
"Cator, the head of the artillery department, and General Cator
"took them to General Burgoyne, the Royal Engineer. Soon
"after that the militia artillery regiments were formed, and
"Colonel Sir Duncan Macdougall, an experienced old Line officer,
"having been appointed lieut.-colonel commanding the Lanca-
"shire Artillery, he went to his friend, General Anderson, to
"recommend to him some unemployed Royal Artillery officer
"who might be induced to take the post of senior major in the
"regiment, in order to conduct the artillery instruction and exer-
"cises. General Anderson mentioned me, as continuing to take
"an interest in the profession, and told him the story of my
"unjust dismissal from the service. Colonel Macdougall sent
"for a copy of the court-martial, and said that if he found that
"I had not disobeyed orders, and my conduct was only that which
"General Anderson had described, he would certainly recommend
"me to the Lord-Lieutenant, then the late Lord Sefton. His lord-
"ship was impressed with the same facts, and desired Colonel
"Macdougall to recommend me to the late Lord Raglan, then
"Master-General, who had been secretary to the Duke of Wel-
"lington at the time of my dismissal, and knew all the particulars
"of the case. Lord Raglan instantly said, '*It is the best thing
"'that can be done*,'* so, under the Lord's providence, I was placed
"in this high post of military trust. I hesitated at first whether
"I should take the commission with the old charges standing
"against me, but there being no pecuniary benefit in the appoint-
"ment, and considering that my acceptance and faithful discharge
"of duty would only place the old military authorities who held
"out against me in a false position, I acceded, and received the
"commission of major in the Lancashire Artillery in 1853.

"   * It will be also judged that Lord Raglan's words were really a testimony
"in behalf of my military character, and of his feelings on the Malta case, as well
"as of the injustice I was suffering; as he could not have approved of an officer
"for such a responsible post who was guilty of disobedience and breach of disci-
"pline; and who was keeping up a constant protest against the proceedings and
"sentence."

"In 1855, after the Crimean war, Lord Lucan demanded a
"court-martial in consequence of the strictures passed upon him.
"The Government refused, on the ground that he had done mili-
"tary duty *after the case in question*, and alleged that by military
"rule no officer could be tried by a court-martial under such
"circumstances. I instantly caught the Government on their
"own principles, and presented my Malta case again on the same
"facts all along shown as in evidence proved before the court-
"martial, namely, that I had *not disobeyed orders*, but that on my
"representation of the idolatrous requisition of the Romish
"church which I found I was required to execute, with my request
"to be exonerated from them, (the Articles of War providing for
"officers making their representations of wrong, and seeking their
"redress,) my commanding officer instantly complied with my
"request, without any censure, and left me in the discharge of
"my military duties for three months after; so that there was
"no disobedience of orders, or breach of military discipline on
"my part. I had also clear military precedents for acting on the
"Articles of War as I did, approved of by Government, and several
"similar remonstrances have been made by officers since—allowed
"by Government. But to my case justice, as yet, has been refused.
"It so happened that my friend, Mr. Joshua Williams, the
"eminent barrister, had been urging me in 1853 to petition par-
"liament again on the subject, and had the case drawn up for
"counsel's opinion. The case and opinions are given in the
"accompanying printed paper. The result of my appeal to the
"then Commander-in-Chief, the late Lord Hardinge, was a letter
"(29th Sept., 1855) stating, in substance, that under all the cir-
"cumstances of the case, and in consideration of the long period
"of my endurance of the penalties of the sentence of the court-
"martial, the prayer of my memorial had been submitted to the
"Queen. I was restored to the rank and pay of captain in the
"Royal Artillery, and permitted to retire on full pay of that
"rank, to date from the 16th June, 1855, but stating *I was with-
"out any claim*, either for arrears of pay, or to be reinstated in
"my original place in the Royal Artillery. I was greatly puzzled
"what to reply to this decision, but thinking it only wise to take
"my restoration to the rank and pay of captain, I wrote to the

"Horse Guards (1st December following) to express my obliga-
"tions to Her Majesty for this restoration, adding, '*that I could
"'not but trust that it had appeared to the authorities that the
"'terms of the charge and sentence under which I had been left so
"'long to suffer could not in truth and justice be maintained
"'against me.*'

"On the retirement of Sir Duncan Macdougall, in May, 1857,
"I was promoted to be lieut.-colonel commandant of the Royal
"Lancashire Militia Artillery, and you will be glad, as an old
"officer, to know that while I was in command I had several
"times the expression of the Duke of Cambridge's high approval
"of the efficiency of the corps, and that he has been known to
"refer to the regiment as an example of the valuable force which
"the country possesses in its militia artillery. Two years ago,
"through my strength then greatly failing, I retired from this
"command, then in my 75th year, when the Lord-Lieutenant
"recommended that I should be appointed the honorary colonel,
"and my officers requested that I would sit for my portrait for
"their mess-room. I state these circumstances, I trust, as truly
"shewing that the same grace of our heavenly Father and King,
"which enabled me and my dear friend to be faithful to His ser-
"vice, honour, and commands, has also its fruits in making a
"soldier faithful and intelligent in the service of his earthly
"sovereign. Not that our sovereign, George IV, at all entered
"into the views of our adversaries—as it is satisfactorily known
"that His Majesty said that 'no act of his reign had caused him
"'such distress as the Malta Trials,' and circumstances show
"that His Majesty *long resisted* the recommendation made to
"him that we should be summarily dismissed the army without
"a trial. The Duke of Wellington in the House of Lords stated
"that the above was his recommendation to the Duke of York,
"and that the Duke of York approved it; consequently it became
"the Duke of Wellington's *duty to take it to the King*. There
"can be no doubt he went, and that the King refused.

"But it is necessary to give the grounds of what I say on
"these important matters. Dr. Collier, private secretary to the
"Duke of Kent, told me, soon after I came home in 1825, in the
"presence of Mr. and Mrs. Alexander Haldane at their house at

"Hatcham, that George IV had said the words I have given
"above, and that there were only two parties between his in-
"formant and the King. Dr. Collier said his communication
"must be considered private. When my friends recommended
"me to bring the case before parliament in 1833, I called on Dr.
"Collier, and, reminding him of his communication, requested
"that I might state it to my friends. He at once said, " You have
"stated what I said correctly, and I think I had it from one of
"the Cavendishes, but I cannot now speak with certainty, as I
"have been suffering much in my head of late.

"The Duke of Wellington, in his statement to the House of
"Lords, said, beside other matters, that he had ordered us to be
"placed under arrest, and had *waited for further information from
"Malta.* Now the documents on the case had been sent to the
"Duke *complete, with every necessary fact for military decision,* by
"Major-General Sir Manly Power, without preferring any charge
"against us, or indeed making any remark on the case, as if simply
"to submit the serious complaints and trouble which the orders
"for the idolatrous ceremonies created in the garrison. Sir Manly
"Power had himself discontinued the orders for the attendance of
"the officers of the garrison at high mass, and joining the proces-
"sions of the host and images with lighted candles in their hands,
"which the preceding lieutenant-governors, with their staff and
"officers of the garrison, had done; showing that Sir Manly
"Power had his own views when sending the documents without
"any charges or remarks against us. And it must occur to every
"intelligent officer that the Duke of Wellington, waiting from the
"8th of October to the 28th of December (that is more than eleven
"weeks) with the papers before him, before he sent the order for us
"to be tried, could not maintain that any military duty had been
"declined, or any breach of discipline committed. Any other
"officer so hesitating to enforce a known military duty, or delaying
"to punish a breach of discipline, would have been cashiered.
"This long hesitation of the Duke is utterly inconsistent with
"their being any military criminality in my hesitating, and
"affords indirect proof that he then saw there were grounds for
"my remonstrance; and *the dishonest suppression of the facts
"of the case,* evidently ordered in England, is further proof of

" this. For, when the charge was made out against me for
" ' disobedience of orders, insubordinate and unofficer-like con-
" ' duct in not carrying *into execution* the orders *for firing salutes,*
" ' and remonstrating against carrying the said orders into
" ' effect ; ' thus keeping out of sight, and out of the charge,
" the popish idolatrous ceremonies and objects of the orders given,
" namely, the tutelar saint worshipped, the tolling of the bell, the
" *church petteraro* salutes only fired on these occasions, and the
" signals and directions of the priests by necessity as well as
" custom involved in the orders, it affords moral proof that
" the authorities in England saw that the popish requisition was
" open to my lawful remonstrance. And this unjust suppression
" of the essential facts of the case being persisted in by the
" authorities at Malta was manifestly to carry out the in-
" structions from England. The proceedings show that I remon-
" strated against this suppression of the facts *before the trials*
" *took place, as contrary to the Articles of War and the practice of*
" *the service,* purposely to prevent me from obtaining evidence
" and obtaining justice at the trial ; and although I wrote to the
" deputy judge-advocate and required, according to the rules and
" practice of the service, all the orders or instructions which I
" received to be set forth in this charge, *my application was*
" *refused.* But I at once saw that this abominable injustice
" would or ought to defeat the charges, as shewing that the matters
" suppressed and attempted to be kept out of sight did not belong
" to our military service, and were illegal to be required or
" enforced on a British Protestant officer, and that the evidence
" would clearly and fully disprove the charges ; as it was mani-
" fest that I had never objected to or remonstrated against an
" order for a *simple salute only without a given object,* as the
" charge set forth, but only against the idolatrous matters which
" the authorities were endeavouring to exclude from the notice of
" the court-martial. Also, it is proved that my *not carrying into*
" *execution* the orders in question *was not from disobedience of*
" *orders,* as stated in the charge, but from my commanding
" officer *having complied with my complaint of wrong,* and with
" my *request to be exonerated* from the *specified* idolatrous and
" unmilitary ceremonies without any censure whatever ; Major-

" General Sir Manly Power also never censured me, but left me
" in discharge of my military duties for three months after;
" demonstrating fully that it was not any military service or
" duty that I had objected to, and that I had not disobeyed the
" orders nor committed any breach of discipline; and I may
" justly observe, that if the Duke and Government objected to,
" and were ashamed of, the idolatrous ceremonies and bell-tolling
" to appear before the army and the British public, it was natural
" and right for me to have objected and to act on the Article of
" War for my protection. Mr. Beckett's letter to the acting
" judge-advocate (page 60 of the Proceedings) states, ' You have
" ' received further directions relative to these trials in two other
" ' letters which I have addressed to you,' and when I applied,
" as entitled by the Mutiny Act, for a copy of the one withheld
" from me it was refused—proving that the officers and court-
" martial were acting under directions from the authorities in
" England that would not bear the light.

" Under the teaching of the prosecutor, the court-martial
" attempted to prevent me having evidence at the trial that the
" host at high mass, and San Lorenzo, the tutelar saint, were the
" great objects of the salutes; that the great bell of the fort was
" tolled with the salutes; and that the petteraroes were not
" military implements, &c.; but I obtained the necessary evi-
" dence on the minutes. The court also refused to receive that
" part of my defence which shewed that the whole of the Romish
" church requisition was for ceremonies which the church and
" state of England declare to be idolatrous, and which the
" sovereign himself, with all officers, military as well as civil,
" were by law solemnly required to declare to be idolatrous before
" accepting their commissions, at the time I entered the service.
" The court, notwithstanding, found me guilty, and sentenced
" my dismissal from the service. The judge-advocate in London
" returned the proceedings, stating that we had ' not had a *full*,
" ' *fair, or legal trial,*' and ordered the court to receive and hear
" the whole of my defence. It did so—but the court-martial
" repeated its former sentence, and I was dismissed the service.

" I have omitted to state that the officer, selected to preside
" at this court-martial, was a Roman Catholic and a foreigner,

"the colonel of a former Sicilian regiment, and then lieutenant-
"colonel of the Malta Fencibles.

"A remarkable incident occurred at Malta, which must be
"kept in mind, as shewing the influence brought to bear on
"Major-General Sir Manly Power, then commanding at Malta,
"and which must have had its influence on the minds of the
"members of the court-martial to act as they did :—After the
"death of the governor, General Sir Thomas Maitland, Sir Manly
"Power had to open all official letters to the deceased governor.
"There was one from the Duke of Wellington, then Master-
"General, respecting Sir Manly Power having forwarded the
"letters of Lieutenant Dawson and myself, remonstrating against
"the idolatrous salutes, bell-tolling, &c. Some one of Sir Manly
"Power's staff caused it to transpire to the officers of the garrison
"that the Duke had stated in that letter, 'We all know Manly
"'Power is a brave soldier, but who would have thought he was
"'such a fool as to act as he has done.' Surviving officers will
"confirm this. I called on Colonel Sir William de Bathe, one
"of the members of the court-martial, before I published this
"fact many years ago, and asked if he did not remember it. Sir
"William immediately said, 'We all had it.' The officers of the
"court-martial would therefore naturally feel that they also would
"be treated as fools if they did not decide according to the
"Duke's views ; not reflecting (on the Duke's flippant remark)
"that if the requisition of the priests for their idolatrous and un-
"military ceremonies had not been clearly open to the remon-
"strances which Lieutenant Dawson and myself had made
"against them, or if a military duty had been objected to by us,
"and Sir Manly Power had neglected to enforce such military
"duty by putting us under arrest for trial, the Duke, instead of
"his remark would have ordered both the major-general and our
"commanding officer, Major Adams, under arrest for neglect of
"duty. And it must be evident that neither Sir Manly Power
"nor the members of the court-martial, under the above circum-
"stances, could attend to the protests of Lieutenant Dawson and
"myself against the illegal and dishonest suppression of the real
"facts of the case, nor to our representations of the law and
"truth of the matter, without incurring the hostility of the Duke

"of Wellington, and perhaps charges of disobedience, for not
"attending to the directions they had received for enforcing the
"charges evidently made out in London.

"But the strangest part of the case remains to be stated.
"General Sir Thomas Maitland, the commander of the forces,
"happening to come to Malta about three months after the
"correspondence respecting the church salutes had been for-
"warded to England, he issued a general order, dated 5th Nov.
"1823, designating the conduct of myself and Lieutenant Daw-
"son '*an unheard-of precedent of insubordination*,' but as the
"matter had been submitted to the Duke of Wellington, then
"Master-General of the Ordnance, he suspended us from all
"duties till a decision were notified from England. Thus it
"happened that the Duke was waiting for more intelligence from
"Malta, and Sir Thomas waiting for a decision from England,
"before this so-called breach of discipline could be dealt with.
"What will thinking men and officers say to this? It also hap-
"pened that Sir Thomas Maitland was much attached to Dr.
"Hennen, the inspector-general of hospitals at Malta, from pre-
"vious service together, and also to his eldest daughter, a remark-
"ably well-read, intelligent, lively young lady, and Sir Thomas
"had them to the palace most evenings when without general
"company. This Miss Hennen was then engaged to be married
"to Lieutenant Dawson. Again it happened that Captain Bayley,
"the military secretary, was very intimate with Dr. Hennen,
"and soon after the issuing of Sir Thomas Maitland's order
"against Lieutenant Dawson and myself, Captain Bayley told
"Dr. Hennen that after the order was handed to him he said to
"Sir Thomas, 'There is no disobedience of orders in this case;'
"to which Sir Thomas replied, '*I know that;*'—and when he
"heard that Lieutenant Dawson was to be married to his young
"friend, Miss Hennen, Sir Thomas expressed to Dr. Hennen *his*
"*deepest regret that he had not known of this engagement before.*
"Does this consist with Mr. Dawson or myself having been
"guilty of any breach of discipline at all? We entertained the
"hope that Sir Thomas would see to the real truth and justice
"of the case, but on the 17th January (two months after) he was
"seized with apoplexy at Malta, and died. Dr. Hennen's other

"daughter, married to a Mr. De la Condamine, (being at Malta
"at the time, though away from her father's house,) I think must
"be able to corroborate these circumstances, and she is still alive.
"Mrs. Dawson is dead, as also her husband.

"It is also strange to state, that the Marquis of Hastings,
"having succeeded as governor of Malta, when the first proceed-
"ings of the court-martial were under consideration in England,
"the marquis sent for the copies of the proceedings kept at Malta,
"and, after reading, returned them to the deputy judge-advocate
"without remark to any one. But *the day after the court-martial*
"*repeated their sentence for our dismissal*, the marquis sent for
"Lieutenant-Colonel the Honourable W. H. Gardner, then com-
"manding the Royal Artillery at Malta, and said that he must put
"a stop to the requisitions of the priests for these salutes; that
"Colonel Gardner must select some place where the priests could
"*fire their own salutes* without danger; but he might have them
"supplied with gunpowder; only having an old gunner in attend-
"ance to see after the powder and magazine. He also ordered
"that the priests might have access to their bell at Fort Angelo, to
"toll it with their ceremonies as their occasions required; and the
"priests after this fired their own salutes and tolled their own
"bell while I was at Malta.

"I published what the marquis had done, in the preface of
"the printed proceedings of the court-martial, (Butterworth, Fleet
"Street; Hatchard, Piccadilly; 1825.) This brought the acts of
"the Marquis of Hastings under the notice of Government, and
"Lord Bathurst, one of the secretaries of state, wrote to the Mar-
"quis of Hastings, disapproving of what he had done, (I forget the
"terms used,) and ordered him to make no alterations in the
"customs observed by his predecessors without orders from the
"Government at home. The Marquis of Hastings forwarded Lord
"Bathurst's letter to Lieutenant-Colonel Gardner, simply and
"without any remark. Colonel Gardner read the letter and re-
"turned it to the marquis also without remark or taking further
"notice of its contents, and the priests were left to toll their bell
"and to fire their own petteraro salutes for their objects of worship
"as the noble marquis had directed. Colonel Gardner's adjutant,
"Lieutenant Drew, to whom the letter was shown, and who was

"cognizant of all, informed me of these particulars when he re-
"turned to England. I have the same particulars from others
"who were at Malta at the time.*

  "Now, here we see a distinguished nobleman, general, and
"statesman, carrying out to the full the objections which Lieu-
"tenant Dawson and myself had made to the popish ceremonies
"in question; and when the Government at home ordered him
"to make no alterations in the customs observed by his prede-
"cessors, he quietly, but firmly, disregarded and disobeyed their
"orders.

  "Here is a case of decided disobedience and continued resist-
"ance on the part of a distinguished general and nobleman,
"which the Horse Guards and the Government quietly suffered,
"while they have maintained the contrived and false charges, and
"the sentence of the court-martial, so contrary to the evidence
"against myself, and when the acts of the noble marquis had
"demonstrated that the Government, as well as the court-martial,
"was altogether in the wrong.

  "I can give a list of most eminent officers, who have from
"the first protested against the sentence of the court-martial;
"and the late Sir Augustus Frazer of the Royal Artillery, a friend
"of my family, and who had a copy of the proceedings of the
"court-martial from my brother, told me that he went to the
"Horse Guards and so argued against the charge of disobedience,
"and the whole proceeding, that Sir Henry Torrens, the adjutant-
"general, got quite in a rage. Sir Augustus also told me that he
"had expressed his views and feelings on the subject also to
"Colonel Cowper, then private secretary to Master-General Sir
"James Kemp; and said, 'Sir James has only to mention your
"'name to me, or in any way refer to the case, and I will as

* I very distinctly recollect speaking to Colonel Gardner about Captain
Atchison's and Mr. Dawson's dismissal, when he was dining at the palace at
Malta, during my visit there in 1826. He was then the officer in command of
the Royal Artillery at Malta, and he told me that Lord Hastings had, before he
had gone on leave to England, put a stop to the required participation by the
officers in these idolatrous ceremonies of the Romish Church. It appears, however, from a subsequent part of this letter, that an order of the main guard at
Valetta, relative to the turning out of the guard to salute the host as it
passed, was, by some mistake, not erased from the board of orders till 1859.
See page 264.   W. LEEKE.

" 'frankly tell him my sense of the great injustice of the proceed-
" 'ings.'

"When I called on General Lord Bloomfield, an attached
"friend of my uncle, Colonel Judgson, to inform him of the cir-
"cumstances of my case, and told him the views of Sir Augustus
"Frazer, and how he had gone to the Horse Guards and expostu-
"lated against the sentence against me, he said, 'That is like
" 'Frazer and his noble conduct in standing by Colonel Oliver,
" '(a religious officer of the regiment,) who had declined the chal-
" 'lenge of a captain of the navy, at Dublin, to fight a duel for
" 'his reply to a lieutenant of the navy, accused of drunkenness by
" 'the sergeant of a guard, when Colonel Oliver happened to come
" 'up as field-officer of the day.' The officer asked, "Am I drunk";
" 'the answer was: "As you ask me, I must say I think so."
" 'Nearly all the officers at Dublin cut Colonel Oliver for not
"fighting."

"Being distantly related to the late Field-Marshal Viscount
"Combermere, and my mother and brother intimate with Mr.
"Carverly Cotton and Lady Corbet Corbet, of Adderley, uncle
"and aunt of his lordship, my case was much pressed on the old
"viscount's attention. At first he said it was nonsense, as an
"officer must obey all orders; but afterwards, when he was led
"to consider the circumstances, he said the case ought to be
"thoroughly looked into. Mr. Woodrooffe, of Lincoln's Inn, then
"one of the committee of the Pastoral Aid Society, also told me that
"the late Lord Chief-Justice Denman had looked into the case,
"and said that it ought to be brought before the Court of
"Queen's Bench.

"I had, as like-minded friends, Colonel Sir George Wood,
"who commanded the artillery at Waterloo; Colonel Sir Alex-
"ander Dickson, the eminent commander of the artillery during
"the Peninsular war, afterwards commandant at Woolwich; and
"General Neville, R.A., surveyor-general of the Ordnance;
"Lieutenant-General Douglas, R.A.; Colonel, afterwards Major-
"General Oliver, R.A.; and Admiral Oliver, with nine other
"officers of inferior rank, gave their names with their sub-
"scriptions in support of Lieutenant Dawson and myself. After

"that, General Sir De Lacy Evans, in the House of Commons,
"voted in my behalf. Then Colonel Sir Duncan Macdougall,
"formerly commanding the 79th Regiment, and quartermaster-
"general under Sir De Lacy Evans, in Spain, after critically ex-
"amining the proceedings on the trial, pronounced there was no
"disobedience of orders or breach of discipline on my part, when
"he was incurring the responsibility of recommending me to be
"the senior major at the formation of the Royal Lancashire
"Militia Artillery; and the no less remarkable expression of
"Lord Raglan, then Master-General, (and who had been private
"secretary to the Duke of Wellington during the whole time of
"the proceedings against me,) when Sir Duncan asked him if
"there was any objection to my being appointed his senior major,
"instantly saying 'It is the *best thing that can be done,*' I think
"shows that his lordship knew and felt, not only that I was
"suffering great injustice, but that the charge of disobedience of
"orders and breach of discipline could not be maintained against
"me. How else could any officer in his high position take the
"responsibility of approving my appointment to such a high
"military position if I had been guilty of any breach of disci-
"pline. His lordship also knew that I continued to maintain
"that I had only acted on my Protestant rights in the service,
"and that the Articles of War provided for my complaint of
"wrong, and seeking its redress; and thus supported my appeal.
"Another important matter on the case requires to be kept in
"view. The late Captain Simmons, of the Royal Artillery,
"author of the book on the 'Constitution and Practice of Courts-
"'Martial,' considered the best one on the subject, and in con-
"stant use in the service, (he was also generally employed, after
"this work was published, as the officiating judge-advocate on
"courts-martial in England,) was quartered at Malta with Mr.
"Dawson and myself until a short time before the case for the
"trials arose. He told me, on my return to England, that he
"had most carefully studied the charges, evidence, and sentence,
"and that at the Royal Artillery mess at Woolwich, and on other
"occasions, he always showed, from the facts proved, that there
"was no disobedience of orders nor breach of discipline on our
"part. It will also be seen, in his able work, (4th edition, pages

"174 to 178,) that he in a very guarded, but firm manner, contro-
"verts the expressions put forth in the King's name to support
"the sentence of the court-martial against our plea that the
"orders were unlawful, namely, 'His Majesty has declared that
"'orders are lawful when issued by authorities legally constituted
"'and competent to give them, responsible to their sovereign and
"'country for their acts and for the exercise of the authority
"'with which they are invested,' and Captain Simmons then
"shows that, as the Mutiny Act demands obedience to the lawful
"commands of a superior officer, and not the commands of a
"lawful superior, '*it is lawful in a military sense to disobey
"an unlawful command of a superior.*' Then how much more
"lawful to present a respectful remonstrance against an unlawful
"command affecting our dearest personal and national rights;
"and in support of his view he gives a memorandum indited
"by the late Duke of York, to confirm the views he thus puts
"forth to the army and the public. I had set forth the same
"truths in vain, and having acted on them am punished and
"denied all justice; yet Captain Simmons was not punished for
"contradicting and opposing the military authorities, but was
"encouraged and employed by them.

    "That I was right in considering that it was *an unlawful
"order* to order me, a British Protestant officer, to execute a
"Romish church requisition; to fire their church petteraro salutes,
"and toll their bell for their specified idolatrous objects of wor-
"ship, under the directions and signals of the priests, *as military
"duty*, I fully demonstrated to the court-martial in my defence,
"pp. 18, 21. It was also proved, by the Marquis of Hastings'
"discarding these requisitions and ceremonies from the Royal
"Artillery, the very day after the court-martial passed their sen-
"tence against me; and I had appealed to the sense of truth
"and honour in the breasts of the court, and claimed their
"indignity at the charge *from its want of truth*: see p. 20—but
"all in vain, through the influence of the Great Duke's promul-
"gated opinion and known directions from England, and the
"prosecutor's doctrine, that an officer is bound, in all cases, to
"obey first and remonstrate afterwards, given in his address on
"Dawson's trial, (mine was after it;) and I had no opportunity

" of replying to this absurdity, which I could have done by a
" remonstrance before obedience, sanctioned by the Judge-Advo-
" cate General, in a case where a general had ordered the mem-
" bers of a district court-martial to act in a way contrary to their
" oaths, as well as to the practice of the service at that time ; and
" other cases have been told me, by an experienced officer, since.
" The *Articles of War* provide for an officer making his complaint
" of wrong and seeking its redress, without any limitation as to
" the time when, or in any other respect.

   " The military authorities received and attended to the re-
" monstrances of other officers in the Greek Islands, and also in
" India, against the similar abominations being enforced upon
" them as military duties ; and in the more recent case of Captain
" Sheffield, of the 21st Regiment, who declined in the most
" marked manner to obey the orders to salute the host as it might
" pass his guard at Malta ; and after being placed under arrest,
" and the case reported to the Horse Guards, an order was
" returned, ordering him to be released, and to return to his
" duties, and the offensive orders to be expunged—all showing
" that they were unlawful to be enforced on a Protestant officer.

   " Had time and the scope of your work allowed, I would have
" given the testimony and opinion of my friends, the late General
" Nevill and Sir Augustus Frazer, that the sentence against me
" was maintained only through the habit of the Duke of Welling-
" ton not to allow any change in matters he had once decided upon ;
" and, in consequence, the other high authorities thought it was
" more politic to let me suffer than to incur his hostility.   Lord
" Raglan, so long the Duke's private secretary, speaking out in
" my behalf, so soon after his death, is some proof of this.

   " I think also, I can make out a pretty strong case of military
" character for intelligence, usefulness, and constant interest in
" the duties of an artillery officer, and in the welfare of the pro-
" fession and of the country, besides the high testimonials which
" I obtained from the seven commanding officers under whom I
" had served, to shew that I was as incapable of disobedience of
" orders, or any breach of discipline, as an officer could be.   If I
" have health and strength, I hope to enter on these subjects as
" useful to the profession and to my country ; and as they may

" prove vindicatory of, and useful to, myself. Yet I am thus
" left to suffer against all law and reason, except as the Lord's
" grace has kept my mind under a constant sense of having acted
" only loyally to the service and to my country, as well as having
" done right in His sight; and in His merciful providence He
" has sustained me, as He did my friend Dawson also, in all
" other respects.

" I cannot conclude without again expressing my heartfelt
" gratitude to you and others, led of the Lord to be our comfort
" and support when we arrived in England, especially Mr.
" Alexander Haldane and his friends in London, who kept the
" case before the public several years. You should know that
" Dawson and myself were entirely dependent on our commis-
" sions. As to Dawson, his mother, relations, and friends, refused
" to see him. Archbishop Sutton was his uncle by marriage.
" His eldest brother was Prebendary of Canterbury. His other
" relations of like grade. *Your contributions enabled him to enter*
" *the Dublin University*, and as soon as he took his degree, the
" excellent Bishop of Winchester took him by the hand, although
" personally unknown, and appointed him as assistant minister
" of St. James's, Guernsey, with a yearly stipend of £150, as good
" as £200 in England. On the retirement of the minister of St.
" James's he was elected in his stead, with double his previous
" stipend. At the end of the five years' engagement, a *party*,
" offended with his faithfulness, elected another minister, when
" the bishop immediately appointed him to a vacant rectory in
" Hampshire, the patron being lunatic. Archbishop Howley then
" appointed him to a new church and district in Kent, which he
" brought into admirable order. Dr. Howley was known to say,
" that he always got more information from Mr. Dawson, as to
" the matters of his diocese, than from any other clergyman.
" His brother and others had then begun to feel his value, and
" not to be ashamed of him, and the vicarage or rectory of
" Orpington, £300 or £400 a year and a good house, falling to
" his gift, he presented it to my valued friend. There he died
" about twelve or thirteen years ago, under circumstances most
" painful for his friends to contemplate, but thoroughly charac-
" teristic of his faithful and consistent life. He had not been

" well when the public fast for the cholera was ordered. He
" conducted all the services, and had *observed the fast strictly,*
" and consequently went to bed much exhausted ; though a very
" large and powerful man, and accustomed to abstemiousness and
" economy on principle. In the middle of the night he was
" called up by a message from his brother the prebendary,
" with a letter and documents shewing that his son had been
" dismissed from his cadetship, with a number of other cadets,
" under a *general sweeping* charge, by the *military authorities,* of
" which the boy not only declared his perfect innocence, but
" also, as I understood, showed grounds for it ; the brother re-
" questing Dawson to draw up a reply for him. I am informed
" that Dawson got up immediately and drew up an admirable
" one, and sent it off without the least delay ; that he was much
" exhausted by the effort ; and that, as a consequence, either
" that day or the following one he was seized with paralysis and
" died. We can well imagine how, and especially in his ex-
" hausted state, and even when striving for Christian patience
" and coolness, his mind could hardly fail to be highly exasper-
" ated against this fresh act of military injustice—how it would
" continue to absorb all his mind and feelings, and so, prevent-
" ing his nerves taking their proper rest, destroy his valuable
" life.

" I could tell you many very interesting things about him,
" all testifying that even in his unregenerate state the Lord had
" endowed him with a highly conscientious and honourable, as
" well as an intelligent and cultivated mind. But he has gone
" to his rest with God in Jesus, and *his works do follow him :*
" especially that of his Protestant protest at Malta, and he was
" my leader, or perhaps I should more correctly say *the imme-*
" *diate example* before me, for the Lord had brought the same
" facts and conclusions to my own soul without any conference
" with him on the principles in question, (we being at distant
" posts when our several convictions and conclusions were
" formed,) and had it not been for his prompt and faithful act, as
" well as that most strange and unmilitary act of the adjutant-
" general at Malta, in telling my commanding officer at Valetta
" to *send me* over to Fort Angelo to execute the orders from

"which he had requested to be exonerated, the trial of my faith
"would not, *then certainly*, and might not at all, have been
"called into exercise. For, as to his work, or the same grace in
"others having *effectually followed* him, you will praise the Lord
"in now learning that, in the spring of the year 1859, Captain
"John Sheffield of the 21st Royal North British Fusileers, on
"the mounting of the main guard at Valetta, Malta, when read-
"ing the board of orders to his guard, and coming to the para-
"graph directing him to turn out his guard and *salute the host* as
"it passed—he instantly returned his sword, *left his guard*, and
"reported to his commanding officer what he had done. He was
"immediately placed under arrest, and the case reported to the
"Horse Guards. After some delay, the authorities in London
"sent an order to Malta, directing Captain Sheffield to be
"released from his arrest and to return to his duty, with further
"directions *to strike out the orders requiring such observances*. We
"must praise the Lord for this result, and for this striking in-
"stance of the fulfilment of His true and certain word,—and
"which we should take to heart for our comfort and encourage-
"ment for faithful discharge of all our Christian duties in Christ
"the Lord, in all the relationships of life. No word of God,
"acted on in faith, falls to the ground, and every act and work
"truly in Jesus will follow us—so manifest in our noble Re-
"formers, and so needed to be kept in mind in these sad days of
"the *essence* and *presence* of popery in the Church on all sides of
"us.

"I must conclude with an outline of my own circumstances
"in some additional respects, to shew also the importance of the
"kind Christian contributions of yourself and friends in my be-
"half, and the wonderful providence and ways of God towards
"myself also.

"My half-brother, Judgson, Fellow of Trinity, Cambridge, on
"the first intelligence, while feeling that there was a great wrong
"in the case, took the prevailing opinion that the Government
"being responsible, I might comply with the orders *on that
"ground*, and he urged me to consider the matter in that light:
"but I felt that that would not discharge my responsibility as a
"Christian man.

"I received the sentence of my dismissal late on the Sunday
" night. A pang came at feeling that I and my three children
" were cast without means on the world; but praised be God, He
" brought His *name*, JEHOVAH JIREH, to my very soul, *imme-*
" *diately*, and I went to bed and slept soundly. The private
" letters, early on the Monday morning, brought one from my
" dear brother, stating that now that he had seen all the circum-
" stances and evidence on the case *he would not have had me to*
" *act differently than I had done.* He said, 'Come home; our
" 'mother has plenty of room for you and your children, and you
" 'shall have at least £200 a year from me until we get you
" 'something better.' You will judge my praise and thankful-
" ness. On arriving at Portsmouth, I received a letter stating
" my brother was ill, staying in London for advice. I had the
" happiness of seeing him for a few hours, and took my children
" to my mother's at Cambridge; and returning to my brother the
" following day, I arrived only to be with him a few hours before
" he died in my arms. With his death went the £200 a year.
" But the *day after*, as I was proceeding to Dulwich, to make
" arrangements for his funeral, I met Dr. Parker of the Royal
" Artillery, a Christian friend, who told me that Lord Lifford, a
" commissioner of excise, had felt greatly for my case, and having
" a small appointment, £100 a year, to dispose of, he would not
" fill it up until I returned to England, as it might be useful to
" me. I felt this also was from the Lord, and accepted it,
" though it went sorely against the feelings of my dear mother
" that I, as she said, should become an exciseman; but my ex-
" planation of the nature of the duties appeased her.

" On opening my dear brother's papers we found that he had
" altered his will materially in my behalf, so that a small estate
" he had intended for an uncle for his life after my mother's death,
" should revert to me at once after her death with all his other
" property. This, with my mother's care and affection to us all,
" gave me the assurance of a future competence as well as a
" present provision; another instance that the Lord is faithful to
" His glorious name, Exod. xxxiv, 5—7, as well as *Jehovah Jireh:*
" and that His promises, in Exod. xxxiii, 13—19, of His coun-
" tenance and presence, and making all His goodness pass

" before the souls of His tried people, are as true and certain
" to us now as to His people of old. So the name of JESUS,
" ' He shall save His people *from their* SINS,' not merely from
" the punishment, as the papists would have it. Oh that
" Christians now would think, and feel, and act on these
" glorious names as we see the prophets and the psalmist
" continually did.

" Under the above happy circumstances and prospects, and
" observing a strict economy, (what will Cambridge and Oxford
" men and tutors say to my assertion that 8s. a week supplied
" me abundantly with my necessary food and sustenance, as my
" accounts will shew—Dawson also did not spend more—and I
" arduously employed at least twelve or fourteen hours a day with
" my publications or other work, and was never stronger in my life,)
" your kind contributions enabled me to carry on my protest, and
" contest with the authorities without stinting any expense, greatly
" supported also by the constant kindness and sympathy of several
" Christian friends in and about London, and by friends frequently
" calling on me from the country, those from the neighbourhood
" of Derby most frequently. Many years ago my books showed
" that I had expended better than £500 in publishing and circu-
" lating papers ; you will therefore see how important your help
" was to me. Dawson having gone to study at Dublin, and with-
" out leisure, and without the prospects I had, I felt that my
" calling was to stand to our case for the great principles that
" were at issue.

" In December, 1827, my dear mother died, and I was enabled
" to marry an excellent woman the following year, with a mode-
" rate allowance from her dear father, the Rev. John Simons,
" Rector of Paul's Cray, enabling us with strict economy to bear
" the charges of our new state. Soon after the abolition of my
" office under the excise in 1836, I was appointed assistant secre-
" tary to the newly formed Church Pastoral Aid Society, which
" just supplied the salary I had then lost, and the year following,
" at the death of my father-in-law, and the settlement of some
" most anxious affairs that lasted several years, the result was
" that, through many providential circumstances and helps from
" Christian friends, we were placed in most comfortable circum-

" stances. My dear wife was called to her eternal rest in Jesus
" five years ago.

" I little thought I should be drawn on to this length when
" I began ; but I am also thankful to say that the medical treat-
" ment I have been under the last fortnight has enabled me to get
" on in a way I did not anticipate, and the interest of the subject,
" with so many occasions of praise and thanksgiving, has also
" carried me on.

" I enclose a photograph of myself, taken last month ; also
" one from a picture of my friend Dawson.   I enter my 79th year
" on the 4th December, 1866, a memorial of so many mercies.

" Yours, my dear Sir,

" Very faithfully,

" THOMAS ATCHISON."

CHAPTER XLVI.

1794—1863.

FIELD-MARSHAL LORD SEATON.

Lord Seaton's services—Letter from him on being made Field Marshal—Letter on my leaving the army—Certificate on selling out—His concern for the welfare of men and officers—Dislike to corporal punishment—Much valued and beloved—The regiment ready to go anywhere with him—Reconnoitring—Fired at by enemy's sentries and videttes—Swimming his horse across rivers—Letters—Religious books—Severe affliction—His death—Notice in the public journals—Intended statue at Devonport.

THE services of Field-Marshal Lord Seaton are stated as follows in the 52nd "Record," at that part of the work which mentions his promotion to the rank of major-general, in May, 1825 :—

"Sir John Colborne had commanded the 52nd for a period "of fourteen years since 1811, and the colours of the regiment had "been borne to victory—and never hurried into defeat—under his "direction during the most exciting period of war since its forma- "tion. He is justly quoted by Napier in the third volume of his "'History' as 'a man of singular talents for war;' and it has been "justly observed of him, 'that the union of talents of such high "'order with such extended experience is rarely to be met with'. . "Here we have an officer entering the army without interest, "without purchasing a single step, a Major and Military Secretary "to the Commander of the Forces in twelve years.' 'Com- "mencing his campaigns in North Holland, in 1799, Sir John "Colborne served next in Egypt, then in the expedition to Naples, "and in Sicily and Calabria in 1806, when he was present at the

"battle of Maida. He was subsequently Military Secretary to Sir
"John Moore in Sicily, Sweden, and Portugal, and in Spain
"during the Corunna campaign. He joined Lord Wellington's
"army in 1809, and was present at the (Spanish) battle of Ocana.
"In the campaigns of 1810 and 1811 he commanded a brigade
"in Sir Rowland Hill's division, and in that command was
"engaged in the battle of Busaco. He commanded the advanced
"guard at the combat of Campo Major, and a brigade at the battle
"of Albuera. He directed and led the attack by which the out-
"work of St. Francisco was taken on the night of the investment
"of Ciudad Rodrigo, and commanded the left brigade of the
"Light Division on the attack and capture of the French en-
"trenched positions at Vera, and also at the battles of the
"Nivelle and the Nive. In the battle of Orthes he commanded
"the 52nd in the decisive attack of that regiment on Marshal
"Soult's position, and commanded the second brigade of the
"Light Division at the combats of Vic-Bigorre and Tarbes, and
"at the battle of Toulouse. Was appointed Prince Regent's Aide
"de Camp in 1814 and Military Secretary to the Prince of Orange,
"Commander-in-Chief of the British Forces in the Netherlands.
"In 1815 commanded the 52nd Light Infantry at the battle of
"Waterloo, and a Brigade on the march to Paris. Has held the
"following appointments:—Lieut.-Governor of Guernsey ; Lieut.-
"Governor of Upper Canada, Commander of the Forces in
"Canada ; Governor-General of British North America ; Lord
"High Commissioner in the Ionian Islands ; and Commander of
"the Forces in Ireland. Has received the Grand Cross of the
"Bath, and of Hanover, and of St. Michael and St. George ; the
"Order of Maria Theresa of Austria, of the Tower and Sword of
"Portugal, and of St. George of Russia ; the Waterloo Medal ;
"the Gold Cross and three Clasps ; the Silver War Medal with
"five Clasps. Was severely wounded at Ciudad Rodrigo."

Lord Seaton was promoted to the rank of Field-Marshal in
April 1860. He was Colonel of the 2nd Life Guards and Gold-
stick-in-Waiting to the Queen ; and, in addition, he became, on
the death of the lamented Prince Consort, Colonel-in-Chief of
the Rifle Brigade.

I received the following letter from him in reply to one

which I had written to congratulate him on his attaining the rank of Field-Marshal :—

"MY DEAR LEEKE,—Accept my best thanks for your letter of "the 10th, which I received with very great pleasure, and for your "kind congratulations.

"My promotion has been accomplished, and notified, in a "way that should be as gratifying, as this approval of my "services can be, to an old boy.

"I called on your brother a few days since, and found Lady "Leeke at home : she gave me a good account of you and of the "flourishing state of your family and parish.   .   .   .   .

"I suppose your son, who is making progress at Trinity College, "is destined for the Church. How satisfactory it must be to "you to know that he is going on well at Cambridge, the first "important trial, which he has to encounter. With Lady "Seaton's kind regards, believe me yours very sincerely,

"SEATON."

I received the following from Lord Seaton in answer to a letter in which I had mentioned my intention to go into the Church :—

"Guernsey, April 18th, 1825.

"MY DEAR LEEKE,—In looking at the date of your last letter, "I think myself inexcusable for not having yet congratulated "you on your happy prospects. I believe you have determined "wisely, and, under all circumstances, I am persuaded that, had "you remained in the army, you would have regretted your loss "of time, and your disappointments would have increased ten- "fold. If the war had continued I might have been of use to "you in your profession, but with the peace my influence was "of course at an end. You have seen much, during your military "career, to improve your judgment, and you can now justly "appreciate the good things of this *bas monde*. I think so "badly of our profession, and the risk of placing a young man "in it is such, that not one of my boys shall turn his mind that "way. [Three of his sons, however, went into the army.] We "are all expecting a brevet on the 23rd instant ; I suppose it "will make me a Major-General ; but whether it will occasion

" my removal from this island I have not yet been informed ; I
" am anxious to remain here, for, in every respect, I find it a
" convenient post.

"Cross has been trying to obtain the rank of Major, but
" without success, and he appears so discontented, and I think
" with reason, that he probably will not join the 52nd again. We
" shall be most happy to see you, if you are inclined to visit
" these islands in the summer. I beg my kind regards to Mrs.
" Leeke and your sister. Believe me, sincerely yours,

" J. COLBORNE."

After being three years at Cambridge, it was necessary for
me to sell out of the army before I took orders, and Sir John
Colborne sent me the following certificate to forward to the
Horse Guards with my application to be placed on full pay for
that purpose :—

" Lieutenant Leeke was appointed to the 52nd Light Infantry
" in the year 1815, and served with his corps till the year 1821
" or 1822 ; he then received permission from the Commander-
" in-Chief to enter the senior department at Sandhurst, where
" he gained very creditable certificates of the progress he had
" made as a student. His regiment being ordered to America,
" he left the College, and, I understand, would have remained
" abroad with his corps had there been any prospect of his suc-
" ceeding in his profession, or had he not lost a step by entering
" the Military College. He was an active and zealous officer
" and much esteemed by his regiment.

" J. COLBORNE, M.-General."

"Guernsey, May 9th, 1828."

In the course of the preceding portion of this work I have
mentioned most of the things which I recollect of Lord Seaton,
which help to display, in a slight degree, the greatness and goodness of his character. There are of course numbers of little
circumstances, which I cannot now recollect, but which have
left on my mind their impression of his noble character and of
his unvarying kindness of disposition.

It used to be said that his chief concern, as a commanding
officer, was about the welfare of the men of his regiment, and

perhaps this feeling might manifest itself, at times, more particularly than did his equally kind feelings towards his officers. I believe there never was an officer, who served under him, whose just claim for due consideration and attention, at the hands of the Commander-in-Chief, he was not always ready to urge. The whole regiment, officers and men, appreciated and loved him, and would have gone anywhere with him, as they also steadily and nobly did, when, at Waterloo, they moved down the British position to their single-handed encounter with ten times their number of the French Imperial Guard. Some years ago I was talking with the oldest 52nd Waterloo officer now surviving, and was observing that I never read that 7th verse of the 5th chapter of the Romans, "For scarcely for a righteous man will one die: "yet peradventure for a good man some would even dare to die," without its bringing Lord Seaton to my mind; and I added that I had always had the feeling, that whatever the danger, and even certainty of death might be, I could never see him in danger, without rushing to his assistance. General Sir William Rowan, for why should I withhold his name, replied, " Well, "that is what I also have always felt about him." But after all many of my readers will feel, that this is what British officers and soldiers would do for any of their comrades who might be in danger. And is not this one of the chief sources, or the chiefest source of the great success which has almost invariably attended our British troops in the various battles in which they have been engaged, that each man knows that his next neighbour and all around him will stick by him under any circumstances of danger in which they may be placed? This statement is made, of course, with the assurance that it is "the "God of battles" who gives the feeling of confidence, and who grants the success.

Lord Seaton had a very great dislike to the infliction of corporal punishment, and when he felt it to be absolutely necessary, he was always anxious that the punishment should be mitigated as far as possible. The men all knew and appreciated this tender-heartedness in their gallant commander, which was so regulated by a sense of what duty required from him, that the discipline of the regiment did not at all suffer from its frequent exercise.

I was telling a fine old sergeant of the 52nd, about whose claims Lord Seaton had interested himself, that I knew he was always ready to make application for any of the old soldiers of the regiment who appeared to have just claims upon the Government, and he replied, rather bluntly, "And he ought to be, Sir, "for we were always ready to go anywhere with him."

When we were at Paris, I was one day riding with Lord Seaton, and another officer of the regiment, on the road leading to the bridge of Neuilly, when we were accosted by a beggar, who was very earnest in his application for assistance, and afforded us some amusement by the high sounding titles which he gave us. He first addressed me as "Monsieur le Colonel," then the other officer as "Monsieur le General," and then Sir John Colborne as "Mon Prince."

Lord Seaton was accustomed, when his regiment was halted for the night, to spend some time in riding over the ground in his front, and now and then he unexpectedly came across the sentries or videttes of the enemy. On the march to Paris, and not very long before we reached it, he was fired at by a French sentry when he was upon one of these expeditions. Either I have heard him at the mess speak of the best method of taking a horse across a deep river, or others have related the circumstances of him. I think on two occasions, when reconnoitring, he only escaped from being taken by the enemy's cavalry, although he did not escape from being fired at, by riding at speed to the river, and forcing his horse into it. His plan was to disengage himself from the horse, and thus to disencumber him, and then to hold on with one hand by the stirrup leather, which was on the downward side of the stream; he maintained that a person in this position was not in danger of being struck by the horse's legs, as a horse always strikes up the stream in swimming across it.

On my dining with Lord Seaton, I think in 1850, he introduced me to Admiral Sir Edmund Lyons, afterwards the first Lord Lyons, as "Mr. Leeke, formerly a very good officer of the "52nd, and now a very good clergyman."

During the last few years of Lord Seaton's life, the Rev. John Yonge, of Puslinch, his brother-in-law, and others, kindly gave

me, from time to time, some account of his health. His power
of enduring a good deal of fatigue was great, after he had passed
his eightieth year. The following is from Mr. Yonge, in July,
1861 :—"Lord Seaton gave me your kind message, announcing
"the death of poor Lady Leeke. I was very sorry to hear it, for
"her loss must be much felt by her family, and by your brother
"especially. I know by experience how great the loss is. Lord
"Seaton is quite recovered from a most alarming illness which
"he sustained in the winter. He and his family are now in
"London, on courtly duty, at the Queen's levees, &c., but Lord
"Seaton will seize the first moment for returning; he takes very
"great interest in improving his plantations and fields."

Lord Seaton wrote as follows, on the 27th of May, 1861, and
I am not sure that it was not the last letter I received from
him :—"It was with great concern we heard of the affliction and
"bereavement in your brother's family, and which is the subject
"of your communication to me of the 24th. Sir Henry must
"derive much comfort from your presence and residence with
"him. It is many years since I have seen your sister Urania ;
"we are sorry to find from your letter that she has met with an
"accident. I am living the life of a farmer at Beechwood, about
"three miles from Plymouth and five from Puslinch. I am still
"able to take my usual rides, which have only been interrupted
"by a severe cold and cough. I hope when you can leave your
"parish, you will be able to visit Beechwood with Mrs. Leeke.
"   . . .   With my kindest regards to your brother,

"Believe me, yours very sincerely,

"SEATON."

My brother and his wife, whose death is referred to in these
letters, and all their family, had received much instruction and
comfort for a long time from some nice little volumes entitled,
I think, "Morning and Night Watches," and the "Bow in the
"Cloud." I took an opportunity of mentioning them to Lord
Seaton, and of sending them to him, and it was with no small
pleasure, that, in a letter from Lady Seaton, received some time
afterwards, I learnt they had been a comfort to Lord Seaton in
his latter days. I would strongly recommend them to the readers
of this work, as also Archbishop Leighton's " Commentary on the

" First Epistle of St. Peter," which I mentioned before as being a favourite book of Lord Seaton's. We may believe that those who can delight in such books must be "spiritually minded," and may expect to have "the Spirit bearing witness with their spirits that " they are the children of God: and if children, then heirs; heirs " of God, and joint heirs with Christ:" Romans viii., 16, 17.

From Lady Seaton, dated, "Beechwood, April 15th, 1862.

" MY DEAR MR. LEEKE,

" My brother has sent, for my perusal, so kind a note " from you, that I cannot but thank you myself for the kind " interest I am so sure you feel for Lord Seaton, and indeed for " all of us, in this our time of anxiety. You will be glad to hear, " and I am most thankful to say, that he is decidedly better than " he was a week since, and that we have much cause for hoping " that God, in his own good time, will restore him to health. In " the mean time he mercifully grants him great patience and sub- " mission to His will, and ourselves much comfort, and I trust we " shall all continue to be granted faith to feel that He who ap- " points us this long trial knows best what is really good for him " who is justly dear to us, as well as for those around him.

" Your nice and valuable little books were great helps to re- " mind us where we should look for comfort and strength, and I " know that Lord Seaton intended writing to you after he received " and first read them; but I am not certain whether he did so or " not. I am sure he would send you his kindest regards, and " join with me in wishing that you may soon lose all remains of " your late illness, which we were sorry to hear you had experi- " enced, if he knew that I am writing to you; but I neither like " to miss a mail, nor to disturb him in a nap he is this moment " indulging in. I beg my kind regards to Mrs. Leeke, and that " you will believe me,

" Yours very sincerely,

" E. SEATON."

A most severe trial was at this time impending over poor Lord Seaton and his family. Six weeks after I received this last letter, I received the following from Mr. John Yonge :—

"Puslinch, 30th May, 1862.

"MY DEAR MR. LEEKE,

"Although Lord Seaton has improved in health since I
"last wrote to you, yet a heavy blow has fallen on him, and on
"my poor sister and all the family, in the unexpected death of
"————, their second daughter, after a very brief illness. She
"rode over to this place about a week since. She died this
"morning. I fear the event will shake the powers of poor Lord
"Seaton a good deal.

"I told him you had, from time to time, written to me, to
"enquire for him, and he appeared much gratified by your regard
"for him.

"He has two sons and two daughters with him, and I hope
"that I shall find that God, in His mercy, extends his support-
"ing hand to them.

"Believe me, sincerely yours,

"JOHN YONGE."

On the 4th of February, 1863, Lady Seaton wrote as follows,
from Torquay, in reply to a letter from me to Lord Seaton, in-
forming him that my eldest son had just been announced as
Second Wrangler in the Cambridge Mathematical Tripos :—
"Lord Seaton begs me to write to you, and I am much pleased
"to do so, as it is to give you his hearty congratulations, in
"which I warmly join, on the great gratification and delight you
"must experience in your son's having so highly distinguished
"himself. Lord Seaton thanks you for believing the interest he
"would take in hearing it—and no one can more justly appreci-
"ate and sympathize with the feelings of a parent on any occa-
"sion of this kind, and which stamps a kind of certainty on a
"son's future career, through life, should it please God to spare
"him a long one.

"You will be very sorry to hear, I know, that Lord Seaton is
"still in a very suffering state, though certainly much better
"than when we left home some weeks since. He had previously
"been a whole year almost entirely confined to his room, and
"plunged into this state of trial very suddenly, from high health
"and vigour, from taking cold in a long ride the end of December,
"1861. Our bitter affliction too, in the loss of one of the most

"devotedly affectionate daughters, has more severely increased
"our sufferings than any words can express; but a merciful God
"has enabled us to feel that it has all proceeded from a Father's
"hand that does not willingly afflict, and has sustained us by
"comfort such as cannot be derived from any other source.
"Your little precious books too have been of much value. It is
"always so cheering to be reminded in a few words of what ought
"to be the mind of everyone who aims at being a sincere follower
"of his Saviour.

"Lord Seaton begs me not to forget his kindest regards. He
"is sorry not to write himself; but we always try to save him
"the exertion of doing so when we can.

"Believe me, yours very sincerely,

"E. SEATON."

Lord Seaton's death took place a few weeks only after this
last letter was written, and it was announced to me in the following letter from his brother-in-law, Mr. Yonge :—

"Sorel, Torquay, 18th April, 1863.

"MY DEAR MR. LEEKE,

"I well know how you valued the public and private
"character of Lord Seaton, and you will not hear, without
"emotion, that he died yesterday. I have not time to descant
"upon a character of so much worth in a public point of view;
"but to you as well as to myself, his private devotedness and
"sincerity of faith (true and lively) will appear to shed a brighter
"lustre than even his public renown. If you will kindly convey
"this event to your brother, Sir Henry Leeke, I shall be obliged.

"Sincerely yours,

"JOHN YONGE."

The following is extracted from "The Times" of April 18th,
1863, the very day after Lord Seaton's death :—

"*Death of Lord Seaton.*

"Another of those worthies has departed, the beginning of
"whose life stretches so far back that in recalling the dates we
"seem as if reverting to fabulous times. Lord Seaton was one
"of the old Peninsular heroes who were engaged in the transac-

" tion of history before the present century commenced.   As we
" look back to those times the fame of Wellington more and
" more dwarfs the reputation of all who served under him ; but
" his subordinates also attained to greatness, and would, but for
" his gigantic proportions, stand out before our eyes in bold
" relief.   John Colborne, Lord Seaton, was an officer worthy of
" his chief, whom he resembled in some points of character, but
" most of all in true modesty and hatred of pretence.   His man-
" ner, like that of most men accustomed to authority, gave one
" the idea of a stern man, but a kinder heart than his never beat.
" There were in his character certain elements which acquired for
" him the esteem of all who could obtain a near view of him.
" Thus, though he had to do with the Canadians in revolt, and with
" the Ionian Islanders in a state of furious discontent, and long
" commanded the army in Ireland, he was never unpopular ; and
" his singular charm of manner may be said to have covered any
" deficiency which he exhibited as a politician."

The services of Lord Seaton, enumerated in " The Times,"
are omitted here, as they have already been mentioned in this
very chapter.

" His chief military feat, however, was performed at Waterloo,
" where he again commanded the 52nd, as part of Adam's
" brigade.   Of his own accord he led the forward movement,
" which determined the fortunes of the day.   When the column
" of the Imperial Guard was gaining the summit of the British
" position, [It was 300 yards below the summit] and was forcing
" backward one of the companies of the 95th, Colborne, seeing
" his left endangered, started the 52nd on its advance.   The
" Duke saw the movement, and instantly sent to desire Colborne
" to continue it.   This fact of Colborne having originated the
" decisive movement is abundantly confirmed.   A French officer
" who accompanied Ney's column of the Imperial Guard has
" stated that although the British troops in front of the Imperial
column showed ' *très-bonne contenance, nous fûmes principalement*
" ' *repoussés par une attaque de flanc très-vive, qui nous écrasa.*'
" This was Colborne's attack at the head of the 52nd, and it
" brought him great renown.

" After Waterloo a soldier seemed to have, as a soldier, no

" more chances in the world; and there was nothing left for Sir
" John Colborne (now a K.C.B.) than the uncertain glories of a
" semi-civil life. Soon after the peace he was appointed Gover-
" nor of Guernsey, where he was the means of reviving Elizabeth
" College, which had fallen into great decay. He was afterwards
" appointed to the command of the forces in Canada, which he
" held from 1830 to 1838. On one occasion, being dissatisfied
" with the conduct of the civil powers in that colony, he resigned
" his command, and his luggage was actually on board the trans-
" port on which he was to have embarked in three days' time,
" when an autograph letter from the King (William IV) arrived,
" requesting him to remain. He was honoured with the Grand
" Cross of the Bath, and he was created Governor-General as well
" as Commander-in-Chief. Having suppressed the Canadian re-
" bellion, he returned to England and was raised to the peerage;
" but he took no part in politics, save once, when he spoke in the
" debate on the union of the Canadas. He expressed himself
" averse from the union, on the ground that it would eventually
" hamper the development of Canada, and, furthermore, prove a
" hindrance to the junction of the North American Provinces
" into a Confederation. Though he took no part in the debates
" of the House of Lords, he was still to have another field for the
" exercise of whatever legislative gifts he might possess. He was
" appointed Lord High Commissioner of the Ionian Islands from
" 1843 to 1849, and there he had, during the revolutionary
" mania of 1848, to deal with the demands of a people continually
" disaffected.

" Since then Lord Seaton has commanded the troops in
" Ireland; in 1854 he was appointed Colonel of the 2nd Life
" Guards; and in 1860 he was promoted to the rank of Field-
" Marshal. He died at Torquay, in the 86th year of his age.
" His life was so prolonged, and latterly was so retired, that
" many persons when they first hear of his death will not know
" who or what he was. He was of the race of heroes who fought
" in the mightiest wars of modern times; who through those wars
" made England glorious and maintained her independence; and
" who have left us an example which is part of our heritage—
" part of our life."

The subjoined notice of Lord Seaton's death is from "Bell's "Messenger" of April 20, 1863 :—

"Another of the famous veterans of the Peninsula and "Waterloo has been taken from us. Field-Marshal Lord Seaton, "died at Valetta House, Torquay, on Friday last. . . . . His "Lordship, with Lady Seaton and family, had been passing the "winter months there for the benefit of his health. He died full "of honours as of years, and the heart of many a weather-beaten "old soldier will throb impetuously as the mention of the great "chief's death conjures up the feats of daring of which Colonel "Colborne, of the Light Division, was the hero."

In "The Illustrated London News" there appeared, in 1865, I think, the following mention of a marble bust of the late Lord Seaton, and, in a subsequent paragraph from "The Times," is given the account of a meeting, convened for the purpose of carrying out a project of placing a bronze statue of Lord Seaton on the Government Parade at Devonport :—

"The English, though behind no Continental or Transatlantic "people in pride of nationality, are not so remarkable as some of "their neighbours for hero-worship. The sentiment is, however, "gaining ground among us, and is especially observable in the "unprecedented demand for monumental commemoration. It "could not, we think, take a more healthy direction. Sculptured "or painted personal memorials of our great dead are the most "natural expression of our admiration, the most direct means of "preserving greatness and worth in our remembrance, and one "of the most legitimate modes of employing and developing art, "notwithstanding some discouraging failures. Still, however, "the popular desire to raise commemorative effigies of various "kinds often seems to spring from not very lofty or unselfish "motives. The fame to be memorialised must generally be re- "cent, or in some way bound up with clique or party. Were it "otherwise, should we not, for example, have heard an imme- "diate requisition for a public monument to the late Lord "Seaton? But the chief services of this gallant veteran were "rendered to the country nearly fifty years ago, and he survived "the vast majority of men old enough to share or to take a more "immediate interest in his achievements. However, there is a

" project on foot, though somewhat tardily conceived, to erect a
" monument to Lord Seaton, and the subscriptions are headed by
" the Prince of Wales and the Duke of Cambridge. Meanwhile
" we are glad of the opportunity of engraving a bust of this dis-
" tinguished officer, though it is destined for no more public
" place than the great hall of the United Service Clubhouse.
" The bust, which is executed in the finest Carrara marble, has
" been presented to the club by the second son of the deceased,
" Colonel the Hon. Francis Colborne, C.B. An inscription to
" this effect is on the red-variegated Belgian marble pedestal on
" which the bust stands.

" This is not the place to enumerate the important services of
" the late Lord Seaton, especially as they were chronicled in our
" pages (see our number for May 2, 1863) soon after his death.
" The reader, however, will remember that, under the family
" name of Colborne, and commencing as a simple Ensign, the
" deceased Field-Marshal served in North Holland, in Egypt, on
" the Neapolitan frontier, in Sicily and Calabria, and through
" great part of the Peninsular War. At Ciudad Rodrigo, where
" he was severely wounded, he performed one of the most gallant
" achievements of the war—the capture, at the head of the 52nd
" Regiment, of the detached fort of San Francisco. In command
" of the same regiment at Waterloo he performed, on his own re-
" sponsibility and at a very critical moment, a brilliant manœuvre
" which decided the fortunes of the day. The column of the
" Imperial Guard had almost gained the summit of the British
" position, [The columns were 300 yards below the position]
" when Colonel Colborne, seeing his left endangered, ordered an
" advance of the 52nd. ' The Duke ' saw the movement, and in-
" stantly sent to desire Colborne to continue it. A French officer
" who accompanied Ney's column confesses that it was this flank
" attack which principally repulsed and crushed the Imperial column.

" After the Peace he was consecutively Governor of Guernsey,
" Commander of the Forces in Canada, (where he suppressed the
" rebellion,) Lord High Commissioner of the Ionian Islands, and
" Commander of the Forces in Ireland. His illustrious and hon-
" ourable life was terminated last summer, at Torquay, at the
" ripe age of eighty-six."

The following is from "The Times" :—

"THE SEATON MEMORIAL.—A meeting of the committee for
"erecting a memorial to the late Field-Marshal Lord Seaton, was
"held in London on the 2nd of June, to receive a report from
"the chairman, Sir Edmund S. Prideaux, and to make definitive
"arrangements for the execution of the work. The chairman
"reported the subscriptions to the Seaton Memorial Fund had
"been constantly increasing and now exceeded £900, and that
"the greater part of this sum is now bearing interest until called
"for. The committee resolved that Mr. Adams should be em-
"ployed to execute a bronze statue of not less than eight feet
"in height. A model of a statue has been prepared by the
"sculptor, and may be inspected at his studio, 126, Sloane Street.
"A favourable opinion of the figure has been expressed by some
"of the most intimate friends of the late Field-Marshal. The
"committee confidently rely on success in obtaining the full
"means of executing satisfactorily the work and placing it, as
"already decided, at Devonport, on the Government Parade,
"where a site has been placed at the disposal of the committee,
"under the sanction and authority of the Secretary of War, who
"has evinced great interest in the success of a memorial in honour
"of the late distinguished Field-Marshal Lord Seaton. The fol-
"lowing are the names of the memorial committee :—The Duke
"of Somerset, K.G., Earl of Devon, Earl Fortescue, Lord Clifford,
"Lord Poltimore, Lord Lyons, K.C.B., Right Hon. Sir John Cole-
"ridge, Lieutenant General Hon. Sir James Scarlett, K.C.B., Sir
"Edmund S. Prideaux (chairman), Sir W. Heathcote, Sir Massey
"Lopes, General Sir W. Rowan, K.C.B., General Sir James Shaw
"Kennedy, K.C.B., General Sir G. Wetherall, K.C.B., Lieutenant-
"General Sir R. Airey. K.C.B., Lieutenant J. Eden, C.B., Colonel
"Owen, C.B., R.E., Major-General Hutchinson, Major-General
"D'Urban, Vice-Admiral Woollcombe, Colonel Harrison, Colonel
"North, &c., and several local country gentlemen and officers."

"September 20, 1866. The colossal statue in bronze of the
"late Field-Marshal Lord Seaton, by Mr. George G. Adams, with
"its granite pedestal, has arrived at Plymouth. The work is at
"once to be placed in the garrison of Devonport."

CHAPTER XLVII.

1815.

LIST OF 52ND WATERLOO OFFICERS AND THEIR SERVICES.

THE following 52nd officers served at Waterloo. They are almost all taken from the Appendix to the 52nd Record, in which the names of those were omitted, whose services could not be ascertained:—

"Lieut.-Colonel Sir John Colborne, K.C.B., Colonel, after-"wards Lord Seaton. Major Charles Rowan, Lieut.-Colonel, "wounded. Captains—P. Campbell, Major; W. Chalmers, Major 'W. Rowan, Major, w.; J. F. Love, Major, w.; C. Earl of March, "(Staff); C. Diggle, w.; J. Shedden; J. McNair; E. Langton; "J. Cross; C. Yorke (Staff). Lieutenants—C. Dawson, w.; M. "Anderson, w.; C. Kenny; G. H. Love; W. Ripley; J. C. "Barrett; W. H. Clerke; G. Hall; W. R. Nixon; G. Gawler; "G. Whichcote; Hon. W. Ogilvy; E. R. Northey; Hon. W. "Browne; E. Scoones; G. Campbell, w.; W. Austin; J. Snod-"grass; J. S. Cargill; W. Hunter; W. C. Yonge; T. Cotting-"ham, w.; C. Holman; G. Moore; E. Mitchell; C. Shawe, J. "Hart; G. E. Scott; H. T. Oakes; J. R. Griffith; J. Burnett; R. "Steward; G. Robson; F. W. Love. Ensigns—J. Jackson; T. "Massie; W. Nettles, killed; J. Macnab; J. Montague; J. F. "May; E. Monins; W. Leeke. Paymaster—J. Clarke, Lieut. "and Adjutant—Winterbottom, w. Quarter-Master—B. Sweeten. "Surgeon—J. B. Gibson. Assistant-Surgeons—P. Jones; W. "Macartney."

Field-Marshal Lord Seaton's services are recorded at the commencement of Chapter XLVI of this work.

"Lieutenant-Colonel Sir Charles Rowan, K.C.B., entered the "52nd in 1798, and served with the regiment in Sicily, Denmark, "Portugal, and Spain. He was for some time Assistant-Adjutant- "General to the Light Division, and as such distinguished him- "self at the action of Almeida. He was present at the sieges of "Ciudad Rodrigo and Badajos, and at the battle of Salamanca, "besides numerous intervening affairs, for which he received the "war medal with clasps. He also served in the battle of "Waterloo, where he was severely wounded. On his retirement "from active service, Sir Charles Rowan undertook the organiza- "tion and management of the new Metropolitan Police, which "task he executed in a manner reflecting the highest credit on "his ability.

"Lieut.-General Sir William Chalmers, K.C.H. and C.B., "served in Sicily in 1806 and 1807, in Portugal and Spain in "1808 and 1809. In the Walcheren expedition ; at Cadiz in "1810 and 1811 ; and in all the succeeding Peninsular cam- "paigns, including the battles of Barossa, Salamanca, Vittoria, "the Pyrenees, Nivelle, and various minor actions and most of "the sieges. He commanded a wing of the 52nd at the battle "of Waterloo, and has received the war medal with eight clasps.

"General Sir William Rowan, G.C.B., entered the 52nd in "1803. Served in Sicily in 1806 ; in Sweden in 1808 ; at "Flushing in 1809 ; in Portugal in 1811, including the action "of Sabugal ; in the Peninsular and France in 1813 and 1814, "including the battles of Vittoria, and the Pyrenees, the attack "of Vera, the battles of the Nivelle, the Nive, Orthes, and "Toulouse, and the intermediate affairs. He has received for "these services the Peninsular war medal with six clasps. He "served also in the campaign and battle of Waterloo, and on the "capture of Paris was appointed Commandant of the first "Arrondissement of that city. Sir William has subsequently "held the high appointment of Commander of the forces in "Canada."

Sir William Rowan is now, in 1866, Colonel of his old Regiment, the 52nd.

"Lieut.-General Sir J. Frederick Love, K.C.B., entered the
"52nd in 1804, and served in the expedition to Sweden under
"Sir John Moore, and afterwards in Portugal and Spain, in-
"cluding the retreat to and battle of Corunna, and the various
"intervening affairs. He served afterwards in the Peninsula,
"and was present at the storming of Ciudad Rodrigo, and in all
"the battles and affairs of the Light Division till 1812. He
"served in the campaign of Holland under Lord Lynedoch, and
"was engaged in the affairs during the advance and unsuccess-
"ful attack on New Orleans, where he was wounded,* He also
"served in the campaign of Waterloo, where he received four
"severe wounds when the 52nd charged the French Imperial
"Guards. Sir Frederick has received the war-medal with four
"clasps for Corunna, Busaco, Fuentes d'Onor, and Ciudad Rodrigo.

"Colonel Charles, Duke of Richmond, K.G., entered the 52nd
"in 1813, having previously, while on the staff of Lord Wel-
"lington, placed himself in the ranks of the regiment with the
"stormers of Ciudad Rodrigo. His Grace was present at all the
"affairs and battles and sieges in which the Duke of Wellington's
"army was engaged from 1810 till 1814, including Busaco,
"Fuentes d'Onor, Ciudad Rodrigo, Badajoz, Salamanca, Vittoria,
"the Pyrenees, the first assault of St. Sebastian, the action at
"Vera, and the battle of Orthes, where he voluntarily left the
"Staff to take command of his company of the 52nd, and was
"severely wounded in the chest by a musket-ball, which was
"never extracted. His Grace subsequently served in the battles
"of Quatrebras and Waterloo as aide-de-camp to the Prince of
"Orange, and after the Prince was wounded he served as aide-
"de-camp to the Duke of Wellington. His Grace has received
"the Peninsular war-medal with eight clasps, and is now, in
"1860, in command of and constantly with his regiment, the
"Royal Sussex (Light Infantry) Militia.' It was owing to the
"repeated efforts of the late Duke of Richmond that the war-
"medal and clasps were accorded to those who had served in the
"general actions of the Peninsula.

* Sir J. F. Love told the author that, after the attack on New Orleans, he
slept in the same room with the dead bodies of the two gallant English generals,
Pakenham and Gibbs, who were killed there.

"Major-General Charles Diggle, K.H. served with the 52nd "in Sicily in 1806 and 1807, and also in the expedition to "Sweden under Sir John Moore. He was present during the "retreat, and in the battle of Corunna, and in the action of the "Coa (Almeida), the battle of Busaco, and the various affairs "when the wing fell back on Torres Vedras. He served in the "campaign of 1813 and 1814, in Holland, and also at Waterloo, "where he was severely wounded. He has received the war-"medal with two clasps."

"Captain and Brevet-Major John Shedden entered the 52nd "in 1804, and served with the regiment in the Peninsula and at "Waterloo." Major Shedden died at Hull in 1821.

"Lieut.-Colonel James M'Nair entered the 52nd in 1804. "Served in the expedition to Sweden in 1808, and afterwards in "Portugal and Spain, and was present during the retreat to, and "battle of Corunna. He afterwards served in the Peninsula "with the 52nd in most of the battles and affairs until the "assault of Badajos, where he volunteered for the storming party, "and was severely wounded. He was promoted to the command "of the 73rd regiment. He commanded No. 9 company of the "52nd at Waterloo.

"Captain Edward Langton served with the 52nd in the "Peninsula, and was present at the battles of Corunna, Fuentes "d'Onor, Ciudad Rodrigo, and Salamanca, for which he has re-"ceived the war-medal with four clasps. He was also present "with the 52nd at the battle of Waterloo.

"Lieut.-Colonel John Cross served with the 52nd in the "Peninsula, and was present at Waterloo. He was afterwards "selected for the command of the 68th Light Infantry.

"General Sir Charles Yorke, G.C.B., entered the 52nd in 1807, "and was present at the battles of Vimiero, Fuentes d'Onor, "Salamanca, Vittoria, the Pyrenees, the Nivelle, (where he was "wounded,) the Nive, and Orthes, (where he was again wounded,) "besides several smaller affairs during the same period. He "served at the sieges of Ciudad Rodrigo and Badajos, at the "latter of which he was wounded. He also served at Waterloo, "on the Staff. He subsequently served in the Caffre campaigns "of 1850 to 1853 as second in command to Sir George Cathcart,

"and was recently military secretary to the Commander-in-
" Chief at the Horse Guards. Sir Charles Yorke has received the
" war-medal with ten clasps.

" Lieutenant Charles Dawson served in the Peninsula and at
" Waterloo, where he commanded a company and was shot
" through the lungs. He died about a year afterwards. The
" name of his gallant brother, Captain Henry Dawson, of the
" 52nd, who distinguished himself at Almeida, and was killed in
" 1812 in defending the position on the Huebra, was often
" mentioned, in after times, amongst the officers of the regiment.

" There is no account of Lieutenant M. Anderson's services in
" the 52nd record; but he was an old Peninsula officer, and at
" Waterloo he commanded No. 5 company, the left-front company
" of the 52nd when in their four-deep line, which extended
" and moved down the British position, and fired into, and first
" stopped the advance of the French Imperial Guard. He lost a
" leg on this occasion.

" Captain Charles Kenny served in the 52nd in the Penin-
" sula and at Waterloo.

" Captain G. H. Love died at Cape Breton in 1830. He
" entered the regiment as ensign in 1810, and served with credit
" during all the Peninsular campaigns till the battle of Orthes,
" when he was wounded in the face. He also served with the
" 52nd in the battle of Waterloo, and was much endeared to his
" comrades by his amiable manners, as well as respected for his
" services.

" Lieut.-Colonel Sir William Henry Clerke, Bart., served with
" the 52nd in the Peninsula, and was present at the battles of
" the Nivelle, Nive, Orthes, and Toulouse, and the intervening
" combats. He was also present at the battle of Waterloo. He
" has received the war-medal with four clasps.

" Lieut.-Colonel George Hall served in the Peninsula in 1811
" and 1812, and again from October 1813 to the end of the
" war in 1814, and was present at the battles of Fuentes d'Onor,
" the sieges of Ciudad Rodrigo and Badajos, (where he was
" severely wounded,) the battles of the Nive, Orthes, and Toulouse.
" He was also present at the battle of Waterloo. He afterwards
" commanded the 72nd Highlanders.

"Lieutenant William Richmond Nixon, entered the 52nd in
"1810, and served with the regiment at the battles of Fuentes
"d'Onor and Orthes, and at the siege of Badajos, where he greatly
"distinguished himself and was severely wounded at the storm-
"ing of Fort Picurina. He also served at Waterloo, and was as-
"sistant adjutant there. He received the Peninsular war-medal
"with three clasps.

"Colonel George Gawler was essentially a 52nd officer. He
"served in this regiment only, and was a type of that steady,
"cool, and gallant set of company-officers, whose attention to
"regimental duty and experience in the field so materially helped
"to place the 52nd amid the most distinguished in the service of
"Britain. Entering the 52nd Light Infantry in November, 1811,
"Colonel Gawler served to the end of the Peninsula war in
"1814, and was present at the storming of Badajos, (when he led
"the ladder party of the 52nd stormers,) at the battles of Vittoria,
"Vera, the Nivelle, the Nive, Orthes, and Toulouse, besides various
"minor affairs. At Waterloo he commanded the right company
"of the 52nd after his captain (Diggle) was placed *hors de combat*.
"He was wounded below the right knee at Badajos, and in the
"neck at San Munos, and has received the war-medal with seven
"clasps. Colonel Gawler was Governor of South Australia for
"several years.

"Major-General George Whichcote served with the 52nd in
"the Peninsula and at Waterloo.

"Captain the Hon. William Ogilvy joined the 52nd in May,
"1811, and was engaged in all the actions in which the regiment
"took part, from Badajos to the end of the war. He also served
"at Waterloo. He received the medal for Waterloo, and the
"Peninsula medal with seven clasps, for Badajos, Salamanca,
"Vittoria, Nivelle, Nive, Orthes, and Toulouse.

"Captain Edward Richard Northey entered the 52nd in 1811,
"and served with the first battalion in every action in which it
"was engaged from 1812, commencing with the retreat from
"Madrid, and at Vittoria was slightly wounded. For these
"services Captain Northey received the Peninsula war-medal
"with six clasps. He also served in the campaign and battle of
"Waterloo.

" The Hon. William Browne served in the 52nd in the Penin-
" sula and at Waterloo.

" Major Edward Scoones served in the 52nd during the
" retreat from Burgos in 1812 ; he was also present with the
" regiment in the Pyrenees and at the battle of Toulouse.
" Major Scoones subsequently served in the campaign and
" battle of Waterloo. He was afterwards a major in the 81st
" regiment.

" Lieutenant Campbell was very severely wounded when ad-
" vancing with the 52nd skirmishers on the French Imperial
" Guard.

" Major William Austen served in the Peninsula in 1811 and
" 1812, in the campaign of Holland in 1814, and in the battle of
" Waterloo. He has received the war-medal with one clasp for
" the siege and storm of Ciudad Rodrigo.

" Lieutenant William Crawley Yonge's services are mentioned
" at page 130 of the first volume.

" Lieutenant Thomas Cottingham served with the 52nd in the
" Peninsula campaigns of 1812, 1813, and 1814, and was present,
" as a volunteer at the storming of Badajos, at the battles of
" Salamanca, Vittoria, the Pyrenees, Nivelle, Nive, Orthes, and
" Toulouse, and also at Waterloo. He has received the war-
" medal with eight clasps.

" Captain Charles Holman served in the Peninsula from
" 1811, and was present at the battle of Salamanca, the siege of
" Burgos, the battles of the Pyrenees, the Nivelle, the Nive,
" Orthes, and Toulouse, and the intervening actions. He was
" also present at the battle of Waterloo, and has received the
" war-medal with six clasps. He had three musket-balls through
" the blade of his sword at Waterloo.

" Lieutenant G. E. Scott served at Waterloo. He was the
" author of a prize poem on the battle of Waterloo.

" Lieutenant J. R. Griffith entered the 52nd in 1813, served
" in the campaign of Holland in 1813 and 1814, and also in the
" campaign and battle of Waterloo, after which he acted as ad-
" jutant in the absence (from wounds) of Lieutenant Winter-
" bottom.

" Major-General Eaton Monins entered the 52nd in 1814,
" and served in the campaign of 1815, and was present at the
" battle of Waterloo, and the subsequent advance on and occupa-
" tion of Paris."

Lieutenant and Adjutant Winterbottom's services are enumerated at pages 325—327 of the first volume.

CHAPTER XLVIII.

1755—1808.

SOME ACCOUNT OF THE 52ND LIGHT INFANTRY FROM ITS FORMATION.

52nd embodied in 1755—In Canada—Bunker's Hill and other actions—Fifteen
years in India—Ferrol, Cadiz, Gibraltar—Made Light Infantry in 1803—
Drill under Sir John Moore—Constant state of readiness for active service—
An additional lieutenant, serjeant, and corporal per company—52nd reviewed by Commander-in-Chief—Unusual amount of promotion given—Sir
John Moore, Sir Harry Smith, and Lord Seaton, and the supporters to their
arms—First battalion goes to Sicily, the second to Copenhagen.

THE 52nd " Record," from which I shall extract much which will
help to form the contents of this and some of the following
chapters, was published in 1860, under the direction of the
following committee of officers who had served in the regiment,
and was edited by Captain W. S. Moorsom :—

His Grace the Duke of Richmond, K.G., Chairman,
Lieut.-General Sir J. Frederick Love, K.C.B., Dep. Chairman,
Lieut.-General Sir John Bell, K.C.B.,
Lieut.-General Sir William G. Moore, K.C.B.,
Major-General Eaton Monins,
Colonel Edward A. Angelo, K.H.,
Colonel George Gawler, K.H.,
Colonel George Napier, C.B.,
Colonel George Campbell, C.B.,
Lieut.-Colonel Sir John Tylden, Kt.,
Lieut.-Colonel Lord Charles J. F. Russell,
Captain W. S. Moorsom, Hon. Secretary,
Captain H. M. Brownrigg,
Captain J. J. Bourchier.

"The origin of the 52nd Regiment dates from the eve of the com-
"mencement of the contest known in history as the 'Seven Years'
"War.' In December, 1755, eleven regiments of infantry were raised,
"and were numbered from the 50th to the 60th inclusive. The
"present 52nd was first numbered the 54th, but on the disband-
"ment, in 1757, of the 50th and 51st, which had only been raised
"for service in North America, it became the 52nd."

The regiment proceeded to Ireland in 1758, and remained
there till 1765. On the 6th of June in that year it embarked at
Cork for North America, and reached Quebec in the August
following. It remained in Canada till about the middle of 1774,
when it proceeded by sea to Boston, to reinforce the army assembled there. In April the flank companies of the 52nd, and of
several other corps, were engaged in destroying the military
stores collected at Concord, and in the affair at Lexington, at
which the 52nd lost three rank and file killed, two wounded, and
one serjeant missing.

On the 17th of June, 1775, just forty years before Waterloo,
the regiment took part in the severe action of Bunker's Hill,
when it particularly distinguished itself. It suffered, however,
severely; the whole of the grenadier company, with the exception of eight men, were either killed or wounded.

"This seems to have been the first occasion on record in
"which the 52nd acted in unison with the 43rd, afterwards so
"honourably linked as their brothers-in-arms on many a field of
"the Peninsula."

In the beginning of July, 1776, the American Congress issued
their Declaration of Independence, and in the next month the
52nd were engaged at Brooklyn, the result of which compelled
the Americans to evacuate New York. They continued in
America till the end of October, 1778, when, having been much
reduced in numbers, in various actions in which they had been
engaged, and many of those remaining having volunteered into
other corps, they embarked for England, and arrived there before
the close of the year.

"A letter dated 31st August, 1782, conveyed to the regiment
"his Majesty's pleasure that county titles should be conferred on
"the infantry, and the 52nd in consequence received the designa-

"tion of the Oxfordshire Regiment, in order that a connexion
"between the regiment and that county should be cultivated,
"which it was considered might be useful in promoting the suc-
"cess of the recruiting system."

The 52nd embarked for India in 1783, and after having been
engaged in various services in that country, during a period of
fifteen years, they returned to England in August, 1798.

"Prior to their embarkation at Madras, the following compli-
"mentary General Orders were issued by the Commander-in-
"Chief :—

"'Head Quarters, Chaultre Plain, 8th February, 1798.

"'His Majesty's 52nd Regiment, being under orders of em-
"barkation for Europe, the Commander-in-Chief, while he feels
"sincere regret at losing so valuable a corps from under his
"command, embraces the opportunity to assure Major Monson,
"the officers, and men, that he shall ever retain a strong impres-
"sion of the discipline and gallantry of that corps during a
"period of fifteen years' service in India.

"'(Signed)   JAMES ROBINSON, Dep. Adj.-Gen.'"

"Fort St. George, February 18th, 1798.

"Upon this occasion the Right Honourable the President in
"Council feels it incumbent upon him to convey to Major Mon-
"son, the officers, and men, of the 52nd Regiment, the thanks of
"this government for the share they have had in supporting its
"authority during a period of fifteen years, and in extending the
"conquests of the nation in the late glorious war against the
"Tippoo Sultaun.

"By order of the President in Council,
"(Signed)   T. WEBB, Secretary."

The 52nd remained in England about two years, during which
period a second battalion was added to it, and it received upwards
of two thousand volunteers from the militia in the course of
twelve months.

On the 25th of June, 1800, the first battalion of the 52nd embarked at Southampton, having been ordered to form part of a
force which was being collected for a secret service. The second
battalion embarked also at Southampton on the 2nd of July, but

returned to that place on the 14th of the same month. Early in
August it again embarked at Southampton, having been selected
to form part of the expedition under Lieut.-General Sir James
Pulteney, Bart.

The armament of which the first battalion formed a portion,
reached the bay of Quiberon on the 8th of July; and the 23rd,
31st, first battalion of the 52nd, and 63rd Regiments landed on
the Isle de Houat, where they remained encamped under the
command of Brigadier-General the Honourable Thomas Maitland
until the 19th of August, when they again embarked and joined
the expedition under Lieut.-General Sir James Pulteney, destined
for the coast of Spain. The strength of the two battalions
amounted to nearly 1800 men. Both battalions landed near
Ferrol on the 25th of August, and on the morning of the 26th
attacked the enemy, and gained possession of the heights above
the town. In the action near Ferrol the first battalion of the
52nd had eight rank and file killed. Captain Samuel Torrens
was wounded, and died in consequence. One serjeant, one drummer, and thirty-eight rank and file were wounded. The second
battalion had two rank and file killed, and three wounded.

Lieut.-General Sir James Pulteney, in his official despatch,
dated, at sea, 27th August, stated :—

"At daybreak the following morning a considerable body of
"the enemy was driven back by Major-General the Earl of
"Cavan's brigade, supported by some other troops, so that we
"remained in complete possession of the heights which overlook
"the town and harbour of Ferrol ; but from the nature of the
"ground, which was steep and rocky, unfortunately this service
"could not be performed without some loss. The first battalion,
"52nd Regiment, had the principal share in this action. The
"enemy lost about one hundred men killed and wounded, and
"thirty or forty prisoners."

The regiment re-embarked on the 27th, and proceeded to the
Bay of Cadiz, where the whole army was ordered into the flat
boats, with three days' provisions in their haversacks, for the
purpose of attacking the town of Cadiz; but the design was
abandoned, and the fleet sailed for Gibraltar, where a force was
selected to accompany General Sir Ralph Abercromby to Egypt;

but the two battalions of the 52nd Regiment, being enlisted for service in Europe only, could not form a part of it, although they immediately volunteered to extend their services to any part of the world; this, however, Sir Ralph did not feel himself authorized to accept, and the regiment returned to Lisbon, where it landed on the 25th November.

In January, 1803, the regiment was made light infantry, which event may be considered to form a new era in its history. The following is a copy of the General Orders relative to the formation of the 52nd Light Infantry :—

"Horse Guards, 10th January, 1803.

" It being his Majesty's pleasure that from the 25th ultimo
" the second battalion of the 52nd Regiment should be numbered
" the 96th Regiment of Foot,

" I am commanded by the Commander-in-Chief to signify the
" same to you, and to desire that in consequence of this arrange-
" ment you will be pleased to give the necessary orders for posting
" a due proportion of the officers of the present battalion of the
" 52nd Regiment to the 96th Regiment.

" In carrying this into effect, his Royal Highness desires that
" the two senior lieut.-colonels may be posted to the 52nd
" Regiment, and that the same rule may be observed with regard
" to the senior majors, captains, subalterns, and staff officers, as
" far as the establishment will allow.

" But although the Commander-in-Chief points out this mode
" of posting the officers, yet should any of the seniors of the
" respective ranks prefer being removed to the 96th Regiment, in
" preference to remaining in the 52nd Regiment, his Royal High-
" ness will not object to their being posted in the 96th Regiment,
" excepting in the case of the two senior lieut.-colonels, both of
" which are to remain in the 52nd Regiment.

" H. CALVERT, Adj.-General."

" Major-General Moore has, in consequence of the instructions
" contained in the letter of which the above is an extract, directed
" a list of the officers of the two battalions to be made out,
" placing the senior of each rank to the 52nd Regiment, and the
" juniors to the 96th Regiment, that the officers may directly see

" their respective situations, and be better able to make the option
" which is given to them by his Royal Highness the Commander-
" in-Chief.

" Memorandum—

" Such of the officers in the list of the 52nd Regiment who
" prefer being removed to the 96th, will give their names to the
" Major-General to-morrow morning.

" (Signed)   JOHN MOORE, Colonel."

" Horse Guards, 18th January, 1803.
" SIR,
             " I have received the Commander-in-Chief's directions
" to inform you that on the separation of the two battalions of
" the 52nd Regiment, for the purpose of nominating the second
" battalion the 96th Regiment, it is his Majesty's gracious pleasure
" that the first battalion, which will then become the entire 52nd
" Regiment, shall be formed into a corps of light infantry, retain-
" ing, however, its present number and distinction of Oxfordshire
" Regiment of Foot, and in every respect its rank in the service.

" You will, therefore, be pleased immediately to select such
" men from the second battalion as you may judge best adapted
" for the light infantry, and replace them from the first battalion
" by men less calculated for such service.

" I shall, hereafter, have the honour to communicate to you
" his Majesty's pleasure respecting the clothing, arms, and accou-
" trements and other appointments of the 52nd Regiment.

" I have, &c.,
" H. CALVERT, Adj.-General.
" Major-General Moore,
    " Colonel 52nd Regiment."

In consequence of the above communication, the men who
were considered unfit for light infantry were transferred to the
second battalion, which was about to become the 96th Regiment,
and were replaced by an equal number of eligible soldiers from
that battalion. Lieut.-Colonel Henry Conran, being the senior
officer present with the regiment, carried the above arrangement
into effect, and afforded every facility in selecting the men for the
52nd Light Infantry. All the necessary arrangements having

been completed, the final separation of the battalions took place on the 23rd of February, 1803, when the first division of the 96th Regiment marched from Chatham to Gillingham to embark, and proceeded to Ireland.

On the 18th of May the 52nd Light Infantry marched from Chatham, and arrived at Canterbury on the 20th, where the regiment halted about a fortnight, and then proceeded to Riding Street barracks.

The following regiments were formed into a brigade, under the command of Major-General Moore, and encamped at Shorncliffe, on the 9th of July, 1803 :—

    4th Foot,
    52nd Light Infantry,
    59th Foot,
    70th Foot,
    95th (Rifle) Regiment.

The most active drill being now about to commence, Major-General Moore explained to the commanding officers of the regiments the system he wished them to adopt. He permitted each commanding officer to fix upon the most convenient hours for drill, but required to be informed at what time the different corps were to be on parade, and he seldom failed to attend, by which means he became acquainted with the systems of the different regiments, and corrected any errors that existed.

In consequence of Lieut.-Colonel Vesey being at this time on the staff in America, Lieut.-Colonel McKenzie had the command of the 52nd Light Infantry, and was indefatigable in superintending the training of it on an entirely new system—to give the soldier a free, unconstrained attitude, and to march with the utmost ease and steadiness, was the primary object.

The country about Shorncliffe was well adapted for the subsequent part of the light infantry drill. And this period of the threatened invasion was peculiarly favourable to the formation of a light corps, as every individual was kept in the same constant state of activity and vigilance as if absolutely in the presence of an enemy; and the careful superintendence of Major-General Moore infused a soul and spirit throughout every rank, which made them perform their various duties with a zeal and alacrity

seldom attained in other corps; and in what degree the 52nd
Light Infantry profited by* those advantages, will be hereafter
shown by a communication from the Horse Guards, after his
Royal Highness had made a minute personal inspection of the
battalion in the month of August, 1804. On the 21st of July,
1803, the light companies of the 4th and 70th Regiments were
attached to the 52nd for the purpose of being instructed in light
infantry drill.

Notwithstanding the unremitting attention that was paid to
drill, every pains was taken to have the brigade in the most
efficient state to march against the enemy in the event of an invasion. The heavy baggage was put into store at Gravesend, and
the officers were only permitted to retain in camp a small port-
manteau each and their beds. One bât-horse per company was
provided for the officers' baggage, and tents were to be carried
with the brigade in the proportion of one for thirty men. The
regiment was accustomed to parade in light service order, and
Major-General Moore detailed very minutely what portion of
necessaries each soldier was to carry.

From the systematic arrangements which were adopted, the
brigade was expected to be formed in column, (with baggage
packed and tents struck,) and the whole ready to move off in one
hour after receiving the preparatory order for march. At this
period the alarm post for troops for the county of Kent was between Dover and Romney Marsh.

On the 1st of August, 1803, his Royal Highness the Commander-in-Chief reviewed the 52nd Light Infantry, formed in
brigade with the 4th, 59th, 70th, and 95th Regiments.

In consequence of a light infantry corps requiring a greater
proportion of officers and non-commissioned officers than a battalion of the line, his Majesty was pleased to order that an
augmentation of one lieutenant, one serjeant, and one corporal,
per company, should be made to the establishment of the 52nd
from the 25th of October, 1803.

Towards the end of November the encampment broke up, and
the regiment went into winter cantonments. On the 26th of this
month the 52nd marched from the camp to Hythe barracks, and
during the time the regiment remained there it was not permitted

to relax in the slightest degree from its former alertness. Arrangements were made to enable the battalion to assemble at the shortest notice, either by day or night; and in order to accustom the soldiers to carry their knapsacks, the regiment marched a few miles into the country twice a week.

1804.

The 4th and 52nd Regiments encamped at Shorncliffe on the 8th of June, and the 43rd arrived on the 15th. His Royal Highness the Commander-in-Chief reviewed the brigade on Shorncliffe on the 23rd of August, and on the following day the 52nd Regiment manœuvred singly in the presence of his Royal Highness, who was pleased to express his entire satisfaction at its very high state of discipline, &c., and the following communication was received from the Horse Guards a short time afterwards.

" Horse Guards, 29th August, 1804.

" My dear General,

" I have the honour of your letter of the 25th ult., " and am commanded to communicate to you, that in consequence " of the superior state of the 52nd Regiment on the Commander- " in-Chief's late personal inspection of it, his Royal Highness has " been pleased to recommend to the King, that the promotion " should be more extensive in that corps than has been usually " granted, and his Royal Highness trusts that this distinguished " proof of his Majesty's approbation will be a strong inducement " to the officers to persevere in the same course of industry, zeal, " and intelligence.

" I have, &c.,

" J. W. Gordon.

" Major-General Moore,
" Colonel 52nd Regiment."

Upon the receipt of this gratifying communication the following Regimental Orders were issued :—

" Regimental Orders.

" Major-General Moore directs the above letter may be inserted " in the orderly book of the regiment, as an honourable record at " once of the superior discipline of the corps, of his Royal High- " ness's approbation, and of the reward which follows.

"The promotion given to the regiment on this occasion "exceeds perhaps whatever, at any one period, has been accorded "to a regiment.

"The officers owe it to their own good conduct, and to the "attention they have paid to their duty, but above all to the zeal "with which they have followed the instructions of Lieut.-Colonel "McKenzie, to whose talents and to whose example* the regiment "is indebted for its discipline and the character it has so justly "acquired.

"(Signed)   JOHN MOORE, Colonel."

Towards the close of 1804 a second battalion was added to the 52nd.

Major-General Moore ever had the most paternal regard for his regiment, which did not fail to produce a reciprocal feeling of esteem on the part of both officers and men; and in the year 1805, when Sir John Moore was created a Knight of the Bath, the officers availed themselves of this favourable opportunity to testify their gratitude and respect by presenting him with a diamond star (value 350 guineas).

The following is a copy of the correspondence which took place on the occasion :—

"Sandgate, 8th April, 1805.

"MY DEAR STEWART,

"Notwithstanding what passed yesterday, I cannot help, "in this manner, again requesting that you will express my best "thanks to the officers of the regiment for the present they have "made me, and that you will assure them, as I feel towards them "the most cordial attachment and the warmest interest in their

---

* The Royal Military Calendar of 1820 states :—" Lieut.-Colonel McKenzie "commenced with the 52nd a plan of movement and exercise in which Sir John "Moore at first acquiesced with reluctance, the style of drill, march, and platoon "exercise being entirely new ; but when he saw the effect of the whole in a more "advanced stage, he was not only highly pleased, but became its warmest sup- "porter. The other light corps were ordered to be formed on the same plan, and "the 43rd and 95th Regiments were removed to Shorncliffe camp to be with the "52nd.

"Letters from Sir John Moore are now extant which corroborate the assertion "that the improved system of marching, platoon exercise, and drill, were entirely "Lieut.-Colonel (afterwards Major-General) McKenzie's."

" welfare and honour, so nothing can be more grateful to me than
" any mark which leads me to hope that I possess their friendship
" and good opinion. I accept the star as a token of their regard,
" and shall wear it with pleasure for their sakes, and in remem-
" brance of a corps of officers already distinguished by their con-
" duct, the knowledge of their duty, and by the manner in which
" they discharge it, and who will, I am persuaded, distinguish
" themselves still more when the opportunity offers, by proving
" to the enemies of their country that, when discipline is added
" to the natural bravery of British soldiers, no troops on earth can
" resist them.

" Ever, my dear Stewart,

" Faithfully and sincerely yours,

" JOHN MOORE.

" Lieut.-Colonel Stewart,

" Commanding 52nd Regiment."

" Shorncliffe, 9th April, 1805.

" DEAR SIR,

" I am directed by the officers of the regiment to say, that
" the very flattering manner in which you have accepted their
" acknowledgment of regard and gratitude, leaves them nothing
" to desire but an opportunity to realize the favourable hopes you
" have formed of their conduct in the field. In this wish I most
" cordially acquiesce, and have only to regret that the indisposi-
" tion of an officer, to whom we all look up with confidence and
" esteem, should, in these times, have deprived us of the benefit
" of his experience, and himself the happiness of making known
" to you the feelings I have endeavoured to express.

" I am, my dear Sir,

" etc., etc., etc.,

" JOHN STEWART,

" Lieut.-Col. Commanding 52nd."

" Major-General Sir John Moore, K.B."

The following letter from Sir John Moore is preserved in the
" Record " of the 92nd Highlanders, and is interesting to the 52nd
as showing the pride their colonel took in the formation of the
" first Light Infantry Regiment," and also as recording the debt
they owe to their gallant comrades of the 92nd :—

"Richmond, November 17th, 1804.

"MY DEAR NAPIER,

"As a Knight of the Bath, I am entitled to supporters.
"I have chosen a Light Infantry soldier for one, being Colonel of
"the First Light Infantry Regiment, and a Highland soldier for
"the other, in gratitude to, and in commemoration of, two soldiers
"of the 92nd, who, in the action of the 2nd of October,* raised
"me from the ground when I was lying on my face, wounded
"and stunned, (they must have thought me dead,) and helped me
"out of the field.   As my senses were returning, I heard one of
"them say, 'Here is the general, let us take him away;' upon
"which they stooped and raised me by the arm.   I never could
"discover who they were, and therefore concluded they must
"have been killed.

"I hope the 92nd will not have any objection (as I have com-
"manded them, and as they rendered me such a service,) to my
"taking one of the corps as a supporter.

"Believe me, my dear Napier, sincerely, etc.,

"(Signed)   JOHN MOORE."

"To Lieut.-Colonel Napier, of Blackstone."

Sir John Colborne, when created Lord Seaton in 1839, took
for his supporters—on the dexter side, a soldier of her Majesty's
52nd (or Oxfordshire) Regiment of Foot, habited and accoutred,
in the exterior hand a musket, all ppr.; and on the sinister side
a Canadian Red Indian, holding in his dexter hand a tomahawk,
and in the exterior a spear, all ppr.

Sir Harry Smith chose two soldiers—the one of the Rifle
Brigade, the other of the 52nd—as the supporters to his arms.

On the 10th of June, the 43rd and 1st battalion 52nd Light
Infantry encamped at Shorncliffe.   The 2nd battalion occupied a
part of Hythe barracks, and, owing to the unremitting attention
which Major Robert Barclay paid to its drill and formation, it
was, on the 15th of August, placed on the same footing as the

---

* 1799, at Egmont-op-Zee, where the 92nd fiercely charged a French brigade,
and a *mêlée* ensued, with victorious result to the Highlanders. Sir John Moore
offered £20 for the discovery of the private soldiers who had thus aided him, but
in vain.

1st battalion in regard to the several allowances and equipments to be issued to regiments fit for service.

His Royal Highness, the Commander-in-Chief, reviewed the 43rd and 1st battalion 52nd Light Infantry at Shorncliffe, on the 26th of August, and those regiments received orders, on the 4th of September following, to hold themselves in readiness for immediate embarkation. In the course of a few days, however, the intention of sending them abroad was given up, and they remained in camp until the 26th of October, when the 1st battalion 52nd Light Infantry marched to Hythe, and the 43rd moved into Shorncliffe barracks.

Towards the end of 1806, the 1st battalion of the 52nd proceeded to Sicily, and in 1807 the 2nd battalion formed part of the expedition to Copenhagen, and returned to England in the month of November. The first battalion landed at Portsmouth from Sicily in January, 1808, and proceeded to Canterbury.

CHAPTER XLIX.

1808, 1809.

THE 52ND IN THE PENINSULA. CORUNNA.

Battle of Vimiero—Convention of Cintra—March into Spain—Retreat in consequence of intelligence of Bonaparte's advance from Madrid—Drunkenness,
plundering, privations—The contents of the military chest thrown down
the mountain side—Kind act of a soldier's wife—Battle and victory of
Corunna—Death of Sir John Moore—The army embarks and returns to
England.

In August, 1808, both battalions of the 52nd landed in Portugal ;
the 2nd battalion, under Lieutenant-Colonel John Ross, landed
on the 19th, just in time to take part in defeating the French,
under Junot, at Vimiero, on the 21st. Sir Arthur Wellesley
states in his despatch that, "On the right of the position the
"enemy were repulsed by the bayonets of the 97th Regiment,
"which corps was successfully supported by the 2nd battalion of
"the 52nd Regiment, which, by an advance in column, took the
"enemy in flank."

After the convention of Cintra, both battalions of the 52nd
formed part of Sir John Moore's army, designed for separate
service in Spain. The army began to leave Lisbon at the end of
October, 1808, and the 1st battalion of the 52nd reached Ciudad
Rodrigo on the 16th of November, and Salamanca on the 21st;
the 2nd battalion was in Major-General Beresford's brigade, and
proceeded to Salamanca by Coimbra and Almeida. Sir David
Baird's corps joined Sir John Moore at Mayorga on the 20th of
December.

I give the whole account of the retreat from Sahagun to Corunna, and of the death of Sir John Moore, from the 52nd " Record ":—

"On the 23rd the British Army, consisting of 25,000 men, was collected between Sahagun, Grahal del Campo, and Vallada, and all the arrangements were completed for attacking Soult's corps, amounting to 18,000 men, very strongly posted behind the river Carrion.

"The different general officers had received their instructions, and about half-past five o'clock in the evening of the 23rd of December, the reserve commenced its march from Grahal del Campo upon the town of Carrion, where the enemy had a strong post of about 5000 men.

"It was expected that this post would be carried early next morning, and that the troops would be able to continue their march the same night upon Saldana, where the principal part of Marshal Soult's force was already concentrated.

"The snow was very deep upon the roads, which impeded the march of the artillery so much that the reserve had made but little progress at midnight, when Captain George Thomas Napier, of the 52nd, arrived from Sahagun with an order for the reserve to return to its former station.

"The column immediately countermarched, and the regiments were in the occupation of their former quarters at daylight in the morning.

"This sudden change was occasioned by the arrival of a courier at Sahagun with intelligence that Bonaparte was in full march on Benavente with the whole of the disposable force he could collect at Madrid. Fortunately this information was received by Sir John Moore at Sahagun two hours previously to the time appointed for the march of the troops from that place. On the 24th those divisions commenced their retreat on Astorga; the reserve followed on the 25th, and arrived at Mayorga late that night.

"The 1st battalion of the 52nd Regiment was quartered in a convent in the town; it rained so heavily that the men could not cook out-of-doors, and they incautiously lighted fires for that purpose in the gallery of the building; at about ten o'clock next morning, when the regiment was falling in to march to Valderas, it was discovered that the hot tiles had set fire to the joists of the floor, but by the exertions of the soldiers it was soon extinguished with very little injury to the convent.

" On the 26th the regiment marched from Valderas to Castro Gonzalo, and early next morning passed the Esla and went into quarters in the town of Benavente.

" At Castro Gonzalo the French cavalry had closed upon the reserve, and there being a very thick fog at the time, it was deemed necessary in that open country for the regiments to march in column of companies at quarter-distance, with flank parties of skirmishers a little distance from the columns; however, no attack was made upon the division during this march, but in the evening a few French dragoons, under cover of the fog, charged a picket of the 43rd without effect, and retired after having cut down a sentry.

" On the 28th, the enemy appeared on the opposite bank of the Esla, and the different regiments repaired to their alarm-posts; but as soon as the enemy had completed the reconnoissance he retired, and the British troops returned to their quarters in the convent.

" The main body of the army marched from Benavente on the 28th, and at about nine o'clock on the morning of the 29th the reserve commenced its march on La Beneza; the cavalry were to follow in the course of the day.

" Shortly after the reserve had quitted the town, five or six hundred cavalry of the French Imperial Guard, under the command of General Le Fèbre Desnouettes, forded the Esla, the bridge having been blown up a few hours before. Lieut.-General Lord Paget, and Brigadier-General the Hon. Charles Stewart, with the cavalry, quickly defeated this force, and in the course of an hour after, the celebrated French cavalry General passed the column of reserve a captive.

" The 2nd battalion of the 52nd Regiment now composed a part of Brigadier-General Catlin Craufurd's light corps which quitted the great route at La Beneza and marched upon Vigo. One hundred picked men from each of those battalions were pushed on by forced marches to secure the bridge of Orense.

"The reserve marched on the 30th from La Beneza to Astorga, and in the afternoon of the 31st moved to Camberos, and waited there the arrival of the cavalry; marched again at midnight, and reached Benbibre next morning, just as the preceding divisions of the army had left it.

"The scene that the reserve witnessed here was the most disgraceful that can be imagined; on entering the town they found the streets and houses full of drunken stragglers from the preceding divisions; parties were immediately employed to collect them all together, and the church being the most convenient building in the town, it was quickly filled with those drunken wretches.

1809.

"On the morning of the 2nd of January, 1809, the reserve marched from Benbibre to Calcabellos, and as the army was now entering into a mountainous country, almost the whole of the cavalry were sent forward to Villafranca on this day, and the arduous task of covering the retreat devolved upon the reserve.

"The recollection of the horrid scene at Benbibre determined every one to check instantly the slightest disposition to plunder or drunkenness; an opportunity was not long wanting, for a short time after the regiments were in their quarters at Calcabellos, three men were found plundering a deserted house in the town. One was a straggler from the Artillery, another from the Guards, and the third was a man of the name of Lewis, of the 1st battalion of the 52nd Regiment.

"Considering this a fit opportunity to make an impression on the minds of the soldiers, next morning, the 3rd of January, Major-General the Hon. Edward Paget assembled the reserve in square, about a mile in front of Calcabellos, and the delinquents were brought out for execution. The ropes were already round their necks, and the unfortunate men were held up in the arms of those who were to perform the execution. The Major-General was pointing out the necessity of enforcing the strictest discipline, when, at this instant, a cavalry officer galloped into the square, and reported the enemy's advance. The General immediately communicated this to the division, and at

the same time declared that if the French cavalry were absolutely ready to charge the square, he should not be deterred
from executing the punishment; but that if the reserve would
now promise faithfully that similar acts should not occur, he
would spare the lives of those unhappy men: and (to give the
greatest solemnity to this engagement) he ended by saying,
'If you mean to fulfil your promise, you will all repeat
'distinctly three times, Yes, yes, yes.' The words resounded
from all parts of the square, and the men were taken down.
But little time was left for reflection, for at the same instant a
second cavalry officer reported that the pickets had been some
time engaged, and were then hard pressed, and commanding-
officers were ordered to march their regiments to the alarm
posts which had been previously assigned to them in the town.

"The man Lewis, of the 52nd, who although a sad plunderer
was a gallant soldier, was afterwards killed at Orthes, by the
side of the present Duke of Richmond, who was in command
of a company of the regiment on that day. He generally contrived to have an attack of rheumatism soon after getting into
action, and thus got out of sight of his officers for the purpose
of filling his haversack.

"Sir John Moore arrived soon after this episode, and withdrew the reserve to a small range of hills, about half a mile
behind the town of Calcabellos, leaving five companies of the
95th Rifle corps to dispute its possession with the enemy; at
about three o'clock P.M. a heavy column of cavalry was observed
winding down the road leading into Calcabellos; the French
chasseurs dismounted as they approached (securing their horses
by throwing the bridle-rein of one over the neck of the other)
and then attacked in light-infantry order.

"The 95th fell back gradually, and although the skirmishing
was very hot in the vineyards behind the town, little loss was
sustained, with the exception of a few riflemen who were posted
in the houses at the entrance of the village, and who neglected to
provide for their own safety in case of retreat. Two British guns
which were posted on the high-road leading to Villafranca, on the
slope of the hill, played upon the French column as it advanced:
amongst others, the French General Colbert fell, by the well-

directed fire of those guns. He was an officer of great promise, and the French bulletin emphatically announced his loss in the following words :—' His hour was come, he died nobly.'

"The skirmishing ceased with the daylight, and the reserve retired upon Villafranca, but without halting there marched to Hererias, where they arrived very much fatigued about four o'clock in the morning of the 4th of January. The men rested until about ten o'clock, when the march was again resumed. This day two companies of the 52nd (Captains Charles Rowan's and Hunt's) formed the rear-guard of the division.

"A great many waggons, loaded with Spanish clothing and other stores for the Marquis of Romana's army, were found unprotected on the ascent of a hill close to Hererias. The stores were destroyed, and the shelving nature of the road at this place afforded a good opportunity of obstructing the enemy's passage. The rear-guard collected the empty waggons and placed them in rows across the road, filling up the intervals with straw, empty casks, and all combustible matter that could be found in the adjoining houses ; as soon as the barrier was completed the whole was set on fire, and the rear-guard followed the division, and had the satisfaction afterwards to know that the enemy's march was retarded several hours by this immense fire.

"The reserve reached Nogales on the evening of the 4th, and at ten o'clock next morning the regiments were formed in column in the streets ready to move off.

"It was found impossible to move the whole of the stores which had collected at this place, and several casks of salt provisions were destroyed.

"The reserve having already suffered many privations, both men and officers now filled their haversacks with salt beef and pork, which fatigue compelled them to throw away a few hours afterwards, and the want of bread was very severely felt at this time.

"The skirmishing with the pickets announced the near approach of the enemy, and as a small part of the military chest was still left without the means of transport, a message was sent to commanding-officers to say that their officers might receive money on account of bât and forage. Colonel Barclay considered the inconvenience (under the existing circumstances) of suffering all the officers to leave the battalion, and judiciously permitted none but the captains of companies to go. Three hundred dollars were issued to each of them on this account, and having no other means of carrying the money, they were compelled to distribute it among their companies, by entrusting a few dollars to the care of each soldier.

"A few miles in rear of Nogales, the road to Lugo leads over a steep mountain; here the weary oxen were unable to drag along the heavy-laden carts, and as the enemy was pressing upon the rear-guard, it was found impossible to save the military chest. Casks containing dollars to the amount of £25,000 were thrown over the precipice on the right-hand side of the road, and rolled from one declivity to another until they at last settled in the bottom of a narrow, rugged ravine, quite out of reach of the column.

"The rear-regiments of the reserve only were present when the money was cast away, and certainly not a man of those left their ranks in the hope of obtaining a portion. This discipline, however, did not extend to the 'followers,' who, as soon as they arrived at the spot where the dollars were rolling over the mountain-side, at once began a scramble, in which the wife of the regimental master-tailor, Malony, (who was a merry one, and often beguiled a weary march to the men with her tales,) was so successful that her fortune was apparently made. The poor woman went through all the subsequent perils and hardships of the retreat, but on stepping from the boat to the ship's side on embarking at Corunna, her foot slipped and down she went, like a shot, and owing to the weight of dollars secured about her person, she never rose again.

"The enemy's advance-guard, in a few minutes after, passed over the very spot on the road where this occurrence took place, and was then entirely ignorant that the treasure was abandoned.

"The fatiguing effects of the retreat now became very apparent; the men had been living for several days on salt provisions, without either bread or vegetables, and the rain fell in such torrents that they seldom had a dry shirt; consequently great numbers were suffering from dysentery, and the very bad state of the roads left many without shoes.

"The present Major-General Diggle, quoting this time of distress, writes : ' Well do I remember the kind act of a worthy ' woman, Sally Macan, the wife of a gallant soldier of my com- ' pany, who, observing me to be falling to the rear from illness ' and fatigue, whipped off her garters, and secured the soles of ' my boots, which were separating from the upper-leathers, and ' set me on my feet again ; even then, decorated as I was with ' the garters, I should have fallen into the hands of the French, ' had not Colonel Barclay sent his horse to the rear for me, being ' unable from weakness to fetch up my lee-way. A year or so ' after this I had the opportunity of requiting the kindness of ' poor Sally Macan, by giving her a lift on my horse the morning ' after she had given birth to a child in the bivouac.'

"The skirmishing continued almost the whole of this day, (the 5th,) and Sir John Moore never quitted the rear-guard for a moment ; whenever the country presented a favourable situa- tion for checking the enemy, a stand was made to give time to the weakly men to get forward.

"The reserve arrived close to the village of Constantino at about four o'clock in the evening. This village is situated on a small elevation, forming a gentle slope down to a stream within musket-range ; beyond this rivulet the road crosses a small valley and ascends the opposite hill in a straight line. On the summit of this hill the rear-guard, with two pieces of artillery, kept the enemy in check, while Major-General the Hon. Edward Paget, with the other regiments of the division, descended into the valley, crossed the bridge, and took up a position with his left resting on Constantino. The enemy followed the rear-guard quickly down the hill, and commenced an attack upon the posi- tion, but after a few discharges of artillery the firing died away, and the men began to cook ; it rained excessively at the time.

"As soon as this hasty meal was finished, an order was sent round for the men to fall in quietly behind their fires ; at eleven o'clock the division marched off in column of companies at quarter-distance with fixed bayonets ; a short time afterwards the pickets were withdrawn from the bridge, the men silently retiring by two or three at a time. Sir John Moore himself rode round the outposts, and directed where fires should be made to deceive the enemy, and the positions were so well chosen, and the arrangements for keeping the fires alight were so well executed, that it was nearly daylight before the enemy discovered that the division had marched.

"The reserve suffered more from the want of sleep on this night-march than on any other during the retreat; the columns moved on, but in what could scarcely be called a state of wakefulness: every instant some one or other unconsciously stalked off the road and fell into the ditches.

"The officers encouraged the men, purposely mentioning in their hearing that they had only a league or two further to march, and at length daylight appeared, but still the march was continued until the reserve passed Lugo a Spanish league; it was then about one o'clock, (the 7th,) rations were issued as expeditiously as possible, and just as the men were beginning to cook, intelligence was received that the divisions which had halted at Lugo were attacked; the reserve got under arms immediately and marched back there, drenched with rain; in this state the troops were crowded into a convent.

"The officers of the 20th regiment, 52nd, and Rifle corps, occupied a room with only one window, and scarcely space enough for the whole of them to lie down, and having shut the door and window, and lighted a charcoal pan to procure some warmth, the adjutant of the 52nd, who was the first to lie down, was seized with convulsions. Being immediately carried out, he recovered, and the rest of the party were thus made aware of the danger which they had escaped—of suffocation from the fumes of the charcoal. Next morning, (the 8th,) an hour before daylight, the British army marched to a position about a mile and a half in front of Lugo, and remained there the whole of the day, offering battle to the enemy's superior force. But Marshal Soult did not think proper to accept the challenge, and soon after dark the British army began to retire from this position and fall back on Betanzos.

"The duty of the rear-guard now became very laborious; it had not only to defend the rear of the army, but the good of the service and other feelings required it also to protect as far as possible those who were unable to keep up with the columns: the stragglers from the preceding divisions being very numerous, some from weakness, others from a manifest apathy or a desire to plunder. Every house contiguous to the road was crowded with these men, cooking flour and apparently enjoying the greatest security. As the reserve came up, they detached small parties to search the houses for stragglers and to warn them of their danger, but the persuasions and entreaties of the officers were heard with cold indifference. In the former part of the retreat there was a mingled feeling of indignation and pity for the loiterers, but now all commiseration was at an end ; the rear-guard had only one object in view, to keep the army as effective as possible, and the soldiers of the reserve were so disgusted with the conduct of those worthless fellows, that they beat and kicked them forwards on the road.

"At daylight next morning (the 9th) the reserve halted upon an extensive table-land behind the river Ladro, and in order to give the stragglers every chance of rejoining the army, the destruction of the bridge was deferred until the enemy were close up to it : all the weakly men were selected from the regiments of this division and sent forward to Corunna under charge of an officer from each battalion ; in the evening the reserve began to fall back slowly upon Betanzos, and in the forenoon of the following day took up a position in front of that town to cover the main body of the army, which went into quarters there.

"Lieut.-Colonel Cadell, in his 'Narrative of the Campaigns 'of the 28th Regiment,' writes :—'On the afternoon of the 9th a 'considerable force of French cavalry came upon some of the 'stragglers. A serjeant of the 52nd, who happened to be behind, 'looking after some of his men, collected a considerable number, 'and gallantly repulsed the cavalry, by which means he saved 'many who would otherwise have fallen into the enemy's hands.' The name of this serjeant has not been preserved.

"On the 11th the army marched from Betanzos to *Corunna*, and Major-General the Hon. Edward Paget followed with the reserve to the village of El Burgo and its adjacents.

"On the 13th the divisions which occupied Corunna marched

out, and the whole army was placed in position about two miles in front of the town, the reserve occupying the small village of Monelos, in rear of the centre of the position on the Betanzos road.

"On the 14th the enemy cannonaded the left of the British line, and on the 15th his whole army made a forward movement, and took up a strong position in front of the British; this evening an affair took place in which Colonel Mackenzie, of the 5th Regiment, fell in endeavouring to take two of the enemy's guns.

"The transports having arrived at Corunna on the evening of the 14th, the embarkation of the sick, the artillery, cavalry, and baggage, was nearly completed on the morning of the 16th, and the reserve had received orders to be in readiness to embark at four o'clock that evening.

"The enemy's line was observed to be getting under arms at a little before two, and shortly afterwards the light troops of both armies were engaged, and the action soon became general.

"Major-General Paget advanced with the reserve to support Lieut.-General Lord William Bentinck's brigade, which the enemy was endeavouring to turn.

"The 52nd Regiment and five companies of the Rifle corps, being part of the reserve, were brought to the front in order to oppose a movement of the French left, which threatened to outflank the right of the British line. The French attack in front on the village of Elvina, held by the British, was repulsed by the divisions of Baird and Hope, while the reserve, after moving to the right of the British line, not only succeeded in repelling the attack of the French, but absolutely established themselves firmly on a part of the enemy's position.

"Near Elvina fell that noble general under whose immediate and personal instruction his regiment, the 52nd, acquired that admirable discipline and that system of light-infantry drill which contributed so largely to the honour of the British army throughout the war of the Peninsula and the campaign of Waterloo, and which have been transmitted through the successors, whose discipline has been conspicuous down to the present times on the ramparts of Delhi.

"'Sir John Moore,' (writes the historian of the Peninsular war,) 'while earnestly watching the result of the fight about the

'village of Elvina, was struck on the left breast by a cannon-shot.
'The shock threw him from his horse with violence, but he rose
'again in a sitting posture, his countenance unchanged and his
'steadfast eye still fixed upon the regiments engaged in his front,
'no sign betraying a sensation of pain. In a few moments, when
'he was satisfied that the troops were gaining ground, his coun-
'tenance brightened, and he suffered himself to be taken to the
'rear. Being placed in a blanket for removal, an entanglement
'of the belt caused the hilt of his sword to enter the wound, and
'Captain Hardinge * attempted to take it away altogether, but
'with martial pride the stricken man forbade the alleviation—he
'*would not part with his sword in the field.*'

"The body of Sir John Moore, wrapped in a military cloak,
was interred by the officers of his staff in the citadel of Corunna.
The guns of the enemy paid his funeral honours, and Marshal
Soult, with a noble feeling of respect for his valour, raised a
monument to his memory.

"The French army having been thus checked at all points,
fell back to its original position a little before dark, and the
52nd, after collecting their wounded by torchlight, marched from
the field about ten o'clok to the place of embarkation at St.
Lucia. The men got into the boats as quickly as possible, and
each pulled off to the nearest transports, but owing to the darkness of the night, and the unfavourable tide, it was nearly two
o'clock in the morning before the last of the regiment got on
board. The company commanded by Lieutenant Diggle had
made prisoners a French captain of light troops, Goguet by name,
and fourteen of his men, and Lieutenant Diggle succeeded in
bringing all of them off as prisoners on board one of the British
frigates.

"On the morning of the 17th, the enemy brought down some
pieces of artillery, and opened a cannonade upon the shipping;
some of the masters of transports precipitately cut their cables
and stood out to sea, but a few hours afterwards the fleet got
collected in the offing, and the signal was made for England.
The first battalion of the 52nd arrived at Portsmouth on the
25th of January.

* The late General Viscount Hardinge, Commanding-in-Chief.

"The 52nd sustained the following casualties at Corunna :— Five rank and file killed, and ninety rank and file missing. Lieut.-General Sir John Moore, Colonel of the regiment, was mortally wounded. Captain Robert Campbell and Lieutenant James Ormsby were severely wounded. One serjeant and thirty rank and file were wounded.

"Both Houses of Parliament voted their thanks to the army 'for its distinguished discipline, firmness, and valour in the 'battle of Corunna,' and the 52nd received the Royal authority to bear on their colours and appointments the word 'Corunna,' in common with the troops employed under Sir John Moore.

"The following extracts from the official despatch and from General Orders, testify to the part taken by the regiment in this battle :—

"Extract from Lieut.-General the Honourable John Hope's Official Despatch.

" 'The enemy, finding himself foiled in every attempt to force 'the right of the position, endeavoured by numbers to turn it. A 'judicious and well-timed movement, which was made by Major-'General Paget with the reserve, (20th, 28th, 52nd, 91st, and '95th Regiments,) which corps had moved out of its cantonments 'to support the right of the army, by a vigorous attack defeated 'this intention. The Major-General having pushed forward the '95th (Rifle corps) and 1st battalion 52nd Regiments, drove the 'enemy before him, and in his rapid and judicious advance 'threatened the left of the enemy's position.'

"Extract from the General Orders issued by Lieut.-General the Honourable John Hope, who succeeded to the command on Lieut.-General Sir David Baird being wounded.

" 'To Major-General the Honourable E. Paget, who, by a 'judicious movement of the reserve, effectually contributed to 'check the progress of the enemy on the height, and to the 1st 'battalion 52nd and 95th Regiments, which were thereby en-'gaged, the greatest praise is justly due.'

"The 2nd battalion, which had embarked at Vigo on the 13th of January, landed at Ramsgate towards the end of the same month and marched to Deal barracks.

"The 1st battalion remained on board their transports at Portsmouth about ten days, waiting for a fair wind to carry them to the Downs.

"The regiment disembarked at Ramsgate on the 14th of February, and marched to Deal barracks on the following day, to recover from the effects of the campaign.

"The advantage of a very superior state of discipline cannot be better illustrated than by noticing that although the 1st battalion 52nd was one of those regiments which covered the retreat of the army from the neighbourhood of Sahagun to Corunna, its loss upon the whole of that harassing march amounted only to one bugler and ninety-two rank and file;* and as a proof of the men's perseverance and patience under fatigue, it may be stated, that a short time after the return of the regiment to England, the return of deaths notified from the different hospitals happened to make on one day an aggregate amount of thirty men.

"The following General Orders were issued to the army by order of his Royal Highness the Commander-in-Chief, eulogizing the life and conduct of the late Lieut.-General Sir John Moore, Colonel of the 52nd Light Infantry.

"'GENERAL ORDERS.

"'Horse Guards, February 1st, 1809.

"'The benefits derived to an army from the example of a dis-'tinguished commander do not terminate at his death; his virtues

---

"* The following duty-state shows how much the regiment suffered from the effects of the retreat to Corunna. In November, 1808, the 1st battalion marched into Spain; effective, 54 serjeants, 18 buglers, 828 rank and file.

"*State of the 1st Battalion 52nd Regiment, 1st March, 1809.*

	Serjeants.	Buglers.	R. & F.
Present fit for duty	26	8	269
With Officers on the Staff	0	0	3
Sick left in Portugal	1	0	4
„ in Hospital	22	8	440
„ at Ramsgate	3	0	21
„ at Portsmouth	2	0	4
On furlough	0	1	1
Missing before 16th January . . .	0	1	92
Missing since 16th January	0	0	11
	54	18	845

The 2nd battalion also suffered severely.

'live in the recollection of his associates, and his fame remains
'the strongest incentive to great and glorious actions.

"'In this view, the Commander-in-Chief, amidst the deep and
'universal regret which the death of Lieut.-General Sir John
'Moore has occasioned, recalls to the troops the military career
'of that illustrious officer for their instruction and imitation.

"'Sir John Moore from his youth embraced the profession
'with the feelings and sentiments of a soldier; he felt that a per-
'fect knowledge and an exact performance of the humble but
'important duties of a subaltern officer are the best foundations
'for subsequent military fame; and his ardent mind, while it
'looked forward to those brilliant achievements for which it was
'formed, applied itself with energy and exemplary assiduity to
'the duties of that station.

"'In the school of regimental duty he obtained that correct
'knowledge of his profession so essential to the proper direction
'of the gallant spirit of the soldier, and he was enabled to estab-
'lish a characteristic order and regularity of conduct, because the
'troops found in their leader a striking example of the discipline
'which he enforced in others.

"'Having risen to command, he signalized his name in the
'West Indies, in Holland, and in Egypt.   The unremitting atten-
'tion with which he devoted himself to the duties of every branch
'of his profession, obtained him the confidence of Sir Ralph
'Abercromby, and he became the companion in arms of that illus-
'trious officer, who fell at the head of his victorious troops in an
'action which maintained our national superiority over the arms
'of France.

"'Thus Sir John Moore, at an early period, obtained with
'general approbation that conspicuous station in which he glo-
'riously terminated his useful and honourable life.

"'In a military character, obtained amidst the danger of cli-
'mate, the privations incident to service, and the sufferings of
'repeated wounds, it is difficult to select any one point as a pre-
'ferable subject for praise; it exhibits, however, one feature so
'particularly characteristic of the man, and so important to the best
'interests of the service, that the Commander-in-Chief is pleased
'to mark it with his peculiar approbation.

"'*The life of Sir John Moore was spent amongst the troops.*

"'During the season of repose his time was devoted to the 'care and instruction of the officer and soldier; in war, he courted 'service in every quarter of the globe. Regardless of personal 'considerations, he esteemed that to which his country called him 'the post of honour, and by his undaunted spirit and unconquer- 'able perseverance he pointed the way to victory.

"'His country, the object of his latest solicitude, will rear a 'monument to his lamented memory, and the Commander-in 'Chief feels he is paying the best tribute to his fame by thus 'holding him forth as an example to the army.

"'By order of his Royal Highness the Commander-in-Chief,
"'HARRY CALVERT, Adjutant-General.'

"Lieut.-Colonel Barclay assembled every man who was capable of leaving the Hospital, and read the above General Orders to the regiment formed in square in the barrack-yard at Deal; there were many soldiers who could not suppress those honest feelings, so creditable to human nature, when they reflected that they had lost a father and a friend, as well as a gallant brother-soldier.

"The officers of the regiment subscribed 150 guineas to obtain a portrait of their lamented Colonel."

CHAPTER L.

1809—1811.

THE 52ND IN THE PENINSULA.

Return to the Peninsula four months after Corunna—Remarkable forced march
to Talavera—The famous Light Division formed—Action of the Light
Division at the Coa—Escape of Dawson's subdivisions—Busaco—Amusing
Anecdote—Miranda do Corvo, Redinha—A sergeant of the 43rd, 52nd, and
95th promoted to an ensigncy—Sabugal—Understanding between English
and French advanced troops—Captain Love and a French serjeant—
French place a straw figure on withdrawing sentry.

On the 25th of May, just four months after its arrival from
Corunna, the first battalion of the 52nd embarked at Dover and
proceeded again to the Peninsula, in company with the first
battalions of the 43rd Light Infantry, and the 95th Rifles. They
landed at Lisbon on the 5th of July, and proceeded, under the
command of Brigadier-General Robert Craufurd, to join Sir
Arthur Wellesley's army, which was then moving on Talavera.
Having marched by Santarem, Abrantes and Oropesa, they
"arrived at Oropesa on the forenoon of the 28th, having that
"morning performed a tiresome march of twenty-four miles. Here
"some of the Spanish fugitives, from the first day's fighting at
"Talavera, spread an alarm of the defeat of their own party, and
"Craufurd, fearing that the British army might be pressed,
"resolved to push vigorously forward. The regiments had just
"bivouacked, when they were ordered to prepare to march again.
"As soon as the men had cooked and eaten their dinners the
"march was resumed, and these regiments arrived in the vicinity
"of Talavera before daylight on the morning of the 29th, having

" performed a forced march of forty-eight miles, in excessively
" hot weather, in addition to the twenty-four miles of the pre-
" ceding day : in all, sixty-two miles in twenty-four hours, each
" man carrying his arms, ammunition and accoutrements, weigh-
" ing between fifty and sixty pounds. This march, one of the
" most extraordinary on record, is said to have been performed
" with the loss of only seventeen stragglers from the three regi-
" ments, 43rd, 52nd and 95th Rifles."

The enemy having retired from Talavera during the night of
the 28th, General Craufurd's brigade marched over a part of the
field of battle towards the alberche and took up an advanced line
of posts near the bridge leading to St. Oballa.

In February 1810 the following General Order was issued by
Lord Wellington :—

"The 1st and 2nd battalions of Portuguese Chasseurs are
"attached to the brigade of Brigadier-General Craufurd, which is
"to be called the *Light Division*."

It was not till the beginning of June that the two regiments
of Caçadores joined Craufurd's Brigade and the famous Light
Division was formed.

On the 10th of July Massena took Ciudad Rodrigo, and the
Light Division, which had been acting as a corps of observation
during the short siege of that place, soon afterwards fell back on
Almeida and came in for its first regular fight as a division, near
that place, on the 24th of July. It has been called the battle of
Almeida, and also the fight at the Coa. It is described as
follows in the 52nd " Record ":—

"Soon after the fall of Cindad Rodrigo, Massena put his
army in movement towards the line of the Upper Mondego, and
Ney's corps advanced upon Almeida, about 20,000 strong in
infantry, with between 3000 and 4000 cavalry, and 30 guns.
Craufurd's division, still acting under orders only as a corps of
observation, consisted of the 43rd, 52nd, and 95th Rifles, the
1st and 3rd Regiments of Portuguese Caçadores, in all about
3200 infantry, with eight squadrons of British and German
cavalry, and six guns, and was disposed on a semicircle in
front of Almeida, towards the Ciudad Rodrigo road, its right
resting on the ravines of the Coa, about three miles above

Almeida, and its left reaching to the same river about three miles below that fortress. On the morning of the 24th of July, Ney drove in the pickets of the division stationed on the Rodrigo road at Val de Mula, four miles east of Almeida, and then showing a front of fifteen squadrons, with artillery in their front, and about 7000 infantry on the right of his advance, while the other troops were seen advancing on his left towards the ravines of the Coa, Craufurd became aware that retreat must be inevitable.

"He seems to have viewed himself as bound to prevent the investment of Almeida if possible, and therefore to have clung to a false position longer than sound military judgment would have dictated if unfettered by such view. Be this as it may, the Light Division was concentrated, on the hour of Ney's attack, between Almeida and the Coa, on a front of barely a mile and a half, with ravines running transversely from the left front to the right rear which to some extent protected the right flank, but which must also be crossed in the face of an overwhelming force, in order to reach the only point then passable over the Coa, viz. the, bridge on the road to Valverde which was about half a mile from the right, and upwards of a mile from the left of the division thus posted. The 52nd were posted in the rugged spurs on the right, except half a company, which was detached under Lieutenant Henry Dawson, in an old stone windmill tower, on which the left flank rested, and at which were also posted two guns of Captain Ross's troop of horse artillery. A Spanish garrison gun was in this tower, and at the first discharge it broke through the floor of the mill, and was afterwards useless. Next to this tower was the 43rd, then the 95th Rifles, and then the 1st and 3rd Caçadores closed the front with the 52nd on the right. Ney's attack was made with an impetuosity which outstripped the orders of Craufurd to retire in echelon of battalions from the left, while he sent his cavalry and artillery first over the bridge. A horse artillery ammunition-waggon was overturned in the road, the 43rd and some of the 95th were thrown rapidly across a knoll which in some degree commanded the road near the bridge, although overlooked by the heights which Ney's troops and artillery had gained; these checked the advance; the 52nd defended each rugged steep, retiring by companies as the ground admitted, and a charge of a company of the 52nd recovered the ammunition-waggon, which Lieutenant M'Donald of the artillery brought off, while the other companies of the regiment, having crossed the bridge, instantly arranged themselves on the left bank among the broken steeps ; the artillery went to the higher ranges of the mountain, wherever Captain Ross could find a place for his guns, and the safety of the division was ensured. No French column crossed that bridge through the death-storm of bullets which swept over it : gallant were the efforts made by Frenchmen to force that pass, and twice repeated with equal gallantry ; a few fine fellows succeeded in crossing, but they were obliged to skulk behind the rocks, and Ney became aware that in face of such troops, now properly posted, the attempt to force the bridge *en masse* was vain ; torrents of rain caused a cessation of fire about four in the afternoon, and during the night the division was withdrawn.

"The half company under Lieutenant Dawson, being unable to retreat at speed with the horse artillery guns, had been cut off in the tower by the rapid advance of Ney's right ; finding his post passed by the enemy and not attacked, Dawson remained quiet till nightfall and then drew off his men under the glacis of Almeida and along the right bank of the Coa, and, without being observed by the enemy, rejoined his regiment by Pinhel,—a fine example of coolness and daring.

" In this affair the Light Division suffered a loss of 30 killed and 270 wounded and prisoners. Marshal Massena states his own loss as having been 'nearly 300 killed and wounded,' but there is reason to believe that it was more than double that number.

" A little after dark, in the night of the 24th of July, the division fell back towards Freixadas without further interruption from the enemy.

" Viscount Wellington stated in his despatch :—

" 'I am informed that throughout this trying day the com-'manding officers of the 43rd, 52nd, and 95th Regiments, Lieut.-'Colonels Beckwith, Barclay, and Hull, and all the officers and

'soldiers of these excellent regiments distinguished themselves.'
In the affair on the river Coa, on the 24th of July, the regiment, commanded by Lieut.-Colonel Robert Barclay, sustained
the following casualties:—Major Henry Ridewood and Captain
Robert Campbell were severely wounded; one rank and file
killed, and sixteen rank and file were wounded; three men
were missing. The Light Division fell back to Freixadas on
the 26th of July, and on the 30th halted near Celerico, where
it remained during the siege of Almeida. The French broke
ground before that place on the 15th of August, and it surrendered on the 26th. At Celerico, on the 4th of August, the
following General Order was issued by Lord Wellington :—

"'The Light Division is to be divided into two brigades, viz.,
'the 43rd Regiment, 3rd Caçadores, and four Companies 95th
'Regiment, in one brigade; the 52nd Regiment, 1st Caçadores,
'and four companies 95th Regiment in the other brigade.

"'Lieut.-Colonel Beckwith of the 95th is to command the
'former brigade, and Lieut.-Colonel Barclay of the 52nd is to
'command the latter brigade.'"

On the 27th of September following the 52nd was engaged
in the general action of Busaco, and with the other regiments
of the Light Division greatly distinguished itself. The following is an extract from Lord Wellington's despatch on the
occasion :—

"On the left the enemy attacked with three divisions of
"Infantry of the 6th corps that part of the Sierra occupied by
"the Light Division commanded by Brigadier-General Robert
"Craufurd and by the brigade of Portuguese Infantry com-
"manded by Brigadier-General Pack. One division of Infantry
"only made any progress towards the top of the hill, and they
"were immediately charged with the bayonet by Brigadier-
"General Craufurd with the 43rd, 52nd, and 95th Regiments and
"3rd Caçadores, and driven down with immense loss.

"In this attack, Brigadier-General Craufurd and Lieutenant-
"Colonels Beckwith of the 95th, and Barclay of the 52nd, and
"the commanding officers of the regiments engaged distinguished
"themselves. The loss sustained by the enemy in his attacks on
"the 27th has been enormous. I understand that the General

"of Division Meste and General Maucune are wounded, and "General Simon was taken prisoner by the 52nd Regiment, and "3 colonels, 33 officers and 250 men."

Private James Hopkins of Captain Robert Campbell's company, to whom General Simon surrendered, was awarded a pension of £20 per annum as the reward of his bravery, and private Harris, who shared in the capture, some years after also received a pension on the representation of his captain, the late Sir Frederick Love.

The following amusing anecdote connected with that period is related in the regimental " Record :"—

"A man of the 52nd, named Tobin, in the company commanded by Lieutenant J. Frederick Love, was found to be absent, and was about to be reported as a deserter. Lieutenant Love, who knew the man well, and was therefore convinced he was not a deserter, but must have been killed or taken prisoner, had him reported as missing. A few days afterwards, when the division was on the march, this man rejoined his company, and when asked where he had been, replied, with a brogue, that he had been 'on a visit to the French Giniral.' Lieutenant Love, not satisfied with this, ascertained from him that between the French and English out-pickets there was a wine-house and still at which the patrols used to meet and take their grog; but one night, drinking more than he ought, he fell asleep, and was taken by a patrol not acquainted with the arrangement, and the better to enable him to make his escape, he said he was a deserter.

"Some time afterwards, previous to the battle of Fuentes d'Onor, an officer in the French service, an Irishman, and aide-de-camp to Marshal Massena, came to the advanced picket with a flag of truce and some letters for the General, and seeing the 52nd on their breastplates, asked Lieutenant Love, who was then commanding the picket, if there was a man in the corps of the name of Tobin. The captain replied that he was in his company, and called Tobin out. The aide-de-camp recognized him, as having been taken prisoner, and gave him a dollar, observing that Marshal Massena had declared, with 20,000 such men he would beat any army double that number. The aide-de-camp then related that Tobin had been brought before the Marshal as a deserter, which from his manner he (the aide-de-camp) saw was not the case, but that he had been taken prisoner, and as he wished to serve a countryman, he affected to treat him as a deserter, and offered to act as interpreter to the Marshal. The soldier answered with clearness the questions put to him, until asked the strength of the Light Division. Here the poor fellow was at fault, and not wishing that his division should be poorly thought of, he replied in an off-hand, Irish way, 'Tin Thousand.' Upon which the Marshal, irritated, exclaimed, 'Take him away—'the lying rascal.' Tobin seeing that the Marshal was angry, said with a *naïveté* of manner, "What's the matter with the 'Ginniral?' I replied, 'He says you are telling lies; he knows 'the Light Division was very little above four thousand when it 'advanced, and as it has been engaged above four times since 'that, it must have lost at least four or five hundred men.' 'Och, thin, the Ginniral don't belave me!' said Tobin; 'till him 'thin to attack thim the next time he meets thim with tin 'thousand men, and see if they don't give him a good licking.' 'When,' said the aide-de-camp, 'I explained this to the 'Marshal, he offered to make Tobin a serjeant if he would take 'service. Tobin asked a day to consider, and having made 'friends with the cook, filled his haversack, and took leave of us 'in the night.'

"In 1811 the Light Division, of which the first battalion of the 52nd formed part, marched from Pombal early on the morning of the 12th of March, and found the enemy's light troops occupying the entrance of the defile and the woods about two miles in front of the village of Redinha, having his main body drawn up on the plain. The corps of General Ney thus formed the rear-guard of Marshal Massena's army.

"The Rifle corps and 52nd advanced through the wood to the left of the road, and succeeded in dislodging the enemy. Having cleared the defile and gained the opposite side of the wood, Captain Mein's company advanced into the plain, and in a few minutes had to sustain the fire of a French battalion in line, being charged nearly at the same moment by a squadron of dragoons, but Captain Mein, with great promptness, rallied the company round him and effectually resisted the charge. However, his loss from musketry was very considerable, having two subalterns and eighteen rank and file killed and wounded. The strength of the ground, and the able disposition of his troops upon it made by General Ney, induced the belief that a stronger force might be in the position than was the case, and Lord Wellington therefore checked the advance of the Light Division on the left, and of the third division, which had been pushed forward on the right to turn the French left, until the rear divisions could come up.

"As soon as this was done the army deployed into two lines, and advanced against the enemy, who fell back under cover of a heavy fire of artillery as the assailants advanced, and withdrew rapidly to the difficult ground on the right bank of the Redinha river, leaving the village itself in flames between them and the pursuers.

"On the 13th the Light Division, under the command of Major-General Sir Wm. Erskine, encamped about a league beyond Condeixa, and next morning, closely following the French rear-guard, directed its march on Miranda do Corvo. Shortly after the division had moved off, it fell in with the enemy near Cazal Novo. Captain William Jones's and Captain George Thomas Napier's companies were the first sent out to force back the enemy's light troops, which were posted behind some stone enclosures, and the heavy fog which prevailed at the time rendered it very difficult to ascertain the exact position which the enemy occupied, but these companies were reinforced by Captain William Mein's, and as the bugles repeated the sound to advance, the companies pressed forward, although engaged against vastly superior forces, and the enemy gave way; but in gaining this first ridge Captains Jones, Napier, and Mein, were wounded, and Lieutenant Theophilus Gifford killed. The fog cleared off, and the French line was discovered again formed on a retired range of hills. Colonel Beckwith's brigade attacked it in front, whilst the 52nd made a movement which brought it full on the enemy's right flank. A vigorous attack at this point forced back a strong body of the enemy, on the road by which his line had to retire, and Captain John Graham Douglas's and Captain James Henry

Reynett's companies continued to pour a destructive fire on the fugitives as they passed along their front. Thus ended this affair of the 14th of March, and the division halted for the night close to Miranda do Corvo.

"The division marched from Miranda do Corvo at about eleven o'clock on the morning of the 15th, and in the evening arrived on the left bank of the Ceira, a short distance from Foz de Aronce. The men had lighted fires, and were making preparations for bivouacking for the night, when the division was suddenly ordered to fall in, and instantly commenced a vigorous attack upon Marshal Ney's corps, which still remained on the left bank of the river.

"The enemy were forced back rapidly upon the bridge, and Captain Joseph Dobbs's and William Madden's companies pressed upon them so closely that their rear was seized with a panic, and in their impatience to escape, great numbers were drowned and trampled upon, but the confusion was completed by the French divisions formed on the opposite bank, who, having in the dark mistaken their own fugitives for the advance of the British, commenced a heavy fire upon them, and it was a considerable time before order could be restored. The bridge was blown up by the enemy during the night.

"The 52nd, commanded by Lieutenant-Colonel John Ross, sustained the following casualties on the 12th, 14th, and 15th March :—Lieutenant Theophilus Gifford and twelve rank and file killed ; Captains George Thomas Napier, William Mein, and William Jones, (all severely,) Lieutenants John Cross, (slightly,) John Winterbottom, Adjutant, (severely,) and Ensign Richard Lifford, (severely,) five serjeants and seventy rank and file wounded. Ensign Lifford afterwards died of his wounds.

"In these affairs the 52nd gained great praise from Viscount Wellington, who stated in his despatch that—

"'Major-General Sir William Erskine particularly mentioned 'the conduct of the 52nd Regiment and Colonel Elder's Caçadores 'on the 12th, in the attack of the wood near Redinha, and I must 'add that I have never seen the French infantry driven out from 'a wood in more gallant style.'

"In relating the occurrences of the 14th, Lord Wellington says,—

"'In the operations of this day, the 43rd, 52nd, 95th Regi-
'ments, and 3rd Caçadores, under the command of Colonels
'Drummond and Beckwith and Major Patrickson, Lieut.-Colonel
'Ross, and Majors Gilmour and Stuart, particularly distinguished
'themselves.'

"'GENERAL ORDERS.

"'March 16th, 1811.

"'No. 1.—The commander of the Forces returns his thanks
'to the General and staff-officers and troops for their excellent
'conduct in the operations of the last ten days against the
'enemy.

"'He requests the commanding officers of the 43rd, 52nd,
'and 95th Regiments to name a serjeant of each regiment to be
'recommended for promotion to an ensigncy, as a testimony of
'the particular approbation of the Commander of the Forces of
'these three regiments.'

"In consequence of the above Order, Serjeant-Major Mitchell
of the 52nd was promoted to an ensigncy in the 88th Regiment,
of which he was appointed Adjutant.

"The Light Division halted on the 16th, and the rear-divisions
of the army closed up.

"On the 17th the Light Division forded the Ceira about a
mile above the bridge, and marched to San Miguel de Poyares;
on the 18th, after a cannonade, it passed the Alva, and bivouacked
near Ponte de Murcella.

"On the six succeeding days the division marched by Morta,
Golizes, St Jago, Pinhancos, and St. Payo to Navazienis, where it
arrived on the 24th and halted there on the 25th. On this day
the second battalion 52nd joined the Light Division, having embarked at Portsmouth on the 26th of January, and landed at
Lisbon on the 6th of March. The division marched to Celerico
on the 26th, halted there on the 27th, and next day marched
upon Sabugal.

"On the morning of the 3rd of April the Light Division
crossed the Coa at a ford about two miles above the town of
Sabugal, with the intention of getting round the enemy's left
flank, whilst two British divisions were to attack him in front ;
but in consequence of the very hazy state of the atmosphere the

movement of the Light Division, then under the command of Major-General Sir William Erskine, was not sufficiently extended, and instead of getting in rear of the enemy's flank, it came in full contact with it, before the other two divisions had arrived at their points of attack.

" Colonel Beckwith's brigade (the 43rd and the 95th Rifles) led the march of the Light Division, and having passed the ford too much to its left became first engaged with the enemy's left, in his front instead of in flank. They were thus opposed to a very superior force, and a vigorous charge of cavalry on his right, and the fire of numerous infantry in his front, compelled Colonel Beckwith to fall back behind some stone enclosures, which enabled him to resist the efforts of the enemy until the arrival of the 2nd brigade, consisting of the two batalions of the 52nd and a battalion of Caçadores.

" The impetuosity of Colonel Beckwith's attack had been such that the 43rd Regiment, in two most daring charges, had driven back the French infantry and captured a howitzer ; but when the 1st brigade was compelled to fall back to the enclosures they were forced to relinquish this piece, and the enemy again surrounded it, and turned its fire on the British brigades.

" The 2nd brigade, however, which had marched somewhat more to the right, and had gained nearly the crest of the ridge without fighting, now formed on the right of the 43rd, and the 52nd advancing at the charge, drove back the enemy's columns which had repulsed the 1st brigade. These columns were supported by cavalry which made a spirited charge upon the 52nd while they were still disordered by their rapid advance ; the cavalry however was repulsed, the 43rd howitzer was recaptured by a company of the 52nd, commanded by Lieutenant J. Frederick Love, and remained in possession of the regiment until it was handed over to the artillery,—not however before Lieutenant Robert O'Hara of the 52nd, who well knew the comfortable practices of the artillery, had relieved the limber of a couple of fine hams and a keg of concentrated *eau de vie*, which were most acceptable as a finish to the action.

" Viscount Wellington thus described this action in his despatch :—

"' Four companies of the 95th and three of Colonel Elder's
' Caçadores drove in the enemy's pickets, and were supported by
' the 43rd Regiment.

"' They were however again attacked with a fresh column with
' cavalry, and retired again to their post, when they were joined
' by the other brigade of the Light Division, consisting of the first
' and second battalions of the 52nd and 1st Caçadores.

"' These troops repulsed the enemy, and Colonel Beckwith's
' brigade and the first battalion 52nd Regiment again advanced
' upon them. They were attacked again by a fresh column sup-
' ported by cavalry, which charged the right, and they took post
' in an enclosure upon the top of the height from whence they
' could protect the howitzer which the 43rd had taken, and they
' drove back the enemy.

"' I consider the action that was fought by the Light Division,
' by Colonel Beckwith's brigade principally, with the whole of the
' 2nd corps, to be *one of the most glorious that British troops were*
' *ever engaged in.*'

"After the action at Sabugal, the French army hastened
across the Agueda, and the regiment marched from Sabugal to
Quadracies on the 4th, to Forcalhos on the 5th, to Albergaria on
the 6th, and went into cantonments at Gallegos on the 9th of
April.

"On the morning of the 23rd of April, the enemy pushed for-
ward a reconnoissance to the right bank of the Azava. Captain
Robert Campbell's company commanded by Lieutenant Henry
Dawson, and a subdivision of the Rifle corps under the command of
Lieutenant Eeles, were posted on picket at the bridge of Marialva,
and Captain Dobbs's company was stationed at the ford of
Malenos de Flores.

"At about seven o'clock A.M. the enemy commenced an attack
upon the Marialva picket, and Captain Dobbs, knowing that
heavy rain had fallen during the night, suspected that the ford
which he was appointed to guard must have become no longer
fordable. He soon ascertained that this was the fact, and leaving
a corporal and three men to watch the ford, at once dashed off
with the remainder of his company to the bridge; at which he arrived most opportunely, the enemy having forced the passage.

Seeing the state of affairs whilst he was coming over the height above the bridge, Captain Dobbs without hesitation charged down on the enemy, who, supposing that his was only the advance of a much larger force, gave way, and recrossed the bridge. On this the companies of the 52nd and the small party of the 95th placed themselves among the rocks on one side of the bridge, and kept up such a fire upon it that the French were unable to force the passage a second time. The manner of the French in advancing was rather singular. A drummer always led, beating what we used to nickname "Old trousers," and as long as "Old trousers" encouraged them they continued to advance, but as soon as the poor drummer fell, they immediately turned tail and ran back, till their officers stopped them and began the same process over again. This continued till the two battalions of the 52nd came up, and effectually secured the passage, when the French force retired. In this affair Ensign Pritchard, one sergeant, and fourteen rank and file were wounded. Captain Dobbs received four shots through various parts of his clothing.

"Napier says the attacking force on this occasion consisted of 2000 infantry and a squadron of cavalry. If they had succeeded much mischief might have ensued, as our horse-artillery were all out foraging, and their cavalry would have got into our quarters at Gallegos.

"On the following day the enemy made another attack upon the Marialva picket, and were again repulsed by Captain Reynett's company under the command of Lieutenant James Frederick Love.

"The following casualties occurred in the 52nd:—On the 23rd of April, Ensign Samuel Dilman Pritchard, one serjeant, and fourteen rank and file were wounded; and on the 24th of April, two serjeants and eight rank and file were wounded.

"*Extract from Lord Wellington's Despatch.*

"'The enemy had on the 23rd attacked our pickets on the 'Azava, but were repulsed. Captains Dobbs and R. Campbell, of 'the 52nd Regiment, and Lieutenant Eeles of the 95th Regiment, 'distinguished themselves on this occasion, on which the allied 'troops defended their posts against very superior numbers of the 'enemy.

" 'The enemy repeated their attack upon our pickets on the 'Azava on the 24th, and were again repulsed.'

" Very early on the 5th of May the Light Division moved to its right, and was posted in support of the 7th (Houston's) division, near Poço Velho, with the British cavalry, scarcely more than 1000 sabres, on the plain above. Massena's attack was led by two corps,—one directed upon the village of Fuentes, the other upon Poço Velho, while large bodies of his troops were seen threatening to turn the British right. The 7th division was pressed step by step out of Poço Velho, and the French cavalry turned the right flank, and drove back the advanced squadrons of the British, and were debouching in force upon the plain. Lord Wellington upon this instantly corrected his front, which it was evident was too much extended. The Light Division, thrown into squares in echelon of battalions, and supported as well as might be by the cavalry, was ordered to cover the retreat of its own horse-artillery and of the 7th division towards Villa Formosa, while the 7th division itself crossed the Turones, and retired by the strong ground on its left bank towards the same point.

" The cross-ridge of rocky hill which runs down to the Dos Casas at Fuentes also runs down to the Turones near Villa Formosa, and on this a new front was to be opposed to the advancing masses of the French left. Never perhaps in modern war was a more beautiful movement made, nor at a more critical moment, than by the Light Division on this occasion. The cavalry of Montburn, numbering 5000 sabres, and flushed with their advantage, pressed round the battalion squares without daring to storm them; the French artillery plunged into their close ranks wherever a clear range could be got : and for nearly three miles these veterans held in their conduct the fate of the British army. But in one hour the rocky points which bounded the plain were reached, a British battery was in position to answer the French guns, and the Light Division, closely connected with the 1st division on its left and with the 7th division on its right,—and now under the command of its old chief, Craufurd, who had rejoined from sick leave,—swept the plain with a fire before which the troops of Massena quailed and withdrew out of range.

"Meantime the French attack on the village of Fuentes had succeeded so far as to give them possession of all but the upper part of the village. Here, however, they could not succeed against the obstinate bravery of the regiments of the 3rd division, which maintained the church and the upper houses, and towards evening a brigade of the Light Division, in which was the 52nd, was sent to relieve them. More accustomed to desultory fighting, these troops soon pushed back the French to the banks of the river, and then, as evening closed in, by that common compact so well known to old friends on opposite sides, the British sentries were posted on the left and the French on the right bank of the Dos Casas without further mutual molestation.

"'I am glad to see you here,' said the French field-officer, on placing his pickets along the right bank, to a captain of the 52nd, across the stream; 'we shall now understand each other. When 'you want water, and our sentries challenge, call out "aqua," 'and you shall have it. Will you give your boys (à vos enfants) 'similar orders?' Of course this was done.

"Soon after dusk a French serjeant, a fine, handsome soldier, was brought in prisoner to the captain (J. F. Love) of the 52nd picket. The report made was that he had come over the line of sentries to take leave of a Spanish girl in the village, and was captured in the act. 'Eh bien! capitaine,' said the serjeant to Captain Love, 'c'est l'amour qui m'a fait votre prisonnier.'* 'Eh 'bien donc!' was the reply, 'pour cette fois-ci nous ne serons 'pas trop exigeants : retournez chez votre capitaine, et dites-lui 'que si l'amour vous a joué un mauvais tour, l'amour vous a 'dédommagé. Je m'appelle Love ; vous ne l'oublierez pas de 'sitôt.'

"These amenities were the small jewels which in that day disguised the blood-stained robes of the God of War.

"During the night of the 5th of May, breastworks were thrown up between the Dos Casas and Turones, which rendered the new front of the British army, in the opinion of Massena, un-

---

* 'Ah, Sir, Love has made me your prisoner.' 'Well, then,' was the reply, 'we will not be hard upon you for once ; go back to your captain, and tell him 'if Love got you into this scrape, Love gets you out again. My name is Love, and 'you will not forget it.'

assailable with any prospect of success; for after hovering about the ground, and idly parading his prisoners, who were chiefly made in Fuentes on the forenoon of the 5th, he gave up the hope of relieving Almeida and retreated.

"In relieving their sentries on this occasion, the French placed a straw figure, with a French cap on its top and a pole by its side, to resemble the barrel of a musket, and the *ruse* was generally successful, so far as to give time to withdraw the rear-guards from their positions."

CHAPTER LI.

1812.

THE 52ND AT THE SIEGE AND ASSAULT OF CIUDAD RODRIGO, AND ALSO OF BADAJOS.

Storming the Francisco redoubt—Assault of Rodrigo—Gurwood leads the forlorn hope—Colonel Colborne wounded—Takes the governor prisoner—Lord Wellington returns to him the governor's sword—Anecdote of the Prince Regent and Gurwood—Fort Picurina—Assault of Badajos—Immense loss of officers and men—McNair and the *chevaux-de-frise*.

"ON the 8th of January, 1812, the Light Division, commanded by Major-General Robert Craufurd, marched from El Bodon, crossed the Agueda, and took up its ground beyond the ridge of hill called the great Teson, on the north side of Ciudad Rodrigo. It was about mid-day, and as the place was not regularly invested, the French garrison in the Francisco redoubt imagined the affair was one of observation rather than in earnest, and amused themselves with saluting and bowing to their English friends. However, at nightfall a party for the purpose of storming the redoubt was formed from each regiment of the Light Division, under the command of Lieut.-Colonel John Colborne,* of the 52nd Regiment, who himself arranged the plan of attack and the details, and saw them effectually carried out. The party was composed of companies commanded by the senior captains of each battalion : two from the 43rd, four from the 52nd, two from the 95th, and one from each of the Caçadore (Portuguese) battalions. Four companies were selected for the advanced guard, to occupy the

"* Now General Lord Seaton, G. C. B."

crest of the glacis and open fire, while the party with the ladders, in charge of Lieutenant Alexander Thomson, of the Royal Engineers, in the rear of those companies, could be brought up and be assisted in placing the ladders for the assault: in the rear of these followed the companies destined for the actual escalade. In this order the whole started and advanced, after a caution had been given by Colonel Colborne with respect to *silence*, and each captain had been instructed precisely where he was to post his company, and how he was to proceed on arriving near the redoubt. An officer of the 95th and two serjeants had been stationed before dark on the brow of the hill, to mark the angle of the redoubt covering the steeple of a church in Ciudad Rodrigo, and this gave an accurate direction to the party in the dusk of the evening. When the party reached the point marked by the officer, Colonel Colborne dismounted, and again called out the four captains of the advanced guard, and ordered the front company to occupy the front face, and the second company the right, and so on. Captain Mulcaster, of the Engineers, then suggested that it would be better to wait for the light ladders which were coming up; Colonel Colborne however thought that no time should now be lost, and proceeded with the very heavy ladders which had been made during the day.   When about fifty yards from the redoubt, Colonel Colborne gave the word double quick.   This movement, and the rattling of the canteens, alarmed the garrison, but the defenders had only time to fire one round from their guns before each company had taken its post on the crest of the glacis, and opened fire.   All this was effected without the least confusion, and not a man was seen on the redoubt after the fire had commenced.   The party with the ladders soon arrived, and placed them in the ditch against the palisades, so that they were ready when Captain Mein of the 52nd came up with the escalading companies.   They got into the ditch by descending the ladders, and then placing them against the fraises.   The only fire from which the assailants suffered was from shells and grenades thrown over from the ramparts.   During these proceedings Lieutenant Gurwood, of the 52nd, came from the rear of the redoubt, and mentioned that a company could get in by the gorge of the redoubt with ladders, on which Colonel Colborne at once desired him to take any ladders he could find. The company at the gorge, however, had forced open the gate, or it had been opened by some of the defenders endeavouring to escape.* The redoubt was entered simultaneously by means of the ladders at the faces, and no further resistance was made ; Captain Mein was wounded, as was believed, by an accidental shot from one of our own companies as he was mounting on the rampart. Most of the defenders had fled to the guard-house, and not a man of them was killed after the redoubt was entered by the assailants.

"The garrison of Ciudad Rodrigo opened a heavy fire on the redoubt the moment it was known to be in possession of the assailants, and the attacking party was then collected outside, and marched by Colonel Colborne down to the rivulet near the foot of the glacis of the place, where it was then disposed so as to cover the working parties opening the first parallel, until moonlight. Such good use was made of the night, that by daylight the redoubt had been converted into an efficient lodgment under cover, with a communication to the rear, and the first parallel was thrown up for a length of 600 yards. Had the redoubt not been thus taken, five days would have been required to attack it regularly ; the governor of the town had been in it about half an hour before the attack, and it was fortunate for his Excellency that his stay there was so short.

"The remarkable success of this assault was probably due to the following points :—the clear conception and explanation of the plan of attack, so that each individual in charge knew what he had to do ; the high discipline and order in which the plan was carried out, under the eye of the officer commanding the party ; and the care taken to cover the redoubt with a sheet of fire while the escalade was being made, rather than trusting to the rush of a few bayonets against many defenders.

"Another instance of similar care in the plan and guidance by its chief, accompanied by success, may be found in the assault

---

"* It afterwards appeared that a serjeant of the French artillery, in the act of throwing a live shell upon the storming party in the ditch, was shot dead : the lighted shell fell within the parapet of the redoubt, and was kicked by some one of its defenders out of their neighbourhood towards the gorge, where, stopped by the bottom of the gate, it exploded and blew the gate open."

of the Picurina outwork at Badajos, on the evening of the 25th
of March, 1812; while the failure in the assault of Fort Chris-
tobal, at the first siege of Badajos, on the 6th of June, 1811, seems
to have been caused by an irregular rush of fine soldiers without
a well-concerted plan, and without sufficient protection from the
means of defence exerted against them during the necessarily
disadvantageous position of assault.

"Viscount Wellington thus referred in his despatches to the
storming of the advanced redoubt of Ciudad Rodrigo:—

"'Accordingly, Major-General Craufurd directed a detach-
'ment of the Light Division, under Lieut.-Colonel Colborne of
'the 52nd Regiment, to attack the work shortly after dark; the
'attack was very ably conducted by Lieut.-Colonel Colborne, and
'the work was taken by storm in a short time; 2 captains and
'47 men were made prisoners, and the remainder put to the
'sword.*

"'We took three pieces of cannon.

"'I cannot sufficiently applaud the conduct of Lieut.-Colonel
'Colborne, and of the detachment under his command.'

"The 1st, 3rd, and 4th divisions as well as the Light Division
were employed in the siege by turns, while the remaining divisions of the army were in observation against the approach
of Marshal Marmont for the relief of the place. The Light
Division thus took its turn in the trenches every fourth day,
being stationed in El Bodon when off trench-duty. The march
to and from the trenches was not agreeable, as the Agueda was
half frozen, and had to be forded to arrive at the ground, so that
a pair of iced breeches were usually the accompaniments of each
man, on twenty-four hours' sharp duty. The riflemen of the 95th
did good service in keeping down the fire of the garrison, and
the saps were pushed forward vigorously, but the approach of
Marmont determined Viscount Wellington to make the assault
at the earliest moment that should present a probability of success; and the counter and enfilading batteries accordingly had to
perform the office of breaching.

---

* This statement in Lord Wellington's despatch is contrary to that of the
52nd "Record," that "not a man of them was killed after the assailants entered the
"redoubt." See preceding page, line 8. W. LEEKE.

"On the 19th of January two breaches were reported practicable, and at nine o'clock at night the Light Division was formed behind the convent of St. Francisco in a double column of sections, and shortly afterwards advanced to the attack of the lesser breach, which was very gallantly carried.

"The forlorn hope was led by Lieutenant Gurwood, of the 52nd, with twenty-five volunteers. The storming-party followed, consisting of 100 volunteers from each regiment; those of the 52nd under Captain Joseph Dobbs, those of the 95th under Captain Samuel Mitchell and Lieutenants William Johnston and John Kincaid, while Captain James Fergusson and Lieutenants John O'Connell, Alexander Steele, and John Bramwell, headed those of the 43rd; the whole under command of Major George T. Napier of the 52nd. These troops entered the ditch opposite a ravelin, which some mistook for the point of attack, and the forlorn-hope diverged to their left along the face of the ravelin, both parties reunited at the flank, and with an impetuous rush the top of the breach was won and the defenders beaten back.

"Captain Ellicombe, Royal Engineers, was in orders to guide the troops to the descent of the ditch, and Lieutenant Alexander Thompson, Royal Engineers, guided the stormers and was wounded at the breach. Lieutenant Theodore Elliott, of the Royal Engineers, at the edge of the ditch finding a party of the stormers were mistaking their directions, most opportunely pointed out to them the true breach and saved the waste of some valuable lives.

"As the supporting regiments mounted the lesser breach, the sections of the 43rd and 52nd wheeled outwards—the 52nd to the left, and the 43rd to the right—towards the great breach, and cleared the ramparts both to the right and left. This advance caused the enemy to abandon the retrenchment behind the great breach, which they had to that moment successfully defended, and in a few minutes afterwards the town was in the possession of the British.

"The following casualties were sustained by the 52nd Regiment, in the attack on Ciudad Rodrigo, on the 19th of January:— The first battalion, commanded by Lieut.-Colonel Colborne, had Captain Joseph Dobbs, and eight rank and file killed. Lieut.-Colonel John Colborne, (severely,) Major George Thomas Napier, (severely, right arm amputated,) Captain William Mein, Lieutenant John Woodgate, one serjeant, and thirty-three rank and file wounded. The second battalion, commanded by Major Edward Gibbs, had one serjeant and three rank and file killed; Lieutenant John Gurwood and five rank and file wounded.

" Lieutenant Gurwood of the 52nd, who led the forlorn-hope, afterwards took the French Governor, General Barrié, prisoner in the citadel. Lord Wellington presented Lieutenant Gurwood with the sword of General Barrié, on the breach by which Gurwood had entered,—a fitting and proud compliment to a young soldier of fortune !*

" In Viscount Wellington's despatch, dated 20th of January, of which the following are extracts, the conduct of the officers and men of the 52nd Regiment was thus noticed :—

"'The 4th column, consisting of the 43rd, 52nd, and part of ' the 95th Regiment, being a portion of the Light Division under ' Major-General Crauford, attacked the breaches on the left, in ' front of the suburb of St. Francisco.

* I have mentioned in my account of Waterloo, that Gurwood had left the 52nd, and had got a troop in the 10th Hussars. The following anecdote respecting him was current in the 52nd in my time, and I remember the particulars very distinctly, as I have often related them since. Some time after the battle of Waterloo Gurwood was stationed at Brighton with his regiment, and frequently dined, as all the officers did, at the Pavilion. One day he was the first person to arrive, and the Prince got into conversation with him, and made him give him the whole history of his leading the forlorn-hope at Rodrigo, of his taking the Governor prisoner, and of Lord Wellington's giving him back the Governor's sword on the breach. When Gurwood had finished his account, the Prince patted him on the back and called him a fine fellow. Shortly afterwards some of his friends advised him to solicit the Prince to obtain a brevet majority for him. This Gurwood took an opportunity of doing, and the very next time he dined at the Pavilion, on one of the invitations sent to the officers of the 10th, the Prince took no notice of him. This continued to be his conduct towards him on two or three occasions afterwards ; at last, one day he came up to him and said, at the same time placing his hand in a friendly manner behind his shoulder " Well ! " my fine fellow, I have settled your business at last, but I have had hard work " to manage it." It was supposed that the Duke of York, for some reason or other, made a great difficulty about giving this brevet step to Gurwood ; and that if the Prince Regent had found it expedient to give way in the matter, he would not have mentioned the subject again, and would have taken no further notice of Gurwood.

See anecdote of the gallant conduct at Rodrigo of the Earl of March, the Prince of Orange, and Lord Fitzroy Somerset, at p. 146, of vol. I.

"'Major-General Craufurd and Major-General Vandeleur, and
'the troops of the Light Division on the left were likewise very
'forward on that side, and in less than half an hour from the
'time the attack commenced our troops were in possession of and
'formed on the ramparts of the place.

"'I have to add to this list, Lieut.-Colonel Colborne of the
'52nd Regiment, and Major George Napier, who led the storming
'party of the Light Division, and was wounded at the top of the
'breach. I have already reported my sense of the conduct of
'Major-General Craufurd and of Lieut.-Colonel Colborne, and of
'the troops of the Light Division, in the storming of the redoubts
'of St. Francisco on the evening of the 8th instant. The conduct
'of these troops was equally distinguished throughout the siege,
'and in the storm nothing could withstand the gallantry with
'which these brave officers and troops advanced and accomplished
'the difficult operation allotted to them, notwithstanding all their
'leaders had fallen.

"'I particularly request your Lordship's attention to Major-
'Generals Craufurd and Vandeleur, Lieut.-Colonel Barnard, 95th,
'Lieut.-Colonel Colborne, Majors Gibbs and Napier, 52nd, and
'Lieut.-Colonel M'Leod, 43rd Regiment; the conduct of Captain
'Duffy of the 43rd, and of Lieutenant Gurwood of the 52nd
'Regiment has also been reported to me.'

"The following officers of the regiment were promoted :—

"Major Edward Gibbs, to be Lieut.-Colonel in the army, 6th
February, 1812.

"Major George Thomas Napier, ditto, ditto.

"Captain William Mein, to be Major in the army, 6th February, 1812.

"Lieutenant John Gurwood, to be Captain of a Company in
the Royal African Corps, 6th February, 1812.

"Lieutenant John Woodgate, to be Captain of a Company in
the Bourbon Regiment, 20th February, 1812.

"The following are the names of the officers who volunteered
for the storming party :—

"Major George Thomas Napier commanded the storming
party of the Division.

"Captain William Jones (afterwards killed at Badajos).

" Lieutenant John Gurwood led the forlorn-hope.

" Captain William Jones ('Jack Jones' of Busaco celebrity) made himself remarkable immediately after the assault of Ciudad Rodrigo. A French officer having surrendered to Jones, Jack made use of him somewhat as Valentine is represented to have used Orson,—to show quarters for his men,—and having placed some of them in a large store, the French officer led the way into the church, in front of which Lord Wellington and some of the staff were collected. Some fire had been lighted already (supposed by Portuguese soldiers) on the pavement, and the Frenchman entering, and seeing the fire, instantly started back, exclaiming, 'Sacré bleu!' and ran out with looks of the utmost horror. Jones, not understanding French, did not catch the idea: 'Sacré bleu' puzzled him, until going further in, he saw powder about the floor and powder-barrels near the fire. 'Sacré 'bleu' became at once identified with *powder*, and he immediately got the help of two or three of his men (whose names are not known,) and carried with his own hands the powder-barrels out of the way of immediate danger. This deed passed unrequited at the time: let the memory of it now receive our admiration!

" Orders having been received to draft the second battalion of the 52nd Regiment into the first, the Earl of Wellington (to which dignity he was raised for the capture of Ciudad Rodrigo) notified that arrangement to the army in the following terms :—

"' EXTRACT FROM GENERAL ORDERS, 23RD FEBRUARY, 1812.

"' No. 3.—The Commander of the Forces having received 'orders to draft the second battalion 52nd Regiment into the first, 'the following arrangement is to be made for that purpose.

"' No. 8.—The Commander of the Forces begs the second bat-'talion 52nd Regiment will accept his thanks for their very dis-'tinguished services. Since they have been in the Peninsula they 'have had various opportunities of displaying their gallantry and 'good conduct, and the Commander of the Forces has had reason 'on every occasion to be satisfied with their behaviour.'   •

" Ten serjeants, 7 buglers, and 487 rank and file were in consequence transferred from the second to the first battalion ; and 10 serjeants, 5 buglers, and 85 rank and file, being unserviceable, were transferred to the second battalion.

"On the 25th of February the skeleton of the second battalion marched for Lisbon on its way to England.

"Ciudad Rodrigo having been placed under the command of a Spanish governor, the British commander determined to take Badajos, if possible, before Marshals Marmont and Soult could unite their forces for its defence.

"On the 26th of February the first battalion, commanded by Brevet Lieut.-Colonel John Philip Hunt, marched from Guinaldo upon Badajos by the following route;—Aldea de Ponte, Sortelha, Escarigo, Alpadrinha, Alcairo, Castel Branco, Niza, Castello de Vide, Portalegre, Monches, and Elvas, where the regiment arrived on the 16th of March.

"Early on the morning of the 27th the Light Division formed on the glacis of Elvas, and started for the siege of Badajos to the enlivening tune, struck up by every corps of buglers, of 'Patrick's 'Day in the Morning.' It crossed the Guadiana by the bridge of boats about four miles from Elvas, and marching onwards for about ten miles, took up its position as the extreme left of the investing army, just beyond long shell-range from the walls. The left brigade was nearly due south of fort Pardeleras, a little in rear of the Sierra del Viento, *à cheval* (astride) on the road to Torquemada. The space between its left and the Guadiana was unprotected, except by a night picket on the Olivenza road.

"Soon after dusk a detachment of the 52nd, marching to its right by a circuitous route parallel to the works of the town, joined near the heights of San Miguel the covering and working parties of 3800 men, which, in a storm of wind and rain, broke ground about one hundred and sixty yards from fort Picurina.

"To the Light Division, and especially to its left brigade, this long route to the trenches across the upper branches of the Calamon and Rivellas, in a cold and very rainy season, formed one of the greatest hardships of the siege. In going to the trenches all of course proceeded in order by the appointed route, but in returning in the evening numerous were the attempts at short cuts homeward, notwithstanding the dashes of the French cavalry and round shot from the town. The Earl of Wellington kindly hu-humoured these irregularities by placing a picket in a covered hollow, to keep the French cavalry at bay.

" On the evening of the 25th the parties going off duty from the trenches, under the command of Major-General Kempt, were ordered to storm fort Picurina, before their relief and departure to camp. The Picurina was a very strong ravelin with flanks, on a mamelon four hundred yards from the covered way of the place, with which it was connected by a covered way of communication.

" One hundred men of the 52nd, under the command of Captain Ewart, headed the attacking parties, with ladders, grassbags, crowbars, and axes. The ditch was so deep, and the escarp so strongly fraised, that the first assault was made on the triple line of thick and high palisades with which the gorge was enclosed. The struggle was very fierce and prolonged, and Ewart fell wounded. At length the support was directed against the salient angle above the fraizes, and made good its footing, while Nixon, Ewart's subaltern, with his axemen broke through the gate of the palisades in rear, Nixon falling severely wounded within it. Another struggle in the narrow interior, and this most important fort, which was calculated to have held out for five days longer, was carried. Captain John Ewart and Ensign William Nixon were wounded, and thirty-four rank and file out of the 52nd hundred were killed or wounded.

" The capture of Picurina placed in the power of the besiegers sites for breaching batteries against the bastions of Trinidad and Santa Maria. The whole front however of the trenches towards these bastions was inundated by means of a dam in a bridge over the Rivellas, close in the rear of the Ravelin of St. Roque. About ten in the evening of the 2nd of April, Lieutenant Blackwood* of the 52nd, with three sappers carrying bags of powder, silently left the advanced trench, and creeping behind the ravelin, lodged the powder with a lighted match upon the dam. They regained the trench in safety, with a harmless shot in the dark from the French sentinel, and the bags exploded—unhappily for some hundreds of valuable lives in the subsequent storming—without sufficient effect.

" Although not armed with the rifle, the shooting of the 52nd

* Robert Temple Blackwood, killed at Waterloo as Captain 69th Regiment, uncle to the present Lord Dufferin.

was sometimes called into play with considerable effect. One of the first counter-batteries was so overpowered by the enemy's fire, that Lieutenant John Dobbs, who was covering the battery in a trench in front of it, was called on to keep down the enemy's guns. He accordingly gave the opposite embrasures in charge of his men, and in twenty minutes the gunners were unable to stand to their guns, and the embrasures were blocked with gabions by the enemy to escape the fire.

" On the 6th of April three breaches were reported to be practicable so long as the fire of the allied batteries prevented the fixing of impediments upon them. These batteries, however, were more than four hundred yards off, with the inundation of the Rivellas intervening, in consequence of which the covered way could not be approached by a direct march, and the counter-scarp seventeen feet deep, with an irregular rocky bottom, remained intact. The ditch, also, for nearly one-half of the front attacked, was filled with water from a branch of the inundation of the Rivellas, which Lieutenant Blackwood and the sappers had so gallantly and ineffectually endeavoured to drain.

" At 9 P.M., on the 6th of April, the Light Division, commanded by Colonel Barnard, and the 4th division by Major-General the Honourable Charles Colville, assembled near the small bridge over the Calamon, a brook tributary to the Rivellas, about a thousand yards from the breaches. The Light Division moved off in columns of sections, the ladder parties, to which were attached engineer officers, (Captain Nicholas and Lieutenant de Salaberry,) leading; then the grassbag, axe, and crowbar men; next one hundred volunteers from each regiment as storming parties, and then the divisions themselves.

" The night was very dark, but as the swollen Rivellas was all the way close on the right hand there was no difficulty in tracking the route. The besiegers' batteries, after firing heavily, suddenly ceased; in this, however, there was nothing unusual. The advance silently neared the covered way. All was very still. The town-clock tolled the hour of ten, and the sentries along the walls successively gave their usual cry of 'Sentinelle, garde à ' vous,' translated by our men into ' All's well in Badahoo.' Suddenly a fireball rising high in air from the bastion of Santa Maria fell near the axe and crowbar parties, but a shovelful of earth at once extinguished it, and all was dark and still again.

"The ladder-party of the 52nd crept quietly through the broken palisades of the covered way, and planted against the counterscarp its six ladders, just in front of the salient part of the proper right face of the unfinished ravelin. The officer of it, Ensign Gawler, the engineer officer leading, Lieutenant de Salaberry, and about twelve or fifteen men were in the ditch, when, with a blinding blaze of light and a regular chorus of explosions of all kinds, the enemy's fire opened. The leading assailants pushed up the unfinished ravelin, in the hope of tracing a practicable passage to the centre breach; but the summit, in the very focus of the fire, was rendered still more untraversable by a field-piece in the flank of Santa Maria, which poured incessant charges of grape across the ravelin, and on to the covered way of the Trinidad, in which now appeared the head of the 4th division endeavouring to plant its ladders. The deceitful inundation below carried away all that were led down, so that excepting some reckless fellows (among whom was Lieut.-Colonel Hunt of the 52nd) who jumped down the counterscarp, and were almost shaken to death, and a few active fellows who scrambled down the remains of one or two narrow ramps which the enemy had cut away, the whole of those who got into the ditch descended by the six ladders planted before the fire opened; of which also the one nearest the salient angle, having slipped into a rocky hole, was too short.

"It then became evident, that the highest discipline and the most devoted courage should not be calculated upon to counterbalance the neglect of those precautions, which long engineering experience has inscribed as essential. Of these the blowing-in of the counterscarp when it exceeds the height of about eight feet, is one.

"The two massive columns were first checked almost hopelessly on the crest of the glacis, under the fire within sixty yards of veteran soldiers well covered, with several firelocks each, and adding to their bullets wooden cylinders set with slugs. Then officers and men, British, Germans, and Portuguese, of various regiments, became practically undisciplined mobs at the foot of the ladders. Then there were desperate rushes, in which the confused mass divided into three part'es, according to each man's fancy for a particular breach. Then came the lighted fireballs and tar-barrels, the explosions of heavy shells, powder-barrels, and fougasses, and the crashes of logs of wood rolled incessantly from above. Then, halfway up the breach, were barrows turned the wrong side upwards, and planks studded with pointed nails. On the summit was a close row of *chevaux-de-frise* of sharp sword-blades well chained together, and from these projected the muzzles of the muskets of grenadiers with their recollections fresh of two previous successful defences.

"The most desperate and persevering gallantry distinguished the assailants; some fell even under the *chevaux-de-frise*. It is not however difficult to conceive that at no one time was any body of men launched against the breach, in sufficient numbers, organization, and unanimity of effort, to overcome the immense combination of obstacles. Captain Currie of the 52nd, a most cool and gallant soldier, seeing the impossibility of success without powerful concert, examined the counterscarp beyond the Santa Maria breach, and having found a narrow ramp imperfectly destroyed, ascended it and sought out the Earl of Wellington, who with a few of his staff was a short distance off. 'Can they not get in?' was the Earl's anxious and emphatic question. On Currie's reply, that those in confusion in the ditch could not, but that a fresh battalion might succeed by the descent he had discovered, one from the reserve was committed to his guidance. From the difficulties of the broken ramp, these men as they got in became mixed up with the confused parties rushing at or retiring from the breaches, and this last hope vanished.

"The buglers of the reserve were then sent to the crest of the glacis to sound the retreat; the troops in the ditch, grown desperate, at first would not believe it genuine, and struck the buglers in the ditch who attempted to sound; but at length sullenly reascended the counterscarp as they could, saved only from complete destruction by the smoke of the expiring combustibles of the defenders, and the foul and worn-out condition of their flintlocks. Cool generosity did not forsake the British soldier to the last,—one of them made a wounded officer of the

52nd take hold of his accoutrements that he might drag him up a ladder, 'or,' said he, 'the enemy will come out and bayonet 'you.' The fine fellow was just stepping on to the covered way, when a thrill was felt by the hand which grasped his belts, and the shot which stretched him lifeless threw his body backward into the ditch again, while the officer whom he had thus rescued crawled out upon the glacis.* As the last stragglers crossed the glacis the town-clock was heard again, heavily tolling twelve; but Picton was in the castle to the right, and Leith in the bastion of St. Vincente to the left, and no French sentinel from that day to this has cried again '*Garde à vous*' from the ramparts of Badajos.

The following is the return of the casualties of the 52nd during the siege and assault of Badajos:—

	Killed.				Wounded							
	Captains.	Lieutenants.	Serjeants.	Rank and File.	Lieut.-Colonel.	Captains.	Lieutenants.	Ensigns.	Serjeant-Major.	Serjeants.	Buglers	Rank and File.
From the 19th of March to the 21st ...				1				1		1		2
„ 23rd to 24th ...		1	1									3
„ 25th				8		1		1		3		34
April 5th										1		4
„ 6th	3	2	3	50	1	3	9	1	1	18	1	261
General total, 415												
Total	3	2	4	60	1	4	9	3	1	23	1	304

Officers Killed.

Captain William Jones.
   „   William Madden.
   „   Clement Poole.
Lieutenant Charles Booth.
   „   Job Watson Royle.

* This man's name is unknown, even to the officer thus saved --the present Colonel Gawler, K.H.

Officers who volunteered for the Storming Party.

Captain William Jones.
Lieutenant James M'Nair.*
„   Charles Booth.
Ensign George Gawler.

Officers Wounded.

Major and Brevet Lieut.-Colonel Edward Gibbs, severely, lost an eye.
Brevet Major William Mein, severely.
Captain Robert Campbell, ditto.
    „   Augustus Merry, ditto, died.
    „   John F. Ewart, ditto.
Lieutenant James M'Nair, ditto.
    „   Charles Kinlock, slightly.
    „   Charles York, ditto.
    „   Robert Blackwood, severely.
    „   Francis John Davies, slightly.
    „   William Royds, ditto.
    „   George Ulrick Barlow, severely.
Ensign William Nixon, ditto.
    „   George Hall, ditto.
    „   George Gawler, slightly.

* I have heard M'Nair, in after days, (i e., four or five years after Badajos, where he was one of the stormers,) speak of the difficulties of the breach and of the impossibility of breaking down the *chevaux-de-frise* made of sword-blades. He went three times to the top of the breach, and whilst attempting, on the third occasion, to break the sword-blades was severely wounded all along the top of his head, but whether it was by a musket-shot, or by the thrust of a bayonet or by a sword-cut over the *chevaux-de-frise*, he could never tell. I think his regimental cap could not be found the next morning; but there were several 52nd officers' caps to be procured, whose former owners had been killed.

CHAPTER LII.

1813, 1814.

THE 52ND AT THE CLOSE OF THE PENINSULAR WAR.

Battle of Vittoria—Northey wounded slightly in the head by a cannon-shot—
Colborne rejoins, having recovered from his wound—The French Emperor
sends Soult to command in Spain—Great loss of the French—Contention
amongst both officers and men, all desiring to be of the storming party at
St. Sebastian's—Major Snodgrass, of the 52nd, in command of a Portuguese
regiment—The action at Vera—Cool gallantry of Sir Harry Smith—Surrender of a French battalion—Great loss of the 52nd—Sir W. Napier's
famous words about the regiment—Affair of the 10th December—Battle
of Orthes on the 27th February, 1814—Torbes, Toulouse, Castel Sarrasin,
Bourdeaux—52nd embark for England—Arrive at Plymouth on the 17th
June, 1814.

AT the battle of Salamanca, which was fought on the 22nd of
July, 1812, the Light Division formed the extreme left of the
British line, and was held in reserve as a check upon the right
divisions of Marmont's army. After this they had a great deal of
outpost duty,—some of it very severe,—until, on the 25th of
November, they went into cantonments at Rodrigo and Guinaldo.

The campaign of 1813, opened about the 20th of May, and
the decisive battle of Vittoria, in which the French army was
utterly routed, was fought on the 21st of June. They lost all but
two out of 153 pieces of artillery, 415 caissons, a large quantity
of ammunition, their military chest, and all their baggage and
papers. The Light Division took up the pursuit, which they
continued for several miles, and the rout was most complete.[*]
The Light Division reached Vera on the 15th of July, and fell

---

[*] Captain Currie, of the 52nd, was killed, and Lieutenant Northey was
wounded in the head by a cannon-shot, at Vittoria.

back to Lesaca on the 20th, where Lieut.-Colonel Colborne, having recovered from his wound received at Ciudad Rodrigo, resumed the command of the 52nd.

"Napoleon was at Dresden during the armistice which, on the 4th of June, 1813, terminated the campaign of Lützen and Bautzen, when the intelligence of Lord Wellington's having passed the Ebro reached him, and by an order dated the 1st of July, he directed Marshal Soult immediately to proceed to take the command of what he still called the armies of Spain.

"The Marshal arrived at his head-quarters on the 13th, and presently commenced his operations for a great offensive movement.

"By the 24th he had collected nearly forty thousand men at St. Jean Pied de Port, with which he designed to penetrate by Roncesvalles; and three divisions more, amounting to about twenty thousand men, under Count d'Erlon, were destined for the attack of the passes of Maya, his object being first to raise the blockade of Pamplona and then to operate to his right, so as to enable the reserve from Irun to join him and relieve St. Sebastian. For this ulterior design he had prepared by bringing with him a large body of cavalry and a great number of guns, neither of which could be used to any great extent in the difficult country between the Pyrenees and Pamplona, and his confidence was expressed in the proclamation issued to his troops setting forth his intentions, and saying, 'Let the account of our success 'be dated from Vittoria, and let the birthday of the Emperor be 'celebrated in that city.' Against him was posted, in the front line guarding the pass of Roncesvalles, Major-General Byng's brigade (not more than 1600 men) of the 2nd division, with 4000 Spaniards; and Byng's nearest support was the 4th division, 6000 strong, under Sir Lowry Cole, three leagues in their rear, the whole distance to Pamplona being only eight and a half leagues, or about thirty-four miles. For the defence of the Col de Maya, Sir R. Hill and the remainder of the 2nd division, about 10,000 men, of which two brigades were in advance guarding its passes, and another brigade (Portuguese) about half way between Maya and Roncesvalles.

"Soult made his onset on the morning of the 25th of July, the day of the unsuccessful assault of St. Sebastian by Sir Thomas Graham; and though, as stated in Lord Wellington's despatch of the 1st of August, the position of the allies was very defective, inasmuch as the communication between the 'several divisions was tedious and difficult, and in case of attack those in the front line could not support each other, and would look for support only in the rear;' yet, in spite of his great superiority of numbers, Soult encountered a most determined resistance, and his progress was not at all equal to his anticipations.

"After a series of attacks made on the scattered brigades and divisions of the allies in the rugged passes of the Pyrenees, Soult's combinations were foiled, partly by foggy weather and partly by want of due concert and vigour among his generals, while, on the other hand, the British divisions obstinately resisted, each on its own ground, and gradually retired until a sufficient concentration of force was effected to resume the offensive. Thus Soult found himself eventually beaten back with the loss of about 15,000 men, and on the 2nd of August his army was cantoned behind the general line of the Bidassoa.

"The enemy's project for relieving Pamplona having thus failed, the Light Division countermarched, and again arrived at Sumbella on the 1st of August, and re-occupied Vera on the 2nd.

"At daybreak on the 30th of August, a considerable French force was assembled on the position above Vera, with a view of drawing off the garrison of St. Sebastian by forcing through the covering army of Spaniards, which were posted on the heights of St. Marcial; the columns soon began to descend the hill, and the Light Division pickets having been driven out of the town, the enemy passed the Bidassoa at a ford a little lower down, where the river forms a kind of elbow, its course at the bridge leading to Lesaca being nearly at a right angle with the ford which the enemy passed. The uncertain result of the operations rendered it inexpedient to destroy the Lesaca bridge; but to secure the brigade from sudden attack during the night, this bridge was partially blocked up with large casks filled with stones, leaving only a narrow passage for one man. The attack upon the Spaniards on the heights of St. Marcial on the 31st having failed, the enemy returned the same night to regain their former positions above Vera, but the heavy fall of rain had rendered the ford which the enemy passed on the 30th impracticable, and his only resource was to force the Lesaca bridge. Favoured by the dark, tempestuous night, he succeeded in disposing of the double sentry of the 95th Rifle corps which was posted on it, and the column commenced passing over as rapidly as the circumstances would permit, his passage being greatly impeded by the 95th picket posted in a house near the bridge. As soon as the enemy's object was ascertained, some companies of the 52nd joined the Rifle corps in a heavy fire upon the fugitives, and at daylight three hundred dead bodies were found near the bridge, and many more of the enemy were drowned in endeavouring to swim across the river.

" Meantime the siege of St. Sebastian had been committed to the 5th division and some Portuguese brigades, and was pushed on as well as the arrival of tardy supplies from England would admit. It was the 19th of August before the Marquis of Wellington received from England the battering train which he had long before demanded, and even then the train arrived without its ammunition. However, a breach having been made in the rampart and wall on both sides of the tower of Mésquitas, and also in the long curtain between the tower of Los Hornos and the demi-bastion of St. Elmo, it was arranged that the assault should take place on the 31st of August, a little before noon.

" It was supposed that the troops engaged in the siege were discouraged by its tedious length and by a former unsuccessful assault, and therefore, besides the 5th division, it was ordered that the storming party should consist of 750 volunteers from the Light and some other divisions,—'men,' in the words of the Marquis of Wellington, ' who could show other troops how to mount ' a breach.' Of these volunteers 150 were from the Light Division, under the command of Lieut.-Colonel John P. Hunt, and the quota of the 52nd was—one captain, Robert Campbell; one subaltern, Lieut. Augustus Harvest; three serjeants, and thirty-five rank and file. As soon as the order was communicated to the regiment, entire companies volunteered, and the captains had a difficult task in selecting the men most fit for such an under-

..aking without hurting the feelings of the others ; in many cases
lots were resorted to to settle the claims of those gallant fellows
who contended for the honour of upholding the fame of their
regiment.

"In the private journal of F. S. Larpent, Esq., Judge Advo-
cate-General of the British Forces in the Peninsula, published in
1853, it is related, on the 19th of August, 1813 :—'There was
'nothing but confusion in the two divisions here last night (the
'Light and 4th), from the eagerness of the officers to volunteer,
'and the difficulty of determining who were to be refused and
'allowed to go and run their heads into a hole in the wall, full of
'fire and danger! Major Napier was here quite in misery, be-
'cause, though he had volunteered first, Lieut.-Colonel Hunt, of
'the 52nd, his superior officer, insisted on his right to go. The
'latter said that Napier had been in the breach at Badajos, and
'he had a fair claim to go now. So it is among the subalterns—
'ten have volunteered where two are to be accepted. Hunt,
'being Lieut.-Colonel, has nothing but honour to look to ; as to
'promotion, he is past that. The men say they do not know what
'they are to do, but they are ready to go anywhere.'

"The manner in which this detachment had been called from
other divisions not engaged in the siege, created such indignation
in the 5th division, that it was said at the time they would bayonet the men of the detachment if they got into the town before
them ; and Major-General Leith, who commanded the 5th
division, and who had the entire arrangements on the day of
assault, in consideration of a feeling in which he in some degree
participated, would not suffer the volunteers from the other
divisions to lead the assault, but disposed them along the trenches
to keep down the fire of the hornwork, which was expected to be
severe on the advance to the breach, while the stormers were
selected from the 5th division.

"At 11 o'clock A.M., on the 31st of August, the storming party
filed out of the trenches. Almost at the same moment a mine
was exploded at the left angle of the counterscarp just as the
forlorn-hope had passed, destroying a few men at the head of the
column, which continued to advance, and covered the exterior
face of the breach. Here they found no access to the town—as

entrenchments had been formed behind the breach—except by climbing the broken extremity of the rampart. The enemy had cleared away the rubbish within the breach so as to render the direct descent perpendicular, while the opposite houses were loopholed, and the crest of the breach was exposed to the fire of shells and grape from the batteries of the castle. The orders had been to form a lodgment inside the breach, but as the rubbish had been cleared away, and no materials for the purpose had been brought up with the assaulting party, it was impossible to do this, and the whole of the surface of the breach was soon completely covered with killed and wounded, while all those who attempted to climb up the rampart were instantly bayoneted by the French and thrown back on the crest.

"Seeing that no progress was made, Sir Thomas Graham directed the batteries on the other side of the Urumea to fire over the heads of the British on the breach upon the French on the ramparts above. This was continued for half an hour, and it was evident that the defence was thus greatly weakened. Fresh troops were then filed out of the trenches to continue the assault, and the detachment of volunteers from the Light Division advanced, together with the 2nd brigade of the 5th division, and after some desperate fighting the former effected a lodgment in some buildings on the right of the great breach; but fortune did more for them than foresight, for soon after an explosion took place behind the rampart of the curtain, (the combustibles gathered there by the French to pour upon the heads of the assailants had accidentally caught fire,) and destroyed many of the defenders. The French were evidently much discouraged by it; the men could with difficulty be kept to the defence, and the officers were seen beating them forwards with their swords. At length the efforts of the British were successful in forcing a way over the ramparts; and, driving the discouraged defenders before them, they succeeded in obtaining possession of the town at about three o'clock P.M., the remains of the French garrison having succeeded with much skill and courage in retiring into the castle.

"While the main attack was being made on the greater breach, Major Kenneth Snodgrass of the 52nd, who then commanded the 13th Portuguese Regiment, had been conducting an assault on the

lesser breach. He had gone down the night before at half-past
ten o'clock, and ascertained (as he had previously suspected) that
the river Urumea was fordable opposite to the lesser breach, the
water reaching somewhat above his waist. Not content with
having ascertained this, he clambered up the face of the breach
at midnight, gained its summit, and looked down upon the town,
contriving marvellously to elude the vigilance of the French sen-
tinels. He applied for leave to lead an attack on the lesser breach,
and was permitted to make the attempt with 300 men of his
regiment, who volunteered for the service, and with whom he
effected an entrance there, nearly at the same time that the principal assault proved successful.

"A detachment, consisting of four serjeants, one bugler, and
sixty-nine rank and file, under the command of Captain John
Sheddon, arrived from England, and joined the first battalion at
Vera on the 1st of September, 1813.

"During the seven or eight weeks that the French occupied
the heights above Vera, they were actively employed in construct-
ing redoubts on the projecting points in advance of their line,
and the position became very formidable.

"On the evening of the 6th of October the plan of attack was
communicated to the officers commanding companies; the redoubts were to be carried by repeated charges of the 52nd in
close column, while the other two regiments of the brigade (the Rifle
corps and the Portuguese Caçadores) were to act as tirailleurs; the
irregularity of the hill where the charging column might find shelter to breathe between its attacks was distinctly pointed out to the
officers. The men took a highly creditable interest in the success
of the operations, and requested permission to leave their knapsacks behind them in the bivouac, and received orders accordingly.

"At eight o'clock on the morning of the 7th of October the
two brigades made a simultaneous attack; the right brigade,
commanded by Major-General James Kempt, advanced by the
Puerto to the right of the town of Vera; the left brigade, commanded by Lieut.-Colonel John Colborne, skirted the left: a deep
rugged ravine which ran down between the ridges of the main
range of mountains prevented all communication between the

brigades, and each had to fight its way independently to the summit of the enemy's position. There were five redoubts sur-mounting each other on the part of the hill which the left brigade was to attack. The Rifle corps and Caçadores spread themselves across the brow of the hill to protect the formation of the 52nd column previous to its attack on the first redoubt. The difficult ascent compelled the men to scramble up singly, and whilst the column was forming up in this manner the enemy rushed out of the redoubt to charge it; five companies of the regiment had just completed their formation, and the sixth was in progress. The shock was parried without hesitation by a countercharge of these five companies, led by Lieut.-Colonel Colborne; the enemy gave way, and the redoubt was carried.

"The assailants having now established a footing at the bottom of the range of hills, a few minutes were allowed for the men to breathe, after which the attack was prosecuted according to the original plan, and each redoubt was captured in succession. On arriving at the last, which formed the enemy's centre, an in-effectual resistance was made by the line of French troops there posted, which, however, soon fled, leaving three small pieces of artillery in the hands of the brigade; but not content with this extraordinary success, the pursuit was continued down the reverse of the hill, and twenty-two officers and nearly four hundred men surrendered themselves prisoners to a part of the regiment led on by Lieut.-Colonel Colborne. Thus ended the most brilliant achievement that perhaps was ever performed by a regiment. The 52nd, in this action, was commanded by Brevet-Major Wm. Mein, who was severely wounded: he was promoted to the brevet rank of Lieut.-Colonel in the army on the 7th of October, 1813.

"The affair of Vera may serve to show how much mutually depends upon good leaders and good troops. Colonel Colborne, during the short time that the camp of his brigade was in this neighbourhood, was constantly on horseback from morning till night, reconnoitring the country over which his brigade might have to act. Thus when he led the troops into action he knew the ground, and was enabled to take advantage of every inequality for cover from the enemy's fire, and of any other accidental irregularity that favoured his movement at the moment. He thus inspired the highest confidence in the mind of every officer and soldier whom he led, that whatever they might have to do would be done in the best manner and with the least possible exposure to loss. On the evening before the attack on Vera, being desirous to examine a point within the enemy's lines which could not be seen from the English side of the valley, he took the adventurous step of going in with a flag of truce, and thus accomplished his object. The capture of a large number of prisoners of the Neuvième Légère* was due in great measure to Colonel Colborne's quick perception of the advantages of ground, as well as to his personal coolness and intrepidity; for Major-General Cole, commanding the 4th division in support of the attack, had sent word that he would not support the advance of the left brigade beyond the crest of the ridge; yet Colonel Colborne, seeing his advantage, kept the 52nd on the high spurs commanding the dips into which the French had run, and summoned them to surrender, where the headmost companies of the regiment, though a few yards behind, had in fact intercepted the retreat of the French, and Lieut J. S. Cargill of the 52nd received on the spot the swords of fourteen of the French officers.

"A writer in the 'United Service Journal' remarks on the affair of Vera,—'The attack was greatly facilitated by numerous 'skirmishers' (95th Rifle corps and Caçadores) 'detached from 'the columns. These having gained the flanks and rear of the 'enemy, rendered by their fire the defence of the entrenchments 'difficult, as these were chiefly open to the rear, and so in propor- 'tion they aided the attack of the columns. The conduct of the 'Light Division, particularly Colonel Colborne's brigade, most 'obstinately resisted, was very praiseworthy. It ascended in the 'finest order in columns, and by deployment, as the nature of the 'ground would admit, it gained the formidable heights, carrying 'the entrenchments defended by the splendid division of Taupin, 'capturing three pieces of cannon, and causing a loss of nearly '900 chosen soldiers, including the officers in command of the '9th and 31st Light Infantry, and the 26th of the line, its own 'loss being not quite 400; a number, considering the strength of

* Napoleon's favourite regiment at Marengo.

'the position, almost incredible, and only to be accounted for by
'the skilful employment of numerous skirmishers; the nature of
'the ground, particularly on our right, favouring very much this
'system of movement.'

"The casualties of the 52nd in the capture of the heights of
Vera on the 7th of October, were one serjeant and eleven rank
and file killed. The wounded were Brevet-Major William Mein,
(severely,) Captains Patrick Campbell, (slightly,) John Graham
Douglas, (severely,) John Sheddon, (slightly,) Lieutenant William
Hunter, (severely,) Ensign Alexander John Frazer, (died on
19th October,) two serjeants, two buglers, and sixty-two rank
and file.

"The Marquis of Wellington, in his despatch, stated that—

"'Colonel Colborne of the 52nd Regiment, who commanded
'Major-General Skerrett's brigade in the absence of the Major-
'General on account of his health, attacked the enemy's right in
'a camp which they had strongly entrenched; and the 52nd,
'under the command of Major Mein, charged in a most gallant
'style, and carried the entrenchment with the bayonet. The 1st
'and 3rd Caçadores and the second battalion 95th Regiment, as
'well as the 52nd, distinguished themselves in this attack.

"'Major-General Kempt's brigade attacked by the Puerto,
'where the opposition was not so severe, and Major-General
'Charles Alten has reported his sense of the judgment displayed
'both by the Major-General and by Colonel Colborne in these
'attacks; and I am particularly indebted to Major-General
'Charles Alten for the manner in which he executed this service.
'The Light Division took 22 officers and 400 men prisoners, and
'three pieces of cannon.

"'These troops carried everything before them in a most
'gallant style till they arrived at the foot of the rock on which
'the hermitage stands, and they made repeated attempts to take
'even that part by storm; but it was impossible to get up, and
'the enemy remained during the night in possession of the
'hermitage.'

"On the 9th of October the regiments of the Light Division
encamped to the right of the road leading through the pass of
Vera, and in a few days afterwards the 52nd Regiment moved up

to the heights of La Rhune, but nothing particular occurred until the 10th of November.

"On the night of the 9th of November the regiment, commanded by Brevet-Major Patrick Campbell, moved from its camp on La Rhune, and silently approached within 300 yards of the advanced point of the enemy's fortified heights of La Petite Rhune. The brigade was commanded by Lieutenant-Colonel Colborne.

"A narrow ravine ran parallel to the head of the column, forming nearly a right angle with the enemy's line of defence on the left side of the hill.

"The signal of attack was made at daybreak on the morning of the 10th, and two companies of the 52nd moved with great rapidity along the enemy's front without firing a shot, until they arrived at the redoubts on the right of this line; in the meantime, the right brigade having moved round the right of the hill, the enemy abandoned his redoubts after a slight resistance, and the Light Division formed on the summit of La Petite Rhune, waiting the appointed time to take its share in the future operations of the day. As soon as the enemy was driven out of the village of Sarre the whole army moved forward to attack his entrenched line. The 2nd brigade of the Light Division advanced against a strongly fortified part of the enemy's position; the flanks of it were covered with impracticable ravines, and the position could be only approached in front over a very narrow low neck, exposed to the fire of two redoubts, and of trenches cut in the hill half-way down the slope. Seeing, however, that shelter could be obtained under a bank on the opposite side, the 52nd, headed by Lieut.-Colonel Colborne, crossed the ridge in single file, regardless of the fire from the defences. When collected under the bank the bugles sounded the advance; and the men ran up the slope with cheers, which had the effect of inducing the enemy to abandon his lines, and the redoubt which supported them.

"In following up this success, the regiment advanced against a very strong irregular star fort, and under a heavy fire from its garrison formed columns of wings, and instantly charged up to the ditch; but the enemy's fire was too powerful, and a trifling

inequality on the slope of the glacis afforded the men sufficient
protection to keep up a fire against the garrison, and in a few
minutes afterwards a second effort was made.

"Upon a preconcerted signal, both wings cheered and rushed
forward; some men of the leading companies leaped into the
ditch, but their efforts were unavailing. The scarp being twelve
feet high it was impossible to ascend it without ladders, and the
regiment was withdrawn a short distance out of the enemy's fire,
by the companies falling back in regular succession, commencing
with the rear. The success of Marshal Sir William Beresford's
operations, however, of whose corps the 3rd division was now
pressing on successfully towards the bridge of Amotz, left no
hope for the garrison to escape, and 560 men surrendered themselves prisoners, laying down their arms on the glacis. The
details of this day's operations are thus related by an eye-
witness :*—

"'The morning of the 9th November, 1813, found the different
'regiments of the Light Division in their usual positions at and
'in front of the pass of Vera; holding La Rhune to their right
'front with a strong detachment, and having their pickets at the
'very base of the ridge, in the plains of France, towards St. Jean
'de Luz and the country to the eastward of it.

"'In the dusk of the evening the columns fell in, and moved
'by wild passes across the lower slopes of La Rhune to within
'two and a half miles of La Petite Rhune. Pickets were thrown
'out, (Captain William Rowan's company for the 52nd,) and the
'men laid themselves down in their blankets.

"'A full hour before daybreak the 2nd brigade fell in, and
'advancing, formed a line of contiguous quarter-distance columns,
'just behind the summit of the last lateral ridge of the Great
'Rhune. Between it and the French fieldworks on La Petite
'Rhune there was only the enormous ravine, which, commencing
'at the little isthmus that connects the two Rhunes, runs for five
'or six hundred yards nearly perpendicular to the face of the
'Great Rhune, and then rounds off towards the north, and
'towards that part of the French position near Ascain.

"'The sky was almost cloudlessly clear; the twilight rapidly

* Lieutenant (now Colonel) G. Gawler of the 52nd.

' brightened, and the mighty outlines of the mountains had be-
' come distinctly marked, when the flash and echoing report of a
' mountain three-pounder on the extreme point of La Rhune gave
' the signal to advance. The columns sprang from their conceal-
' ment, and a few small French pickets, on the face of their
' mountain, commenced a dropping fire.

" ' The right brigade went directly at the French works by the
' isthmus and its western slopes. The second battalion of the
' 95th kept up the communication between it and the 52nd. The
' latter regiment hastened straight down the slope in its front, but
' as soon as it had crossed the rocky watercourse at the bottom,
' brought up its right shoulders, and pushed rapidly on, in a line
' nearly parallel to the watercourse on its left, and to the French
' works, about 500 yards off, on its right.

" ' The enemy, either in the darkness of the mountain shadows
' did not see, or perceiving, had not the presence of mind to
' attempt to check this bold flank movement of Colonel Colborne's
' own devising. The 52nd gained the line of the extreme flank
' of the French works, brought up its left shoulders, scrambled
' up the rocky slope, and stood in rear of the enemy's right, on
' the plateau of the Petite Rhune.

" ' At this point a scene of extraordinary magnificence burst
' upon the view. The sun was just springing in full glory above
' the horizon, and lighting up the boundless plains of the south
' of France. The Pyrenees stretched away to the eastward in an
' abrupt series of enormous sloping walls, and the long lines of
' white wreathing smoke near their bases, showed the simulta-
' neous advance of the whole allied army.

" ' In the foreground, to the right, the 1st brigade of the Light
' Division had done its work, and was rapidly pouring over the
' entrenchments. The French defenders of the last of their Py-
' renean summits were rushing into the huge, rough punch-bowl
' which is bounded by the eastern and western spurs of La Petite
' Rhune. A large portion of the Light Division, in pack-of-
' hounds order, followed down the slope for twelve hundred yards
' in pursuit, but our men were so thoroughly winded, and the
' fugitives, on their part, so fresh, that the results were insignifi-
' cant. An officer and forty or fifty men who garrisoned their

' extreme right redoubt, actually crossed close along the front of
' the leading company of the 52nd (Captain William Rowan's)
' without any loss of consequence, so thorough was the exhaustion
' from the tough struggle up the very rugged mountain's side.

" ' The 52nd collected on the right rear of the now abandoned
' French redoubts of La Petite Rhune. The line of the French
' main position, commencing upon a comparatively low range of
' hills, was in front of the regiment, with an intervening rocky
' watercourse, which, it would seem, was deemed impassable by
' our enemies.

" ' The 52nd moved by threes to the small open ravine and
' wood in their front, under a smart fire of artillery from the ridge
' which was next to be assailed. In front of this wood the
' watercourse was crossed by a small and narrow stone bridge, on
' the opposite side of which was a road running close and parallel
' to the watercourse, with a sheltered bank towards the enemy.

" ' The officers and men of the 52nd crept by twos and threes
' to the edge of the wood, and then dashing over a hundred yards
' of open ground, passed the bridge, and formed behind the bank,
' which was not more than eighty yards from the enemy's en-
' trenchments. The signal was then given, the rough line sprang
' up the bank, and the enemy gave way with so much precipita-
' tion as to abandon, almost without firing a shot, the works on
' the right of the advanced ridge, under, no doubt, the apprehen-
' sion that their retreat would be cut off if they remained to
' defend them.

" ' The 52nd soon paid dearly for this (with the exception of
' the passing of the bridge) easy victory.

" Full eight hundred yards beyond this advanced ridge was
' the main ridge of the enemy's position, and on its most promi-
' nent summit was a large and strong redoubt, garrisoned by a
' battalion of the French 88th Regiment, under its old and veteran
' *chef*. No supports appeared near it, and it was determined that
' the 52nd, single-handed,* (which it had been from the time of
' leaving the position on La Petite Rhune,) should make the
' assault. Moving off therefore in column at quarter-distance,

---

* This is said to have been done in consequence of a mistaken order. See
Napier's " Battles and Sieges in the Peninsula," p. 443.

'left in front, the right wing took a long spur that led to the
'redoubt, and the left wing the next to it, which was so far to the
'left as to menace the enemy's rear.

"'The calculation probably was, that the garrison, like those
'which had been attacked before, would retire rather than risk
'the occupation of its line of retreat. The veteran *chef-de-bataillon*,
'however, remained firm to his charge, and his men to their ram-
'parts. The 52nd, moving up the long-exposed slopes in massive
'formations, suffered fearfully. The great strength of this main
'redoubt became evident, and that it was impossible to surmount
'its nine or ten feet walls if its defenders stood firm. Happily
'for the honour of the old corps, there was between the two
'wings the head of a rounded ravine; into this they obliquely
'moved, and lay down within twenty yards of the edge of the
'ditch.

"After taking breath for a little while, Colonel Colborne
could not refrain from another attempt. The word was passed
to stand up and move on, the leading ranks sprang into the
ditch, but no mere human courage and activity could get further,
and the mass steadily *stepped back* to its cover.

"At this moment an interesting episode occurred. Baron
Alten, seeing from the lower ridge the desperate nature of the
effort, endeavoured to send an order to prevent further attempts.
It was confided to the Brigade-Major, Harry Smith.* Trusting
to the shifting character of the mark of a horseman in motion,
he tried the desperate venture; but it was impossible: no single
living creature could reach the 52nd under the concentrated fire
from the forts. The horse was soon brought down, and Captain
Smith had to limit his triumph to the carrying off of his good
and precious English Saddle, which he performed with his
accustomed coolness, to the amusement of observing friends and
enemies.

"The hairbreadth escape of another fine fellow deserves to
be recorded. Serjeant Mayne, who had volunteered into the
52nd regiment from the Antrim militia, was among the foremost to spring into the ditch of the redoubt. Unable to climb
the ramparts, when his comrades fell back, he threw himself on

* The present Lieut.-General Sir H. G. W. Smith, Bart. and G.C.B.

his face. A Frenchman rising on the parapet, reversed his musket and fired. Mayne had stuck the bill-hook of his section at the back of his knapsack. The tough iron flattened the ball, and, unhurt by the blow, he lived for many years to tell the remarkable tale.

"The precarious position of the 52nd was not of long duration. Colonel Colborne's coolness and ingenuity had not forsaken him. Making a bugler sound a parley, he hoisted his white pocket-handkerchief, and, rising, walked round to the gate of the redoubt. To his summons to surrender, the old chief replied indignantly, 'What! I, with my battalion, surrender to you with yours!'—'Very well,' said Colonel Colborne, in French, 'the artillery will be up immediately, you cannot hold out, and 'you will then be given over to the Spaniards' (some of whom were appearing in the distance). The word 'Spaniards' was all-powerful. Officers and men pressed round their commander till he gave his reluctant assent. In a few seconds the 52nd stood formed in a double line at the gate of the redoubt, to give to the fine old fellow his required satisfaction of marching out with the honours of war. A detachment of the 52nd, under Captain William Rowan, took them down the hill towards Sarre, and gave them over to the British cavalry.'

"After a little manœuvring in advance of the captured redoubt, the 2nd brigade of the Light Division took up its bivouac for the night about a mile and a half to the left front, or rather to the original rear of this redoubt, 'where,' says the historian of the Peninsular war, 'there fell two hundred soldiers of a 'regiment never surpassed in arms since arms were first borne 'by men.'

"On the 10th of November the regiment had two serjeants and thirty rank and file killed. The wounded were, Captain William Rentall, (severely,) Lieutenants Charles Yorke, (slightly,) George Ulrick Barlow, (severely,) Matthew Anderson, (severely,) Charles Kenny and Matthew Agnew, (both slightly;) seven serjeants, three buglers, and one hundred and ninety-two rank and file.

"The Marquis of Wellington again bore testimony to the gallantry of the Light Division, in the following terms:—

" 'I have also omitted to draw your Lordship's attention in 'the manner it deserved, to the conduct of the Light Division, 'under the command of Major-General Charles Baron Alten.

" *These troops distinguished themselves in this as they have upon every occasion in which they have been engaged.*

" 'Major-General Kempt was wounded at the head of his brigade, at the beginning, in the attack of the enemy's work on La Petite Rhune, but continued in the field, and I had every reason to be satisfied with his conduct as well as with that of Colonel Colborne of the 52nd Regiment, who commanded Major-General Skerrett's brigade in his absence.'

" Another distinction was gained by the regiment, the word 'NIVELLE' being conferred on the corps for its distinguished conduct on this occasion.

" After the action of the 10th of November, the regiment halted for the night near St. Pé, and next day encamped near Arbonne, and on the 19th went into quarters in the village. The enemy made a reconnoissance on the 20th, and in this affair of pickets the 52nd had three rank and file wounded.

" Brevet Lieut.-Colonel John Philip Hunt was promoted to Lieut.-Colonel in the 60th Regiment on the 11th of November, 1813, and on the same day Brevet Lieut.-Colonel William Mein was appointed Major in the 52nd Regiment.

" A defensive line of posts being appointed for the different divisions of the army stretching from the sea to Arcangues, the Light Division changed its quarters on the 24th, and the 52nd occupied the château of Castleneur and some farm-houses in the neighbourhood of Arcangues.

" On the 9th of December, Lieut.-General the Hon. Sir John Hope's corps reconnoitred Bayonne closely, and the Light Division drove in the enemy's outposts in front of Arcangues, in order to make a diversion in favour of Lieut.-General Sir Rowland Hill's corps, which passed the Nive at Cambo on this day, and took up a position with its right upon the Adour and its left at Ville Franche.

" Early on the morning of the 10th of December, the Light Division pickets at Arcangues were very vigorously attacked, and the enemy's columns pressed on so rapidly on the flanks that the pickets had no opportunity of making a serious stand until they arrived at the Abattis near the château of Castleneur, behind which Captain John Graham Douglas formed up his company and made a very gallant resistance against the enemy's overwhelming force. Unfortunately he received a musket-shot in the head, of which he died a few days afterwards, much regretted by the regiment; his subaltern, Ensign Frederick Radford, and Major Mein (who was field officer of the pickets) were also wounded in this affair. As soon as the pickets were driven back, the enemy occupied the range of hills at Castleneur, and the Light Division was posted on a parallel ridge in their front, having converted a farm-house, which stood in the centre of the position, into a post of defence. Skirmishing was continued throughout the day, and in the evening the enemy's columns got under arms and made a demonstration of attack, which was not pressed beyond the picket-houses, in the small valley ₐwhich separated the positions of the two armies.

"On both the 10th and 11th the efforts of the enemy were directed against Lieut.-General the Hon. Sir John Hope's corps, which formed the left of the British line on the road to St. Jean de Luz; and having failed in his attempts against this part of the position, on the 13th he attacked Sir Rowland Hill on the right of the Nive, with no better success.

" At the passage of the Nive the brigade was commanded by Lieut.-Colonel Colborne, and the regiment was commanded by Brevet-Major Patrick Campbell, who received the gold medal for this occasion. The casualties were four rank and file killed, six officers, two serjeants, one bugler, and twelve rank and file wounded; and four men missing.

" The officers wounded were :—

" Major and Brevet Lieut.-Colonel William Mein, severely.

" Captain John Graham Douglas, ditto, died.

" Brevet-Major Kenneth Snodgrass, (attached to Portuguese service,) slightly.

" Captain William Henry Temple, slightly.

" Lieutenant Lord Charles Spencer, (on the staff,) severely.

" Ensign Frederick Radford, severely.

" On the night of the 12th two battalions of Nassau troops

came over to the allies, and were received by the pickets of the Light Division.

"The enemy having retired towards Bayonne, on the morning of the 13th, the Light Division went into cantonments on the 14th, and the 52nd returned to nearly the same quarters that it occupied previous to the attack on the 10th of December.

"On the 4th of January the 1st battalion marched to Anainz, on the 5th to Ustaritz, and went into cantonments at Sala on the 8th of that month.

"The 1st battalion broke up from its cantonments at Sala on the 16th of February, and marched by Mobzao, La Bastide, St. Martin, St. Palais, and Etcharry, arriving near Orion on the 24th.

"On the 25th of February, the Light Division arrived close to *Orthes*, and halted upon the heights above the bridge. As soon as a close examination of the loop-holed houses which defended its passage was effected, the division retired into the low ground and encamped for the night. On the 26th the division moved to its right, with the intention of passing the river at a ford above the town, but in the course of the evening the column countermarched, and halted for the night near the village of Berenx. Early on the morning of the 27th the regiment, commanded by Lieut.-Colonel Colborne, moved from its bivouac to the left, in order to strengthen the British left with the Light Division, and crossed the Gave de Pau by a pontoon bridge, which was laid over the river a little below the village.

"The left of the French position rested upon Orthes, and from thence the line was continued along a range of hills in the direction of Dax ; the right terminated on a commanding height behind the village of St. Boes.

"In the early morning the French left was threatened by Hill's corps, which subsequently crossed the river above Orthes, and advanced sufficiently to endanger the retreat of the French being cut off in the afterpart of the day, when the British left had eventually succeeded in driving the French from their formidable positions on the ridges of St. Boes.

"The 4th and 7th divisions attacked the enemy's right, the 3rd and 6th divisions attacked the centre of the French position, and the left brigade of the Light Division (in which was the

52nd) was in reserve, on a spur of the main ridge of St. Boes, partially covered by the old Roman camp. The right brigade, comprising the 1st battalion of the 95th Rifles and the 43rd Regiment, were some miles in the rear, near St. Jean de Luz, receiving their clothing.

"In consequence of the difficult approach to the enemy's right, and the narrowness of the ridge on which alone the leading brigade could deploy, the attack did not succeed at that point, and Cole's leading regiments, after partially gaining the village of St. Boes, were again driven back and cut up by French artillery on their left flank. Neither was the centre making any progress, and a portion of the 3rd division had been repulsed down the hill, when the left brigade of the Light Division was ordered to attack the left flank of the heights which the enemy's right occupied. The Rifle corps (2nd battalion and part of the 3rd battalion) remained on the knoll in support ; the Portuguese Caçadores had been thrown out to the left and were driven back, when the 52nd Regiment moved along in column of threes to the front. The retrogression of the divisions, both on the right and left, placed the 52nd in a very critical situation, and the importance of the movement was known to every individual. The regiment moved up the road to St. Boes from the Roman camp till it arrived close to the ridge on which Major-General Cole was anxiously looking out for support. At this point the regiment deployed to the right across the low and marshy ground under the French position, and advanced in line, wading steadily through the marsh, and accelerating the pace as it approached the hill occupied by the right of General Foy's division. As soon as the crest was attained, the regiment halted and opened its fire on the force opposite, which at once gave way and retired with all its guns. Lord Wellington, who had directed the movement from the Roman camp, instantly sent a message to Colonel Colborne, not on any account to advance further, and to remain in line, and quickly the divisions on the left and right of the 52nd advanced against their now disordered opponents, and the 52nd then occupied the prominent part of the position which had been abandoned by Foy. By these movements five British divisions were united against four of the French. Hill, at the same time, on the British right, was threatening the left and rear of the French, and Marshal Soult skilfully showing a front on each ridge of ground that favoured a stand, to cover the retreat of his now disordered divisions, eventually made good his retreat by Salle-spice, across the river Luy de Bearn, with the loss of six guns and four thousand men.

"This retreat of the French might have been more disastrous to them had not the Marquis of Wellington received a ball in the thigh at the latter part of the day, which materially interfered with his riding.

"To illustrate how much 'fortune' has to do with war, it may be remarked, that the marsh which the 52nd crossed was supposed by the French to be impassable for troops. The peasants said there were rarely twenty days in the year in which it could be crossed by individuals. The mounted officers of the battalion were obliged to ride round by the flanks, and Lord Fitzroy Somerset, who brought orders to the regiment, on trying to force his way through it was bogged, and thrown from his horse.

"The Earl of March,* who was on the head-quarter staff, had been promoted to a company in the 2nd battalion of the 52nd, then at home. He requested to be allowed to join the 1st battalion, and was in command of the leading company in the advance from the Roman fort, and on reaching the crest of the hill, was struck in the chest by a musket-ball, which was never extracted.

"The following passage from the Marquis of Wellington's despatch bears the highest testimony to the 52nd having mainly contributed to the success of the day.

"'St. Sever, 1st March, 1814.

"'Major-General Baron Charles Alten, with the Light Divi-'sion kept the communication and was in reserve between these 'two attacks. ["i. e. of the 4th and 7th divisions on the left, and '"the 3rd and 6th divisions on the right of the reserve."] I 'moved forward Colonel Barnard's brigade of the Light Division 'to attack the left of the heights on which the enemy's right 'stood. This attack, led by the 52nd Regiment under Lieut.-Colonel Colborne, and supported on the right by Major-General

"* The late Duke of Richmond, K.G.

'Brisbane's and Colonel Keane's brigade of the 3rd division, and
'by simultaneous attacks on the left by Major-General Anson's
'brigade of the 4th division, dislodged the enemy from the height
'and gave us the victory.'

"Captain Brialmont, of the Belgian army, in his 'Life of
'Wellington,' says, 'The battle of Orthes appeared lost, when
'Wellington changed his plan of attack and directed Picton's
'two divisions and a brigade of the Light Division against the
'left of the height which was held by Reille's rifle corps. This
'vigorous effort produced an unexpected result, and was particu-
'larly creditable to the 52nd Regiment, which received orders to
'take in flank and rear the troops which were pushing back the
'column from St. Boes. That gallant regiment crossed a marsh,
'under the fire of the enemy, and threw itself with such violence
'upon Foy's and Taupie's divisions that it compelled them to
'retire.'

"In this battle the 52nd had seven rank and file killed, and
seven officers, two serjeants, one bugler, and seventy-six rank
and file wounded. The names of the officers were :—

Brevet-Major Patrick Campbell, slightly.
Brevet-Major Kenneth Snodgrass, (attached to Portuguese
    service,) severely.
Captain Charles Earl of March, severely.
Captain Charles York, severely.
Lieutenant James Price Halford, slightly.
Lieutenant William Richmond Nixon, severely.
Lieutenant John Leaf, severely.

"The regiment halted at Bonnegarde, after the battle of
Orthes, on the 27th of February, and marched next day to near
Montant. On the 1st of March the regiment arrived at Mont
de Marson, and marched the following day in the direction of St.
Maurice, where it arrived on the 3rd, and went into cantonments
at Barcelone on the 9th of the same month.

"The regiment marched to Plaisance on the 19th, to Haget
on the 20th, and on that day attacked the enemy near *Tarbes*.
In this affair Lieutenants Charles Kenny and G. H. Love were
wounded. Two rank and file were wounded.

"During the night of the 21st, the French army retired upon *Toulouse*, and on the 22nd the regiment marched to Lannemezan, pursuing its route by Ganon, Agacen, Sieverer, Plaisance, Cregneaux, and arrived at St. Simon and Portel on the 29th. The division moved to Selle on the 4th of April.

"On the morning of the 10th of April the Light Division crossed the Garonne by a pontoon bridge near the village of Ausonne, and the whole army moved forward to the attack. The Light Division approached Toulouse by the Montauban road, and subsequently moved to its left to the support of Lieut.-General Don Manuel Freyere's Spanish corps, which were destined to attack the heights of La Pugade.

"The Spaniards, having failed in their attack, fell back in the greatest disorder, abandoning the bridge of Croix d'Aurade, but by a forward movement of the 2nd brigade of the Light Division, under Colonel Barnard, the French were checked in their pursuit, and the communication over the river Ers was preserved.

"In the course of the afternoon the divisions of Lieut.-Generals Sir Lowry Cole and Sir Henry Clinton attacked the redoubts of La Pugade, on the Calvinet side, whilst the 52nd and 95th advanced on the opposite side; after a very determined resistance, the enemy abandoned all his works about five o'clock in the evening, and the allied army formed upon the heights overlooking the town.

"The French army retired from Toulouse during the night of the 12th, and the 52nd pickets entered the suburbs of the town at daylight on the morning of the 13th of April; in the course of this day couriers arrived at Toulouse, announcing the decree of the French Senate of the 2nd of April, and on the 18th a convention was agreed upon for the suspension of hostilities between the Marquis of Wellington and Marshal Soult.

"The line of demarcation having been arranged, the 52nd went into cantonments at Castel Sarrasin on the 22nd, and remained there until arrangements were made for evacuating the south of France. On the 3rd of June the regiment marched from Castel Sarrasin and proceeded to Bordeaux. Whilst on the route thither, the two regiments of Portuguese Caçadores (1st and 3rd) which had formed a part of the Light Division for nearly four years, took their departure at Bargas to recross the Pyrenees, and return to their native country.

"The regiment arrived at Bordeaux on the 14th of June, and was reviewed by Field-Marshal the Duke of Wellington on taking leave of the army previous to its return to England. On the 17th of June, the 52nd embarked at Panillac on board his Majesty's ship 'Dublin,' and landed at Plymouth on the 28th. Thus terminated the Peninsular war service of the 52nd, during which, as Napier relates, the army containing 'those veterans 'had won nineteen pitched battles and innumerable combats; 'had made or sustained ten sieges, and taken four great fort-'resses; had twice expelled the French from Portugal, and once 'from Spain; had penetrated France, and killed, wounded, or 'captured two hundred thousand enemies, leaving of their own 'number forty thousand, whose bones whiten the plains and 'mountains of the Peninsula;' but, we may add, whose memory is revered by all in Britain who love to hear or to read of noble deeds, and whose example has left in their regiments an emulation and a spirit to strive after that which is noble as well as daring, which will never be extinguished in the 52nd.

"It was not till the year 1821, that the following letter was received by the regiment :—

"'Horse Guards, 1st of March, 1821.

"'Sir,

"'I have the honour to acquaint you, by direction of the 'Commander-in-Chief, that his Majesty has been pleased to ap-'prove of the 52nd Regiment being permitted to bear on its 'colours and appointments, in addition to any other badges or 'devices which may have hitherto been granted to the regiment, 'the words—

Hindoostan.	Nive	Ciudad Rodrigo
Corunna.	Toulouse.	Salamanca
Fuentes d'Onor.	Vimiera.	Nivelle.
Badajos.	Busaco.	Orthes
Vittoria.		

"'In commemoration of the distinguished services of the regi-'ment in the several actions in which it was engaged in India, 'from September 1790 to September 1793; and in the battle of

'Vimiera, on the 21st of August, 1808; at Corunna, 16th of
'January, 1809; at Busaco, on the 27th of September, 1810; at
'Fuentes d'Onor, on the 5th of May, 1811; at Ciudad Rodrigo,
'in the month of January, 1812; at the siege of Badajos, on the
'16th of March, 1812; at the battle of Salamanca, on the 22nd
'of July, 1812; at Vittoria, on the 21st of June, 1813; in the
'passage of the Nivelle, on the 10th of November, 1813; in the
'passage of the Nive, on the 9th, 10th, and 13th of December,
'1813; at Orthes, on the 27th of February, 1814; and in the
'attack of the position covering Toulouse, on the 10th of April,
'1814.

     "'I have the honour,
      "'etc., etc., etc.,
    "'(Signed) HENRY TORRENS, A.-General.
  "'Officer commanding 52nd Regiment.'"

The words Pyrenees, Peninsula, Waterloo, and Delhi, are also
borne on the colours and appointments of the 52nd.

CHAPTER LIII.

1822—1857.

GENERAL ORDERS AND OTHER DOCUMENTS COMPLIMENTARY TO THE 52ND.

General Orders by Colonel Thornton, Sir John Lambert—Address of the inhabitants of Halifax—General Orders by Sir Samford Whittingham and General Maister—Sir Harry Smith's supporters to his arms—Major-General Anson's inspection—Parting scene when 52nd left Lucknow.

IN the foregoing chapters I have introduced several General Orders, which speak in very high terms of the high character and movements of the 52nd, and although it is contrary to my original intention, and, indeed, inconvenient for me, to swell these volumes with extracts from the 52nd "Record," yet, as that work can only be seen by few persons, comparatively, I think it desirable to insert in this chapter a few similar orders selected from it, and in a subsequent chapter to give a short account of the arduous duties and of the gallant conduct of the regiment in their attack on the Sealkote Mutineers, and at the siege and storming of Delhi.

"In October, 1822, Colonel Thornton inspected the 52nd, and afterwards issued the following order :—

"' Colonel Thornton has derived this day much gratification ' from his inspection of the 52nd Light Infantry Regiment. ' Fully aware of the many years that this corps has been so de- ' servedly pre-eminently distinguished in the excellence of its ' interior economy, clean and soldier-like appearance, steadiness ' under arms, and correctness in movement, his expectations of

'its superiority in those respects were highly raised, and have
'been fully realized, which it will be his pleasing duty to report
'to the Lieut.-General commanding in Ireland.

"'(Signed)   WILLIAM THORNTON, D.-A.-General.'

"On the 24th of April, 1823, the regiment was inspected by
Major-General Sir John Lambert, K.C.B., and the following
'After-inspection Order' was issued :—

"'Assistant Adjutant-General's Office,

"'28th of April, 1823.

"'No. 1.—Major-General Sir John Lambert has no other
'observation to make on the half-yearly inspection of the 52nd
'Regiment, on the 24th instant, than his perfect satisfaction in
'every point connected with the Report which he is called upon to
'forward, and which he shall do in the most unqualified manner.

"'No. 2.—The regiment being about to embark for a foreign
'station, and as circumstances may prevent the Major-General
'again seeing it, he begs the commanding officer, officers, non-
'commissioned officers, and privates, will accept the expression
'of his most sincere wish, that every prosperity may attend the
'corps on whatever service it may be destined for.

"'By order of Major-General Sir John Lambert,

"'(Signed)   C. TURNER,

"'Lieut.-Colonel, A.-A.-General.

"'Lieut.-Colonel Sir John Tylden, Kt.'

"The regiment was inspected by Lieutenant-General Sir P.
Maitland, K.C.B., on the 31st May, 1831.

"The regiment embarked from Halifax (Nova Scotia) for
England, the head-quarters, consisting of the band, buglers, and
five companies, under command of Colonel Fergusson, on board
the 'Marquis of Huntley' transport, and one company on board
the 'Prince Regent' transport.

"The following address was received by Colonel Fergusson
prior to the embarkation of the regiment for England in 1831:—

"'SIR,

"'We, the magistrates and inhabitants of Halifax, cannot
view the departure of his Majesty's 52nd Light Infantry Regi-
'ment without feelings of the deepest regret.

" 'We earnestly request that you will have the kindness to 'convey to the officers, non-commissioned officers, and privates, of 'this distinguished corps, the high feeling of respect which this 'community entertains for them.

" 'The fame acquired by the 52nd, in many a well-fought 'field, had long been the theme of our admiration, and we were 'indeed highly gratified on learning so excellent a regiment was 'to form a part of this garrison.

" 'This gratification, we assure you, Sir, has been greatly en-'hanced by the orderly, quiet, and soldier-like behaviour which 'has so eminently marked the corps during its long residence in 'Halifax, and has led to that perfect harmony which has uni-'formly existed between the regiment and the inhabitants.

" 'We shall, therefore, take a strong interest in the corps, 'wherever its destiny may place it, and shall ever experience 'much pleasure in tracing the steps which may mark its future 'career of military glory.'

"The following letter was received by the regiment prior to marching from Athlone in 1836 :—

" 'GARRISON ORDER.

" ' Major of Brigade's Office, Athlone,

" ' 21st of March, 1836.

" 'The service companies of the 52nd Regiment being to com-'mence their march to-morrow for embarkation, Major-General 'Sir John Buchan cannot deny himself the gratification of ex-'pressing the satisfaction he has derived from having had the 'corps under his command ; although he feels, at the same time, 'that any commendation on his part is rendered almost super-'fluous by the pre-eminent character of the corps, which is known 'throughout the army. But the Major-General trusts that his 'thus publicly expressing his sense of the exemplary good con-'duct and high state of discipline of the corps, will be deemed 'acceptable to the officers, non-commissioned officers, and privates, 'and he sincerely congratulates his esteemed friend, Colonel Fer-'gusson, upon having under his command a corps of officers and 'men, amongst whom the best feeling is manifested by all ranks, 'which has produced the effect of the residence of the regiment

'in Athlone being marked by a total absence of complaint; and
'the Major-General begs to assure the regiment in general that
'his best wishes will accompany them for their welfare in every
'situation they may be placed in.

"'(By order)   J. C. SMITH, Major, M. B.'

"The following extract is taken from No. 2 of the Garrison
Orders, dated Gibraltar, 10th of October, 1838 :—

"'Lieut.-General Sir Alexander Woodford takes leave of the
'52nd with great regret. The general good conduct and efficient
'state of the regiment demand his warm approbation, and he
'requests Major Blois will accept for himself and the corps his
'best wishes for their welfare, prosperity, and honour.'

"On the 9th of January, 1839, the regiment was inspected
in review order for field exercise by his Excellency Sir Samford
Whittingham, and on the following day the General Orders conveyed the extract below :—

"'GENERAL ORDERS.

"'Head-Quarters, Barbadoes, 10th January.

"'The Lieutenant.-General has great pleasure in conveying
'to Major Blois, the officers and non-commissioned officers and
'men of her Majesty's 52nd Regiment, the expression of the
'peculiar satisfaction he experienced at the review of that corps
'yesterday evening.

"'All the movements united activity and precision, and the
'very long advance in line could not be better executed.

"'The 52nd Regiment is, and has long been, one of the most
'brilliant corps of Light Infantry in the British army, and its
'discipline in the field is equalled by its good conduct in
'quarters.

"It is now thirty-five years since the ever-to-be-lamented Sir
'John Moore undertook the organization of the 52nd as a Light
'Infantry battalion. What complete success has attended his
'efforts, the whole British army can testify.

"'The British Light Infantry is now second to none, and the
'52nd Regiment is a beautiful specimen of the master-hand that
'formed it; but to the admirable interior system adopted by Sir

' John Moore, the durability of the superior discipline of the
' regiment must be attributed.

"' The groundwork of the edifice is the elementary drill,
' from the first position of the recruit to the complete drill of the
' company. Without this elementary school, all subsequent la-
' bour will be of little avail. No body of men, not so instructed,
' whatever their length of service, could have made the long
' advance in line and subsequent charge in the masterly manner
' yesterday executed by the 52nd Regiment.

"' But there is another part of the organization of the 52nd
' Regiment, to which the Lieutenant-General is anxious to call
' the attention of all the regiments under his command.

"' It is impossible for any commanding officer to carry on
' *efficiently* the command of the regiment, unless aided and assisted
' by that class of officers who have ever, in all well-organized
' armies, formed the basis upon which military discipline must
' rest.

"' The captains of companies are the responsible agents to
' the commanding officer, for the different portions or divisions of
' which a battalion is composed. But in order to ensure their
' cordial co-operation in the wishes as well as orders of the chief,
' a certain and due proportion of power must be delegated to
' them, and the non-commissioned officers and men of their re-
' spective companies must be accustomed to consider their cap-
' tain, under the superior authority of the commanding officer, as
' the distributor of all minor rewards and punishments.

"' This system, invariably acted upon, has preserved the 52nd
' for thirty-five years in its present splendid condition, and as
' long as that system shall be rightly acted upon, we have a right
' to anticipate for the future the same happy results.'

" On the 6th and 7th of June, the inspection of the regiment
by his Excellency Lieutenant-General Sir Samford Whittingham,
K.C.B., etc., took place, and on the 10th the following General
Order was published :—

"' GENERAL ORDER.

"' Head-Quarters, Barbadoes, 10th June, 1839.

"' The Lieutenant-General commanding has great pleasure in
' communicating to Major Blois, and the officers, non-commis-

'sioned officers, and privates of H. M. 52nd Regiment, his appro-
'bation of the style and manner in which all the manœuvres
'were executed at the Inspection Review of that corps on the
'7th instant.

"'The marching past in slow and quick time, the Light In-
'fantry manœuvring at extended order, the various movements
'of the column at quarter-distance, the rapid and correct forma-
'tions of squares, and the long and perfect advance in line, were
'all excellent.

"'Moreover, it is most satisfactory to the Lieutenant-General
'to have found the interior of this justly-celebrated corps, in all
'its details, in perfect harmony with its splendid appearance in
'the field.'

"On the 6th of February, 1840, the usual half-yearly inspection of the regiment was made by Lieutenant-General Sir
Samford Whittingham, K.C.B., and the following order was
received :—

"'GENERAL ORDER.
"'Head-Quarters, Barbadoes,
"'7th February, 1840.

"'No. 1.—The Lieutenant-General commanding has great
'pleasure in expressing his entire satisfaction with the appear-
'ance of the 52nd Light Infantry Regiment yesterday. The
'steadiness of the regiment under arms, the correctness of their
'movements in line, with the continued alacrity and precision of
'their manœuvring, evinced a degree of individual intelligence in
'all ranks, most creditable to Lieutenant-Colonel Blois, the
'officers, non-commissioned officers, and privates, and fully justi-
'fying the high reputation so long sustained by the 52nd Regi-
'ment for every soldier-like quality.'

"On the 17th of February, the inspection of the regiment by
his Excellency Lieutenant-General John Maister took place, and
the following Order was received :—

"'GENERAL ORDER.
"'Head-Quarters, Barbadoes,
'19th February, 1840.

"'The Lieutenant-General commanding was not disappointed
'at the inspection of the 52nd Regiment on Monday last; the

'cleanliness and good order that pervaded their barracks, hos-
'pital, and every other department; the regularity with which
'the regimental and companies' books are kept, fully met with
'the Lieutenant-General's approbation, and proved to him that
'the same attention which he has already remarked as applicable
'to their appearance and field movements, evidently extends over
'the interior economy and discipline, and has deservedly gained
'them their present high characters as soldiers."

"'The "company system," which had been so justly extolled
'in Sir S. Whittingham's Order of the 10th of January, 1839, as
'receiving in the 52nd a practical illustration of its superiority
'over that system which makes the battalion the unit of organiza-
'tion, and allows little responsibility and no control to the cap-
'tains of companies, was now practically tested by these small
'detachments into which the regiment was divided, and from
'which it was afterwards re-united with efficiency, owing to the
'maintenance of this system, which had likewise been so well
'tested during the Peninsular service of the regiment.'

"The General Order of Sir Samford Whittingham, dated the 10th
of June, 1839, and the General Order of Lieut.-General Maister,
dated the 19th of March, 1842, seem to place the excellence of
this system in a clear light when the extremely detached position
and sickly condition of the regiment in the intervening years is
duly considered.

"The inspection of the regiment by his Excellency Lieut.-
General Maister took place on the 5th of March, 1842, and the
following order was received:—

"'GENERAL ORDER.

"'Head-Quarters, St. Ann's, Barbadoes,

"'19th March, 1842.

"'The Lieut.-General commanding cannot permit the depar-
'ture of the 52nd Regiment from Barbadoes without expressing
'his entire approbation of the orderly and soldier-like conduct
'which has distinguished them on all occasions since they have
'been placed under his command; and although, to his sincere
'regret, the regiment has unfortunately sustained some severe
'losses, both in officers and men, during its service in the West

'Indies, he derives the greatest satisfaction in being able to report
'to the General Commanding-in-Chief that there has been no
'diminution whatever in the excellent system of interior economy
'and discipline, or in that correctness and celerity of movement
'in the field, and state of perfect efficiency in every respect, that
'has so long characterized the 52nd Regiment, and reflects so
'much credit on Lieut.-Colonel Blois especially, and the officers
'of the corps. The Lieut.-General begs them to accept this as-
'surance, that wherever employed, the 52nd will always carry
'with them his best wishes for their prosperity, and for all that
'can be beneficial or gratifying to them as men or as soldiers.'

"The 'company system,' as practised in the 52nd, is but
little understood by officers high in rank in the British army,
who have not had the opportunity of observing it. The results,
as evinced by this order of General Maister after the regiment
had been parcelled out into detachments, and exposed twice to
raging epidemic fevers, will not be lost upon reflecting minds.

"In January, 1843, the following letter was received by the
regiment :—

"'York General Sessions,

"'January Term, A.D. 1843.

"'Resolved, that the magistrates of this county feel most
'sensible of their obligations to Lieut.-Colonel Blois, for his im-
'mediate accession to their request, of allowing two companies of
'the men of his regiment to attend at the County Court House,
'on Tuesday, the 3rd of January inst., for the purpose of pre-
'serving good order, and quelling the violence and force resorted
'to by large assemblages of the populace, and that he be requested
'to convey to Captain Jarvis, Captain Campbell, Captain Pock-
'lington, and Captain Mills, and the officers, non-commissioned
'officers, and men under their command, the thanks of the magis-
'trates of this county, and to express to them the high sense
'which they entertain of the prompt and efficient manner in
'which they acted, and of their firmness and forbearance under
'every circumstance of outrage and attack.

"'Extract from the Minutes,

"'(Signed)   T. DIBBLE, *Clerk.*'

" The following General Order was issued on the departure of
the regiment from Halifax, Nova Scotia :—

" ' GENERAL ORDER.

" ' Head-Quarters, Halifax, September 2nd, 1845.

" ' No. 1.—The 52nd Regiment, Light Infantry, being about to
' proceed to Canada from this command, in which it has served
' upwards of two years, the Major-General commanding avails
' himself of the occasion to express to Lieut.-Colonel Blois, the
' officers, and soldiers, his approbation of the uniformly good con-
' duct by which it has sustained the high reputation hitherto
' borne by this distinguished corps.

" ' (Signed)   JOHN BAZALGETTE,
" ' D.-Q.-M.-General.'

" On the 16th of January, 1846, Lieut.-Colonel W. Blois, who
had commanded the regiment with much credit since May, 1839,
retired on full pay, and was succeeded in the Lieut.-Colonelcy by
Major French.

" In November, 1846, the following letter was received :—

" ' REGIMENTAL ORDER.

" ' Montreal, C. E., 20th November, 1846.

" ' No. 4.—The Commanding Officer need hardly express with
' what pride he takes the earliest opportunity of publishing, for
' the information of the regiment, a copy of a letter received by
' the mail from the Colonel of the regiment, Major-General Sir
' E. Gibbs, K.C.B., addressed to that officer by Major-General Sir
' Harry Smith, Bart., K.C.B., Adjutant-General of her Majesty's
' Forces in India, and hero of " Aliwal."

" ' " Cawnpore, India, 29th July, 1846.
" ' " SIR,
" ' " The honorary distinctions recently conferred upon
' me by our gracious Queen, enable me to take supporters to my
' family arms. I have therefore the honour to acquaint, and to
' request you would make it known to my gallant comrades, the
' 52nd Light Infantry, that in full remembrance of the period I
' was Major of brigade to the 2nd brigade of the immortal Light
' Division of which the 52nd formed so prominent and distin-

'guished a part, involving the glorious contests of the Peninsular
'war; I have adopted a soldier of the 52nd Light Infantry, and
'a 'Rifleman,'—my own regiment. The many affairs and battles
'this brigade so nobly fought in (no man better knows than
'yourself) include the Coa; Pombal; Foz d'Aronce; Sabugal;
'Fuentes d'Onor; siege, storm, and capture of Ciudad Rodrigo;
'siege, storm, and capture of Badajos, where you lost an eye, as
'my brigadier; Salamanca; San Munos; San Millan; Vittoria;
'the heights of Vera, that most irresistible attack, although on a
'fortified mountain. Irun, the crossing of the Bidassoa, Nivelle,
'Nive, the many affairs near Bayonne, Tarbes, Orthes, and Tou-
'louse, with the numerous skirmishes each of these actions
'entailed upon light troops. To this brigade, and to the great
'school of the illustrious Duke of Wellington am I indebted to
'that knowledge of my profession which has led to my present
'aggrandisement, and which has so lately acquired me the appro-
'bation of the Queen, the Duke of Wellington, and an expression
'of thanks from my grateful country. I pray you therefore, Sir
'Edward Gibbs, and the 52nd Light Infantry, to give me that
'credit for the feeling of a grateful comrade I desire to demon-
'strate, and that you and this renowned corps may regard me as
'not unworthy to take a soldier out of your ranks to support me,
'in conjunction with their brothers in arms, a Rifleman, and as
'the means in declining life of remembering the gallant regiment
'who taught me to fight for my country.

"'"I have, etc.,

"'"(Signed)   H. G. W. SMITH,

"'"Major-General."'"

"On the 21st of November the regiment was inspected by
Major-General the Honourable George Anson, Commander-in-
Chief in India, on which occasion his Excellency expressed his
opinion of the regiment in the following terms, conveyed in a
letter from the Adjutant-General to the Major-General commanding the division, and communicated to Lieut.-Colonel Campbell,
commanding the regiment.

" ' Head Quarters, Camp,

" ' Meerut, 8th December, 1856.

" ' From Col. H. Havelock,

" ' Adjutant-General H. M.'s Forces,

" ' To the Officer commanding Cawnpore Division.

" ' I am instructed by the Commander-in-Chief in India, to
' acquaint you that he was highly gratified with the appearance,
' manœuvres, and discipline of her Majesty's 52nd Light Infantry
' at Lucknow, during his recent inspection. His Excellency con-
' ceives that this battalion is, under Colonel Campbell, manifesting
' all those superior qualifications for which it has been highly dis-
' tinguished in peace and in war, throughout the present century.

" ' (Signed)   W. LINDSAY, Major,

" ' Assistant-Adjutant-General.'

" On the 27th of December, in compliance with instructions
received from his Excellency the Commander-in-Chief, the regiment commenced its march to Sealkote, in the Punjab, its strength
being as follows :—1 colonel, 1 major, 5 captains, 9 subalterns,
6 staff, 37 serjeants, 15 buglers, 644 rank and file, 14 women,
and 26 children.

" The parting scene at Lucknow is thus described by the Rev.
H. S. Polehampton, Chaplain of that station :—

" ' Last Saturday week, to my great regret, the 52nd marched
' out of Lucknow, and the 32nd marched in. The 52nd only
' went four miles out the first day.

" ' Colonel Campbell wrote and told me I must now take ser-
' vice at the Barracks of the 32nd, but I told him and Colonel
' Inglis, of the 32nd, that with their leave I would finish the old
' year with the outgoing, and begin the new year with the incom-
' ing regiment. So on Sunday morning (very cold it was) I started
' from Lucknow at seven o'clock and drove to the 52nd camp. I
' arrived there at eight, and found the camp composing a long and
' broad street of tents, at the top of which was that of the Colonel.
' It was a picturesque scene, the men were just falling in for
' church-parade, all in full uniform with their muskets ; and the
' officers, while I celebrated the service, had their swords drawn,

'which I never saw before. There were many camels about,
'ready to take the baggage, and a few huge elephants. Alto-
'gether, the scene had a sort of half-Indian, half-English look.
'Hollow square was formed, and I gave them part of the morning
'service, for the sun was growing too hot to go through it all. I
'preached on the end of the year, the necessity of reviewing the
'past, and of making resolutions of amendment for the future;
'and concluded with a farewell address, recapitulating all that
'we had gone through together; praising the regiment generally
'for its good conduct, and exhorting the really Christian men in
'it to continue in their course, and laying before those who would
'hinder others from joining them our Saviour's fearful warning
'on that head. I never had a more attentive congregation, and
'I believe that I never had truer Christians among any of the
'congregations I have addressed, than in that regiment.'

   "The friendly conduct of Mr. Polehampton, especially during
the ravages of the cholera, had been so esteemed in the regiment,
that on parting a testimonial was presented to him by the officers,
which produced the following letter:—

   "'MY DEAR COLONEL CAMPBELL,

      "'Pray accept yourself, and kindly convey to the officers
'of the regiment under your command, the expression of my most
'sincere thanks for the kind and liberal manner in which you and
'they have shown your appreciation of my services among you
'as a Minister of the Gospel. You may rest assured that your
'gift will be most proudly received, and carefully treasured by
'me, and handed down to those who may come after me as an
'encouragement to exertion, and as a proof of the high esteem in
'which those are held by British soldiers who endeavour to carry
'out that for the performance of which they (and amongst the
'foremost the 52nd Regiment) have ever been renowned, namely,
'their duty in that state of life in which it has pleased God to
'place them. I humbly trust that my ministrations among you
'have not been in vain. But whether in this respect you owe
'anything to me or not, I know that I am most deeply indebted
'to the 52nd Regiment for teaching which is better than precept;

'for example, bright example, not only of conduct becoming to
'the soldier and the gentleman, but also of that which graces the
'consistent Christian.

"'Yours sincerely,

"'HENRY S. POLEHAMPTON.'

"This estimable clergyman afterwards fell a sacrifice to privation and disease, during the siege of Lucknow Residency by
the mutineers and chiefs of Oude in 1857."

CHAPTER LIV.

1857.

THE 52ND IN THE INDIAN MUTINY.

The loyalty of the native troops at Scalkote suspected—Punjab moveable column marches towards Wuzeerabad—Terrific dust-storm—Native troops disarmed—Deserters blown from guns—Utter rout of the Scalkote mutineers—52nd storm the Cashmere gate at Delhi—Victoria cross—Great suffering and loss of life from heat and cholera—Monumental tablet in memory of Captain W. R. Moorsom—Colonel Campbell appointed to a brigade.

" On the 14th of March, 1857, the 52nd arrived at Scalkote, and occupied the barracks. On the 13th of May they received intelligence of the mutiny of the native troops at Delhi; and doubts being entertained of the professed loyalty of the native troops at this station, (consisting of the 9th Bengal Light Cavalry, 46th Native Infantry, and 35th Native Light Infantry,) Captain Seymour Blane's company, made up to 100 rank and file, with Lieutenant Julian attached, was ordered to proceed to the artillery lines for the protection of the guns; and a troop of artillery occupied the barracks vacated by Captain Blane's company.

" On the 16th of May a subaltern's picket, consisting of 50 of all ranks, was ordered to mount every evening at sunset, and proceed to the rear of the cantonments for the protection of the station, and was generally withdrawn at sunrise. At this period the native troops were so far trusted as to be allowed to share in all duties with arms; a cavalry picket (from 9th Light Cavalry, who headed the mutiny at Scalkote on the 9th July, and were subsequently defeated at Trimmoo Ghât) was placed in the

European lines every night, and patrolled frequently under the Captain of the week.

"On the 20th of May the regiment was held in readiness to march to Wuzeerabad, to join the Punjab moveable column under the command of Brigadier-General Neville Chamberlain; and on the 22nd the women and children were sent to Lahore. The officers on leave in the hills were instructed to join, and answered the call with alacrity, and only one remained absent under a new sick certificate: another, having been previously under medical care for some months, was also absent.

"About the same date Lieutenant W. R. Moorsom, of the 52nd, being on leave of absence from the regiment, and employed on a Government survey in Ceylon, heard by express from Calcutta that the Punjab was in insurrection. Upon this he instantly threw up his employment and his leave of absence, drew from his private resources a large sum, in order to travel with the utmost expedition for the purpose of joining his regiment, and took passage by the earliest packet for Calcutta. Here he placed his services at the disposal of Government, and received an immediate commission to repair the telegraph between Benares and Allahabad, which had been destroyed by the mutineers. In this capacity, but still seeking to make his way to his regiment, he joined the column of the immortal Havelock at Allahabad.

"On the 25th of May, Brigadier Chamberlain, commanding the station at Sealkote, directed the regiment to march in as light order as possible, and ordered all the regimental and other heavy baggage (which included the mess, band, library, canteen, and officers' private property) to be deposited in the regimental provost, and a guard from the 46th Native Infantry to be placed over it for its safe custody. As soon as these arrangements had been completed, the regiment marched out at 10 P.M. towards Wuzeerabad; two companies, under the the command of Colonel J. L. Dennis, being left behind for the protection of the station.

"They had not marched for two hours when a most terrific dust-storm overtook the column, and compelled every one to lie down—bullocks, camels, and all. The 52nd were the rear regiment of the column before the storm came on, and upon resuming their march, the 35th Native Infantry, lying in the road mingled with dust and animals, were marched over in the dark without the 52nd being aware of the circumstance until daylight revealed their change of place in the column. This may give some idea of the nature of a dust-storm.

"On the 27th of May the regiment arrived at Wuzeerabad, and joined the Punjab moveable column, which now consisted of the following troops, viz. :—

> 52nd Light Infantry.
> No. 17 Light Field Battery.
> 16th Irregular Cavalry.
> Detachment 2nd Punjab Cavalry.
> 3rd Troop 1st Brigade Horse Artillery.
> No. 1 Light Field Battery.
> Left Wing 9th Light Cavalry.
> 35th Native Light Infantry.

And proceeded *en route* to Lahore, where the column arrived on the 2nd of June. Head-Quarters and the right wing of the regiment occupied barracks at Mean Meer, and the left wing at Annarkullee (Lahore.) Immediately on arrival of Head-Quarters at Mean Meer, the 8th Bengal Cavalry having been already disarmed, were deprived of their horses.

"On the 8th of June Head-Quarters marched at midnight and joined the left wing at Annarkullee; and on the 9th the regiment was paraded at daybreak to witness the execution of two deserters from the 35th Native Infantry, who were blown from guns.

"The march was recommenced in the evening towards Umritzur, which was reached on the 11th. The object of these marches was principally to overawe the disaffected, by making it known that a large body of European troops was at hand in the Punjab.

"On the 13th of June the regiment marched at midnight to Jundiala, *en route* to Jullundur, where it arrived on the 22nd. Captain Seymour Blane of the 52nd was here appointed Major of Brigade to the column. Brigadier-General Nicholson here joined the force, and, although a junior officer to Colonel Campbell, took the command, by virtue of special instructions from the Chief Commissioner of the Punjab. Thus a second time was a high-spirited officer of the 52nd called on to show an example of discipline which should never be called for unless in most urgent cases and with palpable cause. Colonel Campbell did not fail to show an example to his regiment under these trying circumstances.

"In consequence of intelligence having been received of the intended departure of the 35th Native Infantry to join the rebels, the regiment at this period was kept on the alert, and ready to turn out at a moment's notice to intercept their escape, which was not however attempted.

"On the 23rd of June the column marched at midnight towards Phillour, which was reached on the 25th. On arrival, the 52nd and Artillery formed up in line on the right of the road, and the 35th Native Infantry, who were in rear, were ordered to form on the left of the road, in close column, facing the 52nd and Artillery, who were ordered to load. The 35th, thus placed between overwhelming forces, were then made to lay down their arms, and having done so they were dismissed: they were allowed, however, to retain their bayonets, until these were subsequently taken from them by order of Colonel Campbell. About half an hour after this, the 33rd Native Infantry arrived from Hoosheyarpore, having been ordered to join the force, which they did by forced marches, under the impression that they were to accompany the column to Delhi. On arrival, they were formed up in the same manner as the 35th, and were likewise disarmed; the arms of both regiments were conveyed under escort and lodged in the fort of Phillour, now occupied by a detachment of Her Majesty's 8th regiment.

"On the 27th of June the column marched at midnight back to Phugwara, *en route* to Umritzur, where it arrived on the 5th of July.

"On the 8th of July the 59th Native Infantry were disarmed, and their arms lodged in the Fort.

"On the 9th of July two companies of the 52nd, under the command of Captain Bayley, disarmed the left wing of the 9th Bengal Light Cavalry. This was done immediately the intelligence of the mutiny at and plunder of Sealkote (which occurred this morning) reached camp. On this occasion the 52nd lost almost all the property they had left behind at Sealkote, when ordered to form part of the Light moveable column. All the mess-plate and furniture and stock were robbed, and individuals lost all their baggage and furniture. An anecdote of an honest man and gallant soldier must not be omitted. Private Songhurst of the 52nd, who, as servant to Colonel Campbell, had been left in charge of baggage, was living with his family in a small house in the Colonel's compound. On the morning of the 9th of July he put on his accoutrements, loaded his firelock, and putting as many extra cartridges about him as he could, fixed his bayonet and marched his family for about a mile and a half down to the Fort, passing several Sowars of the 9th Light Cavalry who were stationed in order to catch people as they should pass, but who did not seem to like his look. Songhurst got his family down to the Fort in safety, and was going out again, when he was asked where he was going; the reply was, 'Back again to take care of 'the Colonel's property,' which of course was not allowed,—but the intention showed the man.

"On the 10th of July, the regiment marched at night towards Goordasepore, with the view of intercepting the Sealkote muti-neers, who were reported to be about to cross the river Ravée. Goordasepore was reached at four P.M. on the 11th, forty-two miles having been accomplished in less than twenty hours. The heat during this march was most excessive and trying to the troops. Upon arrival of the regiment at Goordasepore, informa-tion was brought that the mutineers were about fifteen miles off on the other side of the Ravée, the ford over which was ten miles from camp. The following Regimental Order was therefore im-mediately published :—

'Camp, Goordasepore, July 11th, 1857.

'The Colonel commanding reminds the regiment that it is 'within a march of the Sealkote mutineers, and he feels sure that 'every individual in it will spare no exertions to come in contact 'with the treacherous and murdering scoundrels.'

"Two companies of the 52nd, under Captain the Hon. D. J. Monson, were left at Goordasepore, to secure the rear, and the march was resumed next morning, when (says Colonel Bourchier of the Bengal Artillery, in his 'Eight Months' Campaign') 'the '52nd, still wearied with their terrific march of the previous day, 'pressed on as if fatigue was unknown to them.'

"On arrival at the Ravée, ten miles, the enemy was found drawn up in line, all being in British uniform and with their colours, on this side of the river, and an immediate advance was ordered to meet them. The guns were in line with large intervals between them: the order from the officer commanding the force was to fill up these intervals with the 52nd, and the regiment was consequently distributed in half-extended order by companies between the guns without support, other than a small party of the Sikh police corps in rear. This formation had hardly been completed when the enemy opened a rapid fire of musketry, to which our artillery replied with grape, the 52nd taking up the firing with the Enfield rifle. The enemy's cavalry attacked on both flanks and in rear: rallying squares were formed between the guns, and a good deal of hand-to-hand fighting occurred with both officers and men. Hardly one of these Sowars escaped. Whilst this *mêlée* was going on, the enemy's right subdivision skirmished up to within thirty yards of our left gun, but were immediately charged and bayoneted by the left subdivision of the 52nd. During this charge one of the 52nd fell, and was afterwards found with four Sepoys dead around him, who had apparently fallen by his individual hand.* The front being thus cleared, the fire of the guns and rifles was resumed, and soon sent the mutineers to the right-about. The main body of the enemy then hastily retired, covered by their sub-divisions, who behaved admirably, and were destroyed while covering the retreat. On re-crossing the river many were drowned, others threw away their arms, and fled to the neighbouring villages, and were soon afterwards given up and executed. Our force on this occasion consisted of about 280 of all ranks, 120 Sikhs, and nine guns. The enemy's force consisted of about 800 infantry and 300 cavalry, of which more than 200 were left dead on the ground, and the remainder took up a position with one 12-pounder on an island in the Ravée.

* "The name of this brave man, unfortunately, has not been preserved by those who witnessed the scene of death.—ED.

" The following is a list of casualties in the regiment on this occasion :—

" *Killed*—5 Rank and File.

" *Wounded*—2 Officers, (slightly,) 16 Rank and File.

" *Died of Apoplexy*—4 Rank and File.

" *Total*—2 Officers and 25 Rank and File.

" Colonel Campbell, commanding the regiment, received a 'contusion from a musket-shot on the left shoulder.' Immediately after the action the column returned to Goordascpore. The heat and exhaustion of the men on this occasion were most severe, and the artillery, although carried on their limbers, were so done up that during the action the men were too weakened to slew round one of their guns to take a shot at a party of flying cavalry. This combat is commonly known as the action of Trimmoo Ghât. The audacity with which the Sepoys and Sowars attacked on this occasion was not repeated in any subsequent action. Colonel Campbell had procured permission, just before leaving Sealkote, to clothe the 52nd in *Karkee-rung*, a native cloth of grey colour, and it is supposed that this very useful and novel dress deceived the enemy as to the character of the troops opposed to them. The 52nd were the first British regiment thus clothed.

" As this was the first occasion on which the 52nd had been in action for upwards of forty years, much interest was felt by the officers and men to show that the glorious character earned for the regiment by their predecessors should be maintained in their hands. The result was that thrice their own numbers were attacked, in a position chosen by the enemy, after the 52nd had suffered from long marching, and were completely routed and driven across the river. It is not the province of this Record to criticise field operations, but it may be remarked that the peculiar disposition of artillery and riflemen in line was not due to the officer in command of the 52nd.

" On the 14th of July the regiment marched in the evening back to the Ravée, to attack the remainder of the rebels on the island ; and on the 16th two boats having with some difficulty been procured, the regiment crossed the river at daybreak, and formed in the following order :—Two companies extended, two in support, and two in reserve. The advance was made over swampy ground, covered with high rushes, and on approaching the gun which the enemy had now brought to bear on the advancing skirmishers, they succeeded in discharging two rounds of grape, but without effect. As they were in the act of re-loading, Captain Crosse's company charged and took the gun, bayoneting some ten or twelve of the enemy who remained to defend it. The remainder fled, pursued by the 52nd, and were shot down or drowned in the river. The village which they had occupied was then burnt, and the troops returned to camp and marched back to Goordasepore at two o'clock the next morning.

"The following is a state of the casualties incurred in this affair :—

"*Wounded severely*—1 Corporal and 1 Private.

"*Wounded slightly*—2 Privates.

"This utter rout of the Sealkote mutineers was looked upon as the consummating stroke to quash any rebellion in the Punjab; and—

"On the 19th of July the column marched towards Umritsur, where it arrived on the 22nd, and on the following morning the whole force marched *en route* to Delhi.

"On the 30th the Sutlej was crossed under considerable difficulties, in consequence of the heavy rains which had now set in.

"On the 2nd of August the column continued on its route from Loodiana, and proceeded by forced marches, sufficient transport having been provided for the whole; and—

"On the 14th of August the column marched into camp before Delhi. The 52nd marched into camp 680 strong, and only 16 sick, but on the 14th of September the effectives of the regiment were only 240 of all ranks, so fearful *ad interim* were the ravages of fever and cholera.

"The force thus added to the camp consisted of the following regiments and detachments :—

"Her Majesty's 52nd Light Infantry.

"One wing of her Majesty's 61st Regiment.

"No. 17 Light Field Battery.

"2nd Regiment Punjab Infantry.

"One wing of the 7th Punjab Police Battalion.

"4th Sikh Infantry.

"250 Mooltanee Horse.

"Siege Guns and Ordnance Stores.

"Treasure—9 Lacs of Rupees.

"On the 13th of September, about midnight, the breaches in the curtain between the Water and Cashmere Bastions were reported practicable, the batteries having at different times between the 7th instant and this day opened fire with great efficiency. Colonel G. Campbell, commanding the 52nd, was appointed to command the third column of assault, which consisted of the following troops :—

"Her Majesty's 52nd Light Infantry—240 of all ranks (now reduced to this number fit for duty from severe sickness).

"1st Punjab Infantry—500 of all ranks.

"Kumaon Battalion—260 of all ranks.

"The object of the column was to storm the Cashmere Gate when blown in by an explosion party, and then to press on through the streets and take possession of and occupy the Jumma Musjid, in the heart of the city, which was one of, if not the most important position to be gained. How far this was attained will be best understood by the following despatch from Colonel Campbell, who was wounded at the head of the column when advancing towards the Jumma Musjid. The conduct of the regiment was admirable : no straggling, which was so much dreaded, took place in the whole advance ; and, on the contrary, the behaviour of the regiment, from the assault to the occupation of the city, was characterized by its steadiness, so much so as to call forth the praise and warm acknowledgments of its commander, as was shown by a Regimental Order issued by him on the subject, on the 5th of October.

"On the 14th of September the 52nd paraded at 3 A.M., and after a delay of at least an hour and a half, occasioned, it was said, by the difficulty in getting the other columns into their proper places, the regiment advanced from camp, heading the third column down the road leading to the Cashmere Gate. Colonel Campbell's despatch, here introduced, gives a detailed and accurate account of the operations of the column under his command. Lieutenant Bradshaw was the only officer of the regiment who was killed. He fell at the head of a party charging a gun placed in a street to obstruct our advance. He was a gallant soldier, and, though he had but recently joined the regiment, was much esteemed by all his brother officers. A little more consideration and experience might have saved him on this occasion, as a party had been sent round to take the gun in flank.

' '*From Colonel G. Campbell, commanding her Majesty's 52nd* '*and the 3rd Column of Assault, to the Adjutant-General of* '*the Army.*

"'Delhi, 16th September, 1857.

"'SIR,

"'I have the honour to report, for the information of the 'Major-General, the operations of the third column of assault 'which was under my command on the morning of the 14th in-'stant, which consisted of the following troops :—Her Majesty's '52nd Light Infantry, 240 strong, under command of Major 'Vigors; the 1st Punjab Infantry, 500 strong, under Captain 'Ramsay; the Kumaon Battalion, 270 strong, under Lieutenant 'Nicholson. On the order being given for the several columns 'to advance, the explosion party at once proceeded towards the 'Cashmere Gate, upon which they advanced with the most fear-'less intrepidity. The explosion was accomplished successfully ; 'but I regret to say that, out of the seven brave officers and men 'who composed the party, five fell. Immediately upon the re-'port of the explosion, the storming party, consisting of a com-'pany of the 52nd under the command of Captain Bayley, 'advanced with a cheer, and overcoming all resistance, speedily 'secured the gateway. The supports, consisting of 50 men of the '52nd, 50 of the Kumaon Battalion, and 50 of the 1st Punjab 'Infantry, followed the storming-party at a distance of fifty yards. 'The entire column having entered the main guard, and re-formed 'as speedily as possible, proceeded to carry out the orders of the 'Major-General, viz. to advance upon the Jumma Musjid, and, if 'possible, to occupy it as well as the Kotwalee. Before quitting 'the neighbourhood of the walls, some of the enemy being still

'within the Water Bastion, I detached a party of the 52nd to
'clear it, which was done at the point of the bayonet, the enemy
'who escaped the bayonet jumping over the parapets on to the
'river-side, where they were destroyed. We cleared the adjoin-
'ing Cutcherry compound, also the houses in its neighbourhood,
'the church, and the Gazette Press compound, the column carry-
'ing everything before it without much opposition. I proceeded
'through the Cashmere Durwaza Bazar, marked out as our line
'of advance. Hearing that a gun was placed in position bearing
'down the street, upon arriving at the point where the gun could
'be seen, I detached a party to get to its rear, through a bye-
'street, but before this party arrived at this point, the gun was
'taken with a rush, without loss, except Lieutenant Bradshaw of
'the 52nd, who, regardless of danger, received a discharge which
'killed him on the spot. We proceeded without opposition
'through the Begum's Bagh. Upon arriving at the gate which
'opens on the Chandnee Chouk, the gate of the Dureeba was
'found to be shut. This difficulty, however, was speedily over-
'come, through the good conduct of a native Chuprassie, Malum-
'Singh, who, accompanied by five men of the 52nd, volunteered
'to endeavour to open it. The column then passed up the
'Dureeba without opposition, except from musketry from a few
'houses. Upon arriving at the turn which brings the Musjid
'into view, and at about one hundred yards distant, the side-
'arches were found to be bricked up and the gate itself closed.
'It was too strong to be forced open without powder-bags or
'artillery, neither of which were with me—the former in conse-
'quence of the engineer and his party having fallen, and the
'latter not having been able to enter the Cashmere Gate, as the
'bridge had been destroyed, and, moreover, the houses on each
'side of the street near the Musjid were filled with the enemy.

"'I remained at this point about half an hour, in the hopes
'of hearing of the successful advance of the other columns at the
'Lahore and Ajmere Gates. At the expiration of this period,
'several men having fallen by the fire from the surrounding
'houses, I judged it expedient to fall back upon the Begum's
'Garden, which we held for at least an hour and a half under a
'heavy fire of musketry, grape, and canister.

"'Captain Ramsay, of the Kumaon Battalion, who had 'diverged to the right from the column, and had been in posses-'sion of the Kotwalee for some time, here rejoined me. Having 'communicated with the Head-Quarters, and ascertained that 'the 1st and 2nd columns had not advanced beyond the Cabul 'Gate, I fell back upon the church.

"'Having detailed the operations of the column, which I 'regret to say were attended with considerable loss, it becomes 'my duty to bring to the notice of the Major-General the gallan-'try and good conduct of all the troops under my command, 'more especially her Majesty's 52nd Light Infantry, who led the 'column from first to last, and who, I consider, fully maintained 'its high reputation. The officers to whom I am more particu-'larly indebted are as follows:—Lieutenant Salkeld of the '(Bengal) Engineers, who personally fastened the powder-bags 'to the gate, fixed the hose, and although fearfully wounded, 'contrived to hand to a non-commissioned officer of the Sappers 'and Miners the light to fire the train ; Lieutenant Home of the 'Engineers, who also accompanied the explosion party ; Captain 'Bayley of the 52nd, who commanded and led the storming 'party, and who was unfortunately wounded on approaching the 'gate; to Captain Crosse of the 52nd, who commanded the sup-'ports ; to Major Vigors, who commanded the 52nd ; to Captain 'Ramsay, who commanded the Kumaon Battalion ; to Lieutenant 'Nicholson, who commanded the 1st Punjab Infantry, and who, I 'regret to say, was wounded shortly after the entry was effected; 'to Captain Synge, 52nd, who acted as Brigade-Major to the 'column.

"'I have, further, the gratification of bringing to the especial 'notice of the Major-General the invaluable assistance I received 'from Sir Thomas Metcalfe, who was at my side throughout the 'operations, and fearlessly guided me through many intricate 'streets and turnings to the Jumma Musjid, traversing at least 'two-thirds of the city, and enabling me to avoid many dangers 'and difficulties.

"'It is difficult to select individuals from the ranks, where 'all behaved so well, who may have particularly distinguished 'themselves ; but I have no hesitation in specifying the follow-

'ing non-commissioned officers and soldiers as deserving of par-
'ticular reward, viz. the non-commissioned officers of the Sappers
'and Miners who formed the explosion party; Serjeant-Major
'Streets of the 52nd, whose gallant conduct was conspicuous up
'to the time that he was severely wounded; Bugler Robert
'Hawthorn, 52nd, who accompanied the explosion party, who
'sounded the signal to advance, and assisted and bound up the
'wounds of Lieutenant Salkeld, and carried him to the rear
'without further injury; Lance-Corporal Henry Smith of the
'52nd, for gallant conduct in carrying a wounded comrade across
'the Chandnee Chouk, under a tremendous fire of grape and mus-
'ketry; Lance-Corporal William Taylor of the 52nd, for con-
'spicuous gallantry throughout the operations.

> " ' I have, etc.,
>
> " ' (Signed) G. CAMPBELL, Colonel,
>
> " ' Commanding 52nd and 3rd Column of Assault.

" ' I regret I am unable to state the names of the non-com-
'missioned officers of the Sappers and Miners who were with
'the explosion party.'

" Lieutenant-Colonel Baird Smith, of the Bengal Engineers,
reported the following names:—Serjeants John Smith and
Carmichael, Corporal Burgess, and Havildar Madhoo. He also
particularly commends Bugler Robert Hawthorn.

" The column fell back about half-past one o'clock in the
afternoon of the 14th, and the 52nd remained in the church that
night, furnishing strong pickets in front of the church.

" On the 15th of September the regiment was engaged, in
concert with the 60th Rifles, in taking up strong posts in houses
and other buildings, and holding them against the enemy as a
base for further advances. The positions to be occupied were as
follows:—1st, the line of the canal from the Cabul Gate eastward
to the ramparts; 2nd, the line of the Chandnee Chouk from the
Lahore Gate to the Kotwalee; 3rd, the line from the Ajmere to
the Jumma Musjid, and on to Deriogunge, if practicable. The
first of these was the line taken up by the 52nd and 60th; and
on the morning of the 17th of September the bank was occupied
and held against the enemy, who kept up a continued and heavy

fire, which gradually decreased towards evening. Up to this period, and indeed until the following day, every position taken up was more or less disputed by the enemy. At about five P.M. of the 17th, the regiment was directed to occupy the magazine, the pickets being relieved by her Majesty's 61st Regiment.

" On the 18th of September the enemy kept up an occasional fire on the magazine with musketry, grape, and round-shot, from guns in position at the palace, but without effect.

" On the 19th the enemy's fire had nearly subsided ; and on the morning of the 20th of September the palace was taken, the city was evacuated by the enemy, and occupied by the British army.

" The following Field Force Order was then issued by Major-General Wilson, commanding :—

" ' Delhi City, 20th September, 1857.

" ' The palace and city of Delhi are in our possession, and the ' labour of the troops has been rewarded.

" ' Major-General Wilson, commanding the force, returns his ' warmest and sincerest thanks to all officers and men for the ' noble and gallant manner they have supported him in the ardu- ' ous struggle in which we have been engaged.

" ' No troops could have behaved better, or undergone with ' greater cheerfulness the fatigue and exposure to which they ' have been exposed, and he will have much pleasure in reporting ' this to higher authority.

" ' The different regiments will be immediately brought to- ' gether and assigned posts in the city, and the Major-General ' looks to commanding officers to preserve the strictest discipline ' among the men.   He calls upon the men themselves not to sully ' their victory by any excesses that will degrade their characters ' as soldiers.'

" *Return of Killed and Wounded from 14th August to 20th September 1857.*

" Aug. 22, 1 rank and file, wounded.

„   27, 3 rank and file, wounded.

„   29, 1 rank and file, wounded.

" Sept. 10, 1 rank and file, wounded.

Sept. 11, 2 rank and file, killed.

„ 14, 1 subaltern, 1 serjeant, 21 rank and file, killed; 1 colonel, 1 captain, 1 subaltern, 8 serjeants, 2 buglers, 52 rank and file, wounded.

„ 15, 2 rank and file, killed.

„ 16, 1 rank and file killed; 2 rank and file wounded.

„ 17, 3 rank and file, wounded.

„ 18, 1 rank and file, wounded.

„ 19, 1 rank and file, wounded.

" Lieutenant Bradshaw, killed on the 14th of September.

" Colonel Campbell wounded in the right wrist on the 14th by a musket-shot.

" Captain Bayley, wounded severely in the left arm when leading the storming-party on the 14th, by a musket-shot.

" Lieutenant Atkinson, wounded slightly in the breast by a spent musket-ball, on the 14th.

" Serjeant Richard M'Keowin died of his wounds on the advance into the city. The Rev. J. E. W. Rotten, Chaplain to the Force, in his narrative writes—' Some time after this I laid Ser-'jeant M'Keowin in his grave, which, for the love and respect I 'bore him, I have marked with a plain stone and an equally 'simple inscription.'

" Ninety-eight men died of cholera and other diseases from the date of arrival in camp, (14th August,) to the date of departure from Delhi, October 5th.

" On the 31st of September a detachment of 200 men proceeded to the Kootub with Brigadier Shower's column.

" On the 5th of October the regiment marched from Delhi towards the Punjab, and on the same day the following Regimental Order relative to the Victoria Cross was published by Colonel Campbell :—

"' EXTRACT FROM REGIMENTAL ORDERS.

"' Camp, Ullepore, 5th October, 1857.

"' 1. The following Order, so honourable to the regiment, as 'well as to the individuals upon whom the distinction has been 'conferred, will be entered in the Record of the regiment :—

"'"FIELD FORCE ORDERS, BY MAJOR-GENERAL A. WILSON,
COMMANDING.

"'" Head-Quarters, Delhi City, 21st September, 1857.

"'"The Major-General commanding the Field Force, in the
'exercise of the powers vested in him by the seventh clause of
'her Majesty's warrant, dated 17th June, 1857, confers, subject
'to confirmation by her Most Gracious Majesty Queen Victoria,
'the decoration of the Victoria Cross, for distinguished valour
'and bravery in action before the enemy during the assault on
'the fortress of Delhi, on the 14th of September, 1857.

"'" REWARD OF VALOUR.

"'"Lieutenants Deacon, Charles Home, Philip Salkeld, (dan-
'gerously wounded,) and Serjeant John Smith, Sappers and
'Miners, for conspicuous gallantry in the performance of the des-
'perate duty of blowing up the Cashmere Gate in the fortress of
'Delhi, in broad daylight, under a heavy and destructive fire of
'musketry, on the morning of the 14th of September, 1857, pre-
'paratory to the assault.

"'"Bugler Robert Hawthorn, her Majesty's 52nd Regiment,
'who accompanied the above explosion party, and not only most
'bravely performed the dangerous duty on which he was em-
'ployed, but previously attached himself to Lieutenant Salkeld of
'the Engineers, when dangerously wounded, bound up his wounds
'under a heavy musketry fire, and had him removed without
'further injury.

"'"No. 2764, Lance-Corporal Henry Smith, her Majesty's
'52nd Light Infantry, who most gallantly carried away a wounded
'comrade under a heavy fire of grape and musketry, in the
'Chandnee Chouk of the city of Delhi, on the morning of the as-
'sault, the 14th of September, 1857."

"'"The Colonel commanding congratulates Bugler Robert
'Hawthorn and Lance-Corporal Smith upon obtaining this very
'enviable badge of distinction, and he is sure that the regiment
'will participate in the strong feeling of pride and gratification he
'feels at the Victoria Cross having been won by two of their
'comrades, upon so important an occasion as the assault of the
'city of Delhi.

" ' He cannot allow this opportunity to pass without express-
' ing his thanks to the regiment generally for the support he has
' received from all ranks in maintaining its reputation during the
' eventful period of the past five months. The regiment has al-
' ways kept inviolate its very high name for discipline and good
' spirit, but a period of forty-two years had elapsed without an op-
' portunity having been afforded by which it could prove the in-
' estimable value of these good qualities when brought into play
' upon the field of battle. At the siege and assault of Delhi, the
' conduct of the regiment has fully realized the most ardent ex-
' pectations of its commanding officer, and it is with the greatest
' joy and pride that he thus testifies to its admirable behaviour.
' Regularity in quarters has prevailed under great temptations ;
' cheerfulness in the performance of arduous duties on picket and
' in the trenches ; and at the assault of the city, its gallantry and
' devotion carried everything before it on its advance. Although
' he has noticed first the more brilliant part of the services of the
' regiment, the Colonel does not forget the praiseworthy conduct
' of the regiment during its harrassing marches and counter-
' marches through the Punjab, as well as its conduct in the en-
' counter with the Sealkote mutineers ; nor can he forget to mourn
' the loss of the many brave and good soldiers who have fallen in
' the performance of these duties.'

" We have only to add to this public testimony of the behaviour of the regiment in general, and of these two gallant
soldiers in particular, that Bugler Robert Hawthorn was attested
for the 52nd Light Infantry on the 15th of February, in the
parish of Moghera, near the town of Londonderry, in Ireland.
Lance-Corporal Henry Smith was attested for the 52nd Light
Infantry on the 9th of February, 1853, in the parish of Ditton, in
the county of Surrey, England. Sergeant-Major Streets, for his
conduct at Delhi, was promoted to an Ensigncy in the 75th Regiment. It is hoped that this record of the way in which these
brave men nobly did their duty, will show to their comrades that
good services in the ranks are appreciated with honour in
the 52nd.

" In narrating the stirring events during the earlier portions
of the history of the 52nd, we have heretofore usually added a

more familiar account than the severe style of the "Record" contained; and the journal of an officer present with the regiment during the whole of the campaign of 1857, enables us to keep up the practice :—

"'Beginning with the 12th of May, at Scalkote we had to go 'out and patrol with parties of cavalry-picket almost every night 'for a couple of hours—not a very pleasant thing, for one had to 'be on the look-out, in case the scoundrels of the 9th Light Cav- 'alry (Bengal) should take it into their heads to quietly pot one. 'We were quite isolated from any other force, and one of the 'Commissioners declared he was informed by his spies that on 'the night of the 12th there was a conspiracy agreed on among 'the native troops to murder every one of us, beginning with the 'Europeans in the mess-house of this same 9th Cavalry, where 'two of us happened to be dining that very night, but they could 'get no one to begin the business. This sort of thing went on 'till the 23rd of May. In the meantime all officers were ordered 'to join. The Colonel arrived about the 18th, just before the 'Simla panic; some others, who could not get a dawk the day 'they wished to start, came in for the Simla affair the next day, 'and were then ordered to remain.

"'Leaving two companies behind under Colonel Dennis, we 'started from Scalkote on the 25th, with the 35th Native Infantry, 'one troop of horse artillery, one light field battery, and a wing 'of the 9th Cavalry, to join the moveable column at Wuzeerabad 'under Brigadier Chamberlain (now Adjutant-General). We met 'other troops at Wuzeerabad, and among them the 24th Queen's, 'but they were ordered back to Jhelum, and with them the troop 'of horse artillery. The Guides, Coke's Regiment, and some 'irregular cavalry, proceeded sharp to Delhi, while we (the Scal- 'kote force) went on to Lahore alone, forming the Punjab moveable 'column. We remained at Lahore a week, and were joined by 'one of the companies left behind. Fraser, with twenty sick 'men, and Songhurst, the Colonel's servant, were the only ones 'left at Scalkote. At Lahore two mutineers were blown from 'guns, after which the moveable column left for Umritsir on the '8th of June, and went on, *via* Jullundur, to Phillour, where 'there is a fort and a bridge across the Sutlej. Here the 33rd

'Native Infantry from Hooshiarpore met us on the morning we
'marched in, and were disarmed, as well as the 35th. Here also
'Chamberlain left us for Delhi, and Nicholson, a splendid fellow,
'came down from Peshawar and took command of the column—
'Blane of ours acting as Brigade-Major. We expected the 35th
'to make a bolt of it to Jullundur, and had parties told off for
'them. We halted two or three days at Phillour, where there
'was a standing drum-head court-martial, to try the mutineers—
'desertion being the general crime. Nicholson here told off a
'force consisting of two guns, eighty of our men with Enfield
'rifles, (of which we had 180,) the men being mounted on extra
'carriages ; and the remainder, amounting to forty men, consisting
'of drivers and others from the troop, acting as dragoons ; the
'battery being supplied with native drivers, who behaved very
'well. This mounted force was to provide for the event of a
'chase, or "*dour*," as the native Indians have it. Crosse had
'command of our men, with Julian as sub. ; we went out on trial,
'and it seemed to be a capital plan. After this, we all marched
'back to Umritsir, leaving the 35th Native Infantry one march
'from the place ; and several of our officers having joined in the
'meantime, we reached that city on the 5th of July, and halted.

"'On the morning of the 9th we heard of the outbreak at
'Sealkote ; and on the evening of the 10th Nicholson, having
'ascertained the direction taken by the mutineers—consisting of
'the 9th Light Cavalry and a wing of the 46th Native Infantry—
'marched us to Goordasepore, forty-two miles, where we arrived
'at five P. M. next day. When we left Umritsir we did not know
'positively where we were going till we got on the road, and then
'we thought our march would be to Buttala, half-way ; but when
'we got there, we were ordered on. Nicholson had some people
'watching at Trimmoo Ghât, where there is a ford across the Ra-
'vee, and from whence he got short despatches almost every hour,
'the ghât being about two miles on the other side of Goordasepore.
'We halted at Buttala a couple of hours, which was a great mis-
'take, for it was in the grey of the morning, when the men can
'march best. However, on we went, the men being carried great
'part of the way ; but from exposure to the sun, which was
'cruelly hot, and for want of food and rest, they were a good deal

'done up, and so were we all. Our Brigadier did not consider
'the season; if he had left it to the Colonel, we might have been
'at Goordascpore by 9 A. M. Fortunately, after we got in, a heavy
'shower of rain came on, and after the men had had their dinners
'they were all right. We were then under orders to march at
'twelve that night, but did not : it would have been awful work
'to get up : we never slept so soundly in our lives, and few of us
'awoke until six next morning. Here Monson and two companies
'were left to secure us from the attack of a mutinous regiment in
'our rear.

"'About 10 A.M. on the 12th of July, Nicholson received in-
'formation that a troop of cavalry were crossing the ford before
'mentioned; and again, that at 9 A.M. the whole of the mutineers'
'force, with their baggage, were crossing. A non-commissioned
'officer of Native Cavalry, in whom great confidence was placed,
'was sent to reconnoitre the ford of the Ravée, and to bring in-
'formation. He was seen by the spies to communicate with
'the mutineers in a way that left no doubt he had given them
'intelligence of our movements, and on his return he was con-
'victed, and immediately hanged. The men had breakfasted at
'six o'clock, and dinners were ordered to be ready at eleven
'o'clock, to provide for the chance of being ordered out sharp; for
'Nicholson never gave a moment's warning. At ten o'clock the
'fall-in sounded; we were formed in a second, and marched off
'in spite of the heat and the previous fatigue, more especially of
'the day before. We had left two companies at Umritsir under
'Vigors, and our muster was now about four hundred. We never
'saw the men march out of a barrack-square at home better than
'they did this day out of the camp-ground of Goordasepore.
'Sufficient it is to say it was in the old 52nd style, and that is
'saying a good deal; and so we went on for some miles, with a
'fearful sun upon us, and not a breath of air. We never felt any-
'thing like it, when the men began to fall out; and before we
'had gone four miles more, about 150—of which about 50 were
'of the 52nd—had fallen out, beat by the sun and the overpower-
'ing heat. A number of horses were also killed by fatigue and
'heat. Several of our men were put on the horses of the 9th
'Light Cavalry, whom we dismounted at Umritsir and left there,

'bringing on their horses; this was on our hearing of the Sealkote
'mutiny; and when we also disarmed the 59th Native Infantry
'at the same place. After this, we crossed a running stream
'above our knees, and there halted for a short time under some
'trees. Nicholson was impatient to get at the scoundrels, who
'were drawn up in line about a mile off waiting for us; and here
'nearly all the men who had fallen out came up again. We then
'formed, with the guns—nine in number—in front, masked by
'Sowars (a sort of irregular lot of horsemen belonging to a Com-
'missioner there, who afterwards bolted—not the Commissioner,
'but the Sowars.) The 52nd came next in quarter-distance
'column, and then fifty of the 6th Punjab Irregulars. We ad-
'vanced to within 250 yards of the enemy, who had a capital
'position, drawn up in rear of a brook, under cover of trees, and
'with cavalry on each flank. It is supposed they had not the
'slightest idea of who we were, or they would not have waited
'for us. The Colonel had got us clothed in *kurkee* the very night
'we left Sealkote, and this probably deceived them into the belief
'that we were anything but the 52nd. Our cavalry were ordered
'about; they obeyed with alacrity, and the guns unlimbered,
'with most of our regiment in skirmishing order among them for
'protection. At that moment the enemy poured in a rattling
'volley, which lasted two or three minutes, and all our casualties
'took place then, with one or two exceptions. They advanced
'on us immediately after this volley; our guns opened with grape,
'and sent them to the right-about in less than a quarter of an
'hour. Some of them behaved very pluckily. We saw one fel-
'low about one hundred yards from the guns, all around him
'having been killed, loading and firing all by himself, till he was
'knocked over. Their cavalry charged on both flanks, and came
'in right among the guns, but were all shot down: they were all
'" bang-ed,"* or would never have done so much. They all made
'a bolt of it across the ford, to an island where they had the
'Sealkote twelve o'clock gun—an old iron twelve-pounder. If
'we had only had a squadron of good cavalry, we should have
'cut them up to a man: as it was, we followed them to the banks
'of the river, and exchanged a few round-shot. They had this

" * Intoxicated with native spirit.

'old gun in position on the island at the edge of the bank. We
'halted a short time, and then marched back. Their numbers
'were estimated at eleven hundred. Of these we killed about
'four hundred, and a number of the wounded were swept away
'in trying to re-cross the river, which at the ford was more than
'breast-high, and was rising every minute. The men behaved
'very steadily, considering it was the first time they had been
'under fire. Our total loss in the force that day was about sixty
'killed and wounded; we lost five men from apoplexy—among
'them was poor old Bates—and we had about twenty men killed
'and wounded. Serjeant Forbes died from his wound; Serjeant
'Sayers was shot through the arm; the Colonel was hit by a
'spent ball in the shoulder, and Troup in the side, both being
'bruised.

"'On the 14th of July we marched again to the scene of the
'late action, and encamped. We heard that a body of the mu-
'tineers had re-crossed the river, and gone off towards Gholab
'Singh's territories, which afterwards proved to be the case, and
'there they were caught and shot.

"'On the morning of the 16th we, with the Sikhs, crossed
'over at daylight to the island by boats: it took us some time, as
'there were only two boats, and we then took the gun, killing all
'on the island, about two hundred in number. We advanced
'with two companies in front, skirmishing. The Colonel the
'previous evening had told Crosse's company off for the gun. As
'we neared them, they turned the gun on us, and fired three
'rounds of grape, which all went over our heads. As they fired
'the third round we closed on them on either side. They were
'in such a hurry, that the man who was ramming down the charge
'was blown to pieces. About six men stood to the gun, and
'fought with tulwars like men, but of course were soon disposed
'of, after wounding five of our men. Many took to the water
'and swam for their lives. As we crossed the river and advanced
'on the island, our guns blazed away at them, but with no effect;
'they answered, making one lucky shot, which killed three horses
'in a waggon. We took a quantity of carriages, buggies, and
'other property of the people at Sealkote, but could find none
'of our own things, neither private property nor mess articles;

'so we thus lost everything—plate, wine, crockery and all. We
'were ordered from Sealkote to march as light as possible, and
'all our mess-things and baggage were put in the Provost, under
'a guard of the 46th Native Infantry; so no doubt they were
'well looked after. Fraser, with his twenty men, took up his
'position in a dead-house in the artillery lines at Sealkote, where
'he was quartered on the morning of the outbreak, and went to
'the fort, where every one had taken refuge, in the afternoon.
'As he was on his way to the fort, he passed the Colonel's house,
'a mile from our lines, and seeing some bazaar scoundrels "loot-
'"ing," he went after them with his men into the house: the
'scoundrels were in such a fright, that they ran to the top of the
'house, threw themselves over, and of course were smashed.

"'On the 17th of July we marched back to Goordasepore,
'and so on, viâ Umritsir and Jullundur, to Delhi. From Loodiana
'we came by forced marches, carried all the way; the battery ac-
'companied us; the troop stopped at Jullundur. We arrived at
'Delhi on the 14th of August, and very glad we were. That
'marching was awful, and the heat in June and July killing;
'the thermometer varying from 100 to 112 degrees in our tents;
'and then the want of rest at night: none of us would have that
'time over again for anything we know. One day we lost two
'serjeants and one man from apoplexy, and the wonder is, we
'did not lose more. At Delhi camp we were brigaded with the
'60th, the Kumaon battalion of Ghoorkas, and Guides. We (the
'52nd) had to furnish 240 men daily for advance pickets on the
'right, where (except the Subzee Mundee, which was not so ad-
'vanced as Sammy House and Crow's Nest) only our brigade were
'sent. Our camp was in front of native lines on the parade
'ground, our pickets extending from Metcalf House on the left
'along the ridge to Sammy House, which was the extreme right
'front picket. The plan of our position and batteries will ex-
'plain this. We used to be on picket two or three days at a
'time. We had one warm day at the Sammy House on the 25th
'of August, when the enemy attacked us from 9 A.M. till 6 o'clock
'in the evening. Swarms of them used to come up, some to
'within one hundred yards of the breastwork, under cover of trees,
'etc., and fire away. They never showed themselves, except in

'passing from tree to tree. On that day they fired round shot
'from the Moree Bastion, and from light guns which they brought
'up. Our casualties were only ten killed and wounded; we esti-
'mated their loss at one hundred: we were well under cover and
'were not allowed to leave the breastwork. A bullet struck
'Paniman's firelock as he was firing, and glancing off, carried
'away the peak of his forage-cap. A round-shot struck the
'breastwork in one place, and knocked in the sand-bags against
'little Clarke, the cricketer, who was bowled over and wound up,
'much to his discomfiture.

"'About the 1st of September we had two hundred men in
'hospital. Delhi is one of the most unhealthy places in India,
'and we were losing men from cholera daily. We lost from this
'cause fifty-three men whilst we were before Delhi. Though our
'pickets were reduced, we could hardly find a relief; the men
'were continually on duty. Our only amusement morning and
'evening was to go to the top of a flag-staff or mosque on the
'ridge, and look out for what was to be seen. The ridge is a good
'two thousand yards from the walls of the city.

"'On the night of the 8th of September we took a jump, and
'erected Brind's Battery of six heavy guns, within seven hundred
'yards of the Moree Bastion, and there opened the next morning.
'The siege-train had arrived three days before from Ferozepore.
'On the morning of the 13th the other batteries on the left, four
'in number, the nearest being a breaching battery about one
'hundred yards from the Water Bastion, next the river, were all
'ready, and opened fire. All but one had been firing for two days,
'principally at the Cashmere Bastion. From the time we made
'the first battery, Pandy seems to have thought it was all up, for
'we erected the others without opposition. The enemy merely
'fired round shot, grape, and shell at the working parties, but
'never attacked. Atkinson had rather a narrow escape one
'night. He was out with the working-party, and whilst sitting
'in a sort of hole from which the earth had been taken to fill the
'sand-bags, a shell landed within a yard or two of him, and burst,
'wounding two of our men. One poor fellow had his leg cut off,
'and died from it; the other lost his arm.

"'On the night of the 13th, at ten o'clock, two engineers went

'to inspect the breach near the Cashmere Bastion, to see if it
'was practicable: they reported it ready, and at twelve o'clock
'we got the order to parade at three in the morning. The attack-
'ing columns had been told off to their destinations in the town
'three or four days before. The Colonel commanded ours, con-
'sisting of the 52nd, Kumaon battalion of Ghoorkas, and Coke's
'regiment of Punjab Irregulars. We could only muster 260 of
'all ranks, the Ghoorkas 200, and Coke's regiment 500 men.
'We paraded at the appointed time, and after some delay marched
'towards the city, a distance of nearly two miles from the camp.
'It was rather an anxious time, as may be imagined. Bayley
'commanded the storming-party, fifty of our men; Crosse com-
'manded the supports, consisting of fifty from each regiment.
'We were to go in through the Cashmere Gate, which was to be
'blown open by the engineers. It was broad daylight when we
'assaulted. The party of engineers, consisting of two officers and
'three serjeants, with Bugler Hawthorn, who was to sound the
'advance when the gate was all right, went on. Out of this
'number one officer and the three serjeants were knocked over,
'and two of the serjeants killed dead. The officer, Salkeld, has
'had his leg taken off, and was very near losing an arm besides.
'Home was the other officer, and was blown up subsequently by
'an accident the other day; he was in orders for the Victoria
'Cross, as also were Salkeld, the remaining serjeant, and Haw-
'thorn. Our advance parties then went on at a run, covered by
'two companies of the 60th, to draw off the fire, and we lay down
'under the glacis of the bastion, waiting for the bugle. We were
'pretty well covered on that side, the glacis being at that spot a
'sort of mound with a few small trees, but we were altogether
'exposed on the other side, and the fire there was "a caution" to
'cool us.

"'The storming party and supports were almost mixed; there
'was such a row, we could not distinguish the bugle, nor did
'we hear the explosion. We then saw the Colonel,* Synge,
'who was acting Brigade-Major, and the head of the reserve,

"* Colonel Campbell, while he covered his men, had placed himself on the
revetment of the sallyport through the glacis, and thus he saw (although he could
not hear) the explosion, and instantly took the critical moment to advance.—ED.

'coming round the corner; so, seeing something was wrong,
'Crosse ran on, meeting as he started Bayley going back, shot
'through the left arm; and after a little check at the Mantlet—
'a door-like affair in the causeway, (which, by the way, was only
'a single beam,) Crosse got in first through the gate, closely fol-
'lowed by Corporal Taylor, who behaved very well in this affair.
'The small spare door that all those large gates have was the
'portion blown in: but the large gates were also partly displaced.
'Inside the covered archway there was only one live Pandy, who
'presented his firelock at Crosse, but it was not loaded. There
'were several others lying dead, evidently killed by the explosion;
'they were all round an eighteen-pounder, the muzzle of which
'was about six yards from the gate. The Colonel and Synge
'were among the first six inside, and we then formed up. Nichol-
'son's column (called the First Column) then came in from the
'other side of the bastion over the breach by ladders, some time
'after we had passed clear of their route: we got the start of
'them, and beat them in. As soon as we had formed in some
'sort of order—and a hard matter it was—we proceeded to the
'left, clearing the Water Bastion, which was cleared before any
'other troops got into the place. We also cleared the ramparts
'as far as the College, where Crosse lost the regiment, being ahead
'with about half-a-dozen men and the Serjeant-Major (Streets).
'We went through a doorway after some fellows; and the Colonel
'with the column, his orders being to take the Jumma Musjid,
'went off to the right towards the Chandee Choke, driving all
'before them, and taking a light gun in one street. Here poor
'Bradshaw was killed in very gallantly charging this gun; At-
'kinson being grazed on the side with a bullet at the same time.
'They crossed the Chandnee Chouk, and went up a narrow street
'to within fifty yards of the Jumma Musjid, which is a very
'strong place, and was full of Pandies. The enemy made a stand
'here, lining the houses and trying to surround us, and as we had
'no means of blowing open the gates of the Musjid, and being
'completely isolated and unsupported—to say nothing of more
'than half the Ghoorkas and Coke's men straggling and looting
'about the town—the Colonel retired across the Chandnee Chouk
'to the Begum's Bagh, in the centre of which is the Bank, (but

'how changed from the picture in the "Illustrated"?) and held
'the gateway looking into the Chandnee Chouk. The column
'crossed the latter, amidst a storm of grape and musketry; Synge
'and Clive had their trousers cut in one or two places; the Colo-
'nel was wounded in the right arm by a bullet near the Musjid,
'during a charge of cavalry. Crosse picked up some Ghoorkas
'and Sikhs, with the men he had of the 52nd, and after driving
'the enemy from the College and places about, made for the
'Chandnee Chouk; and after skrimmaging about for some time,
'they found the regiment, to their great delight. The Colonel
'had sent to the General for supports, but could get no answer,
'and we were losing men at the gateway fast. The enemy got on
'the tops of the houses all round, and had pot shots at us, and
'we could not get at them; so, after waiting for the General's
'answer about two hours, the Colonel retired to the church. We
'got there about one P.M., and had to reinforce the pickets at the
'College, where they were pressing us.

  "'In the meantime, Nicholson's column went round the ram-
'parts to the right (he was to go round to the Ajmere Gate),
'taking the Moree and Burn Bastions. Between the latter and
'the Lahore Gate this column was checked, and did not advance,
'and here Nicholson, as fine a fellow as ever walked, and eight
'officers, were knocked over. The former was in front of all,
'amidst a storm of bullets, in vain trying to encourage the ad-
'vance. They then retired to the Moree Bastion, and held that.
'This was all we got that day, including the intervening houses.
'A force of fifty men of the 60th, some Europeans, and the
'Sirmoor Battalion, (Ghoorkas,) under Major Reid, of the latter
'corps, with about two thousand Cashmere troops, attacked that
'morning the Kissen Gunge, a high position which the enemy
'occupied on our right. This attack failed, and the Cashmeres
'lost their four guns. It was a very difficult position to take,
'and the enemy had a larger force there than was expected, and
'a strong battery, which could only be approached by a narrow
'lane. However, the next day it was evacuated, and the guns
'left.

  "'This force, after taking the Kissen Gunge as was expected,
'was to have entered Delhi by the Lahore Gate, and to have re-

'inforced Nicholson. That (Kissen Gunge) failure had a good
'deal to do with our not gaining more the first day, for as soon
'as the Pandies at the Lahore Gate knew of it, they gained pluck
'and pressed Nicholson, and after checking his column, brought
'their guns and men down the Chandnee Chouk on us. The fact
'of the matter is, we tried a great deal too much. We had not
'more than four thousand men in all in the attacking force, in-
'cluding the reserve, and of this only eighteen hundred were
'Europeans, and what is that in such an enormous place as
'Delhi? If we had contented ourselves with what we actually
'got, it would have been a most successful affair, and we should
'have scarcely lost a man. As it was, the total loss was 62
'officers, and upwards of 1,000 men killed and wounded. We,
'the 52nd, lost four officers and eighty non-commissioned officers
'and men killed and wounded,—nearly one-third of our number.
'Among the killed was Serjeant M'Keowin, of the band. He
'volunteered, and had been doing duty in the ranks for some
'time, and behaved uncommonly well. Brockwell and Howe, at
'the Musjid, Amos and Neale, at the gateway, were also killed.
'Among the wounded, Serjeant-Major Streets, while with Crosse,
'had a most narrow escape. The bullet struck him sideways in
'the stomach, and came out on the left side. He is not quite
'safe yet, but is going on well. Serjeant Thomas was wounded
'in the foot; Serjeant Ellis had his left arm amputated; Serjeant
'Palk was shot right through the cheek and mouth; he has lost
'a few back teeth, but is going on all right. Pitten has his left
'arm amputated; Marshall was shot in the left arm; Corney,
'the same; Selfe in the cheek: he would not retire, but re-
'mained to the last; we all know what a hard little fellow he is.
'Stonor and Dawson were among the wounded during the next
'four days. Bugler Miller was among the wounded on the first
'day; he was the Colonel's orderly bugler, and has since died of
'cholera.

"'From the 15th to the 20th of September, we were working
'our way up streets, over and through houses, etc., till we got
'entire possession of the town. The King left the palace on the
'19th. We were very glad when it was over; that street fight-
'ing is the deuce; the stench from dead blackies in the streets

'and on the tops of houses was awful. We were continually at
'work on detached pickets night and day. The King was taken
'two or three days after the 20th. His two sons and grandson
'were also caught and shot; one of them, a — (we do not know
'a name bad enough for him,) set the example in abusing the
'wretched women and children in Delhi. Does it not make one's
'blood boil to think of the atrocities that have been committed?

"'The mutineers from Delhi have dispersed in different
'bodies. We have only thirteen officers, including two doctors,
'now with the regiment. The others, except Troop and Wing-
'field, who are ahead with sick at Umballa, are all on the sick
'list, and we now stand on an average about eight files per com-
'pany on parade. How different from four years ago, when each
'company was forty-five files! Since we left Sealkote in May,
'we have lost upwards of one hundred and fifty men, of whom
'fifty-three were from cholera and thirty-six killed. That camp
'before Delhi was awful. Every regiment suffered alike, Ghoor-
'kas and Sikhs as well as others. Poor Corporal Taylor, who
'behaved so well, died a day or two ago from fever and
'dysentery.

"'The good behaviour of our men on the 14th and afterwards
'must not be forgotten. An immense number of men were drunk
'about the town, for they found shops full of beer and spirits, yet
'we had not a single case of drunkenness in the 52nd.'"

On their way to join their regiment, on the outbreak of the
mutiny, two officers of the 52nd were detained, and afterwards
fell in action—the one, Lieutenant T. R. Gibbons, at Cawnpore—
the other, Captain W. R. Moorsom, at Lucknow. Both of them
were of distinguished gallantry.

"The young officers of the 52nd may learn from the example
which follows, that a thorough knowledge of all the details of
regimental duty, to which practical professional science is added,
is certain to reap for them distinction in their regiment and in
the army, when field-service shall give the opportunity; but beyond
these, the peculiar attribute ascribed to the character of their late
comrade was a courage and determination in serving alike his
God and his country, which procured the respect of all who
were witnesses of his career.

"The officers of the 52nd, in the year 1860, erected a monumental tablet to Captain Moorsom, in the cathedral of Rochester, which bears the following inscription:—

'TO THE MEMORY OF

WILLIAM ROBERT MOORSOM,

(ELDEST SON OF CAPT. MOORSOM, C.B., LATE OF THE 52ND LIGHT INFANTRY,)*
WHO, WHILE A LIEUTENANT IN THE 52ND LIGHT INFANTRY,
ACTING FIRST AS AIDE-DE-CAMP, AFTERWARDS
AS ASSISTANT-QUARTERMASTER-GENERAL TO

SIR HENRY HAVELOCK,

AND SUBSEQUENTLY AS QUARTERMASTER-GENERAL TO THE DIVISION OF

SIR JAMES OUTRAM,

WAS ENGAGED IN NINE PITCHED BATTLES AND NUMEROUS SKIRMISHES;
WOUNDED TWICE:
HONOURABLY MENTIONED THIRTEEN TIMES IN PUBLIC DESPATCHES,
INCLUDING THE THANKS OF THE GOVERNMENT OF INDIA,
AND PROMOTED TO A COMPANY IN THE 13TH LIGHT INFANTRY
FOR DISTINGUISHED SERVICES.
HE WAS KILLED 11TH MARCH, 1858, IN THE 24TH YEAR OF HIS AGE,
AT THE HEAD OF A COLUMN OF ATTACK ON THE REBEL POSTS OF THE

CITY OF LUCKNOW.

AS A TRIBUTE OF THEIR AFFECTION AND REGARD
THE OFFICERS OF THE 52ND LIGHT INFANTRY
DEVOTE THIS TABLET.'

"On the 1st of April, 1858, Colonel G. Campbell, C.B., gave up the command of the 52nd, and proceeded to Lucknow, having been appointed to the command of the Infantry Brigade there. This command comprised nine battalions, and the circumstance of Colonel Campbell having been recalled from the Punjab to take this position, although one of the junior colonels in the country, was deemed highly complimentary. His departure from the 52nd, which he had commanded for the last five years, was much regretted by all ranks. The welfare of the soldier was

---

* The late Captain Moorsom, the father of the gallant young officer to whose memory the tablet was erected, was the editor of the 52nd " Record."

always in his thoughts, and every officer felt that in Colonel Campbell he had a just and considerate commander in quarters, and a leader in the field under whom the regiment could not fail to maintain the reputation handed down from its predecessors.

" During the severe losses of the regiment in this campaign, the depot company was the source from which these losses were replaced, and the bearing and discipline of the young soldiers sent out to Head-Quarters during the two last years that we have to record, was such as to call forth repeatedly the commendation of the Commanding Officer towards Captain J. J. Bourchier, to whose exertions and attention to the young officers and non-commissioned officers, as well as to the men, was owing an efficiency such as to give the best promise that the character which throughout this Record has been heretofore exhibited by the regiment, will long continue to be maintained by all who have the honour of wearing the uniform of the 52nd Light Infantry."

CHAPTER LV.

1815.

SUNDRY MATTERS CONNECTED WITH WATERLOO, AND WITH THE 52ND AT WATERLOO.

Professor Selwyn's beautiful poem on Waterloo—Its dedication—Lord Seaton's eulogy of British staff-officers—A 52nd corporal's quiet heroism—Mr. Yonge's visit to Waterloo—52nd officer's bones—Drouot's speech in the French House of Peers—Speaks of sixteen battalions of the Guards—Muffling also—Ney's letter to the Duke of Otranto—The four battalions seen by the 52nd close to La Haye Sainte—My ten assertions with regard to the 52nd and the Guards, &c.—Recapitulation of the 52nd movements, &c.—Sir Henry Clinton's despatch—52nd and Imperial Guard meeting between the English and French armies.

THERE are some further matters connected with Waterloo, and several of them connected with the 52nd at Waterloo, which I wish not to omit from this work, and to which I have determined to devote one of its concluding chapters. I must not, however, attempt to place them in any order.

Some months ago Professor Selwyn, of Cambridge, did me the favour to send me a copy of his beautiful poem entitled :—

"WATERLOO:

"A LAY OF JUBILEE FOR JUNE 18, A.D. 1815.

"'It was a day of Giants.'—*Wellington.*

"Cambridge, Deighton, Bell and Co.; London, Bell and "Daldy, 1865."

On the leaf before the title page, he had kindly written :— "To William Leeke, one of those who helped to win the victory "of Waterloo, with the Author's grateful respects. Christmas, "A.D. 1865."

I hope my readers will inquire for this poem. I can promise them great pleasure in its perusal. It occupies, with a few notes, about ninety quarto pages. One Waterloo officer, whom I know, and his wife were moved to tears as they read it. Professor Selwyn has sent it to every Waterloo officer whose address he could discover. He says he has followed Captain Siborne's account of the history of the battle, and consequently he has, as a matter of course, been led into the two mistakes—of the 1st Guards having defeated a first column of the Imperial Guard of France, and of the 52nd having been accompanied by the other regiments of Adam's brigade when they defeated the two columns of the Guard, and also when they subsequently drove off the rear-guard of the enemy.

The following is the dedication :—

> " To those who fell in arms, that glorious day,
> But falling helped to win it ; and to those
> Who shared the triumph, now have gone to rest ;
> To him who sleeps beneath the golden cross ;
> And to the few remaining, ere the last
> Shall pass away from earth,—this thankful lay.
>
> " For brave deeds, held in memory, will revive
> In after days, when peril calls them forth ;
> GOD give us lasting Peace ; GOD save the QUEEN.
>
> WILLIAM SELWYN,
>
> June 18, A.D. 1865."

I will content myself with copying the first seven lines of this heroic poem, to shew my readers how sweetly and smoothly the verses run, and one other portion about the defeat of the French Guard by the 52nd. The whole work is full of heart-stirring passages, which may help to prove that martial ardour and the love of daring deeds burn not alone in the breasts of those who have chosen arms as their profession :—

> " Hark ! 'tis the day of rest ; the matin-bells
> Are sounding forth from every village-tower
> Glad notes of Peace on Earth, good will to men ;
> And in the vale, between two gentle heights,
> A little onward from the forest edge,
> The fields are standing thick with rising corn,
> Rejoicing in the plenteous rain of heaven."

The following lines relate to the charge of the 52nd on the columns of the French Guard. I purposely leave out one line mentioning another corps as joining in the attack, as I know full well, that the 52nd was alone at the time that it charged—not one, but both, and both together—the columns of the Imperial Guard :—

> "The gallant Colborne wheel'd his regiment
> His fifty-second, 'unsurpassed in arms,
> 'Since arms were borne' to make them feel his fire,
> Full on their long extended flank; in front
> They saw the mouths of Napier's battery.
>   " Brave Veterans worthy of a better fate
> And wiser leaders; what could soldiers do
> So closely mass'd, so closely grasp'd in death's embrace?
> They did what soldiers could; they plied their arms,
> Each for himself; they struggled to deploy;
> They faced on Colborne, gave him fire for fire;
> But his strong line, four deep, in firm array
> Full charging, with three British cheers,
> Quite broke their scattered ranks; and opening out
> They covered all the slope in scattered flight;
> And left upon the field where they had stood,
> Their columns' form and measure, sadly traced
> By dead and dying men."

In a letter from Mr. W. Crawley Yonge, I find the following eulogy of the staff-officers of the British army by Lord Seaton, who, contrasting them with the staff of the general officers of one of the foreign armies, of which an officer of high rank had just been speaking in terms of disapprobation, observed, " What " a contrast to our service, when, with so much less pretence at "order, there is so much more reality ; " and he added, " that he " could do our staff-officers the justice to say he had never seen "an occasion when there was the same want that had been de- "scribed—that there never was a moment of hesitation, always a " readiness to carry orders, whenever a communication might be " wanted, into the hottest fire."

Mr. Yonge relates with much feeling the following instance of quiet, unpretending heroism of an old corporal of the company in which he and I were :—" He appeared to be quite worn out " and ill, and suffered greatly from fatigue in the long march

"before Waterloo, and Mc Nair pressed him to go to the rear,
"considering that he was not at all equal to another day's work;
"but he refused, saying, in the quietest manner, that, having
"gone through a good deal of service with the regiment, he would
"rather not leave it on the eve of an action—he was sure it
"would be his last, but he thought he should be able to keep up
"during the day, and so he did, but he went into hospital
"directly after, and from thence was invalided, so that we never
"saw him again."

Little more than six months before his death in 1854, my
poor friend Yonge visited the field of Waterloo. In a letter to
Bentham he mentions that, "In order to make the Belgic mound,
"which was formed on the crest of the British position, not far
"from the left of the 52nd when in line, about 800 yards of
"ground, extending along the crest of the position from the
"Charleroi road to the back of Hougomont, had been scooped out,
"fifty yards wide and seven feet deep," and adds, "It is very
"grievous, for perhaps no other so effectual a mode could have
"been devised for mutilating so interesting an historical record,
"as the place itself would otherwise have always afforded." One
of the guides told him, that in trenching the ground on the
ridge a little deeper than usual, the bones of poor Nettles had
been turned up. They were recognized by the 52nd officer's
buttons, and the man said, it was evident, from his appearance,
that he had been buried just as he fell; the spot he pointed out
tallied very well.

The following most confused account of the defeat of the
Imperial Guard at Waterloo, was given by Count Drouot, Aide
Major-General of the Imperial Guard, in the Chamber of Peers,
at Paris, on the 24th of June, 1815, only six days after the
action. It is translated from "The Moniteur:"—"The emperor
"regards this moment as decisive. He brings forward all his
"Guard: orders four battalions to pass near the village of
"Mont St. Jean, to advance upon the enemy's position, and
"to carry with the bayonet whatever should resist them.
"The cavalry of the Guard, and all the other cavalry at hand,
"seconded the movement. The four battalions, when they
"arrived upon the plateau, were received by the most terrible

" fire of musketry and grape. The great number of wounded
" who separated from the columns, make it believed that the
" Guard is routed. A panic-terror communicates itself to the
" neighbouring corps which precipitately take flight. The enemy's
" cavalry, which perceives this disorder, is let loose into the plain.
" It is checked for some time by the twelve battalions of the Old
" Guard, who had not yet charged, but even these troops were
" carried away by the inexplicable movement, and follow the
" steps of the fugitives, but with more order." [I must make a
few remarks on this speech of Drouot's. In the first place he
probably means La Haye Sainte, and not Mont St. Jean ; La
Haye Sainte is called Mont St. Jean in the French official account. The thought has only just struck me, whilst I am writing this, " Is it possible that Drouot is correct in stating that
four battalions of the Guard did, according to the Emperor's
order, advance towards the British position along the western
side of the inclosures of La Haye Sainte, and could these be the
four battalions seen by us, as I have stated at pages 52 and 53
of the first volume, who remained steady with ordered arms, 300
or 400 yards up the British position on our left, close to the
inclosures of La Haye Sainte, when the whole of the rest of the
French army had given way ? If so, Drouot was misinformed,
and does them very great injustice. The 52nd never saw or encountered any but about twelve battalions of the Guard, and
those they defeated single-handed. These twelve battalions of
the Guard were the first that gave way, and then the whole army
fled, with the exception of four battalions close to La Haye
Sainte, who *may* have been Germans. I wonder whether
Siborne took from Drouot his idea of a first column of four battalions of the French Guard having been defeated by the 1st
British Guards !

We know, however, from the Guards themselves, and from
other sources, that the right battalion of Maitland's brigade of
Guards was stationary when the mass of skirmishers of the
Imperial Guard, and from Donzelôt's division, were driven in by
the left battalion of the brigade, and when we saw the Imperial
Guard skirmishers run down the position, and form about 100
yards in front of their leading column, at the time that the 3rd,

the left battalion of the 1st Guards, retired to the rear of the British position in some confusion, where they were seen by Vivian's Hussar Brigade.

The Guards do not claim, (although Siborne, and many who have copied him, claim it for them,) that the 2nd, the right battalion of the brigade of Guards, joined in any attack upon the French Infantry at Waterloo, excepting always their light company, which, nearly up to that time, had been engaged with the light company of the other battalion in helping to defend Hougomont. The 2nd battalion was stationary, and the 3rd only made the one advance and attack before spoken of.]

"It is very difficult to avoid repetition in speaking of the various mistakes which both English and French writers have fallen into in describing these events, but I will avoid it, as much as possible, in the few additional remarks which I wish to make on the subject of the defeat of the French Imperial Guard.

The more I think of it the more it appears *possible*, that the four battalions we saw up to our left when the 52nd were nearing the Charleroi road, were the four battalions of the Imperial Guard, spoken of by Drouot. If they quietly advanced along the outside of the western enclosure of La Haye Sainte to strengthen Donzelot, and to be prepared, with his division, to attempt to penetrate the British line of battle in advance of that post, at the same time that the two heavier columns should attack our line, 400 yards away in the direction of Hougomont, they would have arrived at the spot where we saw the four battalions (with ordered arms and facing towards the French position) about the time that the two heavy columns, always computed at 10,000 men, gave way before the charge of the 52nd. One difficulty in this theory is, that these four battalions, if French, should not have taken to their heels at the same time that the rest of the French army fled. But then, as they were at the distance of 400 or 500 yards from the British position, there was no cause for any immediate panic, and, if they were battalions of the Guard, their *esprit de corps* especially if they had confidence in their principal officers, might be expected to lead to the steadiness so manifested in them. When the 52nd passed near to the lower corner of the

La Haye Sainte inclosure it was fully 800 yards distant from any part of the British position, and these columns were 300 or 400 yards above them.

I saw them most distinctly, they certainly were not English, from their uniform, nor were they likely to be Germans. What should keep them there, 400 yards or more from the British position, if they were either? And would they be likely to be there, when Donzelot's division, which had been harrassing Alten's troops for two or three hours at least, could not have left the spot more than ten or, at the most, fifteen minutes before? If they were our Allies, why did they not come to our help, when they saw a regiment in red all alone, and must have seen the squares of the Old Guard only 200 or 300 yards in a direct line beyond us? And one may say again—If they were French, why did not these four battalions (notwithstanding that they had seen the flight of the Imperial Guard, and of the whole of the French troops) rattle down upon the left flank of the 52nd, and try to help their friends of the Old Guard to cover the retreat of their army.

I cannot conceive that any English general, commanding four steady battalions, would have missed such an opportunity as that which here presented itself, either of advancing to the assistance, or to the attack, of a regiment circumstanced as the 52nd was. But I may inquire, who but Colborne would have ventured on, and would have carried to such a successful issue, such a feat of daring as was the whole of his advance from the time that he first moved his regiment down the British position to attack the heavy columns of the Imperial Guard, till he brought it across the Charleroi road and led it onward, and up the French position, against the last remaining troops that made a stand—the renowned Imperial Guard, the Old Guard, of France? But Colborne knew his men, and they knew him, and knew each other, and all had confidence in each other! But I must forbear, and apologize for having allowed myself to be so carried away by my *esprit de corps*. My only excuse is, that I should have done just the same, had I belonged to any other gallant regiment which had so distinguished itself. I must however add one word more. Is it not common justice,

that, if matters happened as I have related them, Lord Seaton
and the 52nd should no longer be deprived of the credit and
honour which are their due?　"Should not those, who won the
laurels, wear them?"

But to return for a moment to those four battalions, which
we saw standing, with ordered arms, close to the western inclosure of Hougomont, I would just say, that I think they must
have been a French brigade of Donzelot's division, or *possibly* of
the Imperial Guard, waiting, as I said before, after they had
seen the flight of the heavy columns of their Guard and indeed
of the whole French army, and the daring advance and attitude
of the 52nd, to see how they could quietly get away, without
having to lay down their arms; which by the way, as they were
not disposed to try their strength with us, was perhaps the
wisest thing they could have done.

Drouot, in his speech six days after the battle, although his
account is most inaccurate with regard to details, speaks of
the Emperor ordering *four* battalions of the Imperial Guard to
advance towards the British position, and then he speaks of the
advance of an additional body of troops consisting of *twelve*
battalions of the Old Guard, making out that there were
altogether sixteen battalions of the Guard engaged in the last
attack.

Baron Müffling, the Prussian Commissioner, who was with
the British army during the battle, says, in his "History of the
Campaign of 1815," "The enemy's Guards began to move and
"with sixteen battalions at half-past six o'clock advanced
"towards the platform." [Müffling makes a terrible mistake
with regard to the time, which was very much later.]

Marshal Ney, in his letter to the Duke of Otranto, dated
Paris, June 26th, 1815, says, "A short time afterwards I saw
"four *regiments* [i. e. *eight battalions*] of the Middle Guard arriv-
"ing, conducted by the Emperor himself . . . He ordered me to
"lead them on" . . . He speaks afterwards of "four squares of the
"Old Guard, who protected the retreat."

"A French eye-witness" states that the Emperor's column of
attack "was almost entirely composed of the Old Guard."

It will be seen from all these accounts that the 52nd officers, in addition to their own calculation that the two heavy columns of the French Guard, which they defeated, amounted to about 10,000 men, have the testimony of the earliest French accounts, to shew that more than that number of the French Imperial Guard were in that part of the field, and were engaged at, what has been very properly called by Colonel Gawler, Lord Seaton, and numbers of other gallant and experienced officers, "the crisis "of Waterloo."

The mistakes which have been previously mentioned, which Captain Siborne first fell into, and which the French writers were only too glad to follow, and which so many English historians have adopted, were, that there were two columns of the Imperial Guard, which separately advanced to make the last attack ; that the first was charged and defeated by Maitland's brigade of Guards, and that the second was defeated by a flank attack of Adam's brigade, consisting of the 52nd, 71st, and the 2nd and 3rd battalions of the 95th Rifles, Maitland's brigade attacking them at the same time in front ; and it has been further asserted that both these columns reached the summit of the British position.

I assert that all this is entirely incorrect, and that,

1.   The two columns were seen by the 52nd in close proximity, as shewn in Plan II of this work, the head of the rear column being within thirty paces of that which preceded it.

2.   That the head of the leading column was 300 or 400 yards below the crest of the British position.

3.   That not a man of these columns advanced a single step towards the British position after they were fired into by the 52nd skirmishers.

4.   That no other troops but the 52nd attacked, fired into, charged, and defeated these columns.

5.   That we, who were in the left centre of the 52nd, distinctly saw the skirmishers of the Imperial Guard run down from that part of the British position occupied by Maitland's Guards, and form in front of the leading battalion of the Imperial Guard columns just as the 52nd four-deep line was nearly parallel to the left flank of the leading column, as shewn in Plan II.

6.   That when the 3rd battalion of Maitland's 1st Guards were lying down in square, some distance on the reverse slope of the British position, and were suffering from the fire of a mass of skirmishers of the Imperial Guard, (it is said also that a number of skirmishers from Donzelot's division joined them,) the Duke of Wellington desired the commanding officer of that battalion to "form line on the front face of the square, and drive those "fellows in." That this was immediately done; that the 3rd battalion fired into them, killing and wounding numbers of them, and that they then charged and drove them off the crest of the position, and followed them a short distance down the slope; that then there was a cry of "cavalry," and that some attempting to form square, whilst others had not heard any command to do so, the battalion got into some confusion, and retired in disorder over, and some distance beyond, the crest of the British position, where they halted, and recovered their order.

7.   That this was the only forward movement against the enemy made by the 3rd battalion of the 1st Guards at Waterloo.

8.   That the 2nd, that is the right battalion of the 1st Guards did not join the 3rd battalion in this movement against the Imperial Guard skirmishers, nor did they make any other forward movement against infantry at Waterloo; and that they were at this time "stationary and not firing."

9.   That when the skirmishers of the Imperial Guard were forming in front of their leading column, the 3rd battalion of the 1st Guards must have just re-crossed the British position, as there was a clear view of the ground from the 52nd left centre for 300 yards above the leading company of the Imperial Guard columns, and no troops were visible.

10.   That it was a great mistake which my friend and relative Gawler made, when he assumed that the leading column of the Imperial Guard reached the crest of the British position in front of the 1st Guards, because the dead bodies of Imperial Guardsmen were found lying there the next morning. He did not reflect, when making the statement, that they might be only the dead bodies of skirmishers, but he had no idea of admitting the 1st Guards to a share of the honour of defeating the Imperial Guard. See pp. 84, 85, of Vol. I. Colonel Gawler was on the

extreme right of the 52nd when they advanced from the position, and brought their right shoulders forward, so as to take the Imperial Guard in flank, and consequently he was at a distance from, and, as he states, "did not see the front of the Imperial "column." Hence the *mistake*, which has probably helped to lead Siborne and others into the idea that, if the headmost companies of the Imperial Guard reached the crest of our position in front of Maitland's brigade, it was probable that that brigade should have had a hand in defeating them, particularly when the 1st Guards, and also Sir Colin Halkett's brigade, spoke of having been opposed to troops wearing the bear-skin caps of the French Imperial Guard.

Siborne's correspondent might well remark, as I have before stated, that "If ever truth lies at the bottom of a well, she does " so immediately after a great battle, and it takes an amazingly "long time before she can be lugged out."

I am endeavouring to lug out some of the truth, respecting the defeat of the Imperial Guard at Waterloo, from the mass of conflicting statements under which it has remained encumbered, if not altogether buried, for so long a period.

There are, as might be expected, many and varied difficulties in the way of arriving at the truth in this matter; one of the chief of which has been mentioned before, namely, that of the impossibility which some officers find to distinguish, after the lapse of many years, between what they recollect to have seen, and what they have read of, or have heard from others.

One difficulty, which the 52nd laboured under for years, when individuals amongst them were anxious to substantiate their claim to the full honour due to them for having defeated, single-handed, the heavy columns of the French Guard, arose from their not being able to make out what the 1st Guards really did at Waterloo beyond their having, in common with a great portion of the right wing of the British and Allied army, received and beaten off, in good style, several charges made by strong masses of the French Cavalry.

Immediately on our arrival at Paris, we knew what Lord Hill had said about the Guards being "stationary and not firing," (he was on the right of the Brigade of Guards,) and we knew Sir

John Byng had told Sir John Colborne that he could not bring the Guards forward when the 52nd advanced, because all their ammunition was gone, (rather a lame reason, by the way, for for which the 1st Guards would not thank him,) and knowing also that we had, far away from the British position, defeated, in the lower ground, two columns of the Imperial Guard, containing about 10,000 men, we could not at all reconcile matters.

Sir John Byng probably only referred to the 2nd (the right battalion of the Guards), and possibly knew nothing of the 3rd battalion having been ordered by the Duke to "drive those fellows "off" the position.

Lord Seaton, in writing to Colonel Bentham, as late as October, 1853, (see Vol. I, pages 100, 101,) says:—"I suppose "the Guards must have made some forward movement, and that "many officers must have seen it; but, I contend that the French "column had been checked and thrown into disorder before the "Guards moved. I saw the column of the Imperial Guard "steadily advancing to a certain point, and I observed them "halt, which was *precisely* as the skirmishers of the 52nd opened "fire on their flank."

I think it well to repeat here, from page 102 of the first volume of this work, some further observations of Lord Seaton's:—"The "whole of the Imperial Guard advanced at the same time, and "their flank was first attacked before any forward movement was "made to check them in front. . . . . The Prussians could "not have attracted the attention of the French, so as to cause "the throwing back of their right wing, until after the Imperial "Guard had commenced their attack on our centre. . . . . "No regiment except the 52nd fired on the flank of the Imperial "Guard."

Let me request my readers to look again at the letter of Sir Thomas Reynell, who commanded the 71st, (the right regiment of our brigade,) at Waterloo, (it is at pages 73—75 of Vol. I,) and say if, after reading that, and after considering also what Lord Seaton has written on the subject, they can come to any other conclusion than this: that the whole of the Imperial Guard advanced at the same time, as Lord Seaton declares, that neither of the two heavy columns of the Imperial Guard reached the summit of the British position, but that they were both defeated at "the bottom of the declivity," as Sir Thomas Reynell terms it, by the 52nd alone ?

In bringing this subject to a close, I must beg leave to observe that it is very evident to me that none should venture to become historians of battles, but those who have been present at, and have seen some considerable portion of, the events which they profess to relate.

None but those who, like myself, have some considerable acquaintance with the various movements and incidents which most of the writers on Waterloo profess to relate, and even to give in detail, and which they often give in beautiful and heart-stirring language, can have any idea of the amount of annoyance and disgust I have experienced in reading so many relations and details which I know to be utterly untrue. My belief in the truth of history in general has been most rudely shaken and almost destroyed by reading, in Siborne's account of Waterloo, and in the accounts of others, many statements respecting the 52nd and other regiments, which have no foundation in truth whatever as regards the regiments with which the writers endeavour to connect the movements, or incidents, or exploits, which they record. I do not intend to accuse any of these historians of wilfully mis-stating facts; but the varied information as to events and time which they receive from different persons was sure to lead them into all kinds of error, particularly when they are endeavouring to reconcile, in the best manner they can, these often very contradictory statements.

Possibly it might be a good plan to appoint several officers in each regiment whose especial business it should be to chronicle its proceedings, and more especially when it is on active service. The want of a regularly kept document recording the services of the 52nd, was much felt by different officers who were requested to undertake to write the "Record" of the regiment. The details of circumstances, written down nearly at the time that they occurred, are, of course, more to be depended upon than those recollected many years afterwards. I believe that in a naval action, all the principal events are regularly entered in the ship's log, and why should there not be something of the same sort in the army ?

It appears to be the practice in the British army that, after a general action, only the officers in command of corps, divisions, and brigades, should send in reports for the Commander-in-Chief. The 52nd was in Sir Frederick Adam's brigade, and his brigade was in Sir Henry Clinton's (the 2nd) division, and the 2nd division was in Lord Hill's corps; so in the tenth volume of the supplementary despatches of the Duke of Wellington, edited by his son, we have a report from Lord Hill to the Duke, enclosing Clinton's report of the proceedings of his division, and he again encloses General Adam's report of his brigade, mentioning it at the close of his report as follows :—" *I beg, too, that your lordship,* " *in making your report to the Commander of the forces, will have the* " *enclosed letter from Major-General Adam laid before his* " *Grace.*"

The italics are mine. I would observe that it is a great pity General Adam's letter or report is not given in this volume of the despatches. He was the only general officer who was engaged in the attack and defeat of the Imperial Guard, and it is most probable that his report contained a correct account of its defeat by the 52nd alone. In the following passage Sir H. Clinton refers, I think, to Adam's brigade, when it was posted in squares to the left of Hougomont, from four o'clock till half-past six :—" It then fell to the share of General Adam's brigade to " take its share of the same honourable service. The manner in " which the several regiments—the 52nd, under Colonel Sir John " Colborne; the 71st, under Colonel Reynell; and the 2nd and " 3rd 95th, under Lieut.-Colonels Norcott and Ross—discharged " their duty was witnessed and admired by the whole army." Sir H. Clinton afterwards says: "When the handsome repulse of " the enemy's last attack afforded the opportunity to become our- " selves the attacking body, so judiciously taken advantage of by " Major-General Adam's brigade, under your lordship's immediate " direction, I directed Colonel Halkett to reinforce the attacking " line with the Osnabrück battalion." Clinton says, also, that the Osnabrück regiment "drove the enemy from four guns on the " right of the Genappe (i.e., the Charleroi) road," and that, "during " its advance they got possession of two pairs of colours;" but he omitted to mention—probably he had not heard of it—that

Halkett took the French General (Cambronne) prisoner with his own hands.

Sir Thomas Picton's division, which was posted on the left centre of the British position, and to the left of the Charleroi road, consisted of Sir James Kempt's brigade, containing the first battalions of the 28th, 32nd, 79th Highlanders, and 95th Rifles, and of Sir Denis Pack's brigade, containing a battalion of each of the following regiments :—The 1st, 42nd Highlanders, 44th, and 92nd Highlanders; Colonel von Vincke's 5th Hanoverian brigade also formed part of Picton's division, the command of which, after Sir Thomas Picton's death in the early part of the action, devolved on Major-General Sir James Kempt. I copy the following extracts from his report to the Duke of Wellington, as they give a concise account of one of the most glorious events of the day :—

"Bivouac, near Genappe, 19th June, 1815.

"In consequence of the lamented fall of Lieut.-General Sir "Thomas Picton, (who was unfortunately killed early in the "battle of yesterday, at a very critical moment, while nobly ani- "mating the troops,) the command of the 5th division, and the "troops which had been placed under his orders, devolved upon "me, and it is quite impossible for me to convey, by words, to "your Grace the feelings of admiration with which I beheld the "invincible spirit displayed by the British troops in repulsing "every attack which was made upon the position where I had "the honour to command. The troops were formed in two lines, "supported by Major-General the Hon. Sir W. Ponsonby's "brigade of cavalry. [The 1st Royals; 2nd Scots Greys; and "4th Inniskillings.] The first line was composed of Dutch and "Belgian troops, with the 1st battalion of the 95th Regiment, "under Sir Andrew Barnard, posted on a knoll on the right. "The second line was composed of the 8th and 9th brigades of "infantry, under Major-General Sir Denis Pack and myself, and "the 4th and 5th Hanoverian brigade of militia, commanded by "Colonels Vincke and Best. The enemy having concealed his "attack till the last moment, advanced rapidly in three immense "columns of infantry, covered by 30 pieces of artillery, directing

" their heads on the right, centre, and left of the position to the
" left of the *chaussée*. Our first line, acting as light troops, gave
" way as the columns approached; but the 8th and 9th brigades
" of infantry instantly advanced, and charged the heads of the
" columns just as they had gained the crest of the position : a
" struggle of a few moments ensued, but the invincible spirit and
" determination of the British troops were such, that these im-
" mense masses, directed with the greatest fury, were absolutely
" put to flight by two British brigades, weakened as they had
" been most materially by the severe action which they had fought
" two days before. Major-General the Hon. Sir W. Ponsonby in-
" stantly availed himself of this, and charged in the most gallant
" manner at the head of his brigade. Many prisoners were taken,
" and three eagles." [I suspect that the three regiments of kilted
Highlanders, in these two brigades, astonished the French in no
slight degree. W. LEEKE.]

Shortly after this handsome repulse of the French attack,
Lambert's 10th British brigade was sent to strengthen these
troops, and those on the other side of the *chaussée*, who were
very much harrassed by Donzelôts French division, and by other
troops, who were allowed to maintain themselves in the immediate neighbourhood, and to their left of La Haye Sainte, the
whole afternoon, and up to eight o'clock, when the Imperial Guard
was defeated by the 52nd. The French, as has been mentioned,
took La Haye Sainte at six o'clock : the troops in their front
suffered most severely, and the 27th Regiment, of Lambert's brigade,
which, Kempt says, was unavoidably exposed more than the other
troops, lost an immense number of men. I see by the returns that,
out of 18 officers present, they lost 14 killed or wounded, and, out
of 698 rank and file, they lost 96 killed and 348 wounded ; making
a total of 444 killed and wounded, out of a total of 698 rank and
file present ; and to these 444 may be added 34 officers, serjeants,
and drummers ; making the whole amount of killed and wounded
in the regiment to be 478. This gallant regiment must have
suffered an immensly greater loss than was experienced by any
other regiment at Waterloo.

The ground occupied and passed over by the 52nd at Waterloo, gave to its officers peculiar advantages for observing many of

the principal events which happened during the latter part of the action, from four o'clock in the afternoon till a quarter past nine in the evening.

A reference to the three plans, which will be found at pages 29, 43, and 55 of the first volume, will assist the reader in understanding those leading points of the close and crisis of Waterloo, which I have endeavoured faithfully to describe.

It will be seen, by referring to Plan I, that from twelve o'clock to 3. 30 the 52nd was in reserve a quarter of a mile in front of the village of Merbe Braine, and that they then moved a quarter of a mile to their left and formed square ; this was just at the time that the first great charge of the French cavalry took place, and the 52nd saw them scouring the British position and driving the artillerymen from our guns. The 52nd then moved *in square* over the position, and descended it a short distance, to within 150 yards of the northern inclosure of Hougoumont, where it halted on the narrow cross road to La Belle Alliance and formed squares of wings, which proceeded immediately to take up their forward positions between the 71st and 2nd 95th ; here they remained between two and three hours, when they were ordered to retire over the British position, which they reached about seven o'clock, and having formed a four-deep line by closing the left wing up upon the right wing, they remained in that position (shewn on Plan II by a short dotted line) for about an hour. Here the regiment could see nothing of the field of battle, being forty yards below the crest on the reverse slope of the position ; but during the whole of that period their commanding officer, Sir John Colborne, sat on his horse, partly covered by a bank two feet and a half high, with an excellent view of the whole of the ground between him and La Belle Alliance, watching the formation of the columns of the Imperial Guard, and their subsequent advance in the direction of the right centre of the British line. He appeared to have his eye on them the whole time, as he himself states was the case, except when the officer of cuirassiers rode down the bank and spoke to him, and when, afterwards, the Duke of Wellington rode across our front from the left, and conversed with him for a few minutes, as they both sat on their horses partly covered by the low bank.

At about eight o'clock Sir John Colborne moved the 52nd over the position, and, passing the brigade of guns immediately in their front, they saw, away in the direction of La Belle Alliance, the two heavy columns of the Imperial Guard. The 52nd line did not march straight on these columns, but proceeded some distance down the slope, nearly straight to its front, and then the whole line brought its right shoulders rapidly forwarded, and, about ten minutes after eight, it must have been on the flank of the leading column of the Imperial Guard, as shewn in Plan II. We saw the Imperial Guard skirmishers run in and form in front of the column. The 52nd did not halt, but advanced firing, as I have described it in the third chapter of the first volume. The French returned the fire, and the 52nd lost there about 140 men, killed and wounded, in the course of five or six minutes. They saw the whole French army run in utter confusion, and advanced, as I have before described it, over the masses of the killed and wounded; they were then charged by a mixed body of cavalry. Some French guns fired grape into, and made some havoc in, our advancing line ; then some Prussian or French round-shot struck near the centre of the line, and, immediately after, Sir John Colborne halted the regiment in the low ground, below the inclosures of La Haye Sainte, close upon the Charleroi road, as shewn in Plan III, for the purpose of dressing the line. Some of the Old Guard here made a stand, and opened fire upon us. Lord Uxbridge was wounded. The colour and covering-serjeants were called out and dressed by Nixon, the acting adjutant, but the line was not dressed, for the Duke rode up at the moment and told Sir John Colborne to "go on, "and not give them time to rally." The 52nd advanced to its left of the Charleroi road and of La Belle Alliance, in pursuit of one of the squares, and, after passing through a French column in the hollow road beyond Primotion, who surrendered, they advanced to the farm of Rosomme, three quarters of a mile beyond La Belle Alliance, and there halted for the night, on the very spot on which the Imperial Guard had bivouacked the night before.

There was something interesting in the fact, that the 52nd and the Imperial Guard of France were both in reserve in the early part of the battle of Waterloo, and about as far distant from each other as they well could be—the one being near Merbe Braine, the other at Rosomme—and that, after the battle had raged for seven hours, they should meet in the centre of the field, between the two positions and the two armies, and there decide the fate of the day.

I have always attributed, in some measure, my very clear recollection of the movements of the 52nd at Waterloo, and of so many of the circumstances which occurred at that time, to the fact of its being the only action I was ever in, and that I had no recollections of other battles, as my chief companions, Mc Nair, Hall, Holman, and Yonge had, to interfere with my recollections of Waterloo. Very often when dining and spending the evenings together at Estréeblanche, in our cantonments in the north of France, did they talk over their Peninsular battles and campaigns, and, when Waterloo took its turn, I recollect that I well made up for my only having been a listener to their interesting Peninsular accounts, by taking more than my full share of the discussions which took place with regard to all its remarkable and ever-changing incidents.

I just wish to mention, before I leave the subject of Waterloo, that General Gneisenau, who wrote, by Blucher's order, the Prussian account of their actions on the 16th, 17th, and 18th of June, confirms my statement, made in Chapter IV, page 65, that the Duke of Wellington and Blucher met, after the battle, at *La Belle Alliance.* He writes, speaking of La Belle Alliance, " It " was there also that, by a happy chance, Field-Marshal Blucher " and Lord Wellington met in the dark, and saluted each other " as conquerors."

CHAPTER LVI.

ARTICLES CHIEFLY ON MILITARY OR NAVAL SUBJECTS.

The formation of an army of reserve—Letter to Lord Fitzroy Somerset on the subject—A suggestion with regard to recruiting—Case of a man who became blind from opthalmia contracted in India—Eventually turned adrift without a pension—England can afford to consult the feelings and comfort of her soldiers—Algerian militia, and worship of the host—General Peel and the Sunday employment of workmen at Enfield—Steam rams charged with explosive matter at the prow.

I HAVE observed, I think, in a former part of this publication, that I occasionally forwarded to the Horse Guards, &c., &c., any suggestions on military affairs which occurred to me, and which I thought were calculated to be useful.

The following letter to "The Times" was written about five years ago, and was accompanied by a communication I had made to Lord Fitzroy Somerset in 1852. Some of the proposals contained in the letters appear to have been in some measure recently carried out : —

"THE FORMATION OF AN ARMY OF RESERVE.

" *To the Editor of 'The Times.'*

" SIR,—Nearly ten years ago I forwarded to the Horse Guards " the subjoined rough sketch of a plan for the formation of an " army of reserve, for which I received Lord Fitzroy Somerset's " thanks. Possibly you may not consider it altogether unworthy " of being admitted into the columns of 'The Times,' at the " present juncture, when the whole of Europe is bristling with

"bayonets, and when the nation and our military men especially
"do not feel altogether sure of the peaceable intentions towards
"this country of the Emperor Louis Napoleon. In the not im-
"possible event of his attempting to land three or four bodies of
"50,000 men each, on different parts of our coast nearly at the
"same moment, an army of reserve of 150,000 trained soldiers
"would, of course, be invaluable. If two of the invading forces
"should succeed in landing on points rendering their junction
"feasible, whilst the other attacks would have to be guarded
"against, we should, with only our present resources, have no
"troops that we could effectually oppose to them, until they had
"inflicted the greatest injury and misery on the invaded districts.
"I do not believe that, if 200,000 men could be landed in this
"country, they would ever get out of it again. We should soon,
"as in 1813, have one-tenth, or more, if necessary, of our
"population in arms. I was delighted with, and most proud of,
"our volunteers, when I saw them in Hyde Park last year, and
"they have attended well to their company drill, and in some
"good measure to their battalion drill also; but most of the
"battalions have done nothing yet, and probably will be able to do
"little for the future, with regard to brigade and division move-
"ments; and there would probably be much confusion and loss
"in the event of their having to bear the brunt of withstanding
"any considerable hostile force. I am confident they would do
"their duty, and act as bravely as any troops in the world, but
"an army of reserve of regular soldiers would, in case of invasion,
"be a very pleasing adjunct to our noble and valuable army of
"volunteers. Some of our naval men tell us that it is impossi-
"ble for a French army to land in this country, but after having
"witnessed the rapidity with which the French army was
"concentrated in Italy the year before last, we may easily con-
"ceive that from the eastern and southern parts of France, and
"also from Algiers, most formidable expeditions might be
"unexpectedly sent forth for the invasion of England, the pre-
"parations for such expeditions being made under cover of an
"intended interference in Venetia, in Italy, or in some other
"quarter. As employment is likely to be deficient, the proba-
"bility is that almost any number of recruits might be enlisted

" during the ensuing winter. Why then should we not at once
" commence a system of retirement from the army on some such
" plan as that contained in the following sketch, which would
" cost this wealthy country a mere nothing, and would be consi-
" dered a great boon by thousands of those who, under the present
" system, are necessarily kept away from their country and their
" homes during so many wearisome years :—In some cases men
" might be enlisted for a short period only, with the under-
" standing that at the end of that period they should be dis-
" charged into the army of reserve to serve in it for a certain
" number of years, and to receive a very small, but, perhaps, in-
" creasing weekly allowance, when not embodied, and full pay and
" allowances, with a prospect of pension, whenever they are called
" out. We should thus not only have a considerable portion of
" our population trained to arms, but we should have them ready
" when required, at a very short notice. It seems most desirable
" also that some plan should be adopted of more regularly
" relieving our regiments stationed in India, and in other distant
" parts of the world. The country can afford to do it, and should
" use every effort to have a system of relief constantly going on,
" so that our poor fellows should no longer be subject, except in
" cases of very great emergency, to be kept out of England for a
" longer period than seven years. Indeed, it does not appear to
" be very difficult to make an arrangement by which every man
" should have the option of retiring, after seven years' service, in
" some cases with a conditional, in others with an unconditional
" discharge. It may also, in connexion with this subject, be a con-
" sideration whether men might not enlist for *general* service, so
" that whilst the present system of regiments, and the consequent
" *esprit de corps* are kept up, the younger men might join some
" other regiment, on the withdrawal of their own corps from any
" particular station. Perhaps you may consider the whole sub-
" ject, surrounded as it may be with difficulties, to be worthy of
" ventilation in your columns. Although my communication is
" already a very long one, there are one or two other points to
" which I wish to advert. The one is the additional expense of
" an army of reserve, and a system of more frequently relieving
" our troops stationed at a distance ; I would just observe again,

" with regard to this, that we can well afford, as a country, to
" attend to the comforts and feelings of our soldiers and sailors ;
" for the expenditure of even an additional million sterling would
" only be at the rate of one shilling a head from our population,
" without counting in the population of Ireland. Much of the
" expense and difficulty would be obviated, if the present militia
" adjutants, and staff-serjeants, and barracks, could be made
" available. I presume we should hardly want a militia, if we
" had an army of reserve.

" The men composing the army of reserve might be paid
" twice a year, or quarterly, or monthly, by the staff-officers of
" pensioners, and they might even be assembled periodically, as
" the pensioners are under the staff-officers. Possibly they
" might, when embodied, be occasionally attached to, or brigaded
" with some of the regular regiments. The other point regards
" the doubt which may arise in the minds of some as to whether
" it is well to have so large a portion of those classes from which
" our army is usually recruited, trained to arms ; but, it is a fact,
" proved by the experience of the last fifty years, that those who
" have passed through the ordeal of military service are amongst
" the most loyal and best behaved of her Majesty's subjects.

" I commend the subject to your attention, and to your more
" able pen and advocacy.

" AN OLD 52ND OFFICER.

" November 5, 1861."

" Holbrooke, near Derby,
" February 24, 1852.

" MY LORD,

" Since the debate of Thursday evening on the
" Militia Bill, it has occurred to me that the necessity for a
" militia might be obviated, at least after the lapse of a very short
" time, by the adoption of some plan, first of all for the imme-
" diate increase of the regular army, and then for a gradual
" retirement of a certain portion of it, in order to the formation
" of an army of reserve, which might be kept up at a very
" trifling expense indeed ! I have in a very hasty way thrown
" together a few ideas on the subject in the accompanying sketch
" which I am almost afraid to trouble your lordship with ; the

" ideas MAY, however, be of *some little* use. And I, therefore,
" venture to send them, as also a short note on the subject of
" recruiting.

" I have the honour, &c.,

" W. LEEKE,

" Incumbent of Holbrooke,

" Formerly, for many years, in the 52nd Light Infantry."

" A very rough and hastily written sketch of a proposed system of
" retirement from the army in order to the formation of an
" Army of Reserve, so as possibly to render it unnecessary to
" embody the militia except for a very limited period.

" It is well known that a considerable portion of the soldiers
" of the British army are at all times desirous of being dis-
" charged, either from becoming weary of a soldier's life, or from
" an anxiety to return to their homes. And it is probable that,
" at any time, as many as can be spared of those who have not
" completed, by some years, a sufficient service to entitle them to
" a pension, will gladly retire from the service with a conditional
" discharge, or furlough. The conditions of the discharge, or
" furlough, might be somewhat as follows :—

" 1. That they should be considered still as belonging to her
" Majesty's service, and as forming part of the army of reserve ;
" which, in all cases of emergency, or whenever the proper
" authorities might consider it necessary, should be liable to be
" assembled.

" 2. That they should then be exactly in similar circum-
" stances with the rest of the army, and come under the pro-
" visions of the Mutiny Act ; they might receive the same
" pension for wounds or other casualties.

" 3. In the event of any lengthened or difficult service, some
" distinct expectation of pension might perhaps be held out to
" them.

" 4. They might be formed into companies and regiments
" according to the numbers in each locality. There might be
" some little, but not any great, restriction on their changing
" their residences from one district to another.

" 5. If they deviated from the conditions of their furlough,
" to any extent, they might be punishable by the sentence of a
" court-martial, or otherwise, and perhaps be sentenced to rejoin
" their regiments, or some other corps. In case of refusing to
" attend muster when called upon to do so, they might perhaps
" be treated as deserters. They might be officered from the half-
" pay list. They should be quite distinct from the pensioners.
" Their pay, when embodied should be, &c.

" If the numbers of the infantry of the army were raised at
" once to 200,000, supposing it possible to effect this, either by
" means of recruiting, or, that being unlikely, by means of
" volunteering from the militia, it is calculated that one-third
" of that number, whenever their immediate services could be
" dispensed with, would gladly enter into the regiments in
" reserve, subject to the above necessary, though somewhat
" stringent, conditions. It might, or might not, be desirable
" to give to each man thus volunteering for the reserve, a bounty
" of five guineas, or of sevenpence a-day, (the amount is the same
" to a fraction,) for six months after his arrival at home, so
" that he might not be wholly unprovided with the means of
" subsistence, whilst he was looking out for employment. The
" discharge of 70,000 men on these terms, in the course of five
" years, would only cost the country £70,000 a-year, or the
" discharge of 100,000 in the same period, would cost £100,000
" a-year. The expense would not be great if it should be thought
" desirable to give in some way an additional encouragement to
" the men thus forming an army of reserve.

" If it should be necessary to embody the militia, perhaps
" persons might be allowed to volunteer from it into the line for
" one, two, or more years, with the understanding that they
" would, at the expiration of the given period, receive a condi-
" tional discharge, or furlough, and belong to the army of
" reserve.

" The mode of volunteering from the line for the army of
" reserve might be similar to that adopted after the peace of
" 1815, when the effective men from the reduced battalions
" joined their first battalions. The number, exceeding the
" determined strength of the regiment, were permitted to

" volunteer into other regiments, which had not their full
" complement of men, somewhat in the following manner :—

" The companies were told off into three divisions ; in the
" first were the men whom the captain particularly wished to
" retain. In the second, those who stood the next highest in
" his estimation as good and effective soldiers ; and in the third
" those who, from being married, or weakly, or from other
" circumstances, it was more desirable to get rid of. If the
" number required did not volunteer from the last class, then
" the second were allowed to volunteer, and so on to the first-
" class. Nearly the whole number required were obtained from
" the third class.

" It is a question whether retirement to the army of reserve
" could be permitted as a reward to the *best* conducted of the
" non-commissioned officers and soldiers."

" *Note on the subject of Recruiting for the Army.*

" If it is desired, on an emergency, to raise a large number of
" recruits, it appears desirable that, not only recruiting parties,
" but the regiments themselves should take some part in the
" matter. There are numerous towns and neighbourhoods in
" which a regiment has scarcely ever been, or the band, and
" bugles, or drums ever been heard. If the regiments could be
" quartered in these places, or, at least, some companies, with the
" band attached to one division and the drums or bugles to an-
" other, it is probable that the martial bearing of the soldiers, &c.,
" &c., would have no small effect in inducing a desire amongst
" the young men of the several neighbourhoods to enlist."

The following was Lord Fitzroy's reply.

" Horse Guards, 28th February, 1852.

" SIR,—I have had the honour to receive your letter of the
" 24th instant, and I have to express to you my thanks for your
" communication relative to the formation of an army of reserve.

" I have the honour to be, Sir,

" Your most obedient humble servant,

" FITZROY SOMERSET.

" To the Rev. William Leeke,
" &c., &c.. &c.,
" Incumbent of Holbrooke, near Derby."

In the next chapter, in Appendix No. 4, will be found two cases of old and distinguished soldiers, who had, when discharged, received very inadequate pensions for their services, and whose cases were re-considered, on their being properly represented to the Commander-in-Chief. When I was first speaking to Lord Seaton about Serjeant Housley, he told me he had urged upon the authorities the importance and justice of inquiring into, and adjusting all such claims. About seventeen years ago a young man, belonging to this parish, was discharged with a "very good" character, after four years and eleven months' service, having had his sight nearly destroyed by opthalmia, which he had contracted in India; he first of all received, as an out-pensioner of Chelsea Hospital, "a pension of sixpence *per diem* for one year, when he "was to be again examined."

I felt very much concerned that this young man should, at the age of about five-and-twenty, be left in very destitute circumstances, in consequence of disease contracted in the service of his country, with which disease, but for his service in India, there was no probability that he would have been visited, and I took considerable pains to have his case brought before the proper authorities. After the sixpence a day had been continued to him altogether for two years and nine months, all further payment was refused: the reason given was, that he was of a consumptive constitution, and that had it not been so, the opthalmia would not have turned out so badly. His discharge specifies "that he "is discharged in consequence of medical disability." Certificates were sent to the proper authorities—one from Mr. Douglas Fox, the eminent surgeon, who then resided at Derby, stating that he was not of a consumptive constitution—another from a most respectable neighbouring gentleman, who knew his family well, mentioning that they were a fine, healthy family—I think, also, there was one from myself to the same effect, and I offered to pay his expenses to Chelsea and back, if they would re-examine him, and re-consider his case, but it was all to no purpose; they determined to abide by their first decision, and here he is still, poor fellow, with a parish allowance of eighteenpence and a sixpenny loaf; and notwithstanding the probability that his poor means of subsistence would in the end lead to consumption, he still is in pretty good health, and has lived to prove that the certificates from Derbyshire were correct: his family also continue to be a healthy, fine family. At first there was some hope that he might recover his sight. He was in the Derby Infirmary for three months. He was also enabled by some of us to go to the eye hospitals at Nottingham and Birmingham, but he received no benefit, and he is now quite blind. Now I do maintain that England ought not to treat her soldiers as she has done. She may well find it difficult to get the number of recruits she wants, and is likely to want, if she unfairly leaves them in destitute circumstances when they are discharged. I was informed some few years ago, when speaking of this man's case, that there were two other young men, living some miles from this, who had been discharged in consequence of opthalmia, and who had met with the same sort of treatment as that which he had experienced.

If a soldier loses an arm or a leg on service, he gets a suitable pension. Why should a poor fellow be deprived of a pension, who has become blind in consequence of the effects of the climate he has been exposed to? There must be an alteration in many things, and more regard must be had also to the soldier's welfare when he retires from the service, if it is important that men should be induced to enter the army. This rich and powerful nation can well afford to pay her defenders better than she does, to pension off the deserving soldier with all due regard to his conduct, and to his amount of service and suffering; and also, by providing a larger amount of troops, never to make it necessary to keep regiments for so many years, as is still the practice, from their country and their home. Why, I may ask, should poor fellows, who have become blind in the service, be left to be supported by the parish, be doomed to a life of celibacy and solitariness, and very probably be left to end their days in the union-house?

When Sir Willoughby Cotton, the general commanding at Bombay, was inspecting the batch of invalids about to proceed to England, the man whose case I have been describing, and who was one of them, tells me that he was very kind to them, and said to an officer who was with him, "These young men, when "they get to England, ought to be made comfortable when they "get to their homes, as they have been deprived of their sight."

He says there were a few others, beside himself, who were invalided because they had been suffering from opthalmia. The difficulty of getting able-bodied recruits for the army will, I suspect, greatly increase, and I trust the Government and country will be wise betimes, and not let the great railway and iron companies deprive the army of all the best men the country possesses.* Let the soldier's term of service, and particularly the length of service abroad, be greatly reduced; unless, indeed, men are induced to volunteer to remain longer in the army by the certainty of having a comfortable provision made for them when they leave it, and especially if they should be discharged in a state of health which precludes the possibility of their ever being able to support themselves in comfort. I intend, before long, to bring this poor fellow's case again before the proper authorities. I find that, without my knowing it, he got a friend to make another application for him to the Chelsea board about two years ago: he met with a refusal of relief. His discharge, which I have lying before me, is wrapped and tied up in a torn portion of the reply, the closing words of which are, (in print,) "and the Commissioners "of this Hospital cannot therefore grant you any further relief," and then is added, (in writing,) "of which you have been already "four times informed." Under all the circumstances, they must sound very harshly in the ears of a poor blind man. It is the system, perhaps, rather than the administrators of it, which is to blame.

* At the Derby station, at twelve o'clock every day, except on Sunday, may be seen turning out to their dinners about 20,000 fine fellows, the vast proportion of whom would do credit to any army in the world : and at all the large stations throughout the land, a similar sight, no doubt, may be seen. Why are these companies enabled to take their pick of the healthy and strong men of the country ? The answer is, "they can afford to make it worth the while of these men "to come into their service." I know an engine-driver, who receives eight shillings a day during six days of the week, and, I am sorry to say, he works to some extent also on the Sunday, and is paid in proportion for his work on that day : he is the owner of two good cottages, worth, I should think, about £250 or £300. Surely the British nation must not allow itself to be driven into difficulties with regard to the supply of men for its army, and for the regular relief of its troops in various parts of the world, by the great inducements, in the shape of payments and future prospects of comfort, which large companies or wealthy individuals are enabled to hold out to them.

The following extract from a newspaper of July, 1864, shews that the forced attendance of soldiers on idolatrous religious ceremonies is not unknown amongst the Algerian troops :—

"ALGERIAN MILITIA AND THE WORSHIP OF THE HOST.—A "Paris letter states that sixty men belonging to the National "Guard or Militia of Tlemcen, among whom were a Protestant "and some Jews, were recently ordered to join in the procession "of the Fête-Dieu. The Protestant and several of the Jews "refused to obey; the others, less scrupulous, attended, but "declined to kneel at the moment of the raising of the host. "The officer in command drove the latter from the ranks, but "the Protestant and the Jews, who had not responded to the "summons, were brought before a military court and condemned. "One, however, a Jew, named Haim Ganancia, obtained a new "trial, and this time confided his defence to an advocate. The "latter showed that in the decree of the 9th of November, 1855, "in which the duties of the militia are laid down, no mention is "made of the escort of processions, and that, besides, out-of-door "religious celebrations in Algerian towns are illegal, according "to Art. 45 of the Concordat. The tribunal decided that the "service of following the procession not being necessary for the "maintenance of order and public safety, Haim Ganancia was "not bound to take part in it, and consequently quashed the "judgment."

I have much pleasure in introducing here the following correspondence, which I think does so much credit to General Peel :—

"GOVERNMENT WORK ON THE LORD'S-DAY.

"The Rev. H. Stevens, Secretary of the Lord's-day Society, "writes to us :—

"'Complaints having reached us of a large number of men "'being employed on the Lord's-day, many of them against their "'will, in the Government small-arms manufactory at Enfield, "'respectful representations of the fact were made to General "'Peel, the Secretary of the War Department; the following "'communication was subsequently received :—

"'" War Office, Oct. 5, 1866.

"'" Sir,—I am directed by General Peel to acknowledge the
"' receipt of your letter of the 4th inst., and to express his regret
"' that the exigencies of the service should render it necessary to
"' employ some of the men at Enfield on Sundays, the object
"' being to complete the conversion of as many Enfield rifles into
"' breech-loaders as can be sent out to Canada before the naviga-
"' tion closes. General Peel cannot take upon himself the
"' responsibility of leaving any portion of the regular troops in
"' Canada exposed to the danger of being brought into collision
"' with troops armed with breech-loading rifles whilst they have
"' only muzzle-loaders, if by an exertion it can be avoided. The
"' unusual course of working at Enfield on Sunday is only for a
"' short period and to meet a great emergency; and although
"' General Peel will take care that none of the men are per-
"' secuted or discharged who conscientiously object to working
"' on Sunday, he highly approves of the conduct of those who
"' from patriotic motives and to complete a necessary work have
"' consented to do what may be very distasteful to them.

"'" Your obedient servant,
"'" (Signed)   S. W. H. PEEL."

"' In a reply to a second letter, dated 'War-office, October 16,
"' 1866,' it is further stated :—

"'" General Peel desires me to add, that the shipment of
"' arms to Canada will cease with the stoppage of the navigation
"' at the end of this month, and that he has every reason to hope
"' that the employment of workmen on Sundays, which was
"' rendered necessary by the great emergency of the case, will
"' then be entirely discontinued.

"'" I am, Sir, your obedient servant,
"'" WILLIAM A. PEEL.
"'" Rev. H. Stevens."' "

I think it was in 1864 that I wrote down the following ideas, on
the subject of charging the stems of steam-rams with explosive
matter, which met with about as much consideration as I expected,
from those to whom they were submitted, and who had not the
power of forming any correct opinion of the value, or utter
uselessness of the suggestions :—

It is not known by the writer of this, if the idea has ever occurred to anyone, of loading with powerful explosive matter the stems of the iron-cased ships which are now in the course of construction. Nor does he know if, when the concussion takes place, the chief force of the explosion would take effect upon the vessel run into; *that* possibly might depend, in a measure, upon the degree of velocity with which the iron-cased ship was proceeding. He supposes that in the case of *shells*, bursting whilst in a forward and somewhat horizontal course, the fragments almost always go forwards or sideways, but *not backwards*. It might be the same, to some extent, with regard to an explosion taking place at nearly the most forward point of a steam ram, when it penetrates the side of an enemy's vessel. If the ram should come stem on, on an enemy's *iron-clad* ship, possibly the explosion should be made to take place at an earlier moment after the contact, than would be desirable if the ship attacked were a wooden one, in which latter case a wider and deeper gap would be made, and the explosion taking place more within the ship and near the water line, she would probably be sunk in a very short time.

"The danger to the attacking ram might be obviated, or lessened, by two or three strong water-proof compartments being constructed forward in the vessel. Indeed, compartments throughout such vessels, and also in the *wooden* line of battle ships would enable them to receive the shock of an enemy's ram with some fair probability of surviving it.

"The charge might generally be kept in the magazine, except at night, and when near the enemy. A frame or frames might remain fixed forwards, or might be moveable, into which it should be made to fit. The frame farthest from the stem might possibly be that used in the case of an attack upon a ship not cased with iron, if thereby the explosion would be delayed, till a deeper entrance had been made into its side.

"The writer is totally ignorant of the point of whether a steam ram could so run into a line of battle ship as to sink her without the assistance to be derived from the plan which has occurred to him.

"He does not know that these suggestions may not appear to

men of practical science to be very ridiculous. He has, however, always made a point of making known, in the proper quarters, anything which has occurred to him as being likely to be of service to the country, even at the risk of being laughed at for his pains.

" In order to shew the immense power of a comparatively small charge of powder, he may here mention an anecdote which was related to him by the late Admiral Sir Jahleel Brenton."

I here related the account of Lord Cochrane's method of blowing up Martello Towers, which will be found at page 38 of Vol. II of this work.

I am sorry to find that I have only the rough copy of what I wrote on the subject of steam rams, charged with explosive matter, and that I cannot find the whole of that ; but I recollect another suggestion which might be turned to account was, that small ships might carry in their magazines "infernal machines," capable of blowing up the largest ships, under the bottom of which they might explode, and that these might be used as a means of defence, being submerged, and so connected by means of an extensive floating net-work, that a pursuing enemy should get entangled in them and draw them round him, and that possibly they might be made to explode at the moment of contact, or, if the concussion could not explode them, then, in some way, by means of a connecting wire. If this means of defence could be used by ships out at sea, it is evident that it might much more easily be applied to the mouths of harbours and the entrances of roadsteads. Of course all kinds of plans have been formed, by means of booms and " infernal machines " for the defence of inlets, but my idea refers more particularly to a series of net-work, and to the enemy's vessel getting, as it enters, entangled in it, and drawing under its bows or sides the machines which are to destroy it.

CHAPTER LVII.

MISCELLANEOUS ARTICLES NOTED DOWN FOR PUBLICATION.

Female Club sermon—Duties of wives—Anecdote of two of the judges —Interesting journey with an Egyptian naval officer, &c., &c.—Religious advice
written in the album of one of my daughters—French ambassador's letter
—Letter from Sir Andrew Agnew on the same subject—Dr. Marsh—Importance of the elder children in our schools being taught prayers which
will be of use to them when they are grown up—A suitable prayer.

In making preparation for this work, and also during the progress of writing it, I have noted down various particulars which
occurred to me as suitable for publication. Many of these have
not been introduced into any of the former chapters, and I now
think it well to place the following in a chapter by themselves,
hoping that they may be interesting and useful to those who
read them.

When preaching to the Female Club at Holbrooke, in 1848,
I ventured to take, as a part of my subject, the duty of wives to
obey their husbands, and I think that, in speaking on the last
sentence of Genesis iii, 16, "and he shall rule over thee," I mentioned that there was mercy even in this part of the judgment
upon the woman, considering our fallen state, for had there been
equal authority given to both the husband and the wife, it would
have led to frequent collision and strife. I, no doubt, also spoke
on Ephesians v, 22—25, 33, and, I dare say, that in speaking of
the tender love, mentioned in the last two of these verses, which
the husband should have for his wife, I may also have laid some
stress on the last sentence, "and let the wife see that she reveren...

"her husband." I, probably, also brought forward the passage in the first part of the third chapter of the 1st epistle of Peter. I suppose that the most of the women received what I read and said on the subject, as a portion of the truth of God's Word; but I fear that some one at least must have misunderstood my object, and have imagined that I wished to disparage women; whilst it was to lead them to seek their happiness in striving to obey God's Word in this and in every other respect—for shortly afterwards I received, anonymously, the following simple and beautiful extract, which I find amongst my papers :—

"Extract from Jesse's 'Country Life.'

" 'It is pleasant to reflect on the perfection of the female charac-
" 'ter—to indulge in the remembrance of having seen women
" 'perform those offices of affection and love, which they alone
" 'are capable of shewing. If we refer to the Bible, how delight-
" 'ful are their best attributes there pourtrayed, and how con-
" 'spicuous are they for the warmest and kindliest feelings. It
" 'was a woman who watched over her little brother when he
" 'was hidden in the bulrushes. It was a woman who urged
" 'her father to perform his vow, although her own life might be
" 'the sacrifice. It was a woman who so beautifully said, "all
" ' "was well," when she came to implore the prophet to restore
" 'her dead and only son. It was a woman who followed her
" 'mother-in-law in all her distress and poverty. It was a
" 'woman who offered her last mite in charity. It was a woman
" 'who washed our blessed Saviour's feet with her tears, and
" 'afterwards wiped them with the hair of her head. It was a
" 'woman who said, "Lord, if thou had'st been here, my brother
" ' "had not died." It was a woman who stood at the foot of the
" 'cross. It was a woman who went first to the sepulchre. It
" 'was to a woman our Lord first made Himself known after His
" 'resurrection; and it was *not* a woman who betrayed our Lord
" 'and master.'

" Set this against a sermon preached by Mr. Leeke before the
" Women's Club, 1848.

" γυνή."

Some years back I went to Cambridge to vote at one of the elections, at which there was a very exciting contest. Posting to London early the next morning with three friends, we breakfasted either at the first or second place at which we stopped to change horses. Whilst we were there, a carriage, with four posters, drove up in great haste, on its way to Cambridge, and as we were looking out of the window, to see if any of our friends were in the carriage, the landlord of the inn came in and announced the important piece of intelligence, that Mr. Alderman Paterson was going down to Cambridge to vote. It turned out that the travellers to the election were the two judges, Alderson and Patteson. One of my companions was engaged to dine with Patteson the next day, and promised himself much amusement in relating the anecdote.

About thirty years ago I arranged to escort a lady who was going from the Isle of Wight to London by the Portsmouth mail, and on joining her at Cosham, from Fareham, I found that she had for a fellow-traveller an Egyptian officer, who had been serving for two or three years as a lieutenant in one of our English frigates. He was an intelligent and gentlemanly young man, and spoke English fluently, and well understood the language. We soon got to talk on religious subjects, and he listened with attention to all I had to say for a considerable part of our journey. He mentioned, in the course of conversation, that he was intending to be a week in London, and that he should stay at the Belle Sauvage. When I reached Brailsford, I thought of our conversation, and that I should probably never again see this officer, who was then, I think, on his way to Egypt, and that I should consider whether there was nothing more that I could do for him in the way of leading him to see the folly and delusion of Mahometanism, and of embracing the true religion of Christ. I determined on writing to my bookseller in London, to desire him to call at the Belle Sauvage in a day or two, about nine o'clock, when he would probably find the Egyptian officer at breakfast, and to take with him a small English Polyglot Bible, a copy of the English version of Grotius, (which contains a confutation of Mahometanism, &c., &c.,) and Venn's "Whole Duty of Man," all handsomely bound. The copy of Venn could not be got ready, but "a steady

" friend" found him at breakfast at the hour I had mentioned,
and produced the books, and a letter from me, which, as it was
without an address, he could not at first understand; he, however,
did so immediately, and "took the books very pleasantly:" Ecclesiastes xi, 1, 6. I think it was about fifteen years ago, it may
be more or less, that I read in one of our English newspapers
that a captain of an Egyptian man-of-war had been put to death
for embracing Christianity. I recollect the pang I felt when I
read this paragraph, thinking it possible, perhaps probable, that
the sufferer was the friend whom I met in the Portsmouth mail.
I have the same feeling now, whenever I think of it, but it re-
solves itself, under the influence of faith, into a feeling of joy that
perhaps it was this very young man who was chosen of God to
join "the noble army of martyrs." I have had no means of
verifying the fact.

I give the following entry which I made in the album of one
of my children about twenty years ago, in the hope that it may
be made useful to some of my readers :—

"MY DEAR CHILD,

"If you would be truly happy you must seek your hap-
"piness in God, and in His love and service, for no earthly person
"or thing can give real and lasting happiness. 'Man at his best
"'state,' when he has health, youth, comeliness, friends, riches,
"and honours, 'is *altogether vanity.*' It is in vain that you will
"look for true happiness in any of these things; even if you
"should possess them *all,* they will but afford you gratification
"(and *that* not unmixed with sorrow) for a very little time. These
"things, whilst possessed, will disappoint you of the happiness
"you may have expected from them, they will prove fruitful
"sources of temptation to sin, and, one after another, the most of
"them will fail you in whole or in part; and the time is coming
"when, if any of these things (in which an ungodly world seeks
"its happiness) still remain to you, you yourself will be taken
"from them. Oh, then, make not such things your gods! *Use*
"all the things of this world, but do not *abuse* them, set not your
"heart upon them, but upon the *Lord Jehovah,* Father, Son,
"and Holy Spirit. Seek earnestly the pardon of sin, and the

" favour of your God through the atoning blood of Christ! Live
" upon Christ each day for 'righteousness and for strength!'
" Seek daily the enlightening, purifying, comforting, and strength-
" ening influences of the Holy Ghost, reading diligently, with
" prayer, God's holy Word, which is the Sword or Instrument the
" Spirit uses in His work upon the soul! Be diligent in *private*
" prayer, and in the use of all the appointed means of grace!
" Ask God to teach you *how* to pray to and to praise Him, and
" how to read and hear His holy Word! Thus will you find His
" appointed means of grace to be the sure means of conveying
" spiritual and eternal blessings to your soul. Remember that
" denying yourself, denying your own inclinations in *all* those
" things which are displeasing to God, is one chief part of holiness!
" And recollect holiness is happiness, for it is the seal of the
" Spirit, marking people as the children of God; and if *children*,
" then HEIRS, heirs of GOD, and JOINT HEIRS WITH CHRIST!
" May you, my dearest ———, seek and find this happiness; the
" happiness arising from the sweet assurance that God is your
" reconciled Father and Friend; that your sins are forgiven, and,
" consequently, that you have no occasion to fear death; that all
" things shall work together for good to you here below; and that
" you shall assuredly come into possession of that inheritance
" which is incorruptible, undefiled, and fadeth not away, but is
" reserved in heaven for you.

 " Thus prays your affectionate father,

        " WILLIAM LEEKE.

" Holbrooke, March 2nd, 1845."

 It has been mentioned, in Chapters XLII and XLIII of this
work, that the Committee of the Derbyshire Lord's-day Society
forwarded an Address to the Queen, on the subject of the
desecration of that day in England, by Foreign Princes and
Ambassadors. It was just before the expected arrival of the
King of the French, a copy of the address was sent to the
French Ambassador, who replied as follows:—

 " L'ambassadeur de France a l'honneur d'accuser réception à
" Monsieur Leeke de sa lettre en date du 1er Octobre. Il s'em-
" pressera, dès l'arrivée du Roi en Angleterre, de la remettre à

"la personne de Service auprès de sa Majesté qui est chargée de "placer sous les yeux du Roi les communications qui lui sont "addressées.

"Londres, le 4 Octobre, 1844."

I have found, as I have been writing the above, the following characteristic letter on the subject from the late Sir Andrew Agnew :—

"October 3rd, 1844.

"MY DEAR MR. LEEKE,

"Having been out of town for two days, I can only "thank you for your excellent letter to the *French* Ambassador. "And let me suggest that you take off the *point* by sending "copies of your address to the Queen, to *all* the Foreign Ambas- "sadors, and send a paragraph to '*The Record*,' mentioning that "you have done so—and to other newspapers.

"Please also to send copies to Lord Aberdeen, Sir R. Peel, "and other ministers of the state—and to Prince Albert, through "his private Secretary, Colonel George Anson.

"I see by the Globe this evening, that Mr. Murray, the "*Master of the Household*, has been detained in Scotland by "severe indisposition.

"Faithfully yours,

"ANDREW AGNEW."

The next is a no less characteristic letter which I received from that excellent man, the late Venerable Dr. Marsh, of Beckenham, who was upwards of ninety years of age, when he died :—

"Beckenham, Kent, Nov. 20, 1860, or 1861.

"DEAR MR. LEEKE,

"I thank you for the Address of the Committee of "the Derbyshire Society, which I have just received; I pray for "a blessing on its exertions. I have lately been addressing a "large body of workmen on the four best gifts of God—His Son, "His Spirit, His Word, His Day. The first, to be the propitiation "for our sins.—The second, to renew our fallen nature.—The "third, to make us acquainted with the truth.—The fourth, to "remind us of them continually, ' lest at any time we should let "' them slip.'

"That the devil should be opposed to them might be ex-
"pected. But that the pope (in his official capacity) should be
"opposed to them is a melancholy proof of human folly and
"human wickedness. The first, he opposes by declaring that
"there are also other mediators and modes of justification.—The
"second, by the power said to be possessed by the priest.—The
"third, by discountenancing the circulation of the Holy Scrip-
"tures, and when that church has political power, as in Spain,
"making the reading or giving of a Bible, a crime against the
"state.—The fourth, by making it a day of amusement. The
"judgment on that system now 'of a long time lingereth not.'
"Nor shall we escape if we actually countenance and endow the
"system, and imitate the example.

"But we must pray 'That it may please Thee to lead into the
"'way of truth, all such as have erred and are deceived. That it
"'may please Thee to endue the Lords of the Council, and all the
"'Nobility, with grace, wisdom, and understanding.'

"You will be glad to see as below, that, from time to time,
"some are delivered from the delusion.*

"At present, I am drawn upon much beyond my powers. If
"I live till next April, I shall willingly cast in my mite to the
"cause. God bless all your efforts to win sinners to the Saviour,
"and to lead believers to adorn the doctrine.

"Yours faithfully,

"W. MARSH."

The reading over this letter reminds me of a rather singular
circumstance which occurred to me in connexion with Dr. Marsh,
nearly forty years ago. I had seen him, and had been introduced to him once, but on my going to stay with some friends at
Brighton some time after, they took me to a large evening party
at a house to which Dr. Marsh was also invited. I had not
been long there, when my friend Admiral Hawker introduced
me again to Dr. Marsh, who did not recognize me, with the
evident intention that I should have a little profitable conversation with him. We were left standing alone in the midst of a

* This letter was written on the fly-leaf and title page of "Scripture Truths,"
by Thomas Butler, D.D., and strongly recommended by Dr. Marsh, Honorary
Canon of Worcester.

large number of persons, who were talking to each other, and Dr. Marsh immediately began, "There is a beautiful passage in the 22nd of Job and the 21st verse, which says " Acquaint now thyself with him, [that is, with God] and be at peace ; thereby good shall come unto thee." Just as he had finished this verse, a servant entered and told him that somebody wanted him. He did not return whilst I remained at the party, and I think I have never seen him since, though I seem to have his voice, which was remarkably sweet and clear, still sounding in my ears. I thus had my attention drawn to a most beautiful passage of the Word of God, which I must have read, but had never meditated on before.

In visiting the schools in my rural deanery, I have been much struck with the great importance of endeavouring to make the older children well acquainted with a prayer which shall be suitable for them when they leave school, and indeed during their whole lives. I found the following prayer in the school at Holbrooke, when I came to the parish six-and-twenty years ago, and have had numbers of them printed, on strong paper, at about 5s. a thousand, and have given them to the children, and have otherwise circulated them. I hope many of the readers of this work will alter it as they like, and re-print and circulate it. There are many good prayers which would probably be quite as suitable. My reason for liking this one is, that it contains most of the principal things which we ought to pray for, and that, being intended to be used both morning and evening, the memory is not so much burdened as it is when both a morning and evening prayer are required. We print the first prayers from Watts's Catechism, and the hymns beginning with "Gentle Jesus, meek " and mild," and "Lord, teach a little child to pray," for the little children :—

"*A Prayer for Morning and Evening, suitable for Persons of every age.*

"O Lord God ! I am a helpless sinful creature, but thou hast " invited poor sinners to come unto Thee, who alone art able to " help them. O ! give me a heart to feel the importance of eternal " things ; take away from me the heart of stone, which makes me " so careless about the salvation of my soul, and give me a heart

"of flesh, that I may feel my lost condition through sin, and may
"flee to Christ for pardon. Teach me, O Lord, what Christ is
"made to sinners, and how His death on the cross saves them.
"Wash me in His blood, clothe me in His righteousness, and
"sanctify me by His Word and Spirit. O Lord, send Thy Holy
"Spirit into my heart, incline me to read Thy Word, teach me to
"pray to Thee, and deeply to feel the wants of my soul. Turn
"away my heart from sin and folly, deliver me from the snares
"of Satan, the dangers of evil company, and from my own evil
"tempers and desires. Give the same blessings to all near and
"dear unto me; bless all Ministers of the Gospel, and all Mission-
"aries to the Heathen and to the Jews; bless the Queen and all
"the Royal Family, all who are in authority, and all people
"everywhere; may thy name be known upon earth, thy saving
"health among all nations; have mercy upon all who are afflicted,
"and sick, and dying. Accept my praises and thanksgivings for
"all Thy mercies, make me more and more thankful for them,
"and bring me at last to Thy heavenly kingdom, for the sake of
"Jesus Christ my Lord and Saviour. Amen.

"Our Father, &c."

CHAPTER LVIII.

THE APPENDIX.

My eldest brother killed at Cadiz—Captain Bogue's death at Leipsig—Serjeant Housley's and Private Fell's pensions—Colonel Ponsonby at Waterloo—Hill's French letter of thanks, &c.—Southey's poem on the victory at Blenheim—Closing address.

No I.

Taken from the Gentleman's Magazine for December, 1810.

"LIEUT. SAMUEL LEEKE was the eldest son of the late Samuel Leeke, Esq., of Havant. A fleet of the enemy's armed vessels were discovered entering Puerto Santa Maria, near Cadiz, November 2nd, 1810, and a signal was made for the British gun-vessels to attack. Lieut. Leeke commanded one of them, and most gallantly led the way into the centre of the enemy's fleet. This example of bravery proved fatal to him, he being wounded by a musket-ball, which soon occasioned his death, and deprived his friends of a beloved, good young man, and his country of a valuable officer, whose good conduct ever secured to him the approbation of his superiors in rank, and whose past actions gave great hopes of a brilliant career in the profession he had chosen. He had just completed his twenty-first year. To have been thus early cut off, is the source of great affliction to his mother and family. To alleviate in some measure their distress, and as a memorial of Lieut. Leeke's bravery, his next brother has been promoted to the rank of lieutenant."

Mr. Yorke, the First Lord of the Admiralty, when he heard of his gallant conduct and death, said that, had he survived, he should have been made a commander at once.

No. II.

Death of Captain Bogue at Leipsig.

Letter of Mr James, (son of Sir Walter James, Bart.,) Aide-de-camp to General Sir Chas. Stewart, K.B., to John Hanson, Esq., communicating the melancholy particulars of Captain Bogue's death.

" DEAR SIR,

" A duty most melancholy in its nature, and peculiarly painful to myself, has devolved on me, in making you acquainted with the death of Captain Bogue, which melancholy event happened on the 18th of October, in the victory gained by the Allies over the French in the neighbourhood of Leipsig.

" Out of respect to the feelings, and for the sake of the family of Captain Bogue, I have to regret that this melancholy task has not fallen to the lot of one, who, in entering into the mournful particulars, would be better able than I am, to shew in the strongest light those drops of consolation that are most undoubtedly to be derived from an exit the most honourable — even the most glorious. But, if the afflictions of relatives, and the regret of friends, are to be soothed by the reflection that a duty has been honourably performed, by the conviction that every act of posthumous justice must be rendered to those exertions which contributed in no slight degree to the success of that memorable day, then are the friends of Captain Bogue in possession of a consolation so often wanted in similar events.

" The Rocket Brigade, under the command of Captain Bogue, had been attached, in its general movements, to the body-guard of the Crown Prince of Sweden, under the command of Count Lievitson, with, however, the understanding, that on days of action it was to be more at liberty than that corps, and subjected only to the direction of Captain Bogue. Conformably with this arrangement, at the commencement of the action on the morning of the 18th, Captain Bogue addressed himself to General Winzingerode, commanding the advance of the Crown Prince, expressing his desire to see the enemy, with permission to engage. The General, struck with the gallantry and spirit of the address, granted, as guard, a squadron of dragoons, and requested Captain Bogue to follow his own plans and judgment. Captain Bogue lost no time in approaching to the attack of the village of Paunsdorf, then in the possession of five enemy's battalions; upon whom he opened, in advance of the whole, a most destructive fire. This was returned by musketry, and for some time a very hot combat ensued; when the enemy, unable to withstand the well directed fire of Captain Bogue's brigade, fell into confusion, and began to retreat. Captain Bogue, seizing this moment, charged at the head of the squadron of cavalry; and the enemy, terrified at his approach, turned round, and taking off their caps, gave three huzzas; and every man, to the number of between two and three thousand, surrendered to the Rocket Brigade, not, I believe, exceeding 200 men. The intelligence of this success being communicated to the Crown Prince, he sent his thanks to Captain Bogue for such eminent services, requesting at the same time that he would continue his exertions; and the brigade proceeded, in consequence, to the attack of (I believe) the village of Sommerfeldt, still further in advance. Sir C. Steward accompanied the brigade, and I was of the party. The situation taken up on the flank of the village was exposed to a most heavy fire, both of cannon-balls and grape-shot from the enemy's line, and from the riflemen in the village. A ball from the latter soon deprived us of the exertions of poor Bogue; it entered below the eye, and, passing through the head, caused instantaneous death.

"You will see, I am sure, how impossible it is for me to say anything that can do justice to such actions. I had long been happy in the acquaintance and friendship of Captain Bogue; and no one, I am sure, more sincerely than I do, regrets the loss of a friend and a man whom I was most proud to have it in my power to call a brother-soldier. It remains for me to tell you, that the body was found a few hours afterwards; and decently interred the next morning, at the town of Jaucha, about two miles from Leipsig, all the brigade attending, with the deepest regret, the melancholy ceremony.

"With regard to the horses and effects of Captain Bogue, I hope you will have the frankness to make me, without ceremony, the instrument, on my return, for putting into execution any arrangements you may desire.

"I trust the sufferings of Mrs. Bogue are not so severe as you feared they would be. May I request to have my respects presented to her, and believe me, etc, etc.,

"JOHN JAMES."

No. III.

All that was intended to be said in this number of the Appendix, has been long ago anticipated.—See Vol. 1, Chapter VIII, pages 166—168.

No. IV.

The following correspondence relating to Serjeant Housley's services and claim for an increase of pension will be read with much interest. It helps to prove, as does a similar case which follows it, how ready Lord Seaton always was to attend to the feelings and wishes of those who had served under him :—

Mr. Lecke to Lord Seaton.

"Holbrooke, near Derby,

"May 2, 1851.

"MY DEAR LORD,

"When I called on your Lordship in town, two or three months ago, you kindly said that I might write to you, as the old Commanding Officer of the 52nd, on the subject of a claim made by Serjeant B. Housley.

"He was present with the 52nd in the following actions :—

"Corunna, Busaco, Fuentes D'Onor, Ciudad Rodrigo, (stormer and wounded,) Badajos, (stormer and wounded,) Salamanca, Vittoria, Nivelle, Nive, Orthes, Pyrenees, Toulouse, Almeida, Sabugal.

"He was *wounded three times;* at Rodrigo, at Badajos, and in a skirmish in 1812, between Salamanca and Rodrigo ; but he never was sick or so wounded *as to miss* ANY ENGAGEMENT *or* SKIRMISH *in which the 1st Battalion of the 52nd was engaged during the Corunna retreat, or during the Peninsular war and the Waterloo campaign.* As he has probably seen as much service as any British soldier, has always borne a good character, and is now a very respectable man, I am sure there will be a very great desire on the part of your Lordship, and of his Grace the Commander-in-Chief, to promote his wishes by the further-ance, if possible, of what really appears to be his just claim. His statement is, that he served as a private for nine years and 358 days, as a corporal for three years and six months, and as a serjeant for six years and six months ; that when he was discharged in 1822, he had been twenty years, all but seven days, in the 52nd ; that on his appear-ing before the Kilmainham Board on the 22nd of May, 1822, the president told him he was a young man, and advised him to take the rising pension ; and that he was to appear again in two years and fourteen days, (twice the one year and seven days wanting to complete his twenty-one years' service,) and that he would then get a pension of one shilling and sevenpence-halfpenny a day. This advice he followed, and was discharged, *as serjeant,* on a pension of *fivepence* a day.

"When he appeared *at Chelsea* in 1824, his pension was raised, *not to* a shilling and sevenpence-halfpenny, but only to *one shilling*, and Colonel (Neave, he thinks) told him that, since he was discharged, an Act had been passed determining that no non-commissioned officer, who had not completed twenty-one years' service at the time of his discharge, should receive more than one shilling per diem. He thinks that an *ex post facto* law or regulation ought not to affect him, and that the president's promise to him ought to be fulfilled. He says, the ' Recorder ' at Dublin wrote what he was to have when his time should be completed, and *he would be glad that a copy of any document bearing on his discharge in the ' Recorder's Office ' at Kilmainham should be sent for, to show that his claim is just.*

"The officer commanding the pensioners, once wrote to the Horse Guards or to the War Office on the subject, but nothing was done for him, and I believe no reference made to Kilmainham. This application is made through your Lordship, with the full concurrence of the present officer of pensioners in this district, who speaks very highly of Serjeant Housley.

"As an old 52nd officer, I feel very anxious that this grievance of one who has been present in every action and skirmish in which the 1st Battalion of the regiment was engaged, should meet with every attention. It does appear a great hardship, that a man with *so much service* and with so good a character, who was three times severely wounded, and who served so many years as a non-commissioned officer, and was *discharged as a serjeant* with the understanding that, after two years and fourteen days, he was to receive one shilling and sevenpence-halfpenny a day, should after all be only receiving the same allowance which many privates are receiving who never saw a shot fired.

"I trust he may be enabled to receive the increased pension, and to recover the arrears, or that, if this cannot be done consistently with the regulation, *his good service to his country may be rewarded* in some other way.

"I have the honour to remain, my dear Lord,
"Very sincerely yours,

"WM. LEEKE.

"I find Serjeant Housley ought to have one more bar to his medal, that for the Pyrenees; and also the regimental medal as a stormer at Ciudad Rodrigo. He has that for Badajos, but in some way, from being absent when the medals were determined on, missed that for Rodrigo.

"The *bar* I think your Lordship can kindly obtain for him. The regimental medal, I suppose, would have to be made at Birmingham, after a reference to the regiment. It would be a great pity that such a distinguished veteran should be without any one of the decorations which he is entitled to. If the regiment has no fund from which to supply the medal, the expense of it can easily be managed. Perhaps a letter to the Commanding Officer of the regiment from your Lordship would be the best way of proceeding; or if you think it well, and it would save your Lordship trouble, I can write, perhaps saying that I do so with your sanction. "W. L."

From Lord Seaton.

"Ryde, August 5, 1851.

"MY DEAR LEEKE,

"Lord Fitzroy Somerset acquaints me, in reply to our application, in favour of Serjeant Housley, that he has 'the satisfaction to send me the accompanying copy of a letter from the secretary of the Commissioners of Chelsea Hospital, announcing the increase of *his* pension from one shilling to two shillings per diem from the 21st of July.'

"I think you have reason to be contented with the result of your efforts to assist your client, whose case was so clearly stated by you, that it could not fail to make an impression on the minds of the Commissioners, as to the justice of the claim of a worthy old soldier.

"We are on our route homewards, and intend to call at Otterbourne and remain there Friday and Saturday.

"Lady Seaton unites with me in kind regards to Mrs. Leeke.

"Believe me, yours very sincerely,

"SEATON."

To Lord Fitzroy Somerset.

"Royal Hospital, Chelsea,

"30th July, 1851.

"MY LORD,

"The Lords and others Commissioners of this Hospital having had under their consideration your Lordship's letter of the 5th ult., transmitting one with enclosures, herewith returned, from Lieut.-General Lord Seaton, in behalf of Serjeant Benjamin Housley, a pensioner from the 52nd Foot, together with a report of his examination by a military medical officer, which it was necessary to obtain, and which has unavoidably been the cause of some delay in the decision upon the case—I am now directed to acquaint your Lordship that, in consideration of the serjeant's long service, and the wounds he received in action, the Commissioners have been pleased to increase his pension from one shilling to two shillings per diem, to take effect from the 22nd of this month.

"With respect to the statement that he was promised by the Kilmainham Board that on the completion of his third period of service by absent time, his pension would be increased to one shilling and sevenpence-halfpenny per diem, I am directed to observe that no record or minute to that effect is made in the documents received from Kilmainham, and there is no authority in the regulations for any such promise; a serjeant discharged under such circumstances not being entitled to the additional pension for non-commissioned officer's service granted to a man who has actually completed a third period at the time of his discharge.

"I have, &c.,

"(Signed) A. J. MOORHEAD."

Memorandum, August 8th, 1851.   W. L.

"Serjeant Housley was on detachment at Tamworth, from Lichfield, when the names were given in for the stormers' medals; and his name was omitted for Rodrigo, but not for Badajos. He was in a different company then as serjeant, and thus he thinks the omission occurred. On his return to head-quarters, he spoke about it, when the medals were distributed, but it could not be attended to at the moment, and afterwards, in the changes of quarters, the matter was lost sight of."

The following from Lord Seaton refers to this medal for Rodrigo.

"Deer Park, Honiton,

"September 2nd, 1851.

"MY DEAR LEEKE,

"You will find, from the enclosure, that the claim of Serjeant Housley for a clasp for the Pyrenees, will probably soon be acknowledged by the Board. I think there may be some difficulty in obtaining for your client, at this period, the regimental decoration to which you refer; as it was a medal given by the officers of the 52nd, of the day, without the permission or authority of the Commander-in-Chief.

"Yours very sincerely,

"SEATON."

Several years before this, I met in Lancashire with an old 52nd man, who had been in a great many of the Peninsular battles and severe skirmishes, had been twice very severely wounded; he was a stormer at Rodrigo and eventually received six clasps to his Peninsular medal. He had also fought at Waterloo, and, after all this good service, had been discharged with a pension of fivepence a day. Thus England rewards those who have fought and bled for her. I had known him as a man of excellent character in McNair's company, so I wrote to my friend Yonge, who was also in that company, and requested him to join me in a representation to Lord Seaton on the subject. The following was the result:—

From Lord Seaton.

"Kitley, July 29th, 1842.

"My dear Yonge,

"I have forwarded the petition of William Fell to Lord Fitzroy Somerset; and have requested him to speak to Lord Hill upon the hard case, which I have represented in strong terms, embodying in my note the substance of your letter; and stating that if he will recommend the case for the favourable consideration of the Secretary-at-War, he may be assured that the petitioner is an old soldier deserving the *best* treatment."

To Lord F. Somerset, K.C.B.

"Royal Hospital, Chelsea,

"1st October, 1842.

"My Lord,

"I laid before the Lords and others, Commissioners of this Hospital, at their late meeting, your letter of the 2nd August last, and its enclosures, in behalf of William Fell, an out-pensioner of this establishment, from the 52nd Foot, together with the report of the recent examination, by a military medical officer, of the man in question, when their Lordships, upon considering the same, directed me to acquaint you that, under all the circumstances of the case, they have been pleased to order his pension to be increased from fivepence to ninepence per diem from the 27th ultimo, and directions have accordingly been given to cause him to be paid the difference of fourpence per diem from that date to the 31st December next, and at the increased rate in future, upon his applying to the Collector of Excise for the district in which he resides, for that purpose.

"I herewith enclose Lord Seaton's letter, and

"I have, &c.,

"(Signed) R. NEAVE."

No. V.

Lieutenant-Colonel Ponsonby, of the 12th Light Dragoons, gives the following account of himself on being wounded. He says :—

"In the mêlée (thick of the fight) I was almost instantly disabled in both my arms, losing first my sword, and then my rein ; and, followed by a few of my men, who were presently cut down, no quarter being asked or given, I was carried along by my horse, till, receiving a blow from a sabre, I fell senseless on my face to the ground. Recovering, I raised myself a little to look around, being at that time in a condition to get up and run away, when a lancer passing by, cried out, ' Tu n'est pas mort, coquin !' and struck his lance through my back. My head dropped, the blood gushed into my mouth, a difficulty of breathing came on, and I thought all was over. Not long after, a skirmisher stopped to plunder me, threatening my life : I directed him to a small side-pocket, in which he found three dollars, all I had ; but he continued to threaten, tearing open my waistcoat, and leaving me in a very uneasy posture.

"But he was no sooner gone, than an officer bringing up some troops, and happening to halt where I lay, stooped down, and addressing me, said, he feared I was badly wounded. I answered that I was, and expressed a wish to be moved to the rear. He said, it was against orders to remove even their own men ; but that if they gained the day, (and he understood that the Duke of Wellington was killed, and that six of our battalions had surrendered,) every attention in his power should be shown me. I complained of thirst, and he held his brandy bottle to my lips, directing one of his soldiers to lay me straight on my side, and place a knapsack under my head ; they then passed on into action, soon perhaps to want, though not to receive, the same assistance; and I shall never know to whose generosity I was indebted, as I believe, for my life.

"By and by, another skirmisher came up, a fine young man, full of ardour, loading and firing; he knelt down and fired over me many times, conversing with me very gaily all the while; at last he ran off, saying: 'Vous serez bien aise d'apprendre que nous allons nous retirer. Bonjour mon ami!' ('You will be pleased to learn that we are going to fall back. Good day, my friend!')

"It was dusk, when two squadrons of Prussian cavalry crossed the valley in full trot, lifting me from the ground, and tumbling me about cruelly.

"The battle was now over, and the groans of the wounded all around me became more and more audible. I thought the night would never end. About this time I found a soldier lying across my legs, and his weight, his convulsive motions, his noises, and the air issuing through a wound in his side, distressed me greatly; the last circumstance most of all, as I had a wound of the same nature myself. It was not a dark night, and the Prussians were wandering about to plunder: many of them stopped to look at me as they passed; at last one of them stopped to examine me; I told him that I was a British officer, and had been already plundered. He did not however desist, and pulled me about roughly.

"An hour before midnight, I saw a man in an English uniform coming towards me; he was, I suspected, on the same errand. I spoke instantly, telling him who I was. He belonged to the 40th,* and had missed his regiment. He released me from the dying soldier, took up a sword, and stood over me as sentinel. Day broke, and at six o'clock in the morning a messenger was sent to Hervé; a cart came for me, and I was conveyed to the village of Waterloo, and laid in the bed, as I afterwards understood, from which Gordon had but just before been carried out. I had received seven wounds; a surgeon slept in my room; and I was saved by excessive bleeding."

* This was most probably the same man of the 40th whom I came across, when the 52nd were passing over the killed and wounded of the Imperial Guard.

No. VI.

Lieutenant Hill's French letter.

" De Lichfield en Staffordshire,

"Le 8me Janvier, 1820.

" Ne vous inquietez pas mon ami du sort de la musique, elle est arrivée heureusement il y a quelques jours, et on ne cesse de vous en louer. Les trompettes n'en ont pas encore joué. Mais ces amateurs qui ont eu l'occasion d'assister à l'essai de quelques-uns des Pièces les ont trouvées infiniment jolies. Le Colonel Rowan vient à l instant de passer chez moi pour me prier de vous faire part, qu'il écrivit le jour même de l'arrivée de votre present pour vous en rendre graces. Enfin tout le monde est d'accord que vous meritez autant de *congé* que vous voudrez demander, et nous ne regrettons plus votre absence que pour la perte que nous y faisons de votre societé. Nous nous attendons de passer l'hiver en cette ville, ce qui parait satisfaire aux vœux de tout le monde. Les amitiés que l'on y fait au Regiment n'ont plus de bornes. Les compagnies *Young* et *Yorke* sont à Derby. Celles de Diggle et de Kenny à Nottingham. Mais ces dernières s'attendent à tout moment de se retourner à Derby. C'est avec plaisir que j'apprends, que vous vous portez mieux depuis qui vous êtes de retour en Angleterre. Il ne vous manquait peut-être que le *Rost Bœuf* et tous les *Comforts* que l'on trouve dans notre isle unique. Le soupe maigre et le pain noir de l'Allemagne ne conviennent nullement au temperament Anglais. Allons donc ! buvez et mangez ; réjouissez vous et portez vous bien, par force. Voila les remèdes qui valent bien toute la médecine du monde.

" Ne suis-je pas bien hardi, d'oser m'entretenir avec vous dans une langue dont je ne connais à peine les premiers rudimens, et dans laquelle vous avez sans doutes autant de facilité que dans la votre ?

Très dévouément à vous

R. K. Hill.

" Je trouverai toujours le plus grand plaisir à recevoir de vos nouvelles."

No. VII.

I think I cannot close this work, which contains so much about Waterloo, better than by doing so with Southey's "Price of a Victory."

"The Battle of Blenheim, to which this ballad by the poet Southey refers, was fought, in the year 1704, between the English, under the Duke of Marlborough, and French, under Marshal Tallard. The French were totally defeated, with the loss of 27,000 killed and 13,000 prisoners ; the French commander and 1200 of his officers were among the latter."

"It was a summer evening,
 Old Kasper's work was done,
And he, before his cottage door,
 Was sitting in the sun ;
And by him sported on the green
His little grandchild, Wilhelmine.

She saw her brother Peterkin
 Roll something large and round,
That he beside the rivulet
 In playing there had found ;
She ran to ask what he had found,
That was so large, and smooth, and round.

Old Kaspar took it from the boy,
 Who stood expectant by ;
And then the old man shook his head,
 And with a natural sigh,
' 'Tis some poor fellow's skull,' said he,
' Who fell in the great victory.

' I find them in my garden, for
 There's many hereabout ;
And often when I go to plough,
 The ploughshare turns them out ;
For many thousand men,' said he,
' Were slain in that great victory.'

' Now tell us what 'twas all about,'
 Young Peterkin, he cries ;
And little Wilhelmine looks up
 With wonder-waiting eyes ;
' Now tell us all about the war,
And what they killed each other for.'

'It was the English,' Kasper cried,
  'That put the French to rout ;
But what they killed each other for,
  I could not well make out ;
But everybody said,' quoth he,
'That 'twas a famous victory.

'My father lived in Blenheim then,
  Yon little stream hard by ;
They burnt his dwelling to the ground,
  And he was forced to fly ;
So with his wife and child he fled,
And knew not where to rest his head.

' With fire and sword the country round,
  They wasted far and wide ;
And many a wretched mother, then,
  And new-born infant died ;
But things like that, you know, must be
At every famous victory.

'They say it was a shocking sight
  After the field was won,
For many thousand bodies there
  Lay rotting in the sun ;
But things like that, you know, must be
After a famous victory.

'Great praise the Duke of Marlborough won,
  And our good Prince Eugene ;'—
' Why, 'twas a very wicked thing,'
  Said little Wilhelmine.
'Nay, nay, my little girl,' quoth he,
' It was a famous victory.

'And everybody praised the Duke,
  Who this great fight did win.'
' But what good came of it at last ?'
  Quoth little Peterkin.
' Why, that I cannot tell,' said he,
' But 'twas a famous victory.' "

No. VIII.

My dear Readers,

You must permit me to address the closing words of this book to you. With all its faults—and I am conscious it has many—it has been written with the earnest desire and prayer that it might "help forward the salvation of all" those who should read it. I trust especially, that it may be made useful to many a young officer who may have been as careless and negligent about his God and God's Word, and the salvation of his soul, as I was. May you all be led by God's mercy, if you have not already done so, to make the following most serious inquiries which it is possible for any person to make:—

Have I good ground for thinking that I am in the narrow way of eternal life? Do I fear and love God, and endeavour to keep all His commandments? Do I believe the Bible to be the Word of God? If so, do I read it daily, and meditate in it with prayer that God will by His Holy Spirit bless it to my present and everlasting happiness? Have I learnt from it that I am a grievous sinner before a just and holy God? Have I been humbled for my sins, and have I mourned over them, and have I a true and living and saving faith in Him, who, being God and man, by His death made a full, perfect, and sufficient sacrifice, satisfaction, and oblation for the sins of the whole world?

May you all seek first the kingdom of God and His righteousness: "His kingdom is not meat and drink;" it does not consist in worldly pleasures and enjoyments; though God permits His people to have many comforts and enjoyments and pleasures in this world—indeed we read that He gives us "all things richly to enjoy;" but His kingdom is "righteousness and peace and joy in the Holy Ghost:" Rom. xiv, 17. These are the blessings and enjoyments which He will give abundantly to those who diligently seek Him in His appointed ways.

May the Lord bless you and keep you! May the Lord make His face to shine upon you, and be gracious unto you. May the Lord lift up the light of His countenance upon you, and give you peace now and for evermore. Amen.

www.ingramcontent.com/pod-product-compliance
Lightning Source LLC
Chambersburg PA
CBHW032027120726
47901CB00004BA/1110